THE CONGRESS OF MICRONESIA

NORMAN MELLER
with the assistance of Terza Meller

THE CONGRESS
OF MICRONESIA

Development of the Legislative Process in
the Trust Territory of the Pacific Islands

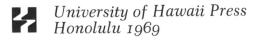
University of Hawaii Press
Honolulu 1969

COPYRIGHT 1969 BY UNIVERSITY OF HAWAII PRESS

Manufactured in the United States of America

LIBRARY OF CONGRESS CATALOG CARD NO. 68–9129

Foreword

IN ORDER TO WRITE a book about the development of legislatures in the Trust Territory of the Pacific Islands, it was first essential to determine how to identify a legislature. Obviously, reliance could not be placed upon names, as evidenced by the Olbiil era Kelulau, the body which functioned in the Palau district between the years 1955 and 1963: translated into English, this would be "meeting place of whispers!" Looking at functions proved equally ineffective. Belying the etymology, early in their histories institutions now referred to as legislatures "had little or no concern with legislation." [1] Even today, if it be accepted that law-making is the measure of a legislature, how can we reconcile the facts that in quantity of output, legislatures are eclipsed by the sheer bulk of quasi-legislation issued by administrative agencies and that the drama of their impact is overshadowed by judicial decisions setting impersonal precedents as binding as statutes for all to observe?

Viewing the same problem from another perspective, at the 1234th meeting of the United Nations Trusteeship Council in 1964, Mr. Shakov, the representative of the Union of Soviet Socialist Republics, declared "no representative legislative body as yet existed in the [American Administered Trust] Territory [of the Pacific Islands] . . . since the Council of Micronesia had turned out to be a purely consultative body" and that the then proposed Territory-wide, bicameral Congress of Micronesia "would be only a consultative body, like the body that already existed . . . [because] no legislation could enter into force until it had been approved by the High Commissioner. . . ." [2] There can be no quarrel with the con-

---

[1] Carl J. Friedrich, *Constitutional Government and Democracy* (Boston: Ginn and Co., 1950), p. 268. See also Charles A. Beard and John D. Lewis, "Representative Government in Evolution," *American Political Science Review*, 26:2 (April, 1932), 231–235; A. F. Pollard, *The Evolution of Parliament* (2d ed.; London: Longmans, Green and Co., Ltd., 1926), pp. 44–60; George L. Haskins, *The Growth of English Representative Government* (Philadelphia: University of Pennsylvania Press, 1948), *passim*.

[2] Trusteeship Council Official Records, 31st Sess., 1234th meeting, June 8, 1964, pars. 14, 15. In future references, these reports will be referred to as TCOR.

tention of the Soviet position if it implied that the exercise of law-making is insufficient per se to identify a legislature. However, the further constraining of the definion of a "legislature" to those bodies in which "the last word about what the law is to be rests" [3] or whose "decision is both necessary and sufficient for the final enactment of a law" [4] ignores the integral involvement of the executive and fails to face the reality of the initiative, referendum, and recall. Such attempts to define a legislature by assigning it a quota of functions or residual powers reawaken the unfruitful attempts by political philosophers of yesteryear to identify the locus of sovereignty. Clearly, the classifier "legislature" carries no undisputed meaning nor necessarily describes any single institution common to various systems of government.

None of the foregoing denies that it is principally through the enactment of statutes that the modern legislature has derived its saliency. A comparable inquiry into primacy put during Cromwell's Long Parliament would probably have prompted a reply referring to the redress of grievances and the subordination of the king. Indeed, there is a strong probability that there are no functional delimitations to the activity of a legislature, be it granting divorces, conducting wars, choosing chief executives, or molding a nation's opinion. Rather, in any political system the legislature performs functions appropriate to that system as they have evolved by virtue of the legislature's representative nature and its characteristic group process.

Of all political institutions, the legislature as a corporate body is most aptly designed to bring the element of representation to political decision-making. Even when the legislature is no more than the agent of a particular stratified level of society, with the legislators bespeaking themselves as well as their class in accordance with its mandate, to that extent their action is bindingly representational. Similarly, the skewing of the legislature's composition through selection of its members by a narrowly restricted suffrage does not prevent it through political fiction from functioning as the representative of the entire constituency. So long as the represented endorse, accept, tolerate, or at least do not openly reject the conduct of deliberations in their name, the decisions of the legisla-

---

[3] K. C. Wheare, *Legislatures* (New York: Oxford University Press, 1963), p. 3.

[4] Inter-Parliamentary Union, *Parliaments* (London: Cassell and Co., Ltd., 1961), p. 116.

ture psychologically are theirs and this in turn legitimizes the legislature's actions. The King's Curia becomes a nascent legislature when to its membership are added those who are recognized spokesmen for the views of others beside the King. Even in the absence of all powers of initiation, a *pro forma* concurrence with an executive-determined program in no way precludes a legislative body possessed of representative character from sanctioning the proposed course of action.

Representation is not confined to the legislative institution. In view of the manner in which constituencies are geographically contorted, fields of candidates partisanly narrowed, and the psychological processes of identification cultivated by modern mass media techniques, on the American scene many constituents may consider the elected chief executive to mirror the views they hold more aptly than do the members of the legislature. However, this constitutes more a dissatisfaction with the style and product of representation than a transference of the basic acceptance of the legislature as the prime representative institution. Not even in the new American state constitutions does the elected chief executive participate in the most fundamental of law-making functions performed by the legislature, the enactment of constituent legislation; and in the case of the United States constitution itself, there has not been any effort to modify the sharing in the task by legislatures on two levels of government, to the exclusion of the executive.

The other distinguishing characteristic of the legislative institution is its collegial nature and the attendant processes it observes. The legislature's structuring reflects its group character by the minimizing of formal hierarchy and the wide internal dispersal of power. In the parliamentary system of government, legislative direction rests in a committee, while Mr. Speaker ought more fittingly be referred to as umpire than as the spokesman his title implies. But whether adopting the British or the American pattern of leadership, the legislature meets collectively and moves to collective decision, be this by simple majority, extraordinary majority, or through consensus to unanimity. When not acting as a body, the legislature typically utilizes smaller groups rather than individuals to further its functions. Committees screen and refine legislative proposals, or at least the latter; when it becomes necessary to reconcile policy differences between the two houses of a bicameral legislature, a conference committee serves the purpose. Duties associated with the administration of the legislature are assigned to accounts committees, rules committees, and a host of other sub-collegial bodies. Delegation is to groups, specialization is formalized through groups, and the individual legislator shapes his conduct accordingly. The member unobservant or defiant of legislative norms soon finds himself subjected to group sanctions and, if the degree of his flaunting warrants, formal censure and expulsion expressed through vote of the legislature. In short, to the extent that all institutional effort embodies both individual and collective aspects, the legislature in its process emphasizes the collegial.

It is against this backdrop of the universal nature of the legislative institution [5] that the legislatures of the Trust Territory of the Pacific Islands may be identified and the development of the legislative process delineated.

[5] For a more complete treatment, see Norman Meller, "The Identification and Classification of Legislatures," *Philippine Journal of Public Administration,* 10:4 (Oct., 1966), 308.

Preface

THIS BOOK COVERS a ten-year period of research. During the course of its preparation, I received the confidences of numerous Micronesians and American administrative personnel in the field. In order to respect their wishes, I have left many sources unidentified and have modified references sufficiently to prevent attribution to specific individuals. Their authors know that I value their contributions as highly as those from people of whom mention could be, and has been, made.

The reader will immediately note that the quotations from materials written in English by Micronesians frequently read a little "quaintly." This but reflects the fact that the people of the Trust Territory of the Pacific Islands are still becoming familiar with the grammar and idiom of the English language. Rather than rewrite these statements correctly, or liberally pepper them with insertions of "sic," I have included them in *haec verba* so that this dimension of Micronesian life may be literally depicted.

There are many limitations to the research upon which this work is based. For one thing, it is of Micronesia as viewed through the eyes of a Westerner. Little systematic inquiry has been attempted by Micronesians themselves since the pioneer effort of Sakuma in 1946 to distribute in Palau what in effect was a public opinion questionnaire, and this attempt was cut short by the objections of the high chiefs. Throughout my decade of study, there has been the continuing risk of influencing findings by the mere playing of the participant-observer. This was borne home in 1956 when, watching the Marshallese congress in session, my probing queries about the authority enjoyed by the Marshallese Holdover Committee unintentionally instigated an effort to limit its scope. At times, however, I have deliberately sought to shape the course of the legislative process in the Trust Territory, as when I trained Micronesian legislators and legislative staff for their tasks, but a conscious effort has been made to prevent this involvement from coloring my analyses.

The account of my indebtedness can never be fully recorded. At various times, financial assistance has been received from the Tri-Institutional Pacific Program, the Legislative Reference Bureau, the University Research Council, the Social Science Research Institute, and the Institute for Technical Interchange of the East-West Center, all either part of or participated in by the University of Hawaii. The Hawaiian and Pacific Collection of the University's Sinclair Library, and its staff, have proven invaluable. The Administration of the Trust Territory has spared no effort in its cooperation. Marion G. Saunders, Dr. Allan F. Saunders and Dr. Robert B. Stauffer greatly facilitated the collection of background data. The New Guinea Research Unit of the Australian National University kindly undertook the duplication of the final draft while I was in that Australian trusteeship studying its "national" legislature. The manuscript itself has been reviewed in whole or in part by Dr. William Alkire, Dr. Ron Crocombe, Fran Defngin, Tom Dinell, Dr. Daniel Hughes, Kurt Ludwig, Dr. Leonard Mason, Dr. Robert R. Robbins, Dr. John L. Taylor, Luke Tman, Kaleb Udui, Raymond Ulochong, Strik Yoma, and John de Young, and the value of their comments and criticisms can here only be cumulatively acknowledged, although I of course stand responsible for any error yet remaining. And finally, how can one number the many courtesies extended to me and my wife by countless people throughout the Trust Territory?

On July 9, 1965, the workshop which preceded the convening of the Congress of Micronesia drew to a close. When I would next see all thirty-three members-elect assembled, they would be congressmen. Many of them were former students at the University of Hawaii, a few even members of my class on legislatures. That memorable Friday afternoon was the eve of their receipt of the power to determine the destiny of the Trust Territory. I held then no reservation about their competence to assume that awesome responsibility—nor do I now.

NORMAN MELLER
Honolulu, 1968

Contents

CHAPTER 1

Micronesia—Past and Present

NORTH OF THE EQUATOR and west of the dateline, spread across an expanse of the western Pacific larger than the whole of the continental United States, lies the Trust Territory of the Pacific Islands. Its thousands of small islands, separated by hundreds of miles of open ocean, prompted Domeny de Rienzi to propose the name of "Micronesia" for this region [1] to the Société de Géographie of Paris.

At that time—1831—it was believed that racial, linguistic, and ethnological factors sharply distinguished the inhabitants of these "micro" islands from the Melanesians (Lemanesia) to the south and from the peoples of the Polynesian Triangle. Later research has revealed Micronesians share few things in common such as the reversible sailing canoe, which set them apart from other inhabitants of Oceania. Rather, basic cultural commonalities with the other Pacific Island peoples negate this three-fold divisional concept of Oceania.[2] Although mutual intelligibility is lacking, all of the indigenous languages have a Malayo-Polynesian root. In short, the Marshalls, Carolines, and Mariana Islands, the three major archipelagoes in the Trust Territory, today are collectively identified primarily as components of a geographic expression which his-

---

[1] To be completely accurate, "Micronesia" also encompasses the Gilbert Islands, now part of the Gilbert and Ellice Island Colony administered by Great Britain, and Nauru, formerly a trusteeship under joint Australian, British, and New Zealand responsibility but now an independent nation. Both are south of the equator. Guam, an unincorporated territory of the United States, lies at the western edge of Micronesia as part of the Mariana Islands but outside the boundaries of the Trust Territory of the Pacific Islands. Recognizing the near concordance of geographic "Micronesia" with the political Trust Territory of the Pacific Islands, the new legislature for the Trust Territory has been named the "Congress of Micronesia." "Someday in the future the terms *Trust Territory* or *Territory* may cease to be used because of a change in the political status of the area. Regardless of change, this area will always remain Micronesia." Recommendation on naming the congress, made by the Working Committee to the Territorial Legislative Committee of the Council of Micronesia, Jan. 9, 1963.

[2] For example, see extensive treatment of Micronesian, Melanesian, and Polynesian material culture in Saul H. Riesenberg, "The Cultural Position of Ponape in Oceania" (Ph.D. thesis, University of California at Berkeley: 1950).

torical happenstance has artificially welded together into a political unit. First under the Spanish, next the Germans, then administered by the Japanese pursuant to a League of Nations mandate, and now governed by the United States in accordance with the Trustee- ship Agreement, these Micronesians have been a subject people under alien rule, until recently outside the stream of the modern world.

Despite having 2,100 islands, the Territory aggregates but 687 square miles of land, an area smaller than the state of Rhode Island, scattered over three million miles of ocean.[3] The low coral islands, frequently strung out in an irregular ribbon around a large lagoon to form an atoll, are sometimes barely awash above the level of the ocean. The volcanic islands, more massive in area, rise to greater elevations, but the tallest, Agrihan in the Northern Marianas, only reaches a height of a little over 3,000 feet. For the most part, the Marshalls are atolls, the Marianas high islands, and the Carolines composed of both. The two largest of the high islands, Babelthuap in the Palaus and Ponape in the Eastern Carolines, together account for two-fifths of the Territory's total land mass. All of this area might be fitted within the single Truk lagoon.

Most of the islands are of either coral or igneous composition and the sedimentary deposits which are the product of the islands' weathering. Some metamorphic rock of continental origin occurs in Yap and Palau, evidencing these islands to be but the tops of great wrinkles in the Asian continental shelf. The soils of the high islands are generally more fertile, while the coral origins of the low islands limit their productive capacities. Nevertheless, the islands with the densest populations tend to be the atolls, a fact which bespeaks a heavy reliance upon fishing for the primary source of protein. The islands' geological formation has set narrow bounds to their mineral resources. With World War II terminating the mining of manganese in the Marianas and of low grade bauxite deposits on Babelthuap, and the cessation of the exploitation of Angaur's phosphate beds a few years ago, the Trust Territory's mainstay is its agriculture, supplemented by its oceanic resources.

All of Micronesia, except for two small, uninhabited islands in the Northern Marianas, falls within the tropics. Here are to be

[3] The limited land available for Micronesian use is further indicated by the fact that over three-fifths of the total area is owned or controlled by the Trust Territory Administration. Title to some of this public domain is dis- puted.

found the South Sea Islands of Hollywood scenarios and romantic novels, with windblown palm trees, azure seas, and wave-lapped, dazzling beaches. Vegetation everywhere is lush and verdant, save on the drier atolls of the northern Marshalls. Temperature remains remarkably equable and the humidity uncomfortably high throughout the year; the winds and rain are the most variable of the climatic elements. The northeast tradewind belt covers the eastern-most part of the Territory, and the remainder falls within the fringe of the monsoon zone of east Asia. Precipitation varies with seasonal shifts of the wind. Rainfall averages eight to fourteen feet a year in the southern-most half, while in the northern islands, which have marked wet and dry seasons, it may not reach half that amount. Micronesia is the spawning ground for Pacific typhoons, and every few years some part of the Territory is devastated or narrowly misses destruction by tropical storm. Relying mainly upon a subsistence economy tied to the products of farm and sea, every untoward climatic variation disrupts the islanders' nicely attuned dependence upon their natural environment, and prolonged drought or heavy storm has proven disastrous to the populations of whole islands.

The origin of the Micronesians remains a matter of conjecture. Voyages into Western Micronesia may have originated from the Moluccas in the East Indies and the Bismarcks northeast of New Guinea several thousand years before the beginning of the Christian era. More likely, the Philippines were the source of hardy travelers who deliberately set sail easterly or, blown off their course, drifted to the islands of Micronesia, some returning to acquaint others of their discoveries. Into the islands these peoples introduced pigs and chickens and brought the roots, seed crops, and trees which had sustained them in their former homes. Adapting these to both high island and low island environments, they also evolved new subsistence patterns which utilized the limited indigenous flora and rich marine resources of their new abode. Although most Micronesians are of medium stature, brown skin, and have straight to wavy black hair, their many sources are revealed by the Mongoloid, Negroid, and Polynesian features encountered. Attesting to the people's manifold origins, the multiplicity of adaptive processes, and to the degrees of spatial dispersion which kept groups isolated, diversities in physical characteristics, languages, and cultural systems today set Marshallese, Ponapeans, Kusaiens, Trukese, Ulithians, Yapese, Palauans, and

Chamorros apart from one another, as well as from the Polynesians who occupy the outliers of Kapingamarangi and Nukuoro.

"Any attempt to reduce the great variety of institutional systems which prevail throughout Micronesia to common denominators would convert them into relatively meaningless categories." [4] However, it is safe to generalize that the Micronesians' political, social, and economic systems were built around kinship ties and, in some places, attendant complex class cleavages, and that these lineage (extended family) relationships continue to play an important role. In the Carolines and the Marshalls, the basic unit of the political-social organization consists of a number of matrilineages, with the members living in small hamlets or dispersed, close to the lands they farm. In the Marianas, the long contact of the Chamorros with the Spanish resulted in the disappearance of traditional lineages and class structure and in their replacement by the Hispanicized, Western-style, nuclear family and amorphous social distinctions depending on wealth.

A hereditary class system in the Marshalls separates the commoner (*kajur*) from those of royal status (*iroij*), and the paramount chiefs (*iroij laplap*) exercise residual feudal authority over their liege subjects.[5] Ponape in the Eastern Carolines was formerly divided into independent kingdoms, each with two parallel lines of nobility, and even to this day most adult males on the island hold titles either within these noble or in commoner lines, which provide them status and a degree of authority in local social life. Notwithstanding missionary contact, the modification of traditional Kusaiean patterns due to depopulation, and that island's complex system of titles' falling into disuse, the former kingship relationship still exerts a degree of influence in socio-political decisions. In the central Carolines, neither Truk nor the atolls lying between the Truk lagoon and Yap, farther west, know the class strata of the other areas. Here the community chief ordinarily is the senior male of the lineage which reputedly first settled on a particular island or attained ascendancy through war. This chief receives a degree of homage in the form of gifts and first fruits from the other lineages but enjoys relatively minimal enhanced prestige and authority. "A similar level of social organization,

[4] John Useem, "Institutions of Micronesia," *Far Eastern Survey*, 17:2 (Jan. 28, 1948), 23.
[5] The traditional chiefly structures of the Marshalls, Palau, and Ponape are described in greater detail in Chapter 5.

except for matrilineal descent, exists on the two Polynesian islands of Kapingamarangi and Nukuoro in the southeastern Carolines." [6]

Stratification reached a peak in the Western Carolines with Yap's [7] nine social classes and sharply partitioned caste relationships. Through Western contact these class cleavages have been somewhat moderated, but they still carry social prestige and leave an imprint upon local political action. In Palau, at the western extreme of the Carolines, the heads of the ten ranking clans of each village, numbering the chief among them, traditionally formed a council (*klobak*) and constituted the local bureaucracy. The villages were loosely linked together into districts, which are today's municipalities, and they in turn had their *klobak* with its paramount chief. Confederations of these districts represented the most extensive form of supra-local political integration found in Micronesia and have been perpetuated in the person of the two high chiefs of the Koror and Melekeok confederations. These chiefs have played prominent parts in the legislature of the Palau district and remain potent forces in matters involving Palauan custom. Reflective of Palauan linkage with Western economy, the upper strata are the wealthy, bifurcated into the *meteet*, who are senior-ranking title holders and their close relatives, and the *merau*, who have amassed fortunes but come from lower ranking clans.

Pre-contact native religious beliefs were promised on reverence of ancestors. Serving as a counterfoil to autocratic abuses, spirit worship and shamanistic practices also controlled over other forms of deviant social behavior. Some of the Outer Islanders in the Yap district continue to hold their pagan beliefs, and a segment of the people in Palau are members of the Modekngei, a movement with dogma somewhat reminiscent of the cargo cult.[8] The great majority of the Micronesians today are Christians, with the Chamorros almost all Roman Catholic, the Marshallese predominantly Protestant, and the balance of the Micronesians divided between these two religions. A strong undercurrent of superstition and

[6] *12th Annual Report [of the United States] to the United Nations on the Administration of the Trust Territory of the Pacific Islands, July 1, 1958, to June 30, 1959*, p. 77. In future references, these reports will be referred to as [*no.*] *Annual Report of the United States to the United Nations*, [*date*].

[7] The caste system of Yap and the nature of the former Yap empire are delineated in Chapter 6.

[8] For extended treatment, see Arthur J. Vidich, "The Political Impact of Colonial Administration" (Ph.D. thesis, Harvard University: 1952), Chap. 10; see also Homer G. Barnett, *Being a Palauan* (New York: Holt, Rinehart and Winston, 1961), pp. 83–85.

taboo persists throughout the area, however, and sorcery accompanied by the simple magic formulas of traditional times is still practiced to some degree.

The colonial powers introduced Micronesia to a commercial money economy in which personal self-advancement replaces the communal values of the traditional society. The Micronesians responded by eclectically accepting the food supplements, minor luxuries, and durable trade goods purchased from the sales of copra, trochus, and handicraft but also retaining their customary measures for living the good life. Subsistence economy, cash economy, and in some favored areas with regular surpluses (as Ponape), prestige economy have all been fitted into a composite, and "because the natives bent without breaking, the acculturation of Micronesia proceeded without the social disintegration which so often accompanies superimposed changes." [9]

Typically in Micronesia, the individual is a member of many different groupings: his immediate household, his lineage, the clan tracing descent from a traditional ancestor, and in the Western Carolines, age-based groups and social clubs. Companies gathered for fishing, farming, and community work projects may be built upon any of these. During the Japanese period, age-graded organizations were encouraged, and to a minor degree their imprint is still felt in athletic activities and the performance of community labor. For the satisfaction of normal wants, cooperation through traditional island organization, with each person's rights and duties defined in relation to the common products and projects, has sufficed. Essential everyday needs for the bulk of the population continue to be met mainly by family effort. It has been only as the Micronesian has adopted the individualism of the West that he has turned to earning his own living and making his way through personal competitive effort. Work for the government and enterprises based on Western patterns have furthered this break from tradition.

Commercial activity in the Trust Territory is chiefly made up of modest family proprietorships and chartered trading companies engaging in import and export business. Some of the latter have grown into extensive operations, with their sales of trade goods each year passing the million dollar mark. Manufacturing is largely confined to cottage-type industries in the subsistence sector. Con-

[9] John Useem, "Governing the Occupied Areas of the South Pacific," *Human Organization*, 4:3 (Summer, 1945), 3.

struction firms are just making their appearance, several districts have small boat building and repair yards, and service-type activities are springing up adjacent to district headquarters throughout the Territory. All of these are Micronesian-owned and fail to rival the large-scale enterprise supported by Japanese capital prior to World War II. The government continues to perform numerous services which elsewhere may usually be found within the private sector of the economy. The repair of equipment, storage and refrigeration facilities, transportation, and electric power are but a few examples. The Kennedy Administration in 1962 opened the Territory to the free entry of United States citizens and American investment, but safeguards precluding exploitation of the region's cheap labor and requirements for Micronesian participation and eventual management have slowed the advent of American enterprise in the area. The most recent development has been the formation by Micronesians of the United Micronesia Development Association to market all of the Territory's copra and, in conjunction with American companies, to operate the Trust Territory's airlines and a chain of tourist hotels. This represents the first effort by Micronesians to undertake an economic venture blanketing the entire Trust Territory.

Territorial imports now total about $10 million annually, with the United States as the country of origin for two-thirds of the foods, machinery, and other products destined for Island consumption. In view of the marketing of most of the Territory's products through Japan as well as the lower price of that country's manufactures, Japan is the second largest supplier of Territorial imports. Each year the value of the Territory's products sold externally falls far short of that of the goods brought into the Islands, and the deficit is offset by governmental expenditures derived from appropriated United States funds. For fiscal year 1967, in part due to the drop in copra sales, external trade failed to equal even one-quarter of the value of imports. Copra constitutes by far the largest component of the Territory's exports, dwarfing the income earned from scrap metal, trochus, cacao, and handicraft. A commercial fishery under American operation has only recently commenced exporting from Palau. It is a somewhat ironic commentary on the state of the Territory's economy that, despite the extensive oceanic resources of the area, imports of canned fish for food annually run more than quadruple the income from external sales and are about equal the value of the total Territorial catch.

The total income of the Trust Territory is unknown: in the words of the high commissioner, "We do not have reliable information on our territorial productivity." [10] Governmental expenditures from all sources for the 1965–1967 period approximated $23.3 million annually, the commercial sector's value of goods and services, about $5.4 million, and the subsistence sector added another $11 million. Not all of this was devoted to providing goods and services available for Micronesian use as, for example, the $1,400,000 in salaries paid to Micronesians which was primarily for military purposes on Kwajalein.[11] But after making adjustments for these and other comparable items, there was a statistical per person average of a little over $400 in goods and services annually available for Micronesian consumption and investment. Given the Micronesian's general access to local food resources and the ubiquity of production and exchange outside of the money economy, these figures substantiate the conclusion reached from casual observation: in the absence of natural disaster, the Territory's inhabitants enjoy a standard of living modestly above subsistence level. On the other hand, they are assured only a fairly simple and monotonous pattern of life, hardly sufficient to satisfy the rising expectations of the educated, younger Micronesians.

Almost 23 per cent of the able-bodied "adult" population falling within the 14 to 65 years of age brackets work for wages and salaries (7,500). A little less than half of these (3,500) are directly employed by the government, and this group includes most of the educated and experienced people in the Territory.[12] Their numbers are swelled by those who share in the monetary economy through full-time, private entrepreneurial effort and by part-time production of copra for export, handicraft, and produce. Cumulatively, though, at least half of the total adult population remains engaged in customary economic pursuits. This hardly offers horizons of opportunity sufficient to accommodate the rapidly expanding population of the Trust Territory or the yearly increasing crop of high school graduates unwilling to support themselves in accordance with traditional Micronesian life-ways.

The present Trust Territory population of close to 91,500 people is growing at an overall rate of almost 4 per cent annually, one of

[10] *Saipan District Panorama*, Oct. 30, 1964, p. 2.
[11] All data are extrapolated from Robert R. Nathan Associates, Inc., "Economic Development Plan for Micronesia" (Washington: 1966), Parts III, IV, pp. 495–507.
[12] *Ibid.*, p. 511.

the fastest in the world. During the Japanese period, the drastic depopulation which initially set in after Micronesian contact with
Westernized civilization was halted, and the destruction and priva-
tions suffered during World War II only temporarily slowed, but
did not reverse, the expansionary trend. The rate has quickened
with American emphasis upon health and sanitation, and even Yap,
the last of the areas to recover from the debilitating impact of Western contact, now registers an increase of inhabitants. It is estimated
that by 1970 the number of the Trust Territory's people will have
doubled since the advent of the American administration, only a
quarter of a century. Already some of the small islands in the Truk
and Ponape administrative districts have become so overcrowded
that a portion of their population has been resettled. "Demographic
imbalance is rapidly becoming the rule rather than the exception
in Micronesia." [13] With half the population now less than 20 years
of age, the ever-mounting pressure upon the Administering Authority for additional school facilities has been one of the reasons for
placing education in the vanguard of augmented governmental
operations.

Under the Treaty of Tordesillas, in 1494 the whole of the Pacific
Ocean nominally came under Spanish influence. This sphere of influence narrowed with the centuries, as Spanish attention focused
upon the island areas north of the equator, and in Micronesia the
Spanish looked to Guam as a port of call along the galleon route
from the Philippines to Mexico. Adjacency led to the inclusion of all
the Northern Marianas under Spanish rule, while Spain was slow
to exercise control over the Carolines and never did establish ascendancy over the more distant Marshalls. Germany, in extending its
empire into the Pacific, moved to fill the vacuum and in 1885 declared a protectorate over the Marshalls, took formal possession of
Yap, and raised its flag on a number of the other islands of the
Central and Eastern Carolines, including Truk, Ponape, and Kusaie.
This clash between Spanish and German interests was referred to
Pope Leo XIII for arbitration. His determination confirmed Spain's
claim to sovereignty over the Carolines on the condition that it
maintain an orderly government. German economic access still
continued, and with the Spanish-American War and the ceding of
Guam to the United States, Germany purchased the balance of the

[13] Roland W. Force and Maryanne Force, "Political Change in Micronesia," in Roland W. Force, ed., *Induced Political Change in the Pacific*
(Honolulu: Bishop Museum Press, 1965), p. 6.

Marianas and the Carolines from Spain for $4.5 million. The American delegates to the Paris peace conference could not agree on the advisability of American possession of all of Spain's Micronesian holdings. There was insufficient American interest in the area, despite the extension of the American Board of Commissioners for Foreign Missions' activities into the Marshalls and Eastern Carolines as early as 1852 and the long contact of American seamen with "American Polynesia," as the central Pacific had been called by many cartographers.[14]

Spanish colonial policy in the Marianas set only minimal objectives: pacification and Christianization of the indigenes, maintenance of a way station for Spanish ships, and preservation at the lowest possible cost of orderly government by the Chamorros and by the Carolinians who had first been allowed to settle on Saipan early in the nineteenth century. In the Carolines, when after papal arbitration Spain belatedly tried to counter Germany's imperialistic ambitions by establishing a system of administration, even less was achieved. Spanish efforts to exploit the area's economic resources never were more than half-hearted. Contrasting with Spain, once its hegemony was assured, Germany pushed beyond constructing a Western system of law and order and concentrated upon economic development of Micronesia through copra production and the encouragement of commerce. The inhabitants were required to plant coconut trees under penalty of punishment by forced labor. Through indirect rule and the exercise of autocratic direction, efficient administration was maintained. Public schools were erected, health measures imposed, and roads extended. German efforts were just beginning to bear fruit when Japanese forces occupied the area early in World War I.

During the initial period of Japanese rule, the naval military government ministered to the needs of the region. At the end of 1920, Japan became formally responsible for the government of the future Trust Territory under a class C mandate from the League of Nations. This designation denoted that the people were not deemed capable of self-governance for the foreseeable future. In 1922, following abandonment by the United States of its advocacy of Yap's internationalization, originally to safeguard American interests in

[14] See Pearle E. Quinn, "The Diplomatic Struggle for the Carolines," *Pacific Historical Review*, 14:3 (Sept., 1945), 290; Earl S. Pomeroy, "American Policy Respecting the Marshalls, Carolines, and Marianas, 1898–1941, *"Pacific Historical Review*, 17:1 (Feb., 1948), 43.

the trans-Pacific cable station there, Japanese civilian rule of Micronesia was instituted under the South Seas Government (*Nanyo Cho*). The naval period turned its attention mainly to the opening up of promising islands by working through indigenous political institutions. With the advent of civilian administration, the Japanese embarked upon an ambitious program of economic exploitation and rapid colonization. Particularly around the district centers, the Japanese encouraged accelerated modernization and deliberately endeavored to undermine many aspects of the traditional political systems by inducing acceptance of Japanese lifeways.

Over the years, the Japanese substituted direct for indirect rule, and the Micronesians were relegated to unimportance in their own governance, frequently holding titular roles with little effective power. Major Japanese attention was directed to converting the economy exclusively to the interests of homeland Japan by tapping the ocean resources and producing the fertilizers, sugar, and industrial alcohol essential to Japan's welfare. Commercial fishing and plantation agriculture were encouraged in the Marianas and Palaus, and the latter became a wintering spa for tourists. The Micronesians were regarded as culturally and socially inferior, and if the movement of Japanese, Koreans, and Okinawans into Micronesia had continued, the indigenes would probably not only have been reduced to a peasant proletariat but also eclipsed in all but the outlying islands. By World War II, Japanese resident civilians outnumbered the natives and on some islands far exceeded them. For example, the single town of Garapan on the island of Saipan had 29,000 Asian residents, almost five times the number of Chamorro and Carolinian inhabitants in the entire Marianas.

The education provided Micronesians stressed Japanese language and customs and was vocationally oriented. Few opportunities for advanced education were afforded. The Japanese honored their obligation to care for the health of the people by introducing free medical care, and they also furnished a number of community services, such as electricity in the urbanized areas. Primarily, the Micronesians profited indirectly from the Japanese presence through improved transportation and communications, designed for furthering colonization and economic growth, and the filtering down of the benefits derived from Japanese commercial and industrial activity. The emphasis placed upon cash cropping of copra and tapioca (manioc) gradually moved many of the Micronesians

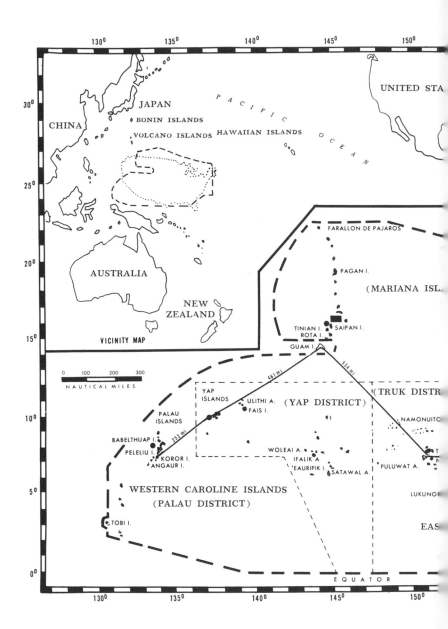

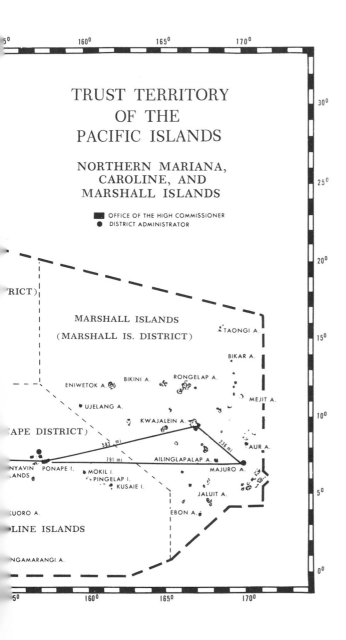

TRUST TERRITORY
OF THE
PACIFIC ISLANDS

NORTHERN MARIANA,
CAROLINE, AND
MARSHALL ISLANDS

■ OFFICE OF THE HIGH COMMISSIONER
● DISTRICT ADMINISTRATOR

NOTE: Broken lines indicate territorial area and districts of jurisdiction and are not to be interpreted as boundaries.

to ever greater dependence upon a money economy, an appreciation of the efficiency of the machine age, and a reliance upon its
products.

In 1935 the Japanese withdrew from the League of Nations, and
military objectives became increasingly dominant. Parts of the
islands were fortified in violation of the mandate conditions,
although the Japanese conscientiously continued to observe other
requirements, such as providing free education, albeit of a limited
nature, and expanding health and sanitation. With World War II,
military defense supplanted economic expansion, and Japanese
efforts were concentrated on military security. As the war continued and conditions deteriorated, the depletion of food supplies
caused the Japanese to adopt ever harsher measures, commandeer-
ing local foodstuffs and other necessary supplies for their military
forces and their colonists. Many of the Micronesians were displaced
from their homes and farms and deprived of medical care and
access to trade sources, and some suffered extreme privation. By
the end of World War II, civilian government had been eclipsed.
In the parts of the Trust Territory where the military forces were
not in direct control, political direction began to be reasserted
through traditional institutions which had previously been undergoing drastic erosion through the Japanese reliance upon direct
police supervision.

In World War II, when the islands came under American jurisdiction, naval military government teams tended to civilian needs,
as had the Japanese military government during World War I.
Over 6,000 Americans were killed wresting Micronesia from
Japanese control,[15] and the temper of the American people hardly
countenanced surrendering the islands to any other nation; conversely, the United States had early declared it sought no territorial
gains from World War II. The placing of the area under United
Nations trusteeship resolved the dilemma, and in 1947, with the
Trusteeship Agreement, the islands technically came under civil
administration. Actually, at the same time President Truman signed
the agreement, he delegated authority on an interim basis to the
Secretary of the Navy and commissioned the Commander-in-Chief,
U.S. Pacific Fleet, as High Commissioner of the Trust Territory, so
that naval personnel continued their administration of the area
until 1951.

[15] See Samuel E. Morison, *History of United States Naval Operations in
World War II*, Vols. VII, VIII (Boston: Little, Brown & Co., 1953).

Shortly after the end of World War II, the general policies to be observed by the United States in Micronesia were announced in a "Pacific Charter" issued by the Pacific fleet commander. This directive provided for the physical restoration of damaged properties and facilities, continued improvement of health and sanitation, encouragement of self-governing communities, institution of a sound program of economic development, and establishment of an educational program.[16] These objectives were more generally augmented by Articles 73 and 76 of the United Nation's Charter. The former declares that the interests of the inhabitants of territories whose peoples have not yet attained a full measure of self-government are paramount and that the members of the United Nations "accept as a public trust the obligation to promote to the utmost within the system of international peace and security established by the . . . Charter, the well-being of the inhabitants of these territories. . . ." Article 76 applies specifically to trusteeships and in part binds the United States "to encourage respect for human rights and for fundamental freedoms for all without distinction as to race, sex, language, or religion, and to encourage recognition of the interdependence of the peoples of the world."

Article 6 of the Trusteeship Agreement for the Former Japanese Mandated Islands spells out the responsibilities of the United States in great detail. In discharging its obligations, the United States is committed to:

1. foster the development of such political institutions as are suited to the trust territory and shall promote the development of the inhabitants of the trust territory towards self-government or independence as may be appropriate to the particular circumstances of the trust territory and its peoples and the freely expressed wishes of the peoples concerned: and to this end shall give the inhabitants of the trust territory a progressively increasing share in the administrative services in the territory; shall develop their participation in government; shall give due recognition to the customs of the inhabitants in providing a system of law for the territory; and shall take other appropriate measures toward these ends;

2. promote the economic advancement and self-sufficiency of the inhabitants, and to this end shall regulate the use of natural resources; encourage the development of fisheries, agriculture, and industries; protect the inhabitants against the loss of their lands and resources; and improve the means of transportation and communication;

3. promote the social advancement of the inhabitants and to this end

[16] *Information on the Trust Territory of the Pacific Islands Under Naval Administration to 1 November 1950* [Honolulu: 1951], p. 5.

shall protect the rights and fundamental freedoms of all elements of the population without discrimination; protect the health of the inhabitants; control the traffic in arms and ammunition, opium and other dangerous drugs, and alcoholic and other spirituous beverages; and institute such other regulations as may be necessary to protect the inhabitants against social abuses; and

4. promote the educational advancement of the inhabitants, and to this end shall take steps toward the establishment of a general system of elementary education; facilitate the vocational and cultural advancement of the population; and shall encourage qualified students to pursue higher education, including training on the professional level.

As the Administering Authority, the United States also agreed under Article 7 of the agreement to ". . . guarantee to the inhabitants of the trust territory freedom of conscience, and, subject only to the requirements of public order and security, freedom of speech, of the press, and of assembly; freedom of worship, and of religious teaching; and freedom of migration and movement." [17]

Felix Keesing identified three schools of thought in native policy: the "zoological park" idea, assimilation into the "superior" society of the dominant group, and a mid-way which fosters the growth of a modernized native society by encouraging only that which is believed desirable in the native culture.[18] In proceeding under the letter of the Trusteeship Agreement, the United States long considered itself to be following the last of these three approaches, not presuming "to determine in advance the ultimate goals of cultural, social, economic and political evolution in Micronesia." [19] In retrospect, in the fields of economic and social development its actions for many years more closely approximated the zoological park policy. The theorem was unquestionably accepted that it was not to the indigenes' interest to accustom them to a standard of living which they would not be able to maintain with their own limited resources. "It is not the intent of the Administration to propagate either a highly sophisticated or a mendicant society in the Trust Territory." [20] As a result of granting aid in a form and at a rate

[17] The United Nations Charter and the Trusteeship Agreement for the former Japanese Mandated Islands are reproduced in U.S. Congress, Senate, *Review of United Nations Charter Collection of Documents*, Senate Doc. No. 87, 83d Congress, 2d Sess. (1954).

[18] Felix M. Keesing, *The South Seas in the Modern World* (rev. ed.; New York: John Day Co., 1945), pp. 81 ff.

[19] G. P. Murdock, *Social Organization and Government in Micronesia*, CIMA Final Report No. 19, Part 3 (Washington: Office of Naval Research, 1949), pp. 5, 6.

[20] U.S. Congress, House, Committee on Interior and Insular Affairs, *Report of a Special Subcommittee on Territorial and Insular Affairs*, 83d Congress, 2d Sess. (1954), p. 26.

which would encourage an integrated socio-economic system and of restricting business activity to Micronesian enterpreneurs, the infra-structure destroyed during World War II remained for the most part unreconstructed, and a long period of economic stagnation ensued. By virtue of the attempt to avoid cultural demoralization and to protect the Micronesians against external exploitation, the Territory never regained the level of economic prosperity enjoyed under the Japanese.

Transference of responsibility from the Navy to the Department of Interior in 1951 introduced some changes in the style of administration observed, but the basic "holding operation" policy remained unaltered. Meanwhile, the "temporary" physical facilities erected by the Navy during the war continued to deteriorate. Much of the effort of the Administering Authority was directed to their patchwork maintenance through stretching the inadequate funds appropriated by Congress, and a large share of all improvements tended directly or indirectly to the needs of American personnel. In the admission of the high commissioner, "possibly the Interior Department erred in contending that it could operate the Trust Territory more cheaply than the Navy and laid a poor basis for getting more money from Congress." [21]

Only in matters pertaining to the national security of the United States was the policy of frugality and non-disturbance of the indigenous inhabitants waived. Under the Trusteeship Agreement, the United States reserved the right to close portions of the area for security reasons and to direct their use to the purposes of the Administering Authority. Whole island populations in the Marshalls were resettled to enable the utilization of their lands for atomic testing and the development of anti-missile defensive systems. Some inhabitants who were not moved were accidentally dusted by radioactive fallout. In the Marianas, the operation on Saipan of a highly classified training ground for Nationalist Chinese guerillas was accompanied by the return of that island from Interior's to Navy's jurisdiction. Rota remained under Interior, while Guam, just outside the Trust Territory's periphery, was granted a greater degree of self-governance as befitting its half century as an American possession. Given the close cultural and family ties of the Chamorro people, that the inhabitants of the Marianas "should be divided into three [separate jurisdictions] seems almost incred-

[21] *Honolulu Advertiser*, Oct. 24, 1965, p. A4.

ible." [22] It was not until 1962, after the discontinuance of the C.I.A. sponsored training activity, that the Northern Marianas were reunited under the Interior Department's administration, which also supervised the Territory of Guam's relationships with Washington.

Except for matters concerned with the national security of the United States, all that has transpired under the trusteeship has in good faith been intended to further the best interests of the Micronesians.[23] As a consequence, past American policy has not redounded to the detriment of Micronesian-American relations. In many respects the United States came to be viewed more favorably than Japan. Although under Japan there had been a wider variety of goods and services and greater opportunities to obtain employment, ceilings had been placed on the modernized aspirations of the Micronesians. Attendance at higher schools had been denied the indigenes, and they were ineligible for other than minor governmental positions. The Japanese attitude of inherent superiority did not sit well, and their deliberate intervention in indigenous affairs disturbed traditional superordinate-subordinate relationships and upset the functioning of the customary social and political organizations. The conscious endeavors by Americans to preserve Micronesian traditional ways, their demonstration of respect for the indigenes as human beings, and the adoption of indirect rule as a system of government collectively served to reassure the Micronesians and to solidify working relationships with the American administrators.

New policy pronouncements from Washington bid well to materially modify this near two decades of American "protectionism." Early in the 1960's, the decision was made to bring the inhabitants of the island complex into the orbit of twentieth century living as quickly as possible, while at the same time exercising precautions to avoid the dangers inherent in such rapid advancement. The means chosen was to accelerate the planned social, economic, and political development of Micronesia, with the last to be undertaken with a view toward the shape of future relationships between Micronesia and the United States. Seemingly, Washington had concluded that it was to the advantage of American security to recast the old policy.

[22] Emil J. Sady, *The United Nations and Dependent Peoples* (Washington: Brookings, 1956), p. 201.

[23] This is not to deny the element of rationalization inherent in the policy followed, for the policy was to the advantage of the national security of the United States and at a relatively nominal cost.

One of the results flowing from this new approach was the place-
ment of the schools in the forefront of deliberately fostered cultural
change, upon the premise that trained manpower is essential for
increased economic activity and the informed citizenry necessary
to assume powers of greater self-government. Under an accelerated
educational program inaugurated in May, 1963, during a three-
year period, over three hundred new classrooms were added to the
Territorial school system, high schools were opened at the headquarters of each of the six administrative districts and in two sub-
centers, recruitment of qualified teachers from the mainland
United States was intensified, and a general upgrading of the
system was begun. Major emphasis was placed upon the teaching
of English. Next scheduled for a similar crash program has been
the improvement of health services. Meanwhile, a survey of the
region's resources by Robert R. Nathan Associates, Inc., provided
a long-range plan for the Territory's total economic development,
and Hawaii Architects and Engineers, Inc., submitted a twenty-
year, $237 million physical development program. A contract
signed in 1968 calls for modernizing air travel through the Territory with jet service, and as the initial stage, the building of
tourist-style hotels in all six of the district headquarters. The dispersal of Peace Corps Volunteers to all parts of the Trust Territory
promises to more than double the number of Americans temporarily residing in the Territory and to influence significantly Micronesian attitudes and aspirations. Contemplated is nothing short of
lifting the peoples of Micronesia out of their "zoo" into a way of
life more attuned to the modern world, and not so incidentally,
patterned in good part on the American model.

Much yet remains to be accomplished before the newly rephrased
objectives for the Trust Territory can be realized. The education
program even though expanded, has not been able to keep pace
with increased school enrollments. According to the Interior Department's own appraisals,[24] "half of the classrooms now occupied
are far below an acceptable standard and many are greatly overcrowded." "Unless secondary school facilities are greatly increased,
by 1972 we will be able to accept in high school only one of every

[24] This and all of the following quotations are official appraisals of the
Secretary of the Interior which have been extracted from his letter and its
accompanying attachment, requesting markedly expanded funds for the Trust
Territory, reproduced in full in U.S. Congress, House, Committee on Interior
and Insular Affairs, Report No. 2172, 89th Congress, 2d Sess. (Oct. 3, 1966),
pp. 18 ff.

four eighth grade graduates." "Fully 43 per cent of all public school
teachers have not graduated from high school, and an additional
30 per cent have only high school diplomas." Despite the attention
now being given to improved health services, "there is still a very
high incidence of filariasis, amebic dysentery, leprosy, and tuber-
culosis—illnesses which are almost unknown or completely controlled in the United States, and which could be controlled in the
Trust Territory. There are almost no registered nurses in the Trust
Territory, and 90 per cent of the doctors are not qualified by medical degrees. The district hospitals. are all overcrowded and three
are wholly inadequate. Most of the 90 outlying dispensaries are
structurally unsound and staffed largely by insufficiently trained
personnel." "Throughout the area there is almost no decent housing
and communities are characterized by the large number of dwell-
ings constructed of leftover World War II corrugated iron. Because
of the low-income level of the people, lack of lending institutions,
and lack of long-range community planning, there has been little
success in launching well-developed housing programs." "Power,
water, and sewage disposal facilities are urgently needed throughout Micronesia. . . . At the present time, less than 10 per cent of the
total population has a protected water supply. While sewage systems do exist on some islands, there is no sanitary disposal system
on any island." "With few exceptions, roads in the trust territory
are generally deplorable. . . ." "Airfields which have been built must
be surfaced and protected from erosion; runway lights should be
installed; the airport at Ponape must be completed. . . .[25] Urgently
needed communication facilities include improved radio equipment
at each district center and regional service center. . . ." "In addition,
courthouses, administration buildings, employee quarters, and legislative buildings are required. Throughout the Trust Territory,
public buildings are in a sorry state."

To help overcome these and other deficiencies, the Secretary of
the Interior in 1966 requested a sum of $172 million for capital
improvements over a five-year period and an additional $152 mil-
lion for expansion of essential services associated with the improvement program. Combined, this represented an amount almost three
times the total of all appropriations made to the Department of the
Interior for the Trust Territory during the previous fifteen years it
had administered the area. The Congress responded by raising the

[25] The Ponape district still depends upon amphibian planes using a water
landing.

appropriation ceiling to $25 million for fiscal year 1967 (from $17.5 million) and for fiscal years 1968 and 1969 to $35 million, with the implication that the greater authorization would continue if the Territory demonstrated it could manage the expenditure of the increased funds. However, the actual augmentation of appropriations has not kept pace (e.g., only $24 million for fiscal year 1968), so the financial needs of the Territory continue.

By the end of World War II the islands of Micronesia had been ravaged, their native economy based on copra destroyed, communications were non-existent, and schooling had all but disappeared. Reclamation of so many islands so widely dispersed presented a colossal task. Under the Trusteeship Agreement, the United States assumed an obligation not just for physical rehabilitation but also for promotion of the political, economic, social, and educational advancement of Micronesia. "Advancement" is a relative term at best, and by today's standards, American past efforts are now being found wanting. Viewed from the perspective of the conditions the United States encountered when it wrested the islands from Japan, these same activities may be judged accomplishments. But whatever the measure, against the backdrop of the restricted self-government permitted the Micronesians by earlier colonial powers and the total absence of any effort to prepare them for determining their own political destiny, the United States' performance stands forth as a positive and significant contribution to the welfare of the Trust Territory. Of all four areas of development, it is in the political realm that the endeavors of the United States have scored their greatest success. It is to political advancement, and the use of the legislative institution as the chosen vehicle for accomplishing this end, that the remainder of this work now turns its attention.

CHAPTER 2

Governmental Strata

IN ITS FIRST ACCOUNTING to the Trusteeship Council, the United States laid before the United Nations its plans for the political advancement of the Trust Territory: initially would come self-governing municipalities, then progressively the powers of regional district bodies would be increased, and finally, Territory-wide organs of self-government in which the indigenous population would play a substantial if not major part.[1] At that time the municipal government structure had already taken shape, and the precursors of today's district legislative bodies were beginning to function. The convening of the Congress of Micronesia on July 12, 1965, represented the implementing of the third stage of this political-development plan by which an ever-expanding scope of self-governance has been transferred to the Micronesians. To the annoyance of some members of the United Nations pressing for ever faster political change, the American personnel still staff the key administrative posts and retain the reins of power, with veto rights over all indigenous political action. Much yet remains to be accomplished before Micronesians assume full responsibility for their own governance. But throughout the two decades of American administration, the United States adhered steadfastly to the broad outline of development sketched before the United Nations, and the ethnocentric horizons of the region's nine major cultures have been ever broadened as the Micronesians have been prepared for participation first in district-wide and then Territory-wide self-government.

Nowhere is the word "democratic," as the measure of the new political structure, written into the sources of authority for the United States' administration of the Trust Territory.[2] They only refer to the promotion of development toward self-government or independence in accordance with the expressed wishes of the Micronesians. Free elections and a share in political decision-making

[1] TCOR, 5th Sess., 19th meeting, July 13, 1949, p. 245.
[2] See John Sandelmann, *Some Observations on the Problem of "Self Government" in the Trust Territory of the Pacific Islands* (Honolulu: 1953), p. 106.

thus are subsumed; coincidentally, these constitute fundamental features of a democracy. Though the basic documents are silent, the United States has entertained no doubts that the government of the Trust Territory should take shape in harmony with the principles underlying its own system, and it has so disported itself. In the fall of 1946 the commander of the Marianas restated and amplified the military government's policies already in effect: [3] democratic processes of government are to be encouraged, but not fostered arbitrarily. Before any move is made, local forms of government must be studied and comprehended. Once the customary governmental system is understood, the logical place to infuse democratic principles is to be determined. After democratic processes are inaugurated in a small way, they will be extended gradually to larger groups and areas. None of this was necessarily antithetical to the indigenous political systems of Micronesia, for some practices traditionally followed had democratic overtones. In addition, in a few cases the Americans had been preceded by the Japanese in proposing the use of elections for choosing "chiefs." [4]

What the American administrators have tended to lose sight of is that "most cultural elements are transferred in terms of objective form stripped of the meaning which is an integral part of them in their original context." [5] Emphasis has been placed upon the implanting of structural changes, with less attention given to ascertaining whether formal adoption has been accompanied by any modification in basic Micronesian political patterns. Because the changes were sponsored by the Administering Authority, the Territory's inhabitants complied in their observance, but to many the new patterns were for long extraneous to the political relationships governing their conduct. Five years after elected municipal government was introduced to Palau, the district anthropologist in Palau advised the district administrator (DistAd), "Until very recently, older and more conservative Palauans have considered participation in elections a kind of favor to the American Administration. . . . Having attended local elections in the past in both

[3] Dorothy E. Richard, *U.S. Naval Administration of the Trust Territory of the Pacific Islands* (Washington: Office of the Chief of Naval Operations, 1957), II, 306–307.

[4] Burt Tolerton and Jerome Rauch, *Social Organization, Land Tenure, and Subsistence Economy of Lukunor, Nomoi Islands*, CIMA Final Report No. 26 (Washington: National Research Council, Pacific Science Board, 1949), p. 48.

[5] R. Linton, ed., *Acculturation in Seven American Indian Tribes* (New York: D. Appleton-Century Co., Inc., 1940), p. 486.

Palau and Yap, I can personally testify that it is embarrassing to watch magistrates and hereditary chiefs act unbidden to marshall all persons to the polling places. . . . The motivation in most cases has sprung from a desire to please and impress the visiting American dignitaries rather than from any deep-seated feeling of civic responsibility." [6] Under these circumstances, it was to be expected that in many districts the innovation of electing local magistrates would return to leadership posts the incumbents who had previously held them by ascriptive right. Only as there developed a sense of political consciousness and of local initiative in the Western sense did these superimposed institutions become more than empty forms.

In their initial zeal duly to recognize the customs of the Micronesians and adapt democratic procedures to the values of the islanders, the American administrators accepted as traditional many of the political configurations they found upon the United States' entry into Micronesia. Municipal government as it was evolved by the Americans in Palau, Yap, and Ponape was premised upon the geographical jurisdiction of each local governmental unit's being coterminous with the districts of the *ancien régime*. In truth, the "independent" divisions of Ponape Island, which the Americans regarded as originating in antiquity, had been increased to five only late during the Spanish and German times; Sokehs was formerly part of Kiti, and Net originally included within U. [7] The ten districts of Yap were delineated by the Japanese when they expanded the eight "traditional" divisions first set up by the Germans. [8] Similarly, the conversion of Palau's "traditional" sixteen districts into municipalities, and the recognition of the Koror and Melekeok confederations, ignored the fact that these groupings had been preceded by other confederations with different geographical delimitations. [9] In fact, the Americans had far greater leeway in identifying the physical boundaries of the new units of municipal government they were sponsoring and need not have

[6] Memo from District Anthropologist Palau to DistAd Palau, July 14, 1953.

[7] William R. Bascom, *Ponape: A Pacific Economy in Transition*, USCC Economic Survey No. 8 (Honolulu: 1946), p. 41.

[8] Stanford University School of Naval Administration, *Handbook of the Trust Territory* (Washington: Office of the Chief of Naval Operations, 1948), p. 77.

[9] See, for example, Arthur J. Vidich, "The Political Impact of Colonial Administration" (Ph.D. thesis, Harvard University: 1952), pp. 80–82. In addition to the fourteen independent districts listed there, Tobi and Sonserol should be added.

believed themselves so restricted. Part of this constraint arose from the Americans' being loath to disturb the customary and hereditary leaders. They believed it would cause less confusion if the present leaders were encouraged to retain their authority while at the same time promoting the election of local officials, thus blending liberal and conservative elements of government.

LOCAL GOVERNMENT

A considerable measure of indirect rule was necessitated by the smallness of the staff during the German regime, and much of traditional local government was retained. The Japanese appeared to follow the German system, but while continuing the form, they eroded the substance. During the Japanese period, local officials of two grades were appointed, village (or island) chiefs and village headmen,[10] the latter nominally supervised by the chiefs. These functionaries submitted reports on local conditions, collected taxes, notified their people of all applicable laws and regulations, and forwarded to higher authority all communications originating in the local area. These posts were normally given to lineage leaders, but in time the Japanese appointed persons more for their amenability to compliance with orders than for their possession of the highest ascribed status. Village policemen and secretaries assisted the officials in many localities. In actual practice, most of the effective authority over local affairs was exercised by the Japanese, and Yanaihara could write that the "office of village chief or village headman retains none of the traditional meaning of chieftain in the gens society, but is merely a subordinate administrative position under the government with purely territorial authority." [11] The structure of local government functioning under the Japanese furnished the matrix for the municipalities founded by the American administration. To the municipalities was returned a greater degree of autonomy, and most units were modified by the addition of a council, a significant incorporation of the legislative function into formal government at the local level.

In December of 1945, at the close of World War II, the naval

[10] Reference to Japanese titles are omitted due to the different terminology encountered: such as *soncho* (atoll magistrate) and *buraku sodai* (village headman) in the Marshalls; *so-soncho* (village chief) and *soncho* (village headman) in the Palaus; and, *soncho* for the mayor and *joyako* for the Chamorro "akonseheros" (councilmen) on Saipan.

[11] Tadao Yanaihara, *Pacific Islands under Japanese Mandate* (Shanghai: Kelly and Walsh, Ltd., 1939), p. 265. Written about Palau, this statement also characterized most of the other areas of the Mandate.

military government was directed to observe that "the inhabitants of the occupied territories be . . . encouraged and assisted to assume as much as possible of the management of their own affairs and the conduct of their own government. Local governments, insofar as practicable, should be patterned on the political-social institutions which the inhabitants have evolved for themselves. . . . Legislation and enforcement machinery should be held to the minimum requisite to the preservation of peace and order, the maintenance of property rights, the enforcement of measures for health and sanitation, and those laws respecting trade, industry, and labor, which are essential to economic well-being." [12] This policy encouraged a resurgence of traditional leadership, but local units continued mainly to coincide with the "traditional" geographic-political divisions drawn during the Japanese era. With the military authorities avoiding as a matter of policy the setting up of a uniform system, the nature of the government which ensued varied widely. "In some cases, the local political system was allowed to continue in operation, with strong chieftains occupying their posts by right of inheritance. In others, a type of local government dating from Japanese or German times was encouraged as customary. In still others, a council form of government patterned along American democratic lines was established." [13]

By 1947 the need to regularize local government was manifest if orderly political development was to be encouraged. "Municipalities" were normally recognized as coterminous with an island or a locally recognized division of a larger island but sometimes could be a combination of several small adjacent islands. Each municipality was to have a magistrate,[14] assisted by a council either appointed or elected. A scribe, or secretary, and a treasurer were to aid the magistrate in keeping records, maintaining vital statistics, collecting taxes, and disbursing municipal funds. Local revenues would be used to pay these officials, policemen in some instances, and school teachers. Election of magistrates was encouraged, and each year the Trust Territory reported an ever larger number of municipalities headed by popularly chosen magistrates. As was to be expected, at first the people selected their hereditary chiefs, but gradually they recognized the value of naming officers

---

[12] Directive of Admiral Spruance, quoted in Stanford University School of Naval Administration, *Handbook . . .* , *op. cit.*, p. 93.

[13] U. S. Department of the Interior, *Management Survey of the Government of the Trust Territory of the Pacific Islands* (Washington: 1951), I, 47.

[14] In a few areas—Ponape, Saipan, Tinian—the name "mayor" is used.

with qualifications other than just ranking hereditary status.[15] Sometimes councilmen were reported "elected" when in fact senior family heads had automatically assumed these posts.[16] These same reports show a slight shrinkage in the number of municipalities as a few were consolidated for purposes of efficiency and economy, until the number firmed around 102.

The indigenous leaders accepted this municipal organization, at first "in many cases, without enthusiasm, for, when all was said and done, they preferred their own system of government." [17] For a period of time these municipalities "served mainly as ineffective one-way channels for the transmission of district orders to the people," with the officers lacking enough personal authority or unwilling to exercise initiative to enforce the orders.[18] Although these local units were to bear the full support of the elementary schools, their resources proved inadequate, and this responsibility was gradually shifted to the district legislatures and finally to the Territorial government. Depending upon the population size of the municipality and the extent of its urban character, the activities of some expanded substantially, with Saipan, the largest, performing functions comparable to those of a small city and listing approximately one hundred persons on its payroll.

Starting in April of 1957, the administration embarked upon an ambitious program of "chartering" municipalities. A multi-purpose objective underlay this effort, namely to delineate municipal boundaries, define authority, specify taxing and legislative powers, set up procedures for the election of municipal officers, and outline their duties. The model, which forms the basis of each local unit's fundamental law, was worked out after taking into account the Micronesian district leaders' comments on the original draft. It presented "few if any new concepts . . . ; essentially it follows the basic ideas contained in the Interim Regulations [under the Navy] and other earlier guides for the establishment of local governments. It does broaden these ideas to meet more advanced condi-

[15] The Micronesians' reluctance publicly to disgrace a traditional leader was well illustrated by the Kusaiens' in 1947 voting the "king" out of office but, to mitigate his defeat, electing his son to the office of chief magistrate. James L. Lewis, *Kusaiean Acculturation*, CIMA Final Report No. 17 (Washington: National Research Council, Pacific Science Board, 1948), p. 61.

[16] E.g., see Marc J. Swartz, "The Social Organization of Behavior: Relations Among Kinsmen on Romonum, Truk" (Ph.D. thesis, Harvard University: March, 1958), pp. 111–112.

[17] TCOR, 8th Sess., 325th meeting, Feb. 16, 1951, par. 40.

[18] Garth N. Jones, "Administration of the Trust Territory of the Pacific Islands" (Ph.D. thesis, University of Utah: 19 1), p. 283.

tions and to some extent standardizes organizational patterns and governmental procedures." [19] Aiming at introducing greater uniformity into the structure and functioning of municipalities, it contemplates that each chartered unit will have an elected council empowered to adopt local ordinances, which become effective upon the concurrence of the district administrator, and to enact emergency ordinances with the sole approval of the magistrate, the local chief executive. The municipal tax levies and the annual budget plan must similarly receive the district administrator's assent. Originally the program anticipated chartering twenty municipalities a year, but the number was reduced to ten as a more realistic annual goal. It was at first thought "highly probable" that all 102 municipalities would be chartered by 1963.[20] Something closer to half of this number have now been chartered, with every Palauan and all but one Ponapean municipality so qualified.

The chartering project was partially undertaken upon the Trusteeship Council's urging that there be more immediate progress toward self-government. An objective appraisal of the program attributes more importance to the understanding gained by Micronesians regarding the processes of government incidental to the effort expended in preparing a community for chartering than to any greater enjoyment of municipal autonomy. Nor were significant structural changes or even modification in day-to-day operations made upon the recognition of the new status. Before a charter is granted by the high commissioner, through an extended series of meetings local leaders are familiarized with their tasks under the charter and with the procedures necessary to be followed. In some cases this has merely meant instructing these officials on operating the local government in the manner the Administering Authority originally intended but which they have failed to observe. The requirement of district administrator approval for local ordinances and annual budgets constituted no innovation, but municipalities, particularly those distant from district headquarters, had been lax in their compliance with these "technicalities."

Through the device of chartering, the personnel of the Administering Authority have been able to gain access to municipal officials to train them in the procedures of Westernized local government. Chartering also gave the Administering Authority an opportunity

---

[19] Memo of HiCom, April 11, 1957, quoted in Thorwald Esbensen, "A Report on Political Education in Truk," [Moen, Truk: circa 1959], pp. 5, 6.

[20] TCOR, 22d Sess., 895th meeting, June 17, 1958, par. 26.

to teach the officials the simple steps in parliamentary maneuver necessary to conduct council meetings and a chance to encourage local incentive by preparing them to play an active role in place of waiting for instructions from above. Today the Administering Authority views the chartering, as exemplified by the new Kolonia Town Charter (Ponape), as responsible for the beginning of a trend toward the increased awareness and involvement of municipal governments in problems of urban development.

The magistrate of the typical municipality, whether or not chartered, continues to provide liaison between his community and the district administration. As the local chief executive, he promulgates the laws of the Trust Territory and of the district and other information addressed to his people, and is charged with seeing that they abide by these laws and the local ordinances. He is accountable for the work of the municipal officers and employees and maintains or supervises the safe keeping of community property and funds. The magistrate also oversees the preparation of municipal tax rolls and the annual budget, the disbursement of funds, and the holding of local elections. In outlying areas where councils serve only as "advisors" to the magistrate, binding directives are normally issued by him after a consensus of the council has been reached. Where elected councils function, as chairman of the council he presides over their meetings, keeps a record of their actions, and directly or indirectly participates in the adoption of local ordinances.

In many of the smaller municipalities, most of the funds collected from head taxes, boat taxes, coconut tree levies, license fees, and other sources of local moneys go to pay the salaries of the magistrate and other municipal officers, with little left over for the funding of community projects. As traditional leaders formerly directed communal activities without need of any financing through taxes and, under the Japanese, the local officials received a small remuneration directly from the branch governments, a degree of dissatisfaction exists over the levying of taxes merely to pay the "keep" of officers of an "American-imposed" municipal government. Non-compliance with local tax laws is widespread. On the other hand, expanded municipal-type services are desired, and there is little inclination to return to the traditional forms and ways of tending to local matters. Today, most project-oriented spending performed for local communities is financed with Trust Territory funds or with grants-in-aid from district legislatures, which leads to frustration when it is not in accord with locally expressed priorities. This is the stuff out of which political interest springs, and it can be through the municipal councils that this public opinion may be expressed and positive steps formulated to take corrective action.

The municipality—whether the chartered variety observing Western political ideas and processes or older ones retaining the traditional political organization relatively unchanged—affords the greatest degree of autonomy of any institution of self-government in which Micronesians play a part. At the district and Territorial levels there are no indigenous executive organs of government. In contrast, at the local level all governmental affairs are conducted by the inhabitants of the Trust Territory, and as a practical matter the district administration does not materially affect the course of day-to-day community government. On islands other than those on which the district headquarters are located, contact with the municipalites becomes less frequent, and district administration knowledge of their operations is ofttimes incomplete. There is even less supervision of those municipalities reached by brief field-trip visits no more than several times a year. Three-sevenths of the Territory's population lives off the islands where the district administration is headquartered, and for them, local government is in good part synonymous with self-government.

DISTRICT ADMINISTRATION

Given the vast distances within the Trust Territory, it was essential for its government that an intermediate level of administration be interposed between the high commissioner (HiCom) and his departments, on the one hand, and the municipalities on the other. When the Germans and Japanese faced the same problem, they utilized the geographical dispersal of the islands into relatively contiguous clusters as the logic for district demarcation. The pattern set by the Japanese was later fairly closely followed by the Americans. Although in Palau, Ponape, and Yap the same sites have served as administrative centers for all three nations,[21] corresponding continuity has not characterized each new administra-

[21] In Truk and the Marshalls, the decision was made to locate the district headquarters on different islands than those used by the Japanese, to avail the Trust Territory of plants built by the American military forces; on Saipan, the town of Garapan was completely leveled during the taking of the island, and the district administrative center was placed close to the military government's temporary civilian camps.

tion's succession to the work of its predecessor. "Except for meager official documents passed on by one government to the next, the informal advice offered by retiring administrators, and the reports of native informants to the incoming group on their feelings toward the predecessors, each new set of rulers was forced to rediscover the nature of native societies." [22]

Originally the high commissioner named four officers as district governors, with two districts, Truk and Ponape, under a single governor for the Eastern Carolines. The Marshall Islands, also under a single governor, were divided, with Kwajalein and the surrounding area as one district and the rest of the Marshalls as the other, with Majuro as its center. Yap was recognized as a sub-district in the Western Carolines, which was under the jurisdiction of a third district governor, and the fourth's jurisidiction covered the Mariana Islands. The Marshalls were eventually combined into a single administrative district, Truk and Ponape were separated, and Yap's status was changed to that of a fully independent district with its own administration. Later in the 1950's, when the Navy regained supervision of part of the Northern Marianas and the Interior Department retained the balance of Micronesia, the Trust Territory for a period was divided into seven districts. Now, at least for the moment, the internal division of the Territory for administrative purposes appears stabilized, with the number of districts again fixed at six: Marshalls, Ponape, Truk, Yap, Palau, and Marianas. How long this will continue remains problematical, for Kusaie in the Ponape district desires separate status as a distinct administrative entity, as do Rota in the Marianas and the Outer Islands in the Yap district.

Relatively little of the literature treating the governance of the Trust Territory considers the exact nature of the district administrator and the agencies operating at the district level. The district administrator occupies a perplexingly ambiguous role. As appointee of the high commissioner,[23] he is his principal's field representative, supervising all district government and responsible for overseeing the activities of the municipalities. Each district is generally organized so as to coincide administratively with the

[22] John Useem, "Applied Anthropology in Micronesia," *Human Organization*, 6:4 (Fall, 1947), 1.
[23] To be accurate, district administrators are appointees of the high commissioner with concurrence from Washington; the latter approval apparently includes involvement of both the executive (Interior) and congressional (committee chairmen) branches.

functional structure of the Trust Territory's Headquarters on Saipan. This results in an anomalous dual supervision, with the district health, education, and agriculture officers looking as much, if not more, to their specialist supervisors on Saipan as to their district administrator. The latter, though, provides the essential supporting services, and in making up the district budget, he prepares the preliminary estimates for the various services; therefore all district departments are dependent upon him. At the same time, he is also the executive officer charged with carrying out the laws passed by the district legislature composed solely of indigenes. However, there have yet to be taken steps to relate the district administrations to these legislative bodies, so as to make them both parts of an integrated institution at the district level.

In the Territory's scheme of government, the district governments are primarily responsible for domestic relations, inheritance, and land law. The construction and maintenance of secondary roads connecting the municipalities and of docks used extensively for travel between the municipalities also fall within the districts' jurisdiction. Liquor control, including the imposition of wholesale license fees and taxes on alcoholic beverages, is assigned to the district. Exclusive issuance of licenses for wholesale businesses, save a named few kept under Territorial supervision, is also exercised by the districts. District revenues may be augmented by sales taxes imposed by act of the district legislature. In the functions of public education and health, the district governments retain an undefined responsibility for support, but in the main these are directly funded through revenues allocated by the Territorial government.

The indigenous inhabitants regard the district administrator and the various executive agencies in the district as part of the American administration, a superimposed government in which they have little part other than as employees. Speaking for the high commissioner, the district administrator is expected to promote the Administering Authority's program. This results in there being no locally accountable political executive, and the district administrator is held in check only by the limits to which the district legislature allows itself to be led and by the degree of enthusiasm with which the Micronesians willingly cooperate with the district administration. There is a growing interest in local selection of the district administrator, possibly by election, which aims toward making him and his administration part of the indigenous government, like the district legislatures which are looked upon as "Micronesian." One of the laws passed by the first Congress of Micronesia provides the vehicle for securing local accountability by providing for the chartering of district governments. In place of a field organization of the Trust Territory, there would emerge at the district level a locally responsible government in a way comparable to state governors and government in the United States and their relationship to Washington. It is open to question whether the Trust Territory's limited resources and population warrant such a Federally modeled form of government; on the other hand, it would promote a greater adaptability to district diversity and would materially encourage the indigenes' sense of commitment to furthering their own governance.

The degree of discretion which a district administrator may exercise in arranging his district's organization and in directing the course of its activities depends upon the scope of power allocated him and the extent to which he has been delegated authority to act without obtaining Saipan's clearance. There has been little consistency in this, as it has varied with both the policies of high commissioners and the personality of the district administrator. Usually the latter is not free to choose the heads for the district departments and has no independent power to reallocate funds inter-departmentally once the annual budget has been fixed at Territory Headquarters. He normally has broad authority in outlining the district organization, but the building blocks remain primarily those functional activities found in all other districts and fall under the policy supervision of Saipan.

One or two assistants aid each district administrator, and he may place some of the district departments directly under them. In the Truk district, for example, the assistant district administrator for Administration supervises finance, supply, personnel, and field trips, while the assistant for Public Affairs works closely with the district legislature, keeps the census, and is charged with political, community, and social development. The major line activities in Truk, such as agriculture, education, public health, and the office of land management, are directly under the supervision of the district administrator.

Gradually Micronesians have risen within the district administration to hold ever higher posts of authority, until in 1965 the first indigene was named a district administrator. It is only a question of time before this will be repeated in the other districts. Meanwhile, in all, indigenes serve as assistant district commissioners. Notwithstanding, so long as most of the major decisions continue to be made at the Territory Headquarters, it remains problematical whether this "localization" of personnel will cause the Micronesians to modify their attitude that the district government is "American."

TERRITORIAL GOVERNMENT

The structural and functional similarities of the Japanese South Seas Government under Mandate status and that erected by the American administration testify to the paramountcy of geography and of need for comparable governmental services over abstract doctrines, no matter how much the two countries' fundamental political philosophies may have differed. The ideological imprint is disclosed more by the manner in which the administering personnel have disported themselves and the way they have related to the Micronesians. The major differences in the activities of the two powers stem mainly from Japan's introduction of thousands of its nationals into Micronesia and its exploitation of the resources of the area for its own advantage; American policy has been to reserve the region primarily for the benefit of its indigenous inhabitants and, until recently, to move no faster in social and economic innovations than the Micronesians themselves desired and were able. In attitude, the Japanese civilian administrators were arrogant and sometimes harsh in their treatment of the Micronesians. To the indigenes the Americans at times may appear no less arbitrary, but the human rights of the Micronesians have been for the most part faithfully observed. In addition to being given political freedom, the Micronesians have also been gradually prepared for the full exercise of political self-determination.

Under Executive Order of the President, as relayed through the Secretary of the Interior, the high commissioner has been charged with the exercise of executive and—until recently curtailed by the convening of the Congress of Micronesia—legislative [24] authority over the Trust Territory. Under the Mandate, the Japanese director of the South Seas Government similarly wielded executive and legislative powers. The Trust Territory is covered by few enactments of the U.S. Congress, so that practically all statutory law in the

[24] See pp. 179–181 for a fuller discussion of the high commissioner's former legislative powers.

Territory falls within the compass of the Trust Territory Code as now augmented by acts of the Congress of Micronesia and urgency orders of the high commissioner. In contrast, the most important laws of the Japanese empire, such as the "Six Codes," were equally applicable in the Mandated territory. In matters affecting the indigenous inhabitants, both Japan [25] and the United States have recognized local precedent and custom as tempering the fiat of the law of the ministering nation.

The United States was remiss in not moving the Headquarters of the high commissioner into the Trust Territory, and the area was administered from Hawaii up to September, 1954, and then from Guam until June 30, 1962, when "provisional" Headquarters were located on Saipan within the Trust Area. Previously, President Truman had designated Dublon in the Truk lagoon as the permanent headquarters site, and technically this decision has never been reversed, although no effort is being made to implement it. In contrast, Japan early placed the governor of the Mandate in the Palaus, so that government could be carried on from within the area. The Japanese administration underwent a number of modifications, but by World War II, the South Seas Government at Koror consisted of the Governor, a Secretariat, the Departments of Domestic Affairs and of Economic Development (or Colonization), and an appellate court. Hospitals, schools, courts, and post offices throughout the Mandate reported directly to Palau rather than to the six branch bureau chiefs of the districts in which they were placed. A Confidential Affairs Section, Archives Section, and Research Section together comprised the Headquarters Secretariat. In the Department of Domestic Affairs was located responsibility for financial affairs, taxation, police, public works, and planning. The Department of Economic Development was similarly divided into sections, administering agriculture and forestry, commerce and industry, communications, and postal matters.[26]

When the Trusteeship was launched, the Federal agencies of the United States undertook direct administration of the postal services and the manning of the weather stations. Except for this and the court system which was divorced to make it independent, the balance of the government was placed under the high commis-

[25] See Peter C. Pauwels, *The Japanese Mandated Islands* (Bandoeng: G. C. T. Van Dorp, 1936), pp. 76–77.

[26] Roy E. James, "The Trust Territory of the Pacific Islands," in Rupert Emerson *et al.*, *America's Pacific Dependencies* (New York: American Institute of Pacific Relations, 1949), pp. 110–111.

TRUST TERRITORY OF THE PACIFIC ISLANDS
Headquarters Organizational Chart
(as of 1/1/68)

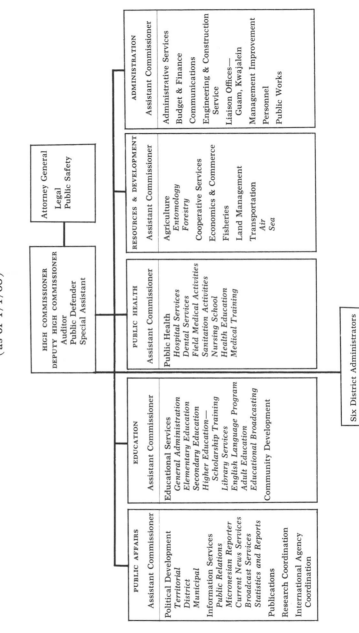

HIGH COMMISSIONER
DEPUTY HIGH COMMISSIONER
Auditor
Public Defender
Special Assistant

Attorney General
Legal
Public Safety

PUBLIC AFFAIRS
Assistant Commissioner

Political Development
Territorial
District
Municipal
Information Services
Public Relations
Micronesian Reporter
Current News Services
Broadcast Services
Statistics and Reports
Publications
Research Coordination
International Agency
Coordination

EDUCATION
Assistant Commissioner

Educational Services
General Administration
Elementary Education
Secondary Education
Higher Education—
Scholarship Training
Library Services
English Language Program
Adult Education
Educational Broadcasting
Community Development

PUBLIC HEALTH
Assistant Commissioner

Public Health
Hospital Services
Dental Services
Field Medical Activities
Sanitation Activities
Nursing School
Health Education
Medical Training

RESOURCES & DEVELOPMENT
Assistant Commissioner

Agriculture
Entomology
Forestry
Cooperative Services
Economics & Commerce
Fisheries
Land Management
Transportation
Air
Sea

ADMINISTRATION
Assistant Commissioner

Administrative Services
Budget & Finance
Communications
Engineering & Construction
Service
Liaison Offices—
Guam, Kwajalein
Management Improvement
Personnel
Public Works

Six District Administrators

sioner and in many ways functionally resembled that of the Japanese. Over the years, modifications in structure have reflected early attempts to set up field headquarters within the Territory for some of the services, and also contractions and augmentations in Federal funding necessitating or permitting such changes. Currently, the Office of the High Commissioner includes the attorney general, the public defender, the internal auditor, and a special assistant (see chart, p. 36). The deputy high commissioner and the assistant commissioners are also located in this office. "The four [now five] Assistant Commissioners and the Attorney General perform both line and staff functions in assisting the High Commissioner in the overall direction of the executive branch. They exercise the authority of the High Commissioner with respect to the activities of the government within their respective areas of responsibility. With the Deputy High Commissioner, they also serve collectively to advise the High Commissioner on matters of policy and program, functioning as a de facto 'cabinet.'

"Under the . . . Assistant Commissioners are heads of departments and specialists who are responsible for the technical direction of their program operations throughout the Territory and for the provision of necessary staff, professional and technical services. The Assistant Commissioner for Public Affairs has basic responsibility for Political Development, Information Services, Publications, Research Coordination, and International Agency Coordination." [27] Education and community development fall within the jurisdiction of the Assistant Commissioner for Education, and public health under an Assistant Commissioner with corresponding title. The Assistant Commissioner for Resources and Development oversees the activities of agriculture and cooperative services, economics and commerce, fisheries, land management, and transportation. The full gambit of administrative services falls within the purview of the Assistant Commissioner for Administration: budget and finance, communications, engineering and construction service, maintenance, management improvement, personnel, property and supply, and the Liaison Offices on Guam and Kwajalein. With few exceptions—such as the plant pathologist on Ponape and the staff entomologist on Palau—all Headquarters staff are stationed on Saipan.

The chain of communications may run directly between the dis-

[27] *18th Annual Report of the United States to the United Nations, 1965*, pp. 24–25.

trict administrators and the high commissioner, or via the department heads at Headquarters and then to the assistant commissioners. The physical dispersal of the Trust Territory over a vast area has of itself raised difficult communication problems, but these have been unduly complicated by the extreme centralization of authority and the limited scope permitted department heads at Headquarters. A survey in 1963 found the latter used essentially as staff officers, exercising no real operating authority and not dealing directly with, or supervising, their counterparts heading functional departments within the districts. The recent addition of the five assistant commissioners potentially only foretells an exacerbation of this centralization on Saipan. The files record inordinate time lags between requests for information emanating from Headquarters, or requests relayed from the field for authorization to take action, and the responding communication. In practice, "home-office"-field relations have never had as a basis a well-demarcated location of authority, and the recent expansion of services associated with the enlarged Federal appropriations has only further revealed this weakness. It is impossible to administer a far-flung area such as the Trust Territory efficiently without great delegation of authority to the field, and this the Administering Authority has been unwilling to grant. There has been a lack of long-range policies with progressive development steps specifically spelled out, and there is no corps steeped in the traditions of a colonial service which would permit broad grants of power to be assigned to the field with confidence. These facts have contributed to this overcentralization at Headquarters and the ambiguity of the district administrator's position.

In order to assure maximum independence for the courts, the judicial branch is placed outside the authority of the high commissioner and the Congress of Micronesia. The chief justice and the associate justices of the High Court are appointed by and accountable to the secretary of the interior.[28] The chief justice supervises an imposing judicial structure, starting with the lowly community courts and culminating in the appellate division of the High Court. The community court judges enjoy a civil and criminal law jurisdiction corresponding roughly to that of the American justice of the peace. Above these courts, the district judges for the six administrative districts may hear all but major felony cases,

[28] As was the high commissioner, until P. L. 90–16 of the U.S. Congress provided for his appointment by the President, subject to Senate confirmation.

civil suits in which sizeable sums of money are at stake, and cases involving a few subjects reserved for the exclusive jurisdiction of the High Court, such as contested land titles and eminent domain proceedings. The High Court has both original and appellate jurisdiction and discretionary review powers over actions of the lower courts. Three Americans staff the High Court, but Micronesians sit with them either as judges on the court or as assessors to advise on local law and custom. Except for these three justices and two American community court judges who hold sessions in the Kwajalein area primarily for cases arising on the anti-missile testing site, the entire judicial branch is staffed by indigenes: 109 community court judges, 24 district court judges, and all court clerks and Trust Territory employees serving the unified court.

The delineation of Trust Territory expenditures by functional categories requires making a number of estimates as well as more or less arbitrary allocations of expenditures. For one thing, geographical dispersal and other contributing factors cause the "overhead" cost element for transportation, communications, and other support services to loom extremely large; it is believed that every government program requires almost $1.00 of overhead expenditure for each $2.00 of direct program cost.[29]

ESTIMATED FUNCTIONAL EXPENDITURES OF TERRITORIAL GOVERNMENT, 1966–67 [30]

Direct services to individuals			
Education		$9,300,000	44%
Health and medical		5,600,000	26
Utility and other			
direct services		2,900,000	14
General government			
Headquarters and			
district executive offices	$600,000		
Protection and enforcement	500,000		
Judicial	200,000		
Overhead	500,000	$1,800,000	9
Direct development programs			
Economic development	$800,000		
Political development	70,000		
Community development	100,000		
Overhead	400,000	1,370,000	7
		$20,970,000	

[29] Robert R. Nathan Associates, Inc., "Economic Development Plan for Micronesia" (Washington: 1966), Part III, p. 533 [modified by author].
[30] *Ibid.*, pp. 534–536.

For this same 1966–67 period, Micronesian governmental expenditures totaled an estimated $700,000, and support for the members and activities of Territorial legislative bodies used up three-fourths of these funds.[31] However, this does not present a fully representative picture because in this year the Congress of Micronesia did not appropriate all moneys available to it for expenditure within the Territory; if these had been computed in, the share of legislative expenditures would have declined to a little under 50 per cent. With augmented funds available to the Trust Territory from Federal appropriations, and with increased Territorial revenues subject to expenditure in accordance with the directions of the Congress of Micronesia and the district legislatures, greater emphasis upon development programs and direct service activities may be anticipated, as well as a marked decrease in the percentage of Territorial revenues devoted to legislative costs.

None of the four nations which have governed the region now included within the Trust Territory established a colonial service in which its personnel was trained for colonial duty.[32] The administration of Micronesia has understandably embodied both a degree of rote copying of the system of government observed by the metropolitan country and a large element of improvisation. The Japanese sent regular civil servants to administer the Islands; United States policy similarly is to employ American citizens under U.S. Civil Service regulations and procedures, except for school teachers and a few others who are hired on a contractual, non-civil-service basis. The Americans work under a grade structure and classification system which follows the U.S. Classification Act of 1949.

Indigenous personnel are employed under a separate title and pay plan, with lower remuneration despite possession of the same technical qualifications, which gives the appearance of treating Micronesians as second-class employees in their own government. This has engendered considerable dissatisfaction on the part of Micronesians, who regard themselves as underpaid and their American superiors as delaying advancement of local personnel in order to preserve their own, more lucrative positions. With the Micronesians taking an ever larger share through the legislative process in setting policy on the district and Territorial levels, it is only a question of time before a unified personnel service will be installed.

[31] *Ibid.*, p. 535.
[32] The short-lived training under the U.S. Navy may be regarded as an attempt to institute a colonial service.

Had the United States a colonial service, displaced Americans might be transferred to other areas or pensioned under a system anticipating this very contingency; as it is, some of the long-time administrators have been content with the *status quo* and reluctant to advocate innovations which might "rock the boat." All this only compounds the bitterness of those indigenous inhabitants now beginning to take an active part in Micronesian politics and pressing for rapid change.

Political institutions recently introduced into Micronesia are more geographically inclusive and more specialized than any the people of the region have ever known. No comparable effort had previously been made to unite Micronesians within and across district and ethnic lines. The specialization to which they are now exposed extends not just to separating the branches of government and the distinct functions of government but also to differentiating the political structure from other social configurations. Elections without reference to caste, class, or other discriminating measure; equality before the law; and the official conceived of as a servant of the people rather than the figure around whom all community prestige turns have interposed an egalitarianism new to the area. It is to be anticipated that this deluge of novel concepts is as yet only partially assimilated. To the followers of a defeated candidate, it may be only logical to refuse to acknowledge the elected magistrate and to maintain they are being deprived of their "Bill of Rights"; that majority rule subsumes cooperation of the defeated minority is still to be fully understood.[33]

Because of all this, for some time to come traditional political systems in each district will continue to function to a greater or lesser degree alongside the new structure of government. Sometimes their respective jurisdictions will be sharply differentiated, with little integration of the two. At other times it will be difficult to know where one system ends and the other begins. Today, if a juvenile from an outlying village commits a crime on Koror, the district headquarters of Palau, the community court will frequently suspend the sentence and allow the Palauan chiefs to proceed through the application of modified custom. The chiefs then summon the father of the delinquent and the chief of his village and publicly shame them for allowing the minor to come to the district headquarters and engage in the anti-social behavior which brought

[33] Recounted in "Second Annual Truk Congress, Sept. 15–19, 1958," p. 2.

him before the judge. The court system here provides a new dimension for the activities of the traditional leaders and a new use for the Palauan sanction of social ostracism; both political systems nicely articulate to face jointly the problem of juvenile delinquency. This represents a more realistic way to accommodate the traditional political structure than any doctrinaire approach, such as "indirect rule," with which the Americans first turned to the task of administering the Trust Territory. After all, even indirect rule is not just "find the chief" but in fact consists of "progressive adaptation of native institutions to modern conditions." [34]

[34] Lucy P. Mair, *Native Policies in Africa* (London: C. Routledge & Sons, Ltd., 1936), pp. 56, 57.

CHAPTER 3

District Legislatures—Antecedents, Powers, and Structure

IN THE PRE-CONTACT PERIOD, Micronesia lived according to custom, but without differentiated institutions for modifying, consolidating, interpreting, or punatively enforcing it. The wrong against the community (crime) was not distinguished from a personal injury (tort), just as kin ties, economic linkages, magic, and the employment of traditional power were part and parcel of a single body of governing rules. Only a decade ago the Palauan district congress was being assured that it could by law punish adultery (the crime) while retaining traditional Palauan prescriptions regulating the obligations of the parties to the adultery (the tort).[1] The exercise of law-making powers by indigenous legislative bodies consequently waited upon the comprehension of the Western conceptual underpinnings of "law," as distinct from custom applied through a reciprocal set of relationships, as much as it did upon the training of Micronesians in the mechanics of legislatures modeled on modern lines. Because of this, and not just the lateness in the express granting of legislating powers, the legislative chambers established by the Americans in the Trust Territory were performing other functions appropriate to their collegial form and representative character before they began enacting laws.

Innovating legislatures as part of governing the Trust Territory did not constitute as onerous an undertaking as it might first appear. Collegial processes and forms in the Micronesian cultures predated the advent of Western rule. The basic institutions in traditional island government contained the seeds of representation, with the clan chief acting on the part of his people, and widespread throughout the region has been the council or group meeting for consultation and often for decision-making. The literal translation of Olbiil era Kelulau, the official name of the Palau district congress between 1955 and 1963, is "meeting place of whispers," perpetuating the reference to the highest political council of the region in which negotiations had been carried on between principals by means of messages whispered to messengers. For

---

[1] See Minutes of Spring Session, 1956, of Palau District Congress.

lower level political undertakings, clan heads met with their paramount chief, following rules of procedure, priorities of debate, and prescribed seating assignments, with their collective decisions announced to the public by the chief as his own determinations. The lore of the *itang* (sage) in the Truk area, by identifying the proper course to follow, facilitated political determinations as well as other forms of communal action; its prescriptions in a way resembled modern parliamentary procedure and its mastery by the relatively few in even advanced Western countries. The high proportion of *alabs* (heads of commoner lineages) elected to the Marshall Islands Congress, coupled with the inclusion of *iroij* (royalty) in that body, imparted to the congress a little of the character associated with traditional consultations of *alabs* with their *iroij laplap* (paramount chiefs).

The prevalence of class structure, with rule by hereditary rank, only superficially was wholly antithetical to the institution of the modern legislature, with its egalitarian features. In spite of the nominal power enjoyed by traditional chiefs, they rarely took decisive action without sounding out opinion from representative individuals and public discussions. Limited forms of representation, reference to public opinion, and familiarity with group processes derived from traditional councils all facilitated the adaptation of the more sophisticated political forms of the West.

By no means all aspects of life in pre-contact Micronesia favored the advent of legislatures. Most Micronesian societies were consensus societies, so that action was frequently deferred until unanimity, or at least the silence of the opposition, was achieved, a slow, time-consuming process. Superior-subordinate relationships did not countenance open challenge or disagreement across status lines and long conditioned subordinates to roles of followers. For this and other reasons, indirection has long been a well-defined course to follow. And probably most discrepant, the people in some of the Micronesian cultures, because of long ingrained patterns of conduct, do not generalize easily; in novel circumstances, rather than run the risk of making a mistake, the tendency is to avoid doing anything at all. When the situation demands action and fixed habits are inappropriate, the response is likely to be vague, evasive, and ambiguous.[2] All this ill-prepared Micronesians to make the

[2] See Thorwald Esbensen, "A Report on Political Education in Truk" [Moen, Truk]: Oct. 6, 1957; Thomas Gladwin and Seymour B. Sarason, *Truk: Man in Paradise* (New York: Wenner-Gren Foundation, 1953), pp. 226, 453.

decisions required of members in a legislature cast in the American mold, presuming open debate, free presentation of views, and majority action.

Facets of one culture, when engrafted onto another, may later prove to be dysfunctional, neutral, or facilitative in ways never contemplated at the time of the transfer. Micronesia's encounters with the West prior to American assumption of jurisdiction over the Trust Territory added a number of institutions which fortuitously helped prepare the indigenes for acceptance of the modern legislature and equipped them with some of the skills necessary for its operation. For a century the Protestant church in the Marshalls and Eastern Carolines inculcated concepts of equality before God and taught democratic processes such as the election of church officials. The deacon and *komat* in the Marshallese church hierarchy merely denote the transformation of the Congregational deacon and committeeman. The Reverend George Lockwood, who was a missionary in the Marshalls between 1928 and 1932, founded the "Eklesia in Marshall" (Association of Marshall Islands Churches), which held biennial all-Marshalls church conferences, and instructed the members in parliamentary procedure through the use of *Robert's Rules of Order*. Governing these Protestant bodies, members became familiar with nominating committees, the rudiments of presenting and voting on motions, and also the employment of dilatory tactics such as "laying on the table." Heavy reliance was placed on the use of committees in running Mission affairs, a fit prelude to American legislative practices.

Probably the first law-making chamber in the Trust Territory [3] was the seven-man elected body which met on Ponape in 1874 under the direction of Missionary Sturges. Although called to pass a law on adultery, its initial legislative action regulated land tenure. The laws it adopted, in addition to property measures, were more or less a codification of the Ten Commandments.[4] The concern for enactment of the decalogue had its historical parallels in

[3] The king of Kusaie, fighting a losing battle to maintain his authority against the inroads of the mission, in 1869 appointed commoners from the island's districts to meet monthly in council with him and the chiefs to deliberate on island affairs. It may be argued that this was the first law-making body. James L. Lewis, *Kusaiean Acculturation*, CIMA Final Report No. 17 (Washington: National Research Council, Pacific Science Board, 1948), pp. 36–37.

[4] See George L. Coale, "A Study of Chieftainship, Missionary Contact, and Culture Change on Ponape, 1852–1900" (M.A. thesis, University of Southern California: 1951), pp. 72–73.

Hawaii a half century earlier.[5] This missionary plan to weaken structurally the chieftainship system on Ponape by introducing democratic forms and processes never fully succeeded, and the reintroduction of the legislature awaited the return of the Americans after World War II.

Both the Spanish and the Japanese experimented with forms of legislative councils, which may be treated as precursors of those founded by the Americans. In the Marianas, first for Guam and then, after 1850, for Saipan and the other Northern Islands, district meetings were held between district "chiefs" and village and ward "chiefs." A method of indirect selection introduced an element of representation into these formal gatherings. As the councils were convened only when unusual problems were to be met, they offered an opportunity for innovative decisions akin to legislating.

On the eastern edge of Micronesia, for the Marshalls the Japanese instituted biennial magistrates' conferences, which gave to the Radak and Ralik chains of islands an incipient sense of Marshallese political unity. Dressed in uniforms supplied by the Japanese and following strict protocol, the Japanese-appointed magistrates kept to a prepared agenda and mainly acceded to that ministering nation's predeterminations by ratifying the resolutions awaiting them. "The magistrates did not meet to make plans"—as one member of the Marshallese Congress differentiated the latter's activities; the main purpose of these island magistrates' meetings under the Japanese was to receive from the administration the instructions for their respective areas. Incidentally, though, the magistrates were alerted to problems beyond the confines of their own atolls, and this indirectly prepared the way for the American-sponsored district congress.

Long recognized as an agent of culture change, the schools played an important role in conditioning Micronesians for accepting and participating in assemblies with law-making power. In addition to communicating factual knowledge about democratic government and the political institutions designed to achieve and maintain it, the schools early founded by American missionaries, and later also those run under public auspices by the American administration, acquainted young Micronesians with both democratic practices and the intricacies of parliamentary action in the

[5] Norman Meller, "Missionaries to Hawaii," *Western Political Quarterly*, 11:4 (Dec., 1958), 788.

making of group decisions. Student leaders were selected for more than their traditional status. Through widening horizons and the development of skills, a grounding favorable to the introduction of district legislatures was being laid. It was undoubtedly his education in Hawaii and close mission ties that were responsible for Henry Nanpei's ambitions to set up a legislature in Ponape during the period of the German administration.[6]

PRECURSORS TO DISTRICT LEGISLATURES

Under American aegis municipal government came into existence much earlier than the district legislatures. However, as the indigenous leaders themselves noted, "it is in this [latter] area that the political growth of Micronesian people is most apparent. The reason for this growth is probably due to the fact that there were no similar bodies previously existing from which attitudes could be formed, habits obtained and outlooks colored which could have caused obstacles to impede development. In short, they do not have 'rivalries' with which to compete. Another reason is the fact that 'they have money.' They levy taxes which they can collect. The money from the revenues collected by these congresses is spent for education, health and other ventures which benefit the people directly." [7]

In most of the Trust Territory, the district legislatures were preceded by some form of advisory body serving above the level of village or municipal government. For the most part, their area of jurisdiction was circumscribed, and their major contribution was as two-way communication channels between the administration and their localities. At best they observed only rudimentary forms of parliamentary procedure. Mainly they were an occasion for local officials to meet with the administration to be "informed, reminded, requested, notified, [and] advised," [8] and to seek clarification of instructions. The early formation of a district legislature in Palau, followed by that in the Marshalls, meant that the lives of these legislative progenitors lasted longer on Truk, Ponape, and Yap. Saipan's municipal council may also be included among the precursors.

[6] See John L. Fischer and Ann M. Fischer, *The Eastern Carolines* (New Haven: Human Relations Area Files, 1957), pp. 41, 50.

[7] "Report of the Political Development Sub-committee to the Council of Micronesia," Oct. 1, 1962, p. 3.

[8] From reference to the Ponape Council of Municipal Officials' meeting in John Sandelmann, *Some Observations on the Problem of "Self Government" in the Trust Territory of the Pacific Islands* (Honolulu: 1953), p. 56.

Soon after the end of the war, the Americans created a Truk atoll council of native leaders, which proceeded to choose an atoll chief. This endeavor to fabricate a unified political structure above the local level collapsed, and in its place a Truk advisory council, consisting of the island chiefs and their assistants, met monthly with the military government. Representing approximately two-thirds of the district's population, they nicely serviced the need of a communication conduit as well as a sounding body for the shaping of administrative decisions by American personnel. As the chiefs would have to execute any proposals they themselves advanced, the council encouraged reasonableness on their part. Gladwin notes the evolvement of informal meetings, after the "official" sessions had adjourned, at which discussion mainly concerned the resolution of inconsistencies between administration policy and local custom.[9] This may be likened to the informal supervision of the administration, which occupies a material part of the modern legislature's attention.

In 1952 an all-Truk Conference of Magistrates was held, and explorations at this time indicated the feasibility of establishing a district council of magistrates to meet annually. Before these conferences were in good part superseded by the Truk District Legislature, they had stretched into week-long sessions, following administration-prepared agendas and with committees reporting to the conference their recommendations on the numerous problems raised. Action proposed did not necessarily require legislation but might call for executive or community measures, and it was not too unusual for these reports to be hortatory in nature. To bridge the year-long interval, the 1953 District Conference of Magistrates elected a Permanent Advisory Committee with "authority to represent all islands in the Truk district in advising the District Administrator and his staff with respect to matters of government. . . ."[10] The committee met as often as once every several weeks for this purpose. In practice, it preferred to refer questions of any importance, especially those having to do with money, to the annual conference rather than taking action itself.

On Ponape, monthly meetings of district chiefs and their representatives with the government administrators to discuss problems pertaining to the whole island date back to the early post-war

---

[9] Thomas Gladwin, "Civil Administration in Truk: A Rejoinder," *Human Organization,* 9:4 (Winter, 1950), 22–23. The same phenomenon was reported for Yap; see Sandelmann, *op. cit.,* p. 119.

[10] *10th Annual Report of the United States to the United Nations, 1957,* p. 26.

period. These sessions of the officers of the five municipalities on Ponape, speaking for almost two-thirds of the people in the district, may be treated as the "beginning of a representative and legislative body." [11] They were succeeded around 1950 by a 22-member representative body elected for the island of Ponape. "All meetings were held with the United States administration officers as the directors of the meetings. There was no division into upper and lower house. Chiefs and common people met together." [12] Later, this was replaced by the bicameral Ponape Island Congress.

The Saipanese, with American assistance, in 1947 adopted a charter for the municipal government of the island. It carried more than municipal import, however, for about seven-eighths of all people in the Northern Marianas live on Saipan. The original document provided for an eleven-member unicameral legislature, called the High Council. Two years later, the civil administration on Saipan appended a second legislative chamber, the House of Commissioners. In the following year the addition of this house was in effect ratified and supplemented by the granting of a second Saipan charter, in which the bicameral body was modeled after the pattern set by the congress on Guam. The new body, with fifteen commissioners in the "lower" house and eleven councilmen in the "upper," actually performed most of its work in joint session. The House of Commissioners as a rule had its way on subjects of local ward nature, but items involving all of Saipan were the concern of the councilmen. The commissioners also had executive duties over their respective wards, so that the legislative body embodied a combination of legislative and executive attributes uncommon to the American scene.

Commentators [13] studying the Saipan congress at mid-century found its deliberations marked by endless discussion and bickering and general ineffectiveness. This was largely because the members' scope of power was never defined vis-a-vis the executive branch, so that their duties and the extent of their authority remained con-

[11] John L. Fischer, "Present and Potential Development of Ponapean Society," Dec. 5, 1950 (University of Hawaii Sinclair Library, Micro. 594, no. 10).

[12] From paper of Oliver Nanpei, read at First Trust Territory Conference on Self-Government (Truk: 1953), p. 16.

[13] Alexander Spoehr, *Saipan: the Ethnology of a War-Devastated Island,* Fieldiana: Anthropology, Vol. 41 (Chicago: Chicago Natural History Museum, 1954), pp. 174–176; also see Robert R. Solenberger, "Continuity of Local Political Institutions in the Marianas," *Human Organization,* 23:1 (Spring, 1964), 58; U.S. Department of the Interior, *Management Survey of the Government of the Trust Territory of the Pacific Islands* (Washington: 1951), I, 51; *6th Annual Report of the United States to the United Nations, 1953,* p. 16.

fused. Much of their time was wasted on procedural and jurisdictional matters rather than spent in taking definitive action to resolve the substantive problems before them. Nevertheless, the experience gained in a legislative body conforming to parliamentary rules and employing a full system of committees prepared the Saipanese for ready assumption of responsibility for the running of a district legislature when one was finally authorized in 1963.

The degree of involvement of American personnel in these early advisory groups varied from district to district. Typically, the American administrators would meet with them at the opening of each session to present the problems currently faced by the administration; thereafter, there was no single pattern which governed the Americans' part in the work of the various bodies. On Ponape, meetings were left almost completely to Ponapeans, who could freely discuss all questions brought before them and would later report to the administrator. In contrast, American personnel took an active part throughout the period of the Truk atoll magistrates' conferences and the Truk District Conferences of Magistrates which succeeded them. The same lack of pattern was to apply to the American administrators' relation to the district legislatures which followed the advisory groups.

These preliminary bodies stimulated the beginnings of a district-wide identity which had never been stirred under the preceding metropolitan nations. The former Administering Authorities had utilized a system of centralized district administration, but it had little meaning for the indigenes who had no share in its direction. Micronesian government was generally local, and at best extended spacially no farther than the confines of the confederations known to Palau. After World War II, across all of Micronesia the inhabitants were for the first time being presented with an opportunity to develop a sense of understanding of district-wide problems and take part in their resolution. Enveloping this may have been a slight aura of play acting, carrying overtones of Gilbert and Sullivan operetta, just as has cloaked the activities of the later district-wide legislatures, but in retrospect, the institution of these preliminary consultative councils was an essential step along the course of alerting the people of the Trust Territory to the potential and procedures of legislating bodies.

FOUNDING DISTRICT LEGISLATURES

Section 41 of the Code of the Trust Territory authorizes the district administrator to create local advisory councils for communities, individual islands, or groups of islands as may seem appropriate. Long before this authorization was promulgated as part of the code in 1952, regional advisory bodies began developing in a rather haphazard way in accordance with the wide administrative latitude allotted each district's civil administration. The initial period under the naval administration was one of experimentation, and there was no disposition to force uniformity. In due time the stamp of approval for the innovations would be obtained from the high commissioner. Some of these advisory groups have already been mentioned as the precursor councils preceding the founding of district legislatures.

Early in the administration of the Territory, the failure of the United States Congress to take action on organic legislation cast a shadow over the whole process of setting up regional legislative bodies. When this constraint was lifted by the Federal Congress' abandoning its efforts at organic legislation, the Territorial administration was free to extend the scope of powers of the district assemblies. Standardization in conformance with the desires of the United Nations and in response to the exchange of knowledge about each district's experiences resulted in greater comparability in regional legislatures as the years passed. The quest for administrative efficiency also looked favorably upon uniformity of charter provisions, and the drafting of a model legislative charter (see Appendix) and a set of model rules by the 1960's foretold that the heterodoxy of the original founding period would continue no longer.

The first district legislatures served groups having cultural cohesion—Palauans, Marshallese, Ponapeans; later legislatures were more heterogeneous in membership. Palau has the distinction of establishing the first regional deliberative body, which through evolutionary steps developed into today's district legislature. The actual founding dates back to May of 1947 when a convention was held on Koror, and the first session of the elected Palau Congress met on July 4, 1947.[14] All this occurred prior to the approval of the Trusteeship Agreement by the United States and while the area was still under Military Government. Indicative of the permissive

[14] For Palau District Congress, see Dorothy E. Richard, *U.S. Naval Administration in the Trust Territory of the Pacific Islands* (Washington: Office of the Chief of Naval Operations, 1957), III, 396–98; Arthur J. Vidich, "The Political Impact of Colonial Administration" (Ph.D. thesis, Harvard University: March 31, 1952), pp. 280–281; Arthur J. Vidich, *Political Factionalism in Palau*, CIMA Final Report No. 23 (Washington: National Research Council, Pacific Science Board, 1949), pp. 78–79.

administration of the period is the fact that the congress was not officially approved until a year later, and a charter did not receive the high commissioner's sanction until September 20, 1948. The organizational plans, devised by the Palauan chiefs and others they called upon for technical assistance, made provision for a partially-elected legislative body, an appointed judiciary, and an administrative council consisting of the two high chiefs of Palau and eight other chiefs to head the departments of the local government. This Palauan government dealt with "all-Palau" problems; all of its policy determinations were subject to approval of the naval administrators. In 1948, the administrative council and its operating functions was replaced by a new council with solely advisory powers (see Palau District Order No. 3–48, Appendix), and a new congress was also introduced (see Palau District Order Nos. 4–48 and 1–49, Appendix). (District Order No. 1–49 incorporates the rules adopted at the 1947 session, as modified over time.) Magistrates were now members; from the inception of the first congress in 1947, the two high chiefs and the paramount chiefs of the Palau districts regularly attended all congressional sessions. Although the Yap area was administratively within the Palau district during this early period, its peoples at no time ever joined in congressional activities. Part of this historical sequence of events has become blurred over time, which helps to explain why in 1957 the Palau district held a "tenth-anniversary celebration" on the "founding of its Congress in *1948* [italics added]." [15]

After the Palau Congress had been in existence for a few years, efforts commenced to revise and refurbish the brief District Order, substituting a new charter spelling out in greater detail the membership, functions, and procedures of the district legislative body. Also, the Palau legislators desired to meet semi-annually instead of only once a year. Resolution No. 7–53 of the Palau Congress would have the Council of Advisors replaced by another body, the Tebechelel Olbiil, responsible to the congress. Resolution No. 8 of the same congressional session called for a council of chiefs, consisting of the two high chiefs and one paramount chief for each of the Palauan communities. Both resolutions recommended that these councils "be incorporated into the structure of the government if and when a charter is granted by the High Commissioner. . . ." A special Palauan charter committee sought to equip each

[15] *Annual Report of the High Commissioner to the Secretary of the Interior, 1958*, p. 28.

council with a distinct mission: the Tebechelel Olbiil was to be a consultant on administrative matters and its members were to serve without vote in the Olbiil era Kelulau, the name to be given to the district congress; the chiefs were to be advisors on custom, with powers to delay for a whole legislative session matters affecting tradition. The president of the congress particularly approved of the Tebechelel Olbiil as a body of executive advisors, as he disliked the exposed position connoted in one-man authority, and Palauan traditions of leadership favored a council over a single individual.

Upon further collaboration between Palauans and members of the district administration in the formulation of the charter, and the suggestion of numerous alternative provisions by the high commissioner's staff, a new charter was issued by the high commissioner in January of 1955. Its fundamental aim was to unite traditional, administrative, and liberal forms "to produce a progressive self-responsibility." [16] This only set up the Olbiil era Kelulau and left vague the status of the Tebechelel Olbiil as advisor to the president of the congress. Both chiefs and magistrates continued as members of the district congress and for eight years participated in its activities, although nominally without ability to vote on resolutions which were to become law. Finally in 1963, with the backing of the district administration to get it through the congress, another charter was adopted which continued the membership of the chiefs, but deprived of power to vote or hold office, and removed the magistrates.[17] At the same time the Tebechelel Olbiil was abolished. Interestingly, the course of this legislative development in Palau was charted partially in light of American experience in Samoa with traditional chiefs participating in the Samoan Fono (legislature) as a matter of right and by the desire to avoid Samoa's failure to tie its units of local government closely with the central administration through legislative membership.

Unlike in the early military government in Palau, in the Marshalls the district administration acknowledged the social position of the *iroij* in the traditional culture, but at first granted them no governmental authority. This policy was reversed with the founding of the Marshall Islands Congress. In March of 1948 a conference of magistrates and scribes of the Majuro district was held to con-

[16] Letter of HiCom to DistAd Palau, June 2, 1964.
[17] For consideration of role of chiefs in the Palau district legislature, see pp. 127–131.

sider subjects of district-wide interest. It was followed by an all-Marshalls conference in 1949, and from the latter arose the administration's sponsorship of a Marshallese congress. In July of 1949 a conference of *iroij* was convoked and within three days "unanimously approved" the draft charter presented to it for review. The deputy high commissioner ratified the charter in 1949, and the first session of the bicameral congress, with one house composed of *iroij* and the other of "elected" representatives, met for the first time in July of 1950.

The pattern of procedure which the Marshallese congress was to follow was set during the preceding 1949 magistrates' conference. Administrative officers first addressed the indigenes, and the latter then engaged in informal, off-the-record meetings, finally reporting their conclusions for formal action. When the congress convened in the following year, after a range of problems had been presented by the administration, the two houses separated to analyze the problems but then in joint session deliberated upon each chamber's proposals, and in this way adopted recommendations to be forwarded to the district administration. From the time of the early 1949 conference, the value of working towards a unified Marshalls district was stressed. Under the Department of Interior's administration, the co-equal role of the hereditary *iroij* with the representative commoners in the Marshallese congress did not meet with favor, and at the urging of the American administrators a second charter was framed in 1958. Much to the Americans' chagrin, the *iroij* basically retained their former role and, in addition, secured protections against revision of traditional rights which the bicameral body could have modified.[18] The reduction in the number of elected members in 1964 only further entrenched the position of the hereditary members.

Almost contemporaneously with the Marshallese, the people of the Northern Marianas expressed their desire to form a governing body for their district. Early in 1950, they laid before the administration a charter with but a single organ of government. The Senate, as it was to be known, would have been endowed with full executive and legislative powers, except for a limited veto, and with judicial powers over local matters. The high commissioner conceded that "the people of Saipan have made excellent progress in political development, but it is believed that they are not at this

[18] For consideration of role of *iroij* in the Marshall Islands Congress, see pp. 132–141.

time prepared to assume the broad powers of government included in the 'Charter for the Marianas Union,' " [19] and he vetoed the novel scheme.

The following year, the high commissioner and his staff prepared a revised charter which granted neither executive nor legislative powers but merely created a body to advise the high commissioner and civil administrator on Saipan. This was in line with the policy of the administration "to encourage a gradual development of democratic processes" and reflected its view that the charter proposed by the Saipanese would have overtaxed their political capacity.[20] Later, the United States reported to the United Nations that "at the request of the various municipal councils, esablishment of a congress for the district of Saipan is held in abeyance for the time being." [21] In view of the impending cleavage of the Marianas district because of a C.I.A. training program on Saipan, one cannot but regard with a little cynicism this explanation that the postponement was sought by the council members to allow them to solve pressing local problems before attempting to institute a legislative advisory body on a district-wide basis. Much later, after the abandonment of the C.I.A. program and as efforts to draft a charter were renewed, protection of the other Mariana islands against being engulfed by the preponderant population of Saipan posed problems to be overcome. A charter was finally formulated for a district-wide legislature to meet in 1963, its jurisdiction covering the reunited Northern Mariana islands. The area's "readiness" for a district legislature was indicated by its easy adoption of rules of procedure, its forming standing committees, and its emphasizing committee work at its initial session.

Like Palau, the Ponape district offered an opportunity for the early structuring of a district-wide legislature. This was postponed for many years by internal factors—both factionalism on Ponape Island and disagreements among members of the high commissioner's staff over the advisability of a legislative body for the whole of the Ponape district. Discussions leading to the formation of a legislature began in 1949 after a referendum favored the preparation of a charter for a district-wide congress. However, the high commissioner disapproved of the draft District Orders creat-

[19] Letter of HiCom, Feb. 24, 1950, quoted in Richard, *op. cit.*, p. 395.
[20] *4th Annual Report of the United States to the United Nations, 1951*, p. 19.
[21] *5th Annual Report of the United States to the United Nations, 1952* p. 15.

ing such a body which were presented to him in 1950 and the charter calling for a bicameral congress, drafted by a "Provisional Ponape Congress" meeting in 1951. Difference of customs in the several parts of the district and the impracticability of members' attending from islands outside of Ponape were reasons expressed for the rejection. A period of confusion ensued, with the Ponape area next opting for an island congress and the high commissioner then disfavoring a body for the island of Ponape alone. Out of this seeming inability to reach a meeting of minds, in May of 1952 there finally emerged a bicameral Ponape Island Congress in which chiefs, elected representatives, and non-voting delegates from the Outer-Island colonies resident on the island of Ponape could all take part.

Dissatisfaction with the resolution of the problem of a district-wide legislature continued on Ponape. At its December, 1953, meeting, the Island Congress declared there should be an all-Ponape district legislature to meet once a year. At the session in November of 1956, Joint Resolution No. 10, which would have converted the Ponape Island Congress into a district congress, was tabled, but the congress appointed a committee to study ways and means of developing a district-wide legislative body. With the two houses "in constant disagreement" [22] over the future organization of the congress, the question was finally settled by calling a convention of representatives of each municipality to undertake the drafting of a new charter which would include all peoples of the Ponape district. The convention decided to eliminate further representation of Ponapean title holders, which resolved the problem of the Outer Islands' not having within their traditional structure persons with comparable titles who could sit in a House of Nobles of a bicameral body. [23] The new legislature for the whole of the Ponape district convened in September of 1958.

As the Trukese were deemed "not prepared to cope with the complexities of centralized government," [24] a district-wide legislative body for that portion of the Trust Territory was late in developing. By 1956 the Truk District Conference of Magistrates unanimously voted to set up a legislature with representatives elected by popular vote. "The granting of the Truk Congress Char-

[22] *1959 United Nations Visiting Mission Report*, par. 55.
[23] For consideration of role of chiefs in Ponape Island Congress, see pp. 123–127.
[24] *3rd Annual Report of the United States to the United Nations, 1950,* p. 17.

ter followed many hours of work and study both on the part of Micronesian leaders and Administration workers in order that the significance of the action might be comprehended by the people and they might be prepared to assume the responsibilities as well as obligations bestowed by the charter." [25] The Secretary of the Interior officially presented Truk's charter when visiting the district in August of 1957, and the first Trukese congress convened on November 4, three years ahead of the estimated target date.

At first, many of these district legislatures were assigned the pretentious title of "congress," and both that name and "legislature" have been employed somewhat interchangeably in Trust Territory terminology. Not all indigenous legislators have been happy with this usage, and in the Marshalls the members volunteered for their body the name of *kwelok*, signifying a gathering or meeting. The district administrator, too, though the title of the Marshall Islands Congress inappropriate and preferred "council" as more properly fitting the body's nature. Nothing came of this, but later charters in other districts have abandoned the name of "congress," and today most of the district bodies are referred to as "legislatures" in their enabling acts, reserving the higher status title for the all-Trust Territory Congress of Micronesia.

The efforts of the administration played a key part in interesting the indigenous inhabitants in the founding of the new legislatures and in preparing them to participate in their operation. There were no exact cultural parallels, and hampered by a language barrier, the indigenes had to be instructed on the significance of the new political institutions. In addition, they had to be assisted through the intricacies of formal voting, fiscal years, and the myriad other elements surrounding the subject matter and process of legislatures, which are taken as a matter of course in more sophisticated areas. As the Micronesians became conversant with the activities of their initial district-wide legislatures, they came to play a more active role in the restructuring of the later bodies which replaced them, so that the current charters today represent a combination of administration-sponsored sections interlaced with indigene-initiated provisions.

The granting of a second or third charter for a district has been occasioned by a number of factors. The local suggestion of a series of basic amendments by a district legislature has sometimes been

[25] *Annual Report of the High Commissioner to the Secretary of the Interior,* 1958, p. 27.

the signal for the drafting of a new charter by the staff of the high commissioner when it is of the opinion that the existing structure has proven unwieldy or that legislative procedures require revision. Contributing to the issuance of new charters has been the long-range administrative objective of institutionalizing the unicameral body throughout the Territory, extending the jurisdiction of each legislature to encompass the whole of its district, and limiting membership to elected representatives as soon as political acculturation has advanced to the point where it permits the elimination in the legislatures of traditional leaders without risk of traumatic disruption of the relationships which govern normal social intercourse. Partially reflecting this, within the districts, efforts toward the redrafting of charters have continuously been encouraged by the district administrators. The granting of four new charters in 1963 also gave evidence of a new-found interest in extending uniformity through a basic matrix of charter provisions, to be modified and expanded as necessary to meet the requirements and idiosyncracies of each district. The involvement of legislators and district administration personnel in the charter granting process assured that the contents of the various charters would remain to some degree dissimilar. It can be expected that in the future the administration will play an ever smaller role in chartering the district legislatures which will succeed the present assemblies, and that because of this, greater variation rather than more conformity will characterize these bodies as they respond to the districts' differing needs.

POWERS

The district legislatures of the Trust Territory well demonstrate that law-making is only one of the properties of legislative bodies. So gradually and unevenly was legislating power acquired that a cross-section of all of the districts at any one time would have revealed no single pattern. This flowed partly from the ambivalence of the Administering Authority, which was willing to facilitate the efforts of indigenes aimed at self-government but at the same time was hesitant to undermine the reserved authority of the high commissioner to control the Trust Territory's course of development. Reference to the charters for guidance is of little aid, for their language, especially as they have been amended, constitutes an uninformative amalgam of Micronesian-prompted phraseology and administration-inspired additions and revisions. As a consequence, legislative powers were expanded more by convention than by express grant.

It has never been clearly understood by either indigenous legislators or the district administration precisely what was to be the district legislature's scope of responsibility. The conceptual separation of powers into legislative, executive, and judicial bundles is completely foreign to customary political practices in Micronesia and, in truth, did not particularly fit the evolving needs of the respective districts. On the other hand, district administrators, formerly enjoying authority in both executive and legislative realms, could only look critically upon the district bodies' intrusion into the latter area except when the legislatures' recommendations coincided with the course they themselves believed proper. The exclusion of Federally supplied funds from the jurisdiction of the district legislatures meant that these bodies perforce had to develop extralegal means if they were to affect the funds' administration in any way. This indefiniteness of the district legislature's part in the system of district government yet remains.

Communications. As initially conceived, the major role of the district legislature was to serve in an advisory capacity to the administration. It was not appreciated that while performing this inchoate legislative function, the individual members and each district body collectively would not only be a source of intelligence for the district administration but also become a major return conduit for the dissemination of information about the district's administration. In the Palaus, the Marshalls, Ponape Island— wherever the early district legislative bodies were chartered—the legislators met informally with constituents and not infrequently with the local government officials prior to coming to the district headquarters for the convening of the district congress. Upon adjournment, they reported back, sometimes to the council of the municipality, at other times to gatherings called for the purpose, so that the people of their area might know what had transpired at the session just adjourned. One of the important reasons for district legislators to attend sessions was to ascertain what was occurring at district headquarters which might be to the benefit of their home municipality. To the legislative halls were brought all the requests and complaints expressed locally, and many of these became embodied in the resolutions formally submitted to the attention of the district administrator. In turn, the administration was heavily dependent upon the district legislators' understanding of the administrative programs and their interpretation of them for the people back home. In a region without newspapers and with only limited radio and postal coverage, such verbal intercourse becomes essential to the processes of administration.

Legislative communication consisted of more than a vertical flow of information between administration and legislator. Inside the legislative body itself, sometimes through the committees, members exchanged points of view and developed expertise in specific subject-matter areas. Via the legislature, then, communications between different sub-regions and groupings within the district's society were facilitated, factual knowledge shared, district opinion structured, and district-wide aspirations fostered.

Contemporaneous with the work of the district bodies' becoming more formalized, journals reporting the legislative proceedings were distributed to the magistrates of the municipalities, and returning members brought back with them both copies of the measures which had been introduced at the adjourned session and materials distributed by the district administration. However, as Micronesia remains primarily an oral-language culture, the information conveyed by word of mouth has most likely exerted more impact than all the written materials distributed. The broadcasting of district legislative sessions now beginning to reach throughout the Territory is but the successor to the first district legislator returning home to inform the people of his community about everything that had happened at the initial session of the district's legislative body.

Formulating and unifying public opinion. Allied to communication, but intrinsically different, has been the material contribution which the district legislatures have made to the structuring of public opinion. Wherever these congresses have been formed, "they represent federations of numerous areas customarily under independent local authorities." [26] Until the district legislatures and their precursor advisory bodies began grappling with district-wide problems, and in turn aided their constituents in looking beyond the boundaries of their village or island, it is difficult to detect the existence of any but localized public opinion. At the first Trust Territory Conference on Self-Government held in 1953, Oliver Nanpei, in a paper referring to the Ponape Islands Congress, noted how its committee system helped give shape to expression of the public

[26] *6th Annual Report . . . , op. cit.,* p. 18.

will. "For example, the committee dealing with fisheries went around and talked to many people who fished around the Island. They learned to get ideas about markets in their minds and to express their thoughts to the administration." [27]

From the founding of the district legislatures, the administration stressed the importance of developing a district-wide outlook, and this helped mold legislative attitudes and actions. In numerous subtle ways, a district identity has emerged from what had been, at best, localized concern. In 1953 the Marshallese were telling the United Nations Visiting Mission that their culture and their district were unique and they did not want to lose themselves in an amalgamation with other Micronesians. By 1956, the *iroij* could propose that the Majuro anthem, "Ij Yokwe lok Ailin eo Ao," be declared the "national anthem for the *entire* Marshalls for the time being [italics added]." [28] Later this same function of promoting regional unity was to be borne by the Council of Micronesia and to reach full flower in initiation of an all-Trust-Territory-identity as one of the contributions of the new Congress of Micronesia.

Island trading companies. Appropriate to the geographic isolation and limited economy of Micronesia, its peoples have been unusually dependent upon trading companies which purchase their copra and other exportable products of soil and sea and in return sell them food and trade goods to supplement their subsistence-type living. All Japanese commercial activity came to a halt in World War II. On take over by the American military forces, a Federal agency, the United States Commercial Company, and later the Island Trading Company, incorporated by the high commissioner under the laws of Guam, furnished these services. Under pressure from United States congressmen to close out I.T.C., it became manifest that indigenous businessmen would have to step into the breach, and both in Palau and in the Marshalls the district legislatures undertook to encourage the setting up of trading companies. The Western Caroline Trading Company was chartered in 1948 through the efforts of the Palau Congress and the Council of Chiefs. MIECO, the Marshall Islands Importing and Exporting Company, was formed through similar cooperative activity in the Marshalls, with the Marshallese congress' having a key role in the

[27] Record of the First Trust Territory Conference on Self-Government (Truk: 1953), p. 18.
[28] Journal of the House of Iroij, 1956 Marshall Islands Congress, Aug. 28 p. 2.

solicitation of capital to found the new company. The Truk district legislature also has shown interest in the financing of the Truk Trading Company.

Historical precedents favored the Marshallese congress' concerning itself in the commercial activity of the district. Government by the Germans was introduced through a private firm, the Jaluit Company's, administering the area; in the Japanese period the Nanyo Boeki Kaisha worked closely with the government. The Americans continued this direct public tie with commercial activity, first with the U.S.C.C. and then the I.T.C. It was only natural for the Marshallese not to draw any sharp dichotomy between the public and private sectors of the economy and, at the first session of the Marshall Islands Congress, to adopt a resolution for the election of MIECO officers and to fix the salary of the MIECO manager. As evidence of its quasi-public nature, for many years MIECO distributed its balance sheet, statement of profit and loss, and statement of net worth to the Marshall Islands Congress when in session, and its manager reported personally to the congress on the year's business just concluded. To this day, the Marshallese congress concerns itself with the management policies and practices of the company. In a way this is reminiscent of the period when, to encourage economic development, American state legislatures blurred the lines between private and public enterprise through grants of public funds to private promoters and followed the course of their activities as though they were public projects.

Administration and administrative supervision. All legislatures engage in a degree of direct administration, tending to their own wants through the activities of their staffs. As illustration, Resolution No. 5–53 of Palau sets up a permanent secretariat responsible for maintaining the records of the congress and, by implication, for caring for congressional facilities. But the district legislatures in Micronesia have engaged in administrative activities wider than their own housekeeping chores, in good part because the nature of the new legislative bodies and the duties of their members were originally not well understood. Many islanders believed the advisory duties with which the legislatures started their careers were of such little moment that the legislators must also be expected to participate in local government. Congressmen in Ponape saw to it that their constituents did their share of community road work, made reports, and otherwise conformed with governmental requirements. The district administrator cited to the 1958 Truk

District Congress five different islands on which legislators had assumed authority over municipal government. In at least one municipality in Palau a congressman, by virtue of his status as a district legislator, was included in the *rubekul* (local government council). Gradually this misunderstanding cleared, but though the district legislators then curbed their direct intervention in local government, they continued in many cases to consult with municipal officials and to be the conduit for contact between municipal government and district headquarters. The result was that the legislators retained their influence over local operations.

A second reason for district legislators' direct involvement in administration arose out of the schism which saw the indigenous population identifying the administration at district headquarters as "American" while the district legislatures were regarded as "Micronesian." Logically, then, greater self-government meant the extension of legislative activity into executive affairs. The ill-fated Charter for the Marianas Union, vetoed by the high commissioner in 1950, would have given the legislature full executive powers in the running of the Marianas district administration. The Palau Congress succeeded to the water transportation equipment of the defunct Palau Association organized under the military government and then entered into a contract with the Western Caroline Trading Company to maintain the system. One of the reasons for the legislators' desiring a permanent secretariat was to ensure the legislature's supervision of these transportation operations. When Palau was granted a new charter in 1955, it expressly authorized the Olbiil era Kelulau to "acquire and administer real and personal property," thereby in effect ratifying the previous legislative action. The gradual assumption of district-wide taxing authority by the congresses was accompanied by the appointment of district treasurers and the establishment of tax collection machinery under legislative aegis. To truncate this expansion of the legislative branch of government, by Executive Order No. 83 the high commissioner in 1962 directed that the office of district treasurer be integrated into the staff of the district administrator and in a single order amended all of the district charters (see Appendix).

A recent example of direct legislative involvement in the details of administration occurred during the 1965 elections for the Congress of Micronesia when, at the request of the district administrator, the members of the Marshall Islands Congress supervised in their respective islands the elections to choose solons for the new Territorial congress. Back in 1962, the political development sub-committee of the Council of Micronesia which toured the Territory reported that "it was observed by the committee that in most of the districts they visited congresses' roles were not clearly defined. Most congresses are assuming responsibilities which should properly belong in the Executive branch." The sub-committee recommended that the problem be dealt with "before it is too late" so that the district congresses could be developed "into bona fide legislative bodies." [29]

As the district chambers through legislation began creating and prescribing the duties of district administrative agencies, the exercise of the legislatures' oversight powers came to resemble more closely the practices of state legislative bodies in the United States. The Palau Board of Education was authorized to issue regulations having the force and effect of law, conditioned upon any regulation's being subject to rescinding by resolution of the Palau Congress.[30] Members of a series of executive boards created by the Mariana District Legislature could be appointed by the district administrator, subject to confirmation either by the district legislature or the holdover committee of that body.[31] In 1964 the Truk District Legislature and the district administrator found themselves engaged in a dispute over an act which would have given the Truk Speaker power to appoint and remove the district tax collector.[32] The district administrator was of the opinion that the legislature was invading his authority; he also disapproved of a legislative proposal specifying the number of police for each municipality within the Truk district.[33]

The district legislatures now have full appropriating powers over moneys collected under their authority or allocated to the district by the Congress of Micronesia. However, the bulk of the expenditures for running the district administration are met out of Federal expenditures. District bodies have no part in either shaping the district administrators' budget requests before they are transmitted to the high commissioner and Washington or in the expenditure of Federal funds by district agencies after they are

[29] "Report of the Political Development Sub-Committee . . . ," *op. cit.*, p. 3.
[30] Resolution No. 13–55, Palau Congress.
[31] See, for example, Acts No. 34–65 and 38–65, Mariana Islands District Legislature.
[32] Act No. 3–64, Truk District Legislature. It should be noted that district legislatures have exercised appointment powers to Territorial administrative bodies, such as the Copra Stabilization Board.
[33] Act No. 4–64, Truk District Legislature.

appropriated by the Congress of the United States and allocated by Headquarters at Saipan. In one district, Truk, the district administrator initiated the practice of referring his preliminary $1,500,000 budget to the Truk legislators for debate and recommendations before it was forwarded to the high commissioner. The legislature summoned the department heads to justify their budget requests and then proposed modifications. However, the high commissioner prohibited continuation of legislative review and also vetoed a bill passed by the first Congress of Micronesia which would have made legislative review mandatory. Although the confidentiality of the Federal executive budget process may now preclude revealing the contents of the Territorial budget to the district legislators in advance of its referral to Washington— the justification for the high commissioner's veto of Assembly Bill No. 2 of the first congress—it would seem only a matter of time before the administrative oversight powers of the district legislatures will be extended in some way to include district budgets, even though the money is not appropriated at the district level.

Another development throughout the Trust Territory has seen the district legislatures calling the personnel of the district administration to account for the manner in which they have undertaken the execution of laws, whether enacted by the legislature or of Territory-wide scope. Early in its life, the Marshallese congress objected to alleged discrimination in health care. In Truk, the district legislators are recipients of numerous petitions of grievances, which they have called on the district administrator to correct, usually without investigation into the accuracy of the petitions' charges. Observation of the Truk solons in action reveals that they look upon the legislature as an instrument for forcing the district administration to mend its ways. The Truk District Legislature has also utilized the device of asking the administration to set up study commissions to make recommendations upon which legislative action may be based. As a variant of this legislative supervision, the Speaker of the Truk legislature has used his office to complain of allegedly lax administration by district agencies and to request that they respond personally to his charges.

The charters of district legislatures now either contain provision for the use of subpoenas in furthering their investigative powers or are being amended to grant the right to issue the writ. The mere possession of this power has strengthened supervisory activities. Under threat of subpoena, the Marianas district administrator directed his public works officer to appear before a legislative committee after the officer had indicated his unwillingness to subject himself to legislative interrogation. In a comparable situation, the Palau district administrator sought to obtain "protection" for his staff members by requiring questions in writing prior to their requested appearance before the legislature. It is only a matter of time before employment of the investigating powers will be coupled with appeals to public opinion to bring pressure upon the district administrators to modify the course of executive action even though the legislatures may not possess direct power over assignment of Federal funds. Illustrative of a related tactic, the Ponape District Legislature now adopts resolutions asking for the enforcement of laws which it previously passed and which it believes are not being administered satisfactorily. With the district administrator now designated as the executive accountable for the enforcement of district legislation under Public Law 1–6 enacted by the first Congress of Micronesia, other district legislatures may adopt this stratagem of chiding the district administration instead of relying upon more direct action through use of their investigatory powers. In any event, the ultimate weapon in administrative oversight is the dispatch of a petition to the Trusteeship Council of the United Nations or a complaint to a U.N. Visiting Mission. Relatively ineffective when used indiscriminately as a blunderbuss, this power arms the district legislatures with a unique potential to sway administrative actions even though they do not possess legal authority to direct them.

Law-making powers. The shift from advisory to full legislating powers happened so gradually that it is recognizable only in retrospect. During the Navy period, the Administering Authority had contemplated giving the district bodies law-making authority subject to the veto of the civil administrators, but it then abandoned the idea. Technically, consultation with the local district bodies supplied only advice to the district administrators, but even before the first district legislature convened, it was recognized that in actual practice the expression of local opinion was likely to carry the weight of legislative decision except "in the relatively rare cases when official policy overrules them." [34] Nevertheless, the fiction of the district legislatures as solely advisory was maintained from the

[34] Stanford University School of Naval Administration, *Handbook of the Trust Territory* (Washington: Office of the Chief of Naval Operations, 1948), p. 106.

time the initial district legislature was convened in Palau until fairly recently. Palau District Order No. 4–48 stated "the function of the Palau Congress is purely advisory to the Civil Administrator," and the supplementary instructions issued as part of Order No. 1–49 declared that the "Congress is empowered only to render opinions and make recommendations to the Civil Administrator." To reinforce this, the latter order added that the civil administrator was not required to follow such recommendations; "however, he will, in all cases, take account of such opinions and recommendations" (see Appendix).

In reporting to the United Nations on the district assemblies, the United States committed itself to expanding their advisory powers "as the people mastered the techniques and procedures of legislation." [35] In fact, the procedure followed had the high commissioner concur with district recommendations phrased in the form of resolutions. This resulted in both American personnel and indigenes' treating the process as akin to legislating, despite the legal fiction that the law-making power resided entirely in the high commissioner. When the "power of resolution upon any subject" was granted to the Palau Olbiil era Kelulau by the new charter of 1955, and then to this was joined the supplemental provision necessitating the high commissioner to act upon these resolutions under penalty of their becoming effective should he fail to do so, "legal" legislating authority was allocated to the district body. The Administering Authority acknowledged that this was only an enlargement of powers already granted and that these powers "would be extended to other district legislative advisory bodies as they advance in experience and their charters are amended." [36]

If the year 1955 be taken as marking the first delegation of the high commissioner's law-making power, full implementation was delayed until the following year. In March of 1956, Section 20 of the Code of the Trust Territory was amended by Executive Order No. 55 to give acts of chartered legislative bodies full force and make a law effective when approved by the high commissioner or otherwise confirmed according to the charter or laws of the Trust Territory. Before this change, after submission and high commissioner ratification, district orders still needed to be prepared and promulgated. The amendment opened the way for legislative en-

[35] *3rd Annual Report . . . , op. cit.,* p. 19.
[36] *11th Annual Report of the United States to the United Nations, 1958,* p. 15.

actments' automatically becoming effective should the high commissioner fail to veto them.

In contrast to the early charter for the Marshall Islands Congress, which specifically authorized the congress to make recommendations on such matters as "civil and criminal law, and regulation of shipping and commerce" (see 1949 constitution, Appendix), the more recently granted charters merely recognize in general terms that the legislative power of the district is vested in their legislatures. Most contain separate authorization for the levying of taxes and the expenditure of the funds, although the allocation of a number of tax sources to the exclusive jurisdiction of the Congress of Micronesia has now reduced the scope of these grants. Almost universally the district legislators look upon their financial powers as their greatest strength, and undoubtedly the district-wide taxes originally imposed pursuant to district legislation and the continued expenditure of funds pursuant to district determination have given the present district legislatures their current political prominence.

For a short while the Administering Authority toyed with precluding the district legislature from concerning itself with traditional matters, in line with the "Barnett thesis." As anthropologist for the Trust Territory, Homer G. Barnett propounded that the customary system of authority should "have jurisdiction over those matters which are traditional, as it always has; and then restricting the authority of the new political order, whatever it is, to the solution of problems that we [Americans], by our presence in their midst, have introduced. . . . There will be simply two parallel patterns of authority functioning in two entirely different spheres of interest. . . . this means continuing to let the old authority deal with all matters that are traditional." [37] It was decided "that the Marshallese Congress should be made the object of an experiment to develop the processes of democratic government without prejudice or damage to native custom." The Marshallese were to be encouraged to consider in their congress "only those matters which are foreign to their culture and outside the scope of traditional controls." [38] Two years later this artificial duality was abandoned, for this conception of two separate cultures existing side by side did not square with reality.

[37] Official Transcript of Proceedings—Conference of District Administrators of the Trust Territory, Feb. 28, 1952, pp. 1–97.
[38] Letter of Dep HiCom to DistAd Marshalls, March 28, 1952.

A vague area of uncertainty still delimits the boundaries of the district legislators' law-making powers. Their actions may not be contrary to the governing provisions of the Trusteeship Agreement, Presidential Executive Orders, Interior Department Orders, or the applicable laws of the United States. Nor may any district legislative body enact laws that contradict the Code and Public Laws of the Trust Territory or Emergency District Orders approved by the high commissioner. Legislature members have been of the opinion that all matters covered by the Trust Territory Code were outside their legislating authority, and with the new Congress of Micronesia succeeding to the legislating powers of the high commissioner, this assumption is now correct. In the past, however, the approval of a district legislative enactment by the high commissioner could have constituted an implied amendment of the Code's provisions. Comparable confusion applied to the relation of the legislatures to district orders, but in compliance with a 1963 memorandum of the high commissioner, all district orders are gradually being reviewed for repeal, amendment, or transformation into district laws. Contemporaneous with the expansion of the district legislatures' powers, the district administrators were directed to curtail their promulgation of district orders; insofar as possible, measures having the force and effect of law were to be submitted to the legislatures for enactment rather than issued as district orders. This form of administrative law-making at the district level has gradually atrophied to the present limited empowerment of the district administrators to issue "emergency district orders."

The delay of the high commissioner in ruling on measures coming to him from the districts caused considerable disgruntlement throughout the Trust Territory. Months would pass while the enactments were reviewed at Headquarters. In defense of the high commissioner, all delay was not the fault of the personnel at Headquarters; some was due to slowness at the district level in preparing resolutions in final form and laboriously translating them into English.

In 1954, when the Marshallese congress met without learning the disposition of the resolutions adopted at its 1953 session, it proposed that a time limit be fixed for action by the high commissioner. The high commissioner suggested modification of this 1954 resolution before it be made effective, but as no session of the congress was held in 1955, somehow it was never implemented. The new charter for Palau, granted in 1955, contained a section fixing a hundred-and-eighty-day maximum for the high commissioner's review, with inaction during that period to be treated as constituting ratification of the measure. Referring to this, when commenting on the delay in approving the 1953 Palau resolutions, the high commissioner noted: "it is regrettable that answers were not given sooner. It is for this reason that we forced our own hand by including [this] section. . . ." [39]

The same mandate was incorporated in the 1958 charters granted to the Marshalls and Ponape and was included in the Yap Island Congress charter of 1959. The period was further shortened in later charters, with a maximum of sixty days specified in the Ponape and Palau charters of 1963. Finally, this was cut to thirty days in the Truk and the Mariana charters of the same year, but it was found that this short a time did not afford a reasonable review period for the high commissioner, and Act No. 2 of the fall 1964 session of the Truk legislature extended the period to sixty days. A civil defense plan for Truk (Act No. 2–64) and a resolution adopted by the Yap Islands Congress (Resolution No. 1–64) became law without signature of the high commissioner in conformance with these charter provisions; whether or not an act passed by the Truk district legislature in the spring of 1963 (Act No. 10–63) became effective by the same route is still a matter of contention. These proscriptions against inaction of the high commissioner do not apply to charter amendments, as attested to by the lag of over ten months between passage and effectuation of the 1963 amendments to the Marshallese charter.

The latest modification in this evolutionary development of the legislative power of the district bodies has been the formalizing of the district administrator's role in granting executive concurrence. Early in the growth of district legislative power, the high commissioner requested receipt of information from the district administrators on enactments forwarded from the district congresses, and he normally followed their recommendations. The charter granted to the Yap Islands Congress in 1959 for the first time provided for veto by the district administrator; if a measure were passed over his objections by an extraordinary majority vote, it was only then to be sent to the high commissioner. This feature was copied in the Palau, Marianas, and Ponape charters of 1963. Truk's charter of the same year allowed the district administrator to veto measures,

---

[39] Letter of HiCom to DistAd Palau, June 2, 1954.

but they were still to be transferred to the high commissioner without further action on the part of the district legislators. The future course of executive approval for district legislative action was foreshadowed by the provisions of the Mariana Islands district charter which left the action of the district administrator as final unless the high commissioner disapproved of the district officer's decision. By act of the Congress of Micronesia, since 1966 all districts now observe the same procedure, which formally elevates the importance of the district administrator in the granting of executive approval. Should he sign the measure before him or fail to take action within thirty days, the bill becomes law without possibility of review by the high commissioner. Only when a district legislature enacts a measure over the veto of the district officer does it now go to the high commissioner for concurrence, and once again a thirty-day period is allowed under legal threat of the measure's becoming law should it not be vetoed. If permitted to exercise full discretion, the district administrator now occupies a crucial position of influence in the course of district law-making.

As the district legislatures began testing their powers, the high commissioner did not hesitate to vary appropriations or question the substantive provisions contained in the resolutions forwarded to him. With the introduction of greater formality and the observance of practices modeled on typically American legislative-executive relations, the right of the high commissioner to revise resolutions unilaterally when signing them became more tenuous.[40] The logic of the express grant of legislating powers to the district chambers dictated that the participation of the district administrator and the high commissioner ought to be limited to acceptance or rejection, once the formal enactment was presented to them. In responding to this, the new charters added item veto powers, allowing the high commissioner to express his approval of a bill while cutting or eliminating its appropriations, which by implication foreclosed his exercise of other amendatory effort. Even this item veto power is not contemplated by the 1966 amendments to the Trust Territory Code which take precedence over the previously granted charters.

Micronesian ignorance of the attributes and processes of legis-

[40] This right of modification was questioned as early as 1955, when the first resolutions adopted by the Palau Olbiil era Kelulau were submitted to the high commissioner. Memo from Staff Anthropologist to Acting HiCom, Aug. 6, 1955.

lative bodies, indigenous cultural patterns which encourage passivity in group situations and abhor frontal confrontation, and the general lack of knowledge concerning the workings of the American-sponsored district government all help explain the limited, incremental growth of district legislatures. Absence of control over the expenditure of Federally appropriated funds and the broad area of action preempted by the scope of the Trust Territorial Code further contributed to discouraging indigenous direction of district affairs. Gradually, the district legislators have begun to appreciate the distinction between legal authority and political influence and the use of the latter to gain ends not achievable through the former. Even to this day, district legislators remain unsure of their formal powers, and their efforts at political manipulation are fairly unsophisticated. With the law-making powers presently at their disposal and their ever greater effort to hold the district administration to account, there is little question that the legislative bodies in all of the administrative districts now possess the potential for playing an aggressive role at this intermediate level of Territorial government.

STRUCTURE

The Administering Authority justified the early charters: "while the bicameral system of advisory bodies may seem unwieldy and unnecessary, it has been approved in recognition of the desires of the people. It will probably be desirable to utilize this type of governmental structure wherever the native customs still recognize and respect the power of chieftain classes." [41] It need not have been so defensive, for though the terminology of the charters called for bicameral district legislatures, unicameralism or a modified version thereof was the practice. The use at the 1949 Marshallese Magistrates Conference of "House of Lords" and "House of Commons" in referring to the contemplated Marshallese congress, and the specification that the Ponape Island Congress was to be composed of a "Nobles' House" and a "People's House" served more to acknowledge the inclusion of traditional chiefs than to require full bicameralism. In both areas the houses met separately to formulate proposals but jointly passed the resolutions which were to be submitted to the high commissioner for his action. The records kept

[41] *5th Annual Report* . . . , *op. cit.*, p. 16.

by these legislative bodies do not reveal this, nor do the titles of the measures they adopted. In Ponape, under the 1952 charter, members from both houses even sat on the joint committees framing recommendations. While the Marshallese did have a degree of cross-communication, the membership of each chamber's committees remained separate. However, once in joint session, the *kajurs* (commoners) could outvote the *iroij* (nobles), and on crucial questions concerning land ownership rights, the *iroij* would not force the issue to a decision when facing adamant *kajur* opposition. Even on Saipan, when the civil administration created a second legislative body called the "House of Commissioners" for the municipality, "at first these two groups met separately, but in order to simplify procedures and achieve a more workable organization they decided to meet together . . . ," [42] and bills were approved in joint session. The United Nations Trusteeship Council looked with favor on a conversion from bicameral to unicameral legislatures, as did the Administering Authority. The composition of the Palau Congress was proof that the traditional chiefs could be accommodated without need of even a formal nod to bicameralism. Thus the former bicameralism for deliberation and unicameralism for definitive decision-making disappeared from the later charters, and today all call for unicameral district bodies (see chart, pp. 76–77).

Unlike the colonial popular assemblies of early America, the number of members in the district legislatures in the Trust Territory has been decreasing over time. Several factors have contributed to this end. There has been little grass-roots demand for increased representation. Until recently, with the legislatures' limited resources, reducing the number of legislators allowed longer sessions and made more money available for the remaining members. Then, too, in Palau, the elimination of the magistrates from the 1963 charter separated the executive from the legislative branch and may be viewed as a strategy to enhance the power of the district legislature vis-a-vis the administration.

Except for the provision made in the 1963 Ponape charter for Kolonia, a splitting of the Saipan municipality, a few electoral precincts in Truk, and the arrangements in the last Palau charter for at-large members, all solons elected to district legislatures have represented single municipalities. Usually, each municipality has

---

[42] Spoehr, *op. cit.*, p. 174.

been granted at least one member, despite its miniscule population, while the more heavily populated areas have been relatively discriminated against even though offered multiple representation. Offsetting the disproportion has been the small size of even the largest election district, facilitating ready contact between the elector and his representative should the voter desire to make his wishes known or the legislator to communicate personally with his constituents. Of course, when an island distant from district headquarters has elected representatives who have physically not resided, and possibly not visited, in that island for many years, the representatives have at best an attenuated sense of identification with "home," and communication opportunities between constituent and legislator have been minimal.

In its effort to encourage political development, the Administering Authority insisted upon no uniform plan for representation, so that Palau could elect twenty-eight members to its congress while Truk, with twice the population, settled upon a twenty-seven-member body. In the Marshall Islands district, after initially setting the ratio of one elected representative for the first five hundred population, a second member for the next five hundred, and a third for all population over a thousand, the 1951 session cut this in half. Except for allowing additional representation for all multiples of two hundred fifty, the ratio was continued in the new charter of 1958. Later even this was found unwieldy, and the Twelfth Marshallese Congress in 1963 recommended reducing the size of the elected membership again to that employed when the district congress was inaugurated. This resulted in a drop in elected representatives from seventy-seven in the 1964 session to forty-one in 1965.

Running counter to this trend toward diminishing size has been the aspiration of the areas around district headquarters, whose populations have expanded greatly, for representation proportionate to their size. Under the 1963 charter, the election of five members at large in the Palau area furnishes Koror with an excellent opportunity to decide their selection while maintaining control over the choice of the five members elected solely from Koror municipality. The Marianas district has recently expressed dissatisfaction with the fixed membership provided by its charter, and would like to substitute the formula of one representative for every eight hundred population on Rota, Saipan, Tinian and the northern islands, which will benefit Saipan, the seat of the district administration.

The first two congresses, those established in Palau and the Marshalls, met annually. This failed to fix a precedent, and today, except in the Marshalls, all of the district legislative bodies convene semi-annually. Although the Truk and Mariana districts face transportation problems and representatives from distant areas frequently arrive late for the sessions, the difficulties encountered in the Marshalls far surpass those of the other districts. July through October have been the favorite months for travel by indigenes in the Marshalls, as the weather then is most suitable for sailing, and the annual convening date of the Marshall Islands Congress was originally fixed with this in mind.[43] In 1955 and in 1959 it was necessary to forego holding sessions of the Marshallese congress due to transportation problems; the latter postponement was also caused by the inability of the congress to finance its costs as well as by the time-consuming, change-over procedures necessitated by the adoption of the new charter. Again in 1966 and 1967 transportation difficulties precluded convening the congress.

The short, three-day meetings of the early Palau and Ponape congresses contrast with the more lengthy sessions of today. As district legislatures have taken up more complicated legislation, they have become accustomed to longer work periods, and in some cases this has roughly doubled the sessions' length. This points up the significance of the ten-day limitation written into the Yap charter of 1959 and the twenty-day restrictions of both the Ponape charter of 1958 (since eliminated) and the current Mariana Islands district charter. The ploy of the Truk district legislature to convene in the Mortlocks in 1965 was given short shrift by the district administrator, who objected that, as the headquarters for the district, Moen Island should properly be the site for all meetings and that it would be too expensive and inconvenient to hold the session elsewhere. Other district legislatures have expressed no dissatisfaction with holding their meetings at district administration headquarters.

All district charters have made provision for the selection of pre-

---

[43] The breadfruit season also originally entered into the fixing of the meeting date. See Notes of 1949 Iroij Conference, Marshall Islands District, p. 8. Currently, the conjunction of the meeting with the summer school vacation is probably a more important consideration.

DISTRICT LEGISLATIVE CHARTERS
(amendments not shown)

	PALAU			MARSHALLS	
	1948	1955	1963	1949	1958
Unicameral/ bicameral	unicam.	unicam.	unicam.	bicam.	unicam.
Frequency of meetings	annual	semi-annual	semi-annual	annual	annual
Size or population unit	(49) [a]	(71) [b]	(44) [c]	(20/39) [d]	(19/66)
Term of office (yrs.)	2	2	4	(1) [i]	2 [i]
Minimum age	26	26	25	—	25
Pay/other benefits	municipal [k]	municipal	by law	[l]	(by law)
Quorum	—	⅔ each	¾	—	⅔
Vote to enact	—	⅔ present	members present	majority members	—
Days within which DistAd [p] must act	—	—	21 [q]	—	—
Days within which HiCom [v] must act	—	180	60	—	180

( ) so interpreted or applied, as ascertained from contemporary sources
   * 1952 Ponape: Ponape Island and non-voting representatives from off-island colonies; Yap: Yap Islands only
   [a] magistrates-chiefs; members elected: 0–199 = 1 representative, 200–499 = 2, all else 3
   [b] 16 chiefs, 16 magistrates, and elected representatives same as [a], except 1 additional for each multiple over 500 with maximum of 5
   [c] chiefs and 28 elected—5 at large, others from municipalities
   [d] *iroij* upper house; 1 from each municipality for lower house until Congress provides more (0–599 = 1, 600–999 = 2, all else 3)
   [e] persons recognised as *iroij;* each municipality, extra for each multiple over 250 (at first meeting in 1960, 9 representatives absent)
   [f] each municipality 1, extra for each multiple over 500
   [g] 25 nobles; 1 from each municipality for lower house, with extra for each multiple over 300, and non-voting delegates for off-island colonies
   [h] each municipality 1, extra for multiple over 400, except that must be over ½ of multiple
   [i] *iroij* for life
   [j] municipality may elect to stagger terms

MARIANA	TRUK		PONAPE			YAP
1963	1957	1963	1952 *	1958	1963	1959 *
unicam.	unicam.	unicam.	bicam.	unicam.	unicam.	unicam.
semi-annual	annual	semi-annual	semi-annual	semi-annual	semi-annual	semi-annual
6	(55) [f]	27	(25/29) [g]	35 [h]	24	20
3	3 [j]	2	(3)	4 staggered terms	4	4 staggered terms
25	30	23	25	25	25	25
by law	by Congress	by law	by law	by Congress	by law	by Congress [m]
4	2/3	3/4	—	3/4	3/4	3/4
members present	2/3 quorum	majority members	majority members [n]	majority members [o]	members present	2/3 present
5 [r]	—	60 [s]	—	—	21 [t]	30 [u]
0	—	30	—	180	60	180

[k] not more than $1 per session day

[l] charter says determined by Congress and approved by Civil Administration; actually municipal payment plus subsistence by district

[m] Congressmen to be compensated equally for actual days service in attendance

[n] 2/3 vote of originating house if disapproved by second house

[o] 2/3 members if at same session as introduced

[p] by Public Law No. 2–26, since 1966 all DistAds have only 30 days to veto; any legislation by 2/3 vote may send to HiCom

[q] may have additional 30 days to consult HiCom; if DistAd vetoes, legislature by 3/4 vote may send to HiCom

[r] if DistAd vetoes, legislature by 2/3 vote may send to HiCom

[s] goes to HiCom even if vetoed

[t] may have additional 30 days to consult HiCom; if DistAd vetoes, legislature by 3/4 vote may send to HiCom

[u] if DistAd vetoes, Congress by 3/4 vote may send to HiCom

[v] by Public Law No. 2–26, since 1966 the HiCom has only 30 days to veto

siding officers from the membership of the legislative bodies. In the Marshalls, the president must be at least thirty years of age, and in Palau it is now declared that only elected members are eligible to serve as officers, effectively disqualifying the chiefs. The charters of the other districts are silent on officers' qualifications. In many of the districts, the presiding officers exert leadership both during the session and in the legislative interim, but only the president of the Mariana Islands district legislature is a full-time officer and compensated accordingly.

A permanent secretary or secretariat has been built into all of the district congresses. In some, a secretary—occasionally called "clerk"—or secretary and assistant, aided by the staff of the district administration, perform all the services that are necessary in carrying on the correspondence of the legislature, preparing notices and reports, keeping legislative and financial records, obtaining supplies, and publishing the journal. The drafting of measures and an embryonic reference service are also lodged with the secretary. Usually, the person serving as secretary has been a non-member, but one of the elected members was named to this post under the 1958 Marshall Islands charter, and the secretary of the Yap Islands Congress is a member of that body. In the Marianas, provision is made for a legislative secretary, who is a legislator and for a non-member executive secretary. Exemplifying the variations found within the districts, the Truk District Congress in 1962 set a term of four years for its secretary, while the charter of the Yap Islands Congress limits the secretary's service to a period of two years or less.

Even though appointed by his district legislature, the district treasurer is now on the staff of the district administrator and subject to removal for cause at any time by the latter. The treasurer receives and disburses funds pursuant to the authority of the legislative assembly and under the direction and supervision of the administrator. At one time the post was sometimes combined with that of legislative secretary, but in all districts today, the collection and accounting for district-imposed taxes is a separate, full-time undertaking. The treasurer remains identified with the legislature as distinct from the district administration, contributing to the ambiguity of his position.

The members of the various district legislatures have had occasion to require the assistance of a parliamentarian, sometimes because of the inexperience of the members and at others because they have become so adroit at parliamentary maneuvering that only a skilled parliamentarian can keep track of the flow of legislative business. In the Marianas and Ponape, one of the elected members is named to serve in this post; in other districts, staff from the public affairs office of the district administration aid. District administration staff have also been utilized for drafting legislative measures. More recently, there is a noticeable trend to hiring legislative counsel to advise their respective bodies on legal matters and to undertake drafting chores, and the services of Peace Corps Volunteers have been called upon for the same purpose. Even with the gradual expansion of the district legislative staffs, the personnel of the public affairs office of each district administration continue to work closely with their respective district legislatures, helping in drafting, factual reference, and in liaison with the district administration.

Committees in the first district assemblies corresponded in number and jurisdiction to the major problem areas outlined by the district administrator at the opening of each session. Following the model draft, the new charters granted in 1963 limit the number of standing committees to four: appropriations, economics, political, and social. The Mariana Islands district is an exception, and in place of the first-named committee, the charter sets up a Holdover Committee; recently an amendment to the charter added an appropriations committee as well. The need for uniformity in committee structure has been more assumed than demonstrated.

Reminiscent of the committees on legislation which were tried in the American colonial legislatures around the period of the Revolutionary War, the 1958 charter for Ponape and that granted to Yap in 1959 called for special committees with bill-drafting duties. Both of these charters contemplated that a member would introduce a proposal for a measure at one session. After being accepted, the measure would be referred to the legislative committee for formal preparation and then could be enacted by the congress at its next regular session. In Ponape, the committee even employed a permanent staff. As this "special feature" was found to be dysfunctional, it was eliminated in the new Ponape charter of 1963 and, in practice, ignored in Yap.

At the same time that the civil administrator in Palau established the first Palau Congress, by District Order he named a council with the inelegantly phrased duty "to keep its fingers on the pulse of the people and so inform the civil administrator on public policy" (see

Appendix). The council was conceived of as advisory to the administrator, and though it might originate legislation, its proposed measures would be presented to the congress via the civil administrator. This prestigeful body, which met on the average of about once a month, in fact also acted as liaison between administration and the Palau Congress and exerted great influence over the latter's decisions. In 1953, the congress adopted a resolution which would make the advisory council responsible to it instead of to the district administrator. The charter granted in 1955 replaced the Palau Council with the Tebechelel Olbiil, to be appointed by the president of the congress with congress' approval and to serve as advisor to the president. The new body, which contained both legislators and non-legislative members, in fact also continued as a consultant group for the district administrator when the congress was not in session. Because of the proximity of these advisors to the seat of administration, this group supplied the impetus for much of the Palauan-inspired legislation, and to eliminate its influence, the Palauans asked that it be abolished when the Palauan charter of 1963 was formulated.

The other districts also felt the need of some form of advisory body composed of indigenes with which the district administrators could meet in the interim between sessions of the district assemblies. In addition, the sore need of the new legislatures for policy leadership, and the necessity of making provision for administrative machinery to plan the holding of each session, encouraged the growth of comparable interim bodies in the other districts. The second session of the Marshall Islands Congress created a Holdover Committee "to study and prepare recommendations for presentation at the next session of the Congress." [44] It was to have other powers to act for the congress in the legislative interim, but these were initially ill-defined and have never been fully clarified other than by everyone's agreement that the committee could not act with relation to Marshallese land rights and other basic customs. The name "holdover committee" was borrowed from terminology employed in Hawaii a few years earlier, and from the Marshalls its usage spread to the other districts. At first the civil administrator tried to limit the committee's membership to a single person upon the grounds of expense and efficiency, but this was reversed, and the size set at ten and later at twelve members.

[44] *5th Annual Report . . . , op. cit.,* p. 15.

Composed mainly of individuals residing on Majuro, the Marshallese Holdover Committee has met informally at least annually with the district administrator and made plans for the calling of each congress and for the items on its agenda. In years when the congress did not convene, it has acted on essential legislative matters, extending taxes and even appropriating funds. It played an important role in the examination of the 1958 charter provisions as originally framed by the administration. A charter amendment was adopted in 1956 specifying that only in case of an emergency which might result in great jeopardy and catastrophe to the Marshallese people was the Holdover Committee automatically empowered to act with full authority of the Marshallese congress; however it has not conformed to this restriction and has turned its attention to far more than the settlement of "any unfinished Congressional business." [45] The 1958 charter's limitation on the Holdover Committee's allocation of district funds other than for purposes for which they were appropriated by the congress has also been observed in the breech. Unlike the Palau advisory group, the Marshallese Holdover Committee continues, although it is less formal a body than the Palau experiment and more a collective name for the Marshallese leaders located at Majuro.

Years before the founding of a district legislature in Truk, a Permanent Advisory Committee of the annual Conference of Island Magistrates served as a consultative body to the district administrator. On the chartering of the Truk legislature in 1957, a Holdover Committee, with members representing the geographical areas of the district, in part carried on the activities of the advisory committee by meeting before the sitting of the Truk Congress to determine its agenda and to prepare measures for consideration; after adjournment, it again convened to wind up the business of the congress. Just as in the Palau district, members from distant islands looked askance at any body serving as advisor to the district administrator if the body's members would be drawn only from those persons residing close to district headquarters, and the Holdover Committee was abolished in 1963.

The Holdover Committee in the Marianas, consisting as it does of the president, the legislative secretary, and the chairmen of the district legislature's four standing committees, exercises pivotal powers of agenda formation and assignment of measures for com-

---

[45] Resolution No. 15–56, Marshall Islands Congress.

mittee deliberation. However, the fact that the bulk of the district's population lives close to administration headquarters has helped obviate both the same suspicion and the same need for an interim consultative body as has been experienced in the Marshalls, Truk, and Palau.

MEMBERSHIP

Almost any citizen eligible to vote in the Trust Territory may be elected to a district legislature. The age and residence requirements are only nominally restrictive. The first Ponape charter (1952) disqualified the holders of the four highest titles in each *wehy* (district) from election to the People's House, since they automatically sat in the Nobles' House, and prohibited all other nobles from holding concurrent seats in both chambers. Neither the Marshallese constitution of 1949 nor the 1955 Palau charter precluded the election of chiefs, but each made special provision for the possibility of their sitting as elected representatives. In recognition of their status in the Marshallese culture, the *iroij* have been eligible as of right to sit and vote in the Marshallese congress since it was founded. In Palau, the 1963 charter has continued the presence in the legislature of the two high chiefs and the paramount chiefs of the municipalities but has now materially restricted their participation to mainly that of debate.

By 1963, holders of elected municipal office were barred from all district legislative bodies other than in the Marshall Islands. Their ineligibility applies only to sitting as a legislator, so that if elected they may resign their municipal posts to accept a district legislative seat. (The language of the Yapese charter remains ambiguous in this regard.) In the Marianas, Palau, and Truk, this prohibition also runs against holding judicial office. Truk by charter extended this disqualification to any person holding a "staff position" in the district administration, which has been interpreted as referring to "a department head, assistant department head and those particular positions immediately on the staff of the District Administrator where policy matters were involved."[46] In a 1963 memorandum, the Truk district administrator identified over two dozen positions covered by this "conflict of interest" provision. The district administrator of Palau went even further than the Truk administrator and, by district directive in 1964, attempted to apply a

---

[46] Memo from Acting Deputy HiCom to DistAd Truk, Oct. 25, 1963.

blanket disqualification to any member of the executive branch; his prescription was later rescinded as the district charter provided no basis for its issuance.

At the instigation of the Administering Authority, in all elections for the office of district legislator held after December 31, 1968, judges, members of the insular constabulary, and employees of the Trust Territory or district administration in positions of assistant department head or higher will be ineligible as candidates. Originally, the administration had suggested that the cut-off date be fixed at 1966, on the grounds that it was advisable for the separation between the three branches of government to "be accomplished as soon as possible." The misgivings expressed by the Congress of Micronesia were occasioned by such practicalities as that two-thirds of the Ponape legislature might be disqualified by the new limitations.[47] As a result the deadline prohibiting such dual service was postponed to the end of 1968.

The compromise extension may have delayed the day of decision, but it also incorporated an unfortunate feature not found in any of the charter provisions. In the future, a person occupying a position in either the judicial or executive branches must elect to sever his relations before running for a legislative post, rather than deciding to do so after having been successful in his bid for a legislative seat. Given the limited opportunities for employment in the Territory, for some time to come this may have the unfortunate consequence of discouraging the movement of top personnel from the executive and judicial branches into the political arena of the legislature.

Considering the Micronesian attitude towards age as a measure of competence, the charters have all set fairly minimal age requirements for candidacy. Truk's first charter in 1957 declared a representative had to be at least thirty years old to serve, but in the following year an amendment reduced the minimum age to twenty-six. Except for a further lowering of the age to twenty-three by the Truk charter of 1963, all other districts now require a uniform minimum age of twenty-five years.

Mr. Rifai of the United Arab Republic in 1961 raised the question in the Trusteeship Council whether there should not be greater uniformity in representation and lengths of service. According to him, the existing situation "was not conducive to the creation of a

[47] *Saipan District Panorama*, July 30, 1965, p. 1.

territorial conscience and the feeling that the inhabitants were part of a single territory." [48] If an analogy is drawn with the American experience of diversity in state legislative bodies, this criticism may not be accorded much weight, but it correctly assessed the lack of any general pattern in the length of terms for district legislators. They have varied from one to four years. Over time, the four-year term has come into favor and, with the 1967 amendment to the Marianas charter, is now found in five of the six districts. Only Truk with a two-year term prescribes a shorter period of legislative service, but the Ponape district legislature has begun to discuss establishing a comparable term. The lengthening of terms probably can best be attributed to the members' realization that a longer time in office facilitates mastering the procedures and subject matter with which they are called upon to deal. A new addition to both the Palau and Ponape charters, although from the records unused to date, is the right to recall an elected representative during his term in office.

Not all members entitled to seats in the district assemblies have appeared each year. Transportation difficulties account for part of this failure. The limited legislating power of the beginning congresses, with a concommitant lack of status, and the members' dependence upon the local municipality's collecting money to help defray their costs while at the district center undoubtedly discouraged attendance. As in the early legislatures of Europe, the support of a representative was treated as an obligation of the municipality enjoying the benefit of his services. Even though the district administration might furnish transportation and subsistence for the period the legislature was in session, in areas like the Marshalls where members have had to wait months at Majuro before obtaining deck space back home, attendance at a session constituted a personal financial burden.[49]

While the Palau charter authorized members to receive compensation and allowances from their municipalities, and in nearly all cases congressmen were receiving "some token salary," the Palau Olbiil era Kelulau at its first meeting initiated the payment

[48] TCOR, 27th Sess., 1148th meeting, June 14, 1961, par. 47.
[49] As illustrative of the monetary contribution made by the municipalities of one district to their representatives, for the thirty-eight members of the 1956 Marshallese House of Assembly for whom data are available (out of a total of 42), nine received nothing and another eleven less than $30. The mean average payment was $44; three assemblymen were each recipients of $100 or over for attending this session.

of a per diem.[50] Since then, the charters of all district legislatures have been amended to authorize legislators' remuneration from district collected revenues, and the pattern has been for members' per diem to increase over time. Between 1955 and 1963 the daily rate doubled in Palau from the munificent sum of $1.50, with a fourteen-day maximum, to $3.00, without any maximum prescribed; by the latter date, an additional $3.00 a day was also allowed for committee sessions and for an extra two-day period before and after each committee meeting. Larger sums have been allotted by other legislatures, as the Marianas' provision of $12.00 a day for each session attended and a per diem of $10.00 for members "traveling away from their home-islands on legislative business." [51] The district legislatures look upon these payments not as salaries but primarily as reimbursement for expenses incurred. As a case in point, a 1962 Truk act furnished $5.00 a day but required $3.50 to be deducted for each day of meeting a representative did not attend. In no district is the specified remuneration so large that it refutes the generalization that members normally stand for office because of the prestige associated with the legislative post or because of a sense of public obligation rather than for their own financial betterment.

The physical accommodations for district offices in the Territory have never been more than minimally adequate, and usually the legislatures have met in temporary chambers at district headquarters under disadvantageous conditions. This is changing as structures have been set aside for legislative use or district tax moneys have been appropriated for the construction of congressional halls. As of now, a survey of legislative facilities across the Territory reveals great disparities. Just as the members are now allotting larger stipends to themselves, so have they been turning attention toward improving their physical facilities. Even air conditioning for the legislative hall, a luxury for the Trust Territory, was proposed by the Mariana district legislature in its 1966 budget. It is only a matter of time before each legislative body will have its own vehicle (usually a truck) and miscellaneous minor extravagances such as a Polaroid camera, presumably for its staff's use.

The model charter states that "members of the legislature during

[50] Letter of Assistant DistAd Palau to HiCom, May 19, 1955. Prior to 1955, the Palau Congress had few funds at its disposal and "discussions which surrounded the proposed expenditures of monies collected were marked by a strong and not altogether undesirable note of parsimony." *Ibid.*
[51] Act No. 3–63, Marianas District Legislature.

their attendance at the Legislature and in going to and returning from the same, shall not be subject to civil process and shall, in all cases except felony or breach of the peace, be privileged from arrest. No member shall be held to answer before any tribunal other than the Legislature itself for any speech or debate in the Legislature" (see Appendix). This section has been incorporated into all of the charters granted in 1963, and it may be anticipated that it will be added to the charters for the Marshalls and Yap when the constituent legislation of these two districts is modified. A few of the district legislators involved in minor traffic violations during a period when they were engaged in the performance of their legislative duties have already had occasion to resort to this grant of privileges and immunities for protection.

Few women have been members of the district legislatures.[52] In 1950, Palau elected two female members, and it is reported "both showed an intelligent and intense desire to participate actively in government." [53] Although the Marshallese women are interested in politics and will participate in local political discussions, none has ever been elected; however, as many as five *leroij* (female paramount chiefs) have sat at one time in the House of Iroij of the Marshall Islands Congress. Two women ran for representative in the 1966 Truk elections, and their success foretells that more women will regularly fill legislative posts. Their number will most likely always remain fewer than the male component for, just as in the United States, Micronesian cultural patterns do not encourage a woman's holding an elected political post.

At the various workshops and instruction sessions which the district legislators have attended, the necessity for acting for the district as a whole, rather than for their respective municipality, has been emphasized and reemphasized. Probably as frequently, it has been stressed that "when voting on a resolution, do not allow your personal desires or opinions to influence your decisions. Vote as you know the people who elected you want you to vote." [54] It therefore might be expected that when a district legislator is queried as to his representational role, he will reply not as he

[52] In 1955 the high commissioner indicated about fifteen women, or approximately 10 per cent, were members of various councils and congresses. If applicable only to district legislatures and their progenitors, this number appears too high. See TCOR, 16th Sess., 617th meeting, June 16, 1955, par. 95.

[53] Richard, *op. cit.*, p. 482.

[54] Address of the DistAd, Proceedings of the Fifth Ponape Island Congress, Nov. 13–22, 1956, p. 15.

actually views himself as a legislator but as he has been instructed to behave. Two surveys conducted almost a decade apart reveal that members of two of the district legislatures in the Territory consider that they adhere to representational roles similar to those reported in comparable studies of American state legislatures.[55] Of the seventeen members of the House of Assembly interviewed in the Marshalls in 1956 and the twenty-six members of the unicameral Truk district legislature similarly surveyed in 1965, the largest components thought of themselves as able to decide issues in accordance with their own judgment (Trustee role), irrespective of the wishes or instructions of constituents. Far smaller components of each legislative body stated they felt duty bound to comply with their constituents' wishes (Delegate role) or indicated an ambivalence which showed constant adherence to neither polar type (Politico role).

LEGISLATIVE ROLE CONCEPTS

Legislative Role	Marshall House of Assembly (17 responses) 1956	Truk District Legislature (26 responses) 1965	Truk Constituents * (26 responses) 1965
Trustee	12	12	2
Politico	2	8	—
Delegate	3	5	20
Not Classified	—	1	4

* Views legislators thought their constituents held about the role legislators should observe.

When the Truk district legislators were queried as to how the people of their districts expected them to perform their role, over three-quarters replied that their constituents believed them bound to follow instructions received from the voters. It is not known whether this is an honest assessment or represents a structuring of responses so as to echo the various hortatory intructions which they have received from American administrators.

The Marshall Islands Congress of 1956 is illustrative of both the type of persons who sit in that district legislature and the contrasts between the popularly chosen representatives and the hereditary chiefs within that body. Compared to the population as a whole,

[55] For fuller discussion of this, see pp. 284–287.

PROFILE OF 1956 MARSHALL ISLANDS CONGRESS
(in percentages)

	HOUSE OF IROIJ (n = 28)	HOUSE OF ASSEMBLY (n = 42)
Education:		
In Missionary Schools	75.0	83.3
In Japanese Schools	28.6	28.6
In American Schools	21.4	21.4
None or not indicated	7.1	2.4
Travel:		
Trust Territory—yes	50.0	45.2
Trust Territory—no	35.7	33.3
Trust Territory—not indicated	14.3	21.4
Japan	25.0	16.7
Hawaii	14.3	2.4
Mainland U.S.	10.7	—
Language Ability (spoken):		
English	28.6	35.7
Japanese	28.6	42.8
German	17.9	—
Other Micronesian	10.7	16.7
Government Employment:		
Present		
District	10.7	16.7
Local office	10.7	40.5
Previous		
American	53.6	59.5
Japanese	35.7	21.4
Teacher or former teacher	14.2	42.8
Religion:		
Protestant	71.4	90.5
Catholic	28.6	4.8
Not indicated	—	4.8
No religious office	75.0	57.1
Deacon or *komat*	17.8	42.8
Not indicated	7.1	—
Married	96.4	95.3

PROFILE OF 1956 MARSHALL ISLANDS CONGRESS (Cont'd)
(in percentages)

Age:		
Median	52.0 years	44.0 years
Mean	51.3 years	45.0 years
Median number of children	3	5

the legislators were better educated, more traveled, enjoyed a greater command of English and, through present or former employment, were more conversant with the operations of government introduced by the Americans. In cross-house comparisons, the elected representatives were noticeably younger, more closely mirrored the prevailing Protestantism of the Marshalls, and had often been prepared for public office by service as school teachers. A goodly component of the representatives were also occupying municipal posts. Although the upper chamber nominally consisted of *iroij laplap* or *leroij*, in fact they constituted only fifteen of the twenty-eight members present. The House of Assembly did not represent a cross-section of the body politic but, rather, was heavily weighted toward persons of importance in traditional Marshallese society. Half of the forty-two assemblymen were *alabs* (heads of the *bwij*—lineage—entitled to work the land) or *iroij erik* (lesser nobles), and another ten were in the *bwij errito* (the oldest lineage), and thus close in line to become *alabs* upon the death of the incumbents.[56]

In mid-1956 the Marshall Islands Congress consisted primarily of members with status associated with land. Representation of their own interests or of their class loomed large, for most of the assemblymen were selected indirectly by municipal councils made up of *alabs*. Since then, direct election of assemblymen has spread through the district, but the resulting representation of the more diffuse electorate was accompanied with relatively little change in the composition of the Marshallese congress. The members elected to the 1965 unicameral body were still almost all Protestant, about half were deacons and *komats*, a little larger percentage spoke English, and if anything a higher proportion of their numbers enjoyed positions of status associated with customary land rights.

---

[56] See Jack A. Tobin, *Land Tenure in the Marshall Islands*, Atoll Research Bulletin No. 11 (Washington: Pacific Science Board, National Research Council, rev. 1956), p. 15.

The greatest apparent difference from a decade previously was that experience as a school teacher had dropped in importance as an avenue for the political socialization of elected assemblymen. The wedding of the traditional and the introduced political systems in the structuring of the congress continued to bring to the legislative hall persons distinguished by their prescriptive claims to leadership.

CHAPTER 4

District Legislatures—
Their Procedures and Process

ELEMENTS ENCOURAGING both uniformity and diversity contributed to shaping the procedures followed by today's district legislatures. Lack of knowledge and multiplicity of innovative effort provided centrifugal forces, while the basic body of parliamentary practice common to all American legislative bodies added a centripetal pull. What has finally emerged is a mixture of customary conduct and introduced methods, with the latter more an overlay than comprising part of an alloy. Careful observation of the district legislatures at work continues to reveal the presence of traditional patterns, notwithstanding the letter of the formal rules which proport to govern all legislative actions.

A concerted effort was made in most districts to equip the members of the new legislative bodies with an understanding of the rudiments of parliamentary affairs. At the very first meeting of the Marshallese congress, in 1950, naval administration personnel gave "instructions" to the neophyte members. At the next session, a former Hawaiian legislator continued the training by drawing up for the members' use a set of rules which borrowed some of that other Pacific Territory's unique practices [1] and applied them to the Marshallese scene.

Once the legislatures commenced functioning, impromptu meetings and organized workshops have been held by the administrators in the different districts when they have believed turnover in the composition of the legislative assemblies warranted mounting another program in parliamentary procedure. Coaching in the running of local councils, as part of the municipal chartering project, included the preparation of handbooks for municipal officials' use and furthered the exposure of district legislators to parliamentary methods. From all this there emanated a series of simplified legislative manuals published in district languages, some of them literal translations of published trade handbooks, others the em-

---

[1] Such as *ijab bojak*, a direct translation of Hawaii's *kanalua* (undecided). See p. 310.

bodiment of staff members' understanding of parliamentary procedure, modified as was thought necessary to fit local needs. Basic to many of these, as well as to the model standing rules prepared at the Headquarters of the high commissioner, was *Robert's Rules of Order,* even though it is primarily intended for use by clubs and informal organizations and leaves much to be desired when applied to parliamentary bodies.

ORGANIZING

The format followed in organizing each newly elected legislature is fairly similar throughout the Territory. The opening day normally sees an invocation, presentation of credentials for the seating of members, and the selection of officers. The endeavor to obtain formal credentials has not been very successful, and legislative records bearing entries that a member has been disqualified because of improper or inadequate documentation are rare. The previous session's presiding officer may chair the meeting until new officers are chosen. The naming of committees generally waited upon an itemization by the district administrator or his representatives of subjects to be considered, but this is unnecessary as the new charters now prescribe a fixed number of standing committees. The opening day of the district legislature may find the district treasurer reporting on district-levied revenues, and the secretary, on unfinished legislative business. In most districts, all the steps necessary to organize the legislature are commonly observed in the session which follows an election; in the other sessions, practices may be telescoped.

The presiding officer is chosen primarily because of personal support based upon friendship, community status, relative capacity, competence in oral English, and, sometimes, a willingness to stand up to the district administrator. The last quality is valued because the officer, whether called Speaker or President, assumes the responsibility of "speaking" for his body vis-a-vis the administration, a task which most Micronesians are culturally conditioned to shun. Not uncommonly, a number of persons are placed in nomination, and the candidate receiving a plurality by secret ballot is declared elected. At first the administration, covertly or openly, influenced the selection of the presiding officer, but the district legislatures have become jealous of their powers and of the right to choose their own officers. Maneuverings in advance of the session line up support for potential candidates, but it has only been with the emergence of parties that pre-organization caucusing has taken on a formal pattern.

Election, appointment, and even drawing members by lot were methods employed in naming committees as the district legislatures first got under way. The trend has been to assign the selection of chairmen and members of each committee to the presiding officer, although a charter provision granting this power has not prevented such officers' calling for nominations and votes' being taken to determine committee membership. Before naming anyone to a committee post, the presiding officer may consult with the prospective appointees, and as a rule all designations are premised upon the interests and capacities of the legislators. The presiding officer will also try to secure a degree of geographical spread within each committee, and in districts where there are admitted cleavages, as in Ponape, each area's delegation may be asked to indicate its choices for committee seats. Seniority rules do not apply to district legislatures. Unlike in their American state counterparts, where promises for committee chairmanship or preferred committee assignments may be the currency for garnering political support, in many of the district legislatures committee service is regarded as onerous, and the members approached may have to be cajoled into accepting. As the legislatures become integrated into their respective district's power structure and the prestige of committee chairmen grows, it may be anticipated that members will vie for committee posts, a development which has already begun in some districts.

While most of the work of the first legislatures turned around matters presented by the district administrators, some issues were brought to the legislative halls by the members themselves. Later, holdover committees or the officers of the district bodies began preparing the legislative agenda prior to the convening date. In some districts, such as Palau, the presiding officer distributed a tentative agenda in advance of the session to allow the members to discuss it with their constituents, to propose additions and modifications, and come prepared to act upon the matters finally agreed upon for discussion. All of this was necessary to impart an impetus to the new legislative bodies, for as expressed by a member who attended the first session of the Marshall Islands Congress, "We didn't know quite what to discuss at the meeting, so we asked them [Navy Administrators]." Matters now come quite spontaneously to the district legislatures; they are either relayed by legislators from their constituents or originate with the members themselves. The opening address of the district administrator remains a guiding factor in pointing the attention of the legislators to the major difficulties facing the district and in acquainting them with the administration's viewpoint on those problems. The more recent accompaniment of such messages with drafts of legislation further facilitates legislative deliberation and assures at least attentive scrutiny of the proposals, if not final passage. While in the United States there has been a shift in initiative from the legislature to the executive, the opposite has been occurring in the Trust Territory as district legislators become conversant with their bodies' procedures, more aware of their own powers, and less dependent upon the administration's designation of items to which to turn their attention.

The district legislatures all employ the services of committees to screen the matters before them and to recommend appropriate action. Here, again, a change has taken place. Within the first few days of the session, the early assemblies referred as many as possible of the subjects before them to their committees. This was followed by a protracted series of committee meetings, while plenary sessions were deferred, and all committees then reported back to their parent body. Now, the district legislatures usually meet briefly each day before adjourning to allow their committees to complete their work loads, and references to committee are made throughout the course of the session. The Marianas legislature, which is the most sophisticated in its methods, each day follows an agenda of thirteen items, starting with roll call, communications and petitions, messages from the district administrator, reports of committees, introduction and first reading of measures, special orders of business, and second reading of bills, and winds its way, finally, to adjournment for the day, when committees are once again free to sit.

LEGISLATIVE MEASURES

From their inception the district legislatures have been uncertain with both the form and content of legislative measures. Part of this confusion stems from the legislatures' nominally advisory character, according to which their role was merely one of "requesting" or "recommending" governmental action. Despite the law-making powers they have now been granted, due to the inability of district legislatures to direct the expenditure of Federal money, they perforce have to continue framing requests.

Another element adding to the confusion has been the lax employment of terminology in the charters and in legislative practice. The original charter to Palau in 1949 refers to "bills," even though this body was only an advisory council. The next congress structured, the Marshallese, could submit "recommendations in writing in the form of resolutions." The Marshalls used four different forms of resolutions. While a measure referred to as an "Iroij Resolution" or "Assembly Resolution" normally was adopted by only the one house named, there was no assurance of this, and the distinction between concurrent and joint resolutions never became manifest to legislators or administration. Nor did the administration appreciate that sometimes the appellation "joint" was reserved for a resolution redrafted when the houses of the Marshallese congress were sitting in joint session. To compound the uncertainty, four types of resolutions were employed under the Ponape charter of 1952.[2] This form of confusion continues to this day, for the most recent Palau charter (1963) carries references to "bills, resolutions, and memorials," the Marianas charter of the same year recognizes "bills, resolutions and recommendations," the 1958 Marshalls charter acknowledges that some "*acts* of Congress" (italics added) may not have the force and effect of law, and the Yap Islands Congress of the following year refers to "bills becoming resolutions" and also to "representations of congress." Even where charter provisions are more carefully drawn, as in the 1963 Truk charter which provides for only bills and resolutions, the drafting practices followed confuse the two. Bill No. 1 of the 7th Truk District Congress of 1963 was "a resolution," while Bill No. 2 of the same congress was "an act." The Trukese legislators appear to appreciate that the resolution format is to be employed when they cannot or do not want to legislate, but nonetheless, all measures still carry a "bill" designation. Upon adjournment, when the measures are sorted out for district administrator action and referral to the high commissioner where necessary, some are then relabeled as "acts" and others as "resolutions."

District legislators are just learning that more than an expression of legislative intent is necessary to constitute a law. Under the circumstances which surround social enforcement of custom, the

---

[2] See Proceedings of the Fifth Ponape Island Congress, Nov. 13–22, 1956, pp. 66–67.

inclusion of administrative detail is unnecessary, for the traditional system can readily implement any modification or innovation. However, in enactments by legislative bodies, the manner in which and the agency by which the legislative will is to be enforced must be stated, or at least the measures must be fitted into the matrix of existing law and administration so that it will automatically bridge what would otherwise be a fatal hiatus. Unfortunately for achieving enactment through the latter method, many of the district legislators are not familiar with either the Trust Territory Code or district laws, or with the activities of the district administration in executing laws. A further hindrance is the fact that many Micronesians do not formulate their preferences clearly, both because they are not trained to think that specifically and because of reluctance to take positive stands publicly. As a result of this trinity of inexperience, ignorance, and intent, the legislative product is vulnerable to the criticism of ambiguity. The disqualification of persons with posts in the administration from sitting in the district legislatures will only exacerbate this shortcoming until members receive the assistance of skilled legislative counsel.

When the members attempt to supply the detail they believe necessary for adequate drafting, they easily fall into one of a number of traps. Sometimes they assume that the law has cognizance of what is known to them, only to find that their proposal is fatally defective because of vagueness. Resolution No. 2–61 of the Yap Islands Congress would make it a crime to refuse to perform or purposely ignore community duties pursuant to Yapese custom. The high commissioner rejected this on the grounds that the customs must be set out to enable the courts to have notice of them and the constabulary to enforce them. Another common error, becoming too precise without regard to the future impact of the proposed measure, results in the absurdity or incongruity of the detail incorporated. The Marshallese House of Assembly in 1953 "resolved that each delegate should have a minimum of two terms [and] that each delegate should be chosen from those persons who have attended a previous Congress as a delegate."[3] In both cases the intent of the indigenous legislators was relatively clear, and probably adequate as a petition for encouraging the Administering Authority to take corrective action. As legislation, these efforts of the district bodies were found wanting.

[3] Resolution No. 3, 1953 Journal of Marshall Islands Congress.

A member usually presents a measure to the legislature in fairly general form, expecting that before it is adopted it will be redrafted as required to accomplish its purposes. As a rule he is the sole sponsor, not necessarily because there can be only one but because this conforms to custom. Indeed, in the Marianas there is even the fear that if more than two authors were permitted, this might result in the political parties automatically lining up behind their respective members to endorse all legislation. The rewriting which occurs after a measure is introduced is usually performed by the legislative staff and the personnel assigned by the district administration. As noted,[4] some of the district assemblies went through the same stage of evolution as American colonial legislatures, with members in effect offering only the substance of a proposal, and if the proposal were accepted by the legislative body, a drafting committee then putting it into shape for legislative action. This formalistic division has now disappeared.

The charter of the Yap Islands Congress expressly calls for holding a measure over for two sessions unless an extraordinary majority vote approves earlier passage. Much the same practice occurs in the other district legislatures which meet semi-annually, as the members approach problems cautiously, in part because of cultural antipathy to precipitous action and also due to the advice long tendered by administration personnel. If difficulties are encountered, or a general feeling of uncertainty prevails with regard to a particular program, the district legislators commonly postpone passage for one or more sessions until most everyone is satisfied, or at least willing to refrain from voicing any strenuous objections. A minimal degree of delay is required by the newest charters granted in 1963, which mandate two readings on separate days before a measure may be adopted. However, in all district legislatures there is generally little danger of hasty passage, for in the absence of unusually strong administration or constituent demands, and without legislative leadership firmly directing the course of legislative business, the work of the district bodies drags slowly along to the last few days of each session. It may even be generalized that one of the problems resulting from the proclivity of the district legislatures to postpone decision-making is how to keep them fully engaged throughout the whole period scheduled for their sessions.

Following the example of the United States Congress and also

[4] P. 79.

of some state legislatures, the Trust Territory's district bodies have been encouraged to authorize appropriations in separate measures, and then, by a single budget bill, appropriate out of district revenues the moneys necessary to finance all programs for the next fiscal period. This has the advantage of relating expenditures to estimated revenues, but it may discourage adequate funding after the initial drive for passage of a program has been spent. In the Marianas district, bills containing money authorizations are sometimes held after passage until the budget act is firmed up, and it is only then that they are forwarded to the district administrator for approval.

The presiding officer, during the course of the daily session, carries a heavy burden of factual explanation and psychological prompting of members to definitive action. He keeps up a running chatter of comment, supplying background information and pointing out implied concurrences in the remarks of speakers, all to aid the members in understanding the issue and reaching a collective decision. This style of leadership, besides being peculiarly compatible with Micronesian mores, may be fundamental to making the legislature work, corresponding to the experience reported for another institution, the local council.[5] In Palau, where classes of members are barred from balloting on some issues, before a vote, the presiding officer may remind the chamber of the disqualification. Similarly, the size of the vote necessary for affirmative action may be announced by the presiding officer before tallying commences. Presiding officers endeavor to maintain harmony in their chambers and adopt a variety of stratagems to this end. One of their chores is to prevent the members from wandering too far into irrelevancies during the course of debate. Sometimes they bring issues to a head by indicating they believe discussion has proceeded sufficiently long; it is rare for any member to stop debate by moving the "previous question." During the course of the session, the presiding officer may attend committee sittings to assist in their work and may even meet with their chairmen to speed up the flow of legislative business, but this is not standard practice. In the main, the speakers of the district legislatures are well styled as "presiding officers," for they believe it is more important to act

[5] See, e.g., Conrad Bentzen, *Land and Livelihood on Mokil*, CIMA Final Report No. 25, Part II [Washington: National Research Council, Pacific Science Board, 1949], pp. 164–169.

as a referee, until a consensus takes shape, than as a protagonist favoring one side or the other of any question. The presiding officer's role may be expected to change as district legislatures become more programmatic in concern and constituents look to their representatives for ever more concrete accomplishments.

COMMITTEES

Rather than being "little legislatures," committees of the district legislatures are merely devices for tackling portions of the work load of their parent bodies. As explained to the Fourth Annual Conference of Truk Island Magistrates a decade ago, if every member of the family participated in each part of the operation of gathering breadfruit, building a fire, cooking the fruit, pounding it, and then looking for leaves to wrap the breadfruit, a much longer time would be required than if each member were assigned a fraction of the total operation. Correspondingly, if the work of a legislature is divided among committees, more can be accomplished than if the whole body devotes attention seriatim to each problem before it.[6]

From the founding of district bodies, committees have been employed to spread the burden. Committees have suggested appropriate solutions for the various problems raised and have phrased in more apt terminology the ideas voiced by individual members during the opening days of each session. While the prime service of the committees has been to provide factual background and to develop solutions for the district's difficulties, they have not been denied power to screen the measures introduced by individual members. In the main, though, the function of the standing committees has been one of proposing and refining, rather than evaluating policy, so that it has been exceptional for them to reject legislation referred to them because of their disagreement with the measures' sponsors over policy. After committees have prepared their reports, the district legislatures have not hesitated to return measures for further refinement in accordance with the legislature's instructions. Committee chairmen do not necessarily carry the burden of defending the committee report upon the floor of the legislature, but should questions arise, they often take the brunt of general session discussion.

[6] Proceedings of Fourth Annual Conference of Truk Island Magistrates, Jan. 17–24, 1956, p. 2.

Committees of the Territory's legislatures have depended heavily upon the collective knowledge of their members. Sometimes this has been because of a lack of familiarity with the means of obtaining outside assistance; other times it has been due to a lack of rapport with those from whom such aid might be obtained. Then, too, there are legislators who seem to believe that a need to seek information and solutions outside the circle of their committee membership constitutes an admission of personal inadequacy. Possibly because of limited facilities, committee meetings have been somewhat casual, occasionally held in a member's house or consisting of visits by some or all of the membership to the offices of the administration. The appointment of non-legislators to committees, as in Palau, expanded committee competence but also introduced an element of potential irresponsibility, which led to the discontinuance of the practice. Over time there has been a gradual systemization of committee action, but most committees still engage in little advance planning and somewhat naïvely expect the administration to respond immediately, without preparatory notice, to their call. Different committees of the same legislative body may investigate identical subjects, despite the exclusive jurisdiction delineated for each. In some districts, standing committees carry on their work between sittings, continuing their study of measures and preparing the ground work for future legislation at subsequent sessions.

As the legislative process has grown more sophisticated, nongovernment "interests" have begun appearing before committees to state their positions favoring or opposing legislation. The legislature's relations with the district administration have become more regularized to assure the flow of information from the administration to the committees. Concomittantly, informal contacts between district administration personnel and subject-matter committees have been built; where this has not occurred, their lack has constituted a potential friction point between legislature and executive. Some district administrators have assigned personnel with whom the committees may work in finalizing bills and resolutions. The latest stage in the evolution of committees has been their use for shaping and mobilizing public opinion through hearings, investigations, and the issuance of public statements.

In the absence of positive legislative leadership, the administration of each committee has been no stronger than its median member. Without any seniority system and with members disinclined to adopt forceful directory roles, many committees have not appreciably eased their parent bodies' burden both because they are reluctant to bottle up measures and because they report measures out after only incomplete study. Also, since they have failed to satisfy fully the need to narrow viewpoints to a single solution, their members do not necessarily feel bound to support the committee's report and in the legislative chamber may oppose the recommendations with which they concurred in committee. On the other hand, given the relative inexperience of the Micronesian legislators with modern government, the early structuring of committees into the district legislatures materially facilitated the legislative process and the refinement of the legislative product.

FLOOR ACTION

The format of debate and decision-making called for by the district legislatures sharply contrasts with that followed in traditional council meetings. At the district sessions there is only limited time available for reaching decisions and for engaging in the customary formalities. Free expression of viewpoint, confrontation to sharpen the issue, and voting to reach a determination where unanimity cannot be achieved all run contrary to traditional norms. Customary practices had to be replaced by the parliamentary procedures of the West. All this contributed to the interminable debate, the speaking in circles like an *amaidechedui*,[7] the liberal use of metaphor, and the irrelevancies commented upon by observers of the early district legislatures, which continue to a degree. For a considerable period, the legislator, on rising, would comply with the traditional forms of avoiding giving offense by delivering a lengthy assurance of accord with the preceding speaker, and only gradually would he get around to disagreeing. Vestiges of a consensus society, in the form of debate continuing after a majority vote has been obtained, linger on. When to all of this is added the members' lack of subject-matter knowledge over the novel questions brought to their attention and their general insecurity in dealing with the government of the Americans, dis-

[7] An *amaidechedui* is a small Palauan lizard which climbs in a spiral; the simile is used to describe the culturally patterned circumlocution typical of Palauan debate. See Roland W. Force, *Leadership and Cultural Change in Palau*, Fieldiana: Anthropology, Vol. 50 (Chicago: Chicago Natural History Museum, 1960), p. 143.

cussion on the floor of the district legislatures understandingly has been prolonged and positive decisions arrived at only with difficulty.

In the early Ponapean congress, it was reported that "the common people thought that they could not express their own opinion, for under Ponapean custom, ordinary people do not have the choice of talking before the high chiefs." [8] Informants advise that a sense of hesitation continues to this day on the part of some commoners. In Yap, differences in rank do not prevent members from posing an issue or speaking on a matter before the congress, but there is a tendency to be circumspect in challenging the position of a higher status person. (No one from a low caste yet sits in the Yap Islands Congress.) Reluctance of some of the members from the Low Islands to take a strong stand has been observed in the Truk district legislature. In Palau, persons from high ranking families play a prominent part in debate. The chiefs, who as a rule are old, "senior" citizens, sit in the back of the chamber and forego an active role. A position taken by one of the high chiefs may be disputed, but at times members have been unwilling to commit themselves when a sharp difference of opinion has arisen between the chiefs in the Palau district legislature. In these and other ways, Micronesian traditional status relationships complicate and prolong the debate of a legislative session.

The district legislators are exhibiting an ever greater degree of familiarity with the more common motions and strategies of parliamentary procedure, although they sometimes employ practices which might cause raised eyebrows in more experienced legislative bodies. The successful adoption of an amendment may carry the original motion to which it was made. When a series of alternatives are under discussion, the members may be afforded the opportunity of registering their preferences, and the one receiving a plurality is accepted. The practice identifies the single most popular choice, but not necessarily that on which a majority of legislators might be willing to compromise. Oral amendments offered from the floor still cause confusion, sometimes because they will be phrased as suggestions rather than as formal motions to change the specific terminology of the matter under debate, and other times because the amendment does not harmonize with the remainder of the text. But, overall, there has been an air of camaraderie, a sense of joint sharing in an undertaking unaccustomed

[8] Paper of Oliver Nanpei, read at First Trust Territory Conference on Self-Government (Truk: 1953), p. 16.

to all, and a willingness to experiment with the new rather than sullen or resigned rote performance, all of which augur well for the continued success of the district assemblies.

The charters of all of the district legislatures require more than a simple majority for a quorum necessary to undertake legislative business. With the exception of the Marshall Islands Congress (two-thirds), a quorum of three-fourths of the total membership is mandated. Some of these charters do not prescribe agreement of a majority of the legislature's total membership for enactment of a measure but only a majority of the quorum. Voting is ordinarily by the raising of hands; secret ballot votes are not unknown when the members do not wish to publicize their individual preferences. Legislative records report that measures have been defeated because of failure to obtain the requisite vote, testifying to the observance of the charter requirements.

Use of roll calls to tally members' votes is now general practice. However, incorporation of the roll call into the permanent legislative journal in order to publish an account of each member's decision yet remains something of a novelty. A decade ago, when the introduction of the roll call was attempted in the Marshalls, each member treated the calling of his name as an invitation to rise and state his stand on the measure being voted upon. Roll calls, permanently committed to writing, probably will not become part of the established procedures of the district bodies until constituent interest grows and a member's voting record becomes of political moment to his future election.

All of the district legislatures have employed legal or extra-legal procedures for putting measures they have adopted into final form for submission to the district administrator and the high commissioner. In the Marianas, modification after enactment may affect only grammar, punctuation, and comparable matters, and no substantive change may be made. In contrast to this, some of the earlier district legislatures did little more than voice approval of a principle, without any details for administrative implementation, and after adjournment this bare skeleton would be materially expanded. In the Palaus, the office of the district administration would undertake the revision; the draft would then be reviewed by a committee named for the purpose, which would accept or reject it, depending upon whether the committee believed it conformed with the ideas of the congress. If the committee did not concur, it would direct the manner in which the draft should be amended. In the Marshalls, to this day the final draft may not be firmed up for over two months after adjournment. Reference to the contents of measures submitted to the high commissioner can be misleading, for measures may embody provisions not even discussed within the legislative chamber but believed necessary by the staff of a district administration to implement the legislative intent. With the legislative employment of staff skilled in drafting, and with the legislative and executive branches of government drawing apart so that the district legislatures are now more concerned over the exact detail of the measures they adopt, this form of extra-legal refinement of district legislative enactments will probably disappear.

The objective of complete and accurate record keeping has never been fully understood by the staffs of the Micronesian district legislatures, and most minutes of sessions have been sketchy at best. On occasion, gaps in the formal accounts have been filled in with volunteered material solely to have some data on record, as required by the district administration. Since neither legislators nor the courts have exerted pressure to improve legislative records, this will await the staffing of district legislatures with personnel whose professional standards prompt them to achieve a more careful accounting of legislative actions.

Most of the districts keep summary journals, sometimes published only in a Micronesian language. In the Marianas, a tape record is kept of the entire proceedings, which is later broadcast, and from this the staff prepares a verbatim journal, but the latter operation falls far behind the holding of the legislative session. Currently, in the Marshalls, the radio station of the District Education Department cuts a tape of all legislative proceedings for broadcasting, and the secretary has been using this as the source for his summary journal. These journals contain little but reference to the addresses by the district administrators, the bills and resolutions introduced and some history of their passage, and proof that the necessary vote has been achieved for each measure enacted.

In multi-lingual districts, legislative debates are in the dominant language, as Ponapean in the Ponape district and Chamorro in the Marianas. In the latter, the rules read that "English shall be the preferred spoken language of the legislature," but they also add that another language is not precluded, and members debate primarily in Chamorro. The original records of the district legislature are kept in the language used for floor debate, and translations into English may be made for the convenience of the American administration. Relatively few indigenes associated with the district legislatures have complete mastery of the English language, so careful comparison between the English and Micronesian language versions of legislative records reveals discrepancies. In 1916, a commentary on the use of the Hawaiian language in Hawaii's legislative debates and official documents noted that it made "the carrying on of government more difficult and expensive." [9] This has of course disappeared from the Hawaiian scene, just as has the Chamorro language from the debate on Guam, and similar reliance on English by Micronesian district legislators will probably occur in the future.

Until recently, schisms within the membership of a district legislature have primarily reflected personality clashes and the presence of cliques following the lead of key members. The disparate growth of the areas around the district headquarters has meant that their needs have become different from those in the outlying areas. This differentiation has caused a degree of friction within the district legislatures and sometimes shows in divisions between "urban" and "rural" blocs, with the latter objecting to the predominant allocation of public improvements to the headquarters' areas.[10] The fight in the Palau legislature over reestablishing some form of a holdover committee to meet with the district administrator in the interim between legislative sessions carried overtones of anti-Koror feeling. The members who would be appointed to such a committee would have to be legislators from Koror or closely adjacent areas, and it was believed this would lead the district administration to attach too much importance to the views of Koror people. On Ponape, there are not bitter divisions between the representatives from Ponape, Kusaie, and the low islands, but the existence of these three groupings is acknowledged. The Kusaie and low island delegations each tend to hold together, while the members from Ponape Island frequently divide their vote. The Marshalls' geographic cleavage between the Radak and Ralik chains has not assumed major importance in separating members

[9] Report of the U.S. Commissioner of Labor Statistics, *Labor Conditions in Hawaii*, Senate Doc. No. 432, 64th Congress, 1st Sess. (1916), p. 67.

[10] Or see the decision of the Ponape Island Congress not to meet in 1955, as a result of the difficulties arising out of the dispute between Kolonia (the Ponape district center) and Net Municipality, until the issue was resolved. *1956 United Nations Visiting Mission Report*, pars. 143, 144.

into opposing camps,[11] although the variance between the two chains with respect to land and copra rights does differentiate their outlook. The technique sometimes adopted in the Marshallese congress to avoid a decision on which opposition is anticipated has been to suggest that it is a problem peculiar to one or the other island chain and should be settled by the people of that area.

The birth of political parties in the Palaus and Marianas has seen members dividing along party lines, both on issues and on the organizing of their respective bodies. However, officer and committee posts are not reserved solely for the majority party in either body, and in the absence of recorded roll call votes, it is not possible to demonstrate any partisan differences which sharply separate the members of the rival political organizations. Occasionally "religious groups have expressed a stand with respect to specific measures, such as the manufacture and use of alcoholic beverages," [12] but it is exceptional for legislators to split neatly into religious groupings opposing each other within the legislative halls. In some districts, teachers' organizations have been successful in shaping legislative decisions, enjoying access through the teachers and former teachers found in the legislative membership. Businessmen's organizations are appearing in the Trust Territory, and the position of some legislators, favoring or opposing the administration's plans, has mirrored the views of these business organizations as communicated to or shared by the businessmen-members of the district legislatures. Unlike with party and pressure group activity in the United States, relatively little of district legislative activity can be traced directly to these groupings.

Faced with the uncertainties of a novel political institution and repeatedly reminded that the district legislatures are of critical importance to the people of Micronesia in realizing greater self-government, district legislators have inevitably emphasized the formal side of running a legislature and have been less sensitive to the substance of power which may be exercised through the legislative process. Prescriptive decorum has always surrounded important traditional institutions in Micronesia, and this has led the new legislatures similarly to stress formalism. Also, it is easier

[11] Early in the history of the Marshall Islands Congress, an issue over the payment of medical charges ended with a rump session of Ralik members held on Ebeye in the Kwajalein atoll, and their decision that each person should be responsible for his own hospitalization costs.

[12] *11th Annual Report of the United States to the United Nations, 1958,* p. 34.

to transfer the trappings and the institutionalized procedures associated with a Western-style legislature than it is to equip legislative members with an understanding of the scope of power they are receiving and a sense of assurance as they grasp it. Workshops can communicate the former, but power relationships themselves must be restructured to achieve the latter.

The formalism of the district legislatures follows no single pattern. To many, the tape recorder is something of a toy, and though proceedings are faithfully recorded, the use of these tapes in any way has been relatively limited. Public address systems add decibels to the soft-spoken Micronesian. The Palau legislature in 1960 announced a contest for the purpose of selecting its official seal. Marshallese legislators early requested distinctive identification badges, only to be embarrassed by the administration's innocent supplying of markers "similar to the wooden tags which the Japanese administrators forced malefactors to wear publicly as partial punishment." [13] In the Marianas, formalism is manifest in the manner in which the presiding officer is addressed and references are made to other members. In all districts, befitting the importance of the legislative body, as well as consonant with Micronesian custom, dignity of dress is exaggerated as measured in relation to the clothing ordinarily worn by the members. The shifting of major interest from compliance with form to substance must await the understanding by the members themselves of the significance of the expanding jurisdiction of the district legislature and their fuller exercise of the powers now available to them.

SUBJECT-MATTER INTEREST

The quantity of legislation adopted by the district legislatures has not been particularly impressive. For example, the first three sessions of the Marshallese congress in total passed only sixty-three resolutions—thirty-four so-called "joint," another eleven "concurrent," and the balance either "Iroij" or "Assembly." The two sessions held in Truk in 1964 adopted but fifteen acts and thirty resolutions, while from 1963 through 1965 the Mariana Islands District Legislature added forty-nine acts to that district's laws.

Since their founding, almost every conceivable subject has in some manner come before one or more of the district legislatures. Even though the legislatures have been precluded from legislating

[13] Memo from District Anthropologist to Acting DistAd Marshalls, Sept. 15, 1953.

on a wide range of matters, this has not prevented them from expressing their collective views in what, in effect, are legislative resolutions. As illustration, "requests for action by the United States Congress" are now handled by the Territorial Government; [14] nevertheless, the Marianas sent a delegation to Washington in the spring of 1966 to urge amendments of United States laws governing enlistment of men from the Marianas in the U.S. Armed Forces. For the most part, the district legislative output has been directed toward governmental activities and has shown relatively little interest in relationships among private persons, relationships with which government at best is involved only in fixing the approved rules of conduct, acting as umpire, and ensuring enforcement of these rules. As the legislators have become cognizant of their political roles, like their counterparts in the United States, they have begun adopting congratulatory resolutions and expressions of condolence in an effort to build personal popularity.

The first Marshallese congress which met in 1950 adopted twenty-seven resolutions. Illustrative of the scope of concern of this early legislature, five resolutions involved trade stores and commercial activity, an equal number applied to traditional rights and customs, three to health and sanitation, three to agriculture and conservation, and two each to taxation, school support, and the judicial system. The balance covered a swath of miscellany. The original Ponape legislature dealt with such matters as raising the interest rate on savings accounts, maintenance of a road around Ponape, and the expenditure of tax moneys; the following year this island congress turned its attention to exempting the sale of kerosene from taxation, returning guns to the people, and requiring all persons to follow the practice of using two names. The spring session of the 1955 Palau congress adopted resolutions on taxes, alcoholic beverage importation, firearm control, establishing local government title to lands and roads, as well as enacting an inheritance law, taking a number of conservation measures, and limiting liability under Micronesian custom. Greater sophistication in subject matter is revealed as the sessions passed, so that by 1961, provision was being made for a loan fund to furnish economic assistance for homesteaders, the promotion of coconut, cacao, and mahogany planting, and the codification of the laws and resolutions enacted by district legislatures.

[14] Public Law 1–6 of 1965, Congress of Micronesia.

The tax system of the Trust Territory has developed in a chaotic way, encompassing levies by municipalities, the Territorial Government, and the district legislatures. Until recently, when the Congress of Micronesia interjected an element of rationality into the tax structure in line with the recommendations of the Solomon Report, many of the district taxes were imposed on products already taxed by other levels of government. Early, the Palau legislature placed a sales tax on "luxuries," such as fountain pens, large ornamental vases, and expensive shoes. License fees, sumptuary levies on cigarettes and alcoholic beverages, and import and export taxes yielded the districts sufficient revenues to release the municipalities from part of their responsibility for education. Until the Territorial Government accepted the burden of educational costs, the district legislatures spent "a rather large proportion of their budgets on teachers' salaries." [15] More recently, a marked increase has been noted in the proportion of the district budget expended by the legislators for themselves. "Support of the legislature . . . (with personal services payments, building and office expenses) has left little available for project spending in most districts." [16]

BUDGETED EXPENDITURES, DISTRICT LEGISLATURES, 1965–66 [17]

DISTRICT	LEGISLATIVE	OTHER PURPOSES	TOTAL
Mariana	48.9%	51.1%	$ 47,224
Marshalls [a]	30.2	69.8	132,848
Palau	59.3	40.7	22,935
Ponape	34.6	65.4	46,988
Truk [b]	21.4	78.6	78,387
Yap [c]	28.8	71.2	95,007

[a] Marshalls for calendar 1965.
[b] An additional $17,500 for "Other Purposes" was vetoed.
[c] "Legislative" includes $20,000 for "Municipal Government Building."

As the district legislators constitute a virtual bridge between the traditional and Western political systems, of interest has been the extent to which they have turned their attention to traditional subjects. In the main, the endeavors of the district legislatures have been more to exhort the Micronesians to continue to support local customs than to make customs legally mandatory. A resolution de-

[15] As commented upon by Mr. Edmonds, New Zealand; TCOR, 27th Sess., 1148th meeting, June 14, 1961, par. 67.
[16] John R. Tabb, "Public Finance in Micronesia," prepared as part of report of Robert R. Nathan Associates, Inc., 1966.
[17] Ibid., extropolated from pp. 10–12.

claring that law and order should be preserved, respect for custom ought to be given by all, and everyone should have the right to be honored [18] could hardly be objected to by the Administering Authority on grounds of the principles enunciated. But declarations such as this are too vague to allow enforcement through either the courts or the administrative machinery of the Territory Government, so that at best they have only served to reinforce the customs singled out for attention through the constraints of traditional social structure. More effective in gaining compliance has been the deliberate adoption of a law paralleling a traditional norm, such as the Palauan law on incest, so that mere charge and judicial trial will bring punishment through social disapproval expressed in customary manner, and not necessarily through a fine or imprisonment imposed by a court upon conviction. An allied variant has been the careful evaluation of proposals for new laws to ensure they are in harmony with traditional relations still being observed. The draft of a Ponapean law on intestacy, and the declaration that magistrates should determine the persons entitled to succeed to land in such cases, were amended to recognize the right of the *nanmarki* to make the award, thus avoiding further erosion of the *nanmarki's* chiefly position.

Despite the Barnett thesis that the district legislatures should limit themselves to problems arising out of Western contact and that these new institutions should forbear traditional matters,[19] the Micronesian legislators have long taken steps "to overcome through legislation certain cultural practices which are essentially opposed to behavior more appropriate to independent political status." [20] Thus the burden of traditional food and money exchanges has been a subject of interest to the Palauan congress on a number of occasions, as they have come in conflict with new ways. Declaration No. 1–62 of the Palau Congress reads:

A DECLARATION OF HIGH CHIEFS AND OTHER CHIEFS OF THE PALAU DISTRICT TO ELIMINATE UNNECESSARY CUSTOMARY PRACTICES

Whereas, the Olbiil era Kelulau at its Fall Session of 1962 discussed

[18] Resolution No. 25, First Marshallese Congress, referred to in Dorothy E. Richard, *U.S. Naval Administration in the Trust Territory of the Pacific Islands* (Washington: Office of the Chief of Naval Operations, 1957), III, 404.

[19] See p. 68.

[20] Roland W. Force and Maryanne Force, "Political Change in Micronesia," in Roland W. Force, ed., *Induced Political Change in the Pacific* (Honolulu: Bishop Museum Press, 1965), p. 12.

the possibility of eliminating certain unnecessary customary practices in the Palau District; and

Whereas, the fourteen hereditary chiefs, . . . after carefully studying and observing the matter noted that food preparations connected with such customary practices often constitute unnecessary economic wastes and are harmful to living conditions and the economic stability of Palau.

It is therefore declared by all the chiefs of the Palau District and endorsed by the Olbiil era Kelulau that the following practices, *kall ra sis, kall ra chomengades, kall ra ngasech ra mlechel* and *senk ra ngalk* are not obligatory and therefore they do not have to be performed nor do we have to spend money for them under customary obligation.

Passed by unanimous vote of the members of the Olbiil era Kelulau present and voting at its Fall Session of 1962.

Here, through the district legislature, the chiefs were proclaiming that the economic burdens associated with wakes, honoring the grave, the first child ceremony, and presentation of gifts to the baby need no longer be borne. The declaration neither prohibited the practices nor declared any punishment; the legislature was being utilized as the appropriate forum through which to announce a modification in traditional obligations, and by endorsing the modification, the status of the legislature was added to that of the chiefs in overcoming any resistance to the change. Previously, in 1955, and again in 1959 and 1963, individual or family social liabilities under Palauan custom were declared modified through action taken by the district legislature. Through resolution of the Ponape district legislature, a somewhat parallel effort to ban some types of feasts, because of their competitive character resembling the "potlatch" of the Northwest American Indians, failed to pass. Unlike that in Palau, the Ponape legislature did not approve of using its process to revise traditions which depended only on social sanctions for their enforcement.

A degree of similarity is increasingly revealed in the concerns of the various district legislatures. For example, by 1958, five had passed laws setting the minimum salary schedules for teachers, this before the costs of the educational system were transferred to the Trust Territory Government. Alcoholic beverage control is now administered in all of the districts pursuant to district legislative enactment. Under the statutes adopted by the Congress of Micronesia, an ever greater degree of parallel action by all six district legislatures may be expected. It may even be hypothesized that there is a commonality of subject-matter interest in all Pacific

Island legislatures, giving due account for developmental time lags. At the November, 1951, session of the provisional Ponape legislature, antedating the official approval of the Ponape Island Congress, "the dog tax was abolished as discouraging food production." [21] Exactly half a century before, the first legislature of the Territory of Hawaii earned the name of "lady dog legislature" because of spending most of its time wrangling over dog taxes. Its members were not as frank in admitting that roast dog was still an important part of the Hawaiian *luau*.

THE DISTRICT LEGISLATURE'S WEB OF RELATIONSHIPS

A legislature presents a multiplicity of aspects, depending upon the viewer's perspective. To the legislators' constituents favoring or resenting the legislature's enactments, to the local governmental officials who may regard the legislator as competitor or ally, to the personnel of the Administering Authority who ambivalently view the development of self-government through the legislative process as both an accomplishment and a threat, and to the high commissioner who must defend the actions of the district legislatures as well as his replies to them before national and international review, the district legislature is a many-faceted institution.

Of necessity the high commissioner has had to rely upon the district administrators and his staff at Territorial Headquarters for guidance in responding to the district legislative enactments submitted to him for approval. This inevitably led to the scrutinizing of legislative enactments for their disadvantageous elements and contributed an in-built administrative bias towards conservatism. To offset it, the high commissioner has had to add a counterbalancing viewpoint designed to encourage indigenous expression even when district legislation may be thought inopportune and its formulation technically deficient. Without undertaking any statistical analysis, the impression gained is that over the years a sizeable number of measures have been vetoed by the high commissioner and that these vetoes have been based less on the technical objections of his staff than on the substantive issues they have raised. Picking examples at random, of the sixteen resolutions adopted by the Marshallese congress at its 1956 session, six were in effect vetoed, five for policy reasons. At approximately the same period,

[21] *Kolonia en Pohapey,* Dec. 6, 1951.

a representative of the Tebechelel Olbiil (Administrative Council) explained to the Olbiil era Kelulau (Palau Congress) the high commissioner's reasons for disapproving parts of the 1955 Palau budget adopted that spring:

It is not approvable by the Government to build up a Budget to support the Municipalities.

It is not approvable to pile more upon the boat license fees.

By the resolution cigarettes would bear too much tax.

Per diem rate for the members of the Olbiil era Kelulau is little too high and reduction must be considered next session.

Taxation on cigarettes and perfumery should be collected by a different system, that is to tax all the other imported goods equally with the cigarettes and perfumery.[22]

A decade later the high commissioner was still vetoing an appreciable number of measures, many times for policy reasons. After the spring 1964 session of the Truk district legislature, seven acts were approved and two were vetoed for technical reasons; in the following fall, of the six acts adopted by this district legislature, four were disallowed, only one for irregularities; the spring 1965 session saw nineteen acts sent to the high commissioner, of which he signed all but four, and two of the latter were disapproved on policy grounds. The Mariana Islands District Legislature passed seventeen acts at its spring session in 1965, and the high commissioner disagreed with the objectives of three and vetoed a fourth on a technicality. The amendment of district charters to allow the district administrator to veto measures, and the district legislatures to pass them again over his rejection, assures that the procedurally deficient bills will be detected at the district level, while the high commissioner will increasingly be called upon to deal only with basic policy issues. Regardless of the growing competence of the district legislatures, disagreements over programmatic issues will continue, and the district assemblies will thereby be in position to play an ever more important role as a mediating institution between the United States administration and the Micronesian people. To the Administering Authority, the actions of the district legislatures will continue to be viewed with a degree of trepidation, as a necessary part of political self-expression but

[22] Minutes of the Tenth Convention of the Olbiil era Kelulau, Oct., 1955.

subject to the gnawing doubts of a parent toward the adequacy of an offspring's efforts.

The effectiveness of the district legislature has depended in large degree upon the nature of the informal relationships existing between it and district administrator. By positing agenda items and proposing drafts of measures, the district administrators have significantly influenced the content of the legislative output. Their advice has not been taken lightly, for the legislators realize they must rely upon the administration to help them arrive at decisions. The district administrators in turn know that the legislators serve as a bridge between their municipalities and the district center, and the administrators are dependent upon this aid to facilitate the districts' administration. With law-making through District Order now almost completely foreclosed, the district administrators have become even more reliant upon the district legislatures. The district administrators have not been adverse to using the legislators as a "front" to support programs which the high commissioner has not favored. When district legislature and district administrator join ranks in close policy agreement, they present a hard combination for the high commissioner to turn—as witness the high commissioner's reversing himself in finally approving Resolution No. 3 of the 1955 Marshallese congress, which set up a local option plan for alcholic beverages, after first rejecting it.[23] In short, the relationship is a symbiotic one, and each of the parties derives an advantage from maintaining a good working association with the other.

On the other hand, it is natural for the district administrator to view the district legislature as a challenge to his authority for, given the course of the Trust Territory's political development, this was the very purpose for having legislatures. Once glimpsing the promise of self-governance, the Micronesian legislators have looked upon the Administering Authority as delaying the movement of indigenes into positions of responsibility and their attainment of ever greater policy-making powers. The district administrator easily may become the symbolic embodiment of all such resentment, and this but adds greater friction to the articulating of the two branches of government essential to the American-devised system in the Territory. A lack of cordial personal relationship between legislators and district administrator only aggravates the latent suspicion and distrust of the former, while the latter in turn comes to

[23] See letters of DistAd Marshalls to Deputy HiCom, March 3, 1955, and Deputy HiCom to DistAd Marshalls, May 2, 1955.

regard the legislators as deliberately meddling in the running of the district and taking every opportunity to needle the administration. Legislative inexperience becomes synonymous with personal incompetence, and the interdependence of the two branches sometimes becomes lost in personal animosity.

The emergence of organized politics adds another dimension, one which can widen the distance between a popularly chosen legislature and commissioner-appointed district administrator. However, as more Micronesians are selected for district administrator posts and provided that their ties with the district legislatures are cooperative and not antagonistic, there may develop within each district a sense of solidarity of purpose which is at best only nascent among Micronesians at the present time.

With the chartering of the district legislatures, the center of power has potentially shifted from the municipalities, the other political unit introduced by the Americans and staffed wholly by indigenes. In a district like the Marianas, where the Saipan municipality had grown into the most complex of all local government in the Trust Territory, the Mariana Islands District Legislature has had difficulty in establishing saliency, let alone primacy. Even today, some of the people on Saipan do not consider a post in the district legislature to be necessarily higher than one on the Saipan Municipal Council, and whether a person runs for one or the other legislative body may depend on how strongly he feels an interest in solely Saipanese affairs. In other districts where local government has not advanced much beyond the scope of activities performed traditionally, the district legislators have more easily moved to the vanguard of indigenous political leadership. The establishing of the Truk district legislature in 1957 was followed the next year by the Truk atoll magistrates' voting to discontinue their monthly meetings. It was not thought profitable to call the annual Palau Magistrates Conference into session between 1962 and 1966. As foreseen by the district administrator when talking to the Truk chiefs in 1956, a representative sent to district headquarters to attend the district legislature "will come in here each year for a week or so and spend a week talking about the district problems and he will go back to his island probably better informed about the district problems than the chief [magistrate] would be." [24]

There has always been a degree of consultation between the dis-

[24] Proceedings of Fourth Island Conference of Truk Island Magistrates, Jan. 17–24, 1956, p. 47.

trict legislators and the municipal officials of their constituencies. Magistrates have directed attention to many problems which have become the basis of measures considered by the district legislatures; indeed, for the fifteen years that Palauan magistrates were members of that district's legislature, they could introduce such measures directly. The removal of the magistrates from that body signaled that they were too closely identified with the Executive branch and that they did not properly belong in a legislative body. Not so incidentally, they also constituted an elected group and so were a threat to the popularly-chosen legislators. The disqualification of elected municipal officers in the legislative charters more recently granted by the high commissioner only attests to the intention to further limit municipal officers to local policy matters.

A late development has been the organizing of local officials to present measures to the district legislatures. The magistrates of Ponape have formed a committee to draft desired legislation so that the wishes of the municipal officials may be formally brought to the attention of their district body. The district administrator of Palau reactivated the Palau Magistrates Conference in 1966, in part to "discuss and coordinate with the magistrates possible legislation to be submitted to the Spring Session [1966] of the Palau District Legislature." [25] Municipalities' taxing powers have now been limited, and in addition to their having to come to the district legislatures for authorization to impose and collect excise taxes, they must look to their districts' solons for other forms of financial assistance if they are to continue furnishing accustomed municipal services. The competition betweeen officials originally inherent in the structuring of two levels of government, one local and the other district, has not been eliminated, but the position of the district legislator has recently been enhanced in comparison to that of the municipal officer.

At least initially, few people understood the purpose of the district legislatures or the function of the representatives. The first Marshallese congress in 1950 did not include the "best leaders" from some of the atolls because it was felt "they would probably be without voice and the whole affair would be dictated to by the [Civil Administrator] CivAd and his various Department Heads." [26] Today most Micronesians continue to know relatively little about how the legislature of their district runs its business or the place it

[25] *Palau Post*, March 25, 1966.
[26] Memo of CivAd Marshalls to HiCom, Oct. 9, 1950.

occupies in the district's government. The voters were, and in many of the outlying areas still are, willing to send representatives to the district headquarters primarily because the Administering Authority tells them it is important they do so, and because this direction is reinforced by the word of their traditional leaders who still command their respect. However, even in the outlying reaches, each year the schools graduate more and more of Micronesia's youth who have been instructed in the rudiments of democratic government and the key role of the legislature in a democratic system. Moreover, wherever their homes, the people of the Territory have learned that the district legislatures can accomplish things which affect them personally, and for whatever the specific reason, throughout the whole of Micronesia there has been a growing respect for the legislature as a vehicle of change.

A decade ago, the Fischers wrote that public confidence in the Ponape Congress would depend "on the experience of the congress, the issues which it takes up for discussion, the quality of the decisions which it makes, the support which it receives from the American administration, the degree of responsibility which it is permitted and a number of other factors which cannot be predicted in detail. . . ." [27] The same statement could as well have been applied to all of the other district legislatures in the Trust Territory and have been expanded by reference to such items as the number of measures which are vetoed and the extent to which the district legislature becomes identified as the champion of the rights of the district inhabitants. What has transpired is that, in many of these areas, the district legislatures have deported themselves in ways which have brought them, if not eminence, at least prominence.

As problems have grown bigger than the confines of a single municipality, they have gravitated to the legislative forum for resolution. This has not always strengthened public regard for the competence of the legislature, as its jurisdiction may not extend to these subjects. Locally generated requests to the legislators for an increase in the price of copra or for greater administrative services which are funded out of Federal moneys do not lead to enhancing the district legislature's status. At best, all that the district legislature may do is adopt a resolution. But in the Marshalls the people know the congress played a major part in organizing MIECO, the

[27] John L. Fischer and Ann M. Fischer, *The Eastern Carolines* (New Haven: Human Relations Area Files, 1957), p. 187.

district's largest trading company, and in this and other districts they understand that the burden of local school salaries was transferred, by the legislatures, from the municipal to the district level. With money to appropriate, the district bodies can now provide scholarships, construct radio stations, and aid local public works, all of which make for greater impact on the average Micronesian than their passage of a law regulating abstract obligations owed between private parties. Of course, the imposition of taxes means an added burden on the constituents and easily furthers the contention that they are levied just to support the "politicians"; like citizens the world over, the Micronesians would prefer to enjoy the benefits which legislatures bring without having to pay their costs. Perhaps the best measure of how Micronesians regard the district legislatures is that they hold them as "ours," while the executive and judicial branches of the district government are the "Americans' government."

A final dimension just taking form in a district legislature's web of relationships is its link to other Micronesian legislative bodies. Observation of the practices of other districts' legislatures commenced with the founding of the first regional assemblies. In 1957, for example, it was reported that inter-legislature visits, "which are encouraged and sponsored by the Administration, took place . . . in all districts where congresses held sessions." [28] Knowledge that some administrative districts had been granted legislatures spurred their founding in others. However, efforts at cross-district legislative cooperation still remain premature. Concerted action was proposed in 1962 through an exchange of correspondence initiated by the president of the Truk District Congress, enclosing a draft resolution calling for the turn over of the Trust Territory copra processing tax to the district legislatures. Though it did not succeed in its purpose, this is but the forerunner of comparable endeavors to come.

Precisely how the district legislatures will dovetail their work with that of the new Congress of Micronesia remains uncertain. In anticipation of the congress' convening, a few district enactments were vetoed by the high commissioner on the ground that their subjects would be covered in bills to be brought before the congress for enactment as Territory-wide laws. The order of the Secretary of the Interior which established the congress materially curtailed the district tax base, and the taxing laws have had to be revised

---

[28] *11th Annual Report . . . , op. cit.*, p. 16.

accordingly. At its first session, the congress provided for the sharing of Territorial import and export collections with the districts, to be expended as budgeted by the district legislatures, so that cooperation rather than competition has distinguished the founding of the new Territory-wide congress. The general feeling of district good will toward this historic congress was marked by the passage of legislation in three districts (Palau, Truk, and Yap), and analogous action of the Holdover Committee in the Marshalls, to appropriate moneys to their respective congressional delegations as an entertainment fund for appropriately feting the new Territorial body. Whether relations will continue as cordial after district legislators are denied the privilege of running for election to the Congress of Micronesia remains problematical. Most probably, this will see the appearance of a new overlay of politicians who give their major attention to Territory-wide matters but are dependent for support upon the resolution of the problems of their home constituencies. This in turn is likely to be followed by an ever greater dependence by the district legislatures upon the directions and subventions flowing from the Territorial congress.

CHAPTER 5

Traditional Leaders and the District Legislatures

TO THE EXTENT basic "principles" have guided American administration in the Trust Territory, one has been to allow the maximum amount of self-rule to the indigenous society compatible with the maintenance of law and order. The Americans entered the area with the preconception that the chiefs were the legitimate rulers, but they misunderstood the nature of that leadership within Micronesian society. They not only countenanced the continuation of chiefly authority when not overtly conflicting with American democratic concepts but also initially strengthened the chiefs' functional role which had been eroded during the German and Japanese periods. Sometimes it was even expanded over that theretofore enjoyed, due to the American failure to reintroduce the restraints on arbitrary use of power formerly an essential part of the traditional society.

When the Americans took control of Micronesia, they found no single pattern of indigenous leadership. In the Marianas, all that remained of the high chief or noble class was the perpetuation of their name, "Chamorri," since applied by the Spanish to all the peoples of the archipelago. In contrast, the chiefs in the Yap region, particularly in the low islands to the east in the mid-Carolines, continued to exercise much the same authority over their peoples as when first subjected to Western rule.

The Truk atoll furnishes an excellent example of how the American administering personnel helped perpetuate an "invented" chiefly structure and how that structure disappeared from the legislative scene with the chartering of a congress for the district. Aboriginally, chieftanship in Truk was "largely local and personal,"[1] with attributes of authority vested in a number of classes,

[1] Marc J. Swartz, "Personality and Structure: Political Acquiesence in Truk," in Roland W. Force, ed., *Induced Political Change in the Pacific* (Honolulu: Bishop Museum Press, 1965), p. 17. For other material on Truk, see Marc J. Swartz, "Leadership and Status Conflict on Romonum, Truk," *Southwestern Journal of Anthropology*, 15:2 (Summer, 1959), 213; John L. Fischer and Ann M. Fischer, *The Far Eastern Carolines* (New Haven: Human Rela-

the village the largest permanent political unit, and the geographical jurisdiction of a chief of one type not necessarily coinciding with that of another. The traditional chief was the oldest capable man in the chiefly lineage, and obvious senility constituted the measure of incompetency. This proved inadequate for the purposes of an administering country, whether German, Japanese, or American. All three recognized indigenous leaders, starting with the "flag" chiefs established by the Germans, responsible to them for an island or a group of islands; thus, they brought into being an office for which there was no precedent in the Trukese culture. The superior physical power of the metropolitan nation and traditional patterns of subservience and respect combined to secure the cooperation of the village chiefs. Persons with hereditary claim to some chiefly title might be selected by the Trukese for these new posts, or leaders might be named by the area administrator without regard to local preferences.

Under early American military and civil government, the Administering Authority for a while was dealing with an artificial seven-level hierarchy, headed by a chief for all islands in the Truk lagoon. American reorganization of this Truk political structure eliminated some of the layers, and it was finally simplified into recognition of a single "chief" for each of the Truk atoll islands except Falo, which voted to remain under Moen. Over time these administrative leaders had assumed many of the characteristics of the old local chieftans, including being tendered the respect and owed the traditional obligations of local groups.

The importation of elections by the Americans was not followed by any immediate replacement of incumbents, and when it was necessary for popular choice to name new office holders, succession followed along hereditary lines or, if not appropriate, then at the direction of the retiring chiefs. When a matrilineal line was unable to nominate a suitable person, the office might pass to the incumbent's son, as in the case of the renowned leader of Moen Island, Chief Petrus Mailo, who described himself as "not a chiefly

tions Area Files, 1957); John L. Fischer, "Totemism on Truk and Ponape," *American Anthropologist*, 59:2 (April, 1957), 250; Thomas Gladwin, "Civil Administration on Truk: A Rejoinder," *Human Organization*, 9:4 (Winter, 1950), 15; Edward T. Hall, Jr., "Military Government on Truk," *Human Organization*, 9:2 (Summer, 1950), 25; Edward T. Hall and Karl J. Pelzer, *The Economy of the Truk Islands*, USCC Economic Survey No. 7 (Honolulu: 1947); George P. Murdock and Ward H. Goodenough, "Social Organization of Truk," *Southwestern Journal of Anthropology*, 3:4 (Winter, 1947), 331.

person" but only a "bush-dweller." [2] The council of Truk atoll chiefs and later the all-Truk Magistrates Conference served as precursor legislative bodies, but when a wholly new institution in the form of an elected district-wide congress was set up, it was relatively easy for a group of younger leaders to come to the fore. There was no compelling reason for the Administering Authority to make any special provision to accommodate the island chiefs in the district legislature, as a different leadership role was being structured to which they had no vestige of traditional claim. Upon holding elections, the voters chose few of them for the new posts. Significantly, the atypical Chief Petrus, whose personal qualifications and behavior well fitted him for a place in the new institution, emerged as speaker of the first Trukese legislature.

In the Palau, Marshall Islands, and Ponape districts, the American administrators believed it would be advantageous to assure customary leaders membership in the respective congresses. The standing of the legislative bodies would be enhanced by their presence, and with the chiefs automatically represented, the voters would feel no obligation to elect them and so would be free to choose commoners. Then, too, not sharing the diffidence of the commoner in presenting their views to the American administration, the chiefs would be less reluctant to voice their thoughts upon controversial issues clearly and frankly in public. The presence of the chiefs would provide spokesmen for traditionalism, at the least guaranteeing that more than the viewpoint of one status group would be brought to the legislative halls, and would interject a conservative element into legislative debate and decision. Each of the three districts embraced status societies which knew varying degrees of mobility but in which political power was expressed through the persons occupying the positions of highest authority. The Administering Authority hoped that the incorporation of these symbolic representatives would ease the founding of the new institutions which contemplated full popular participation by all adults without regard for status distinction.

[2] "Speech of Chief Petrus Mailo before Truk High School Students" [Moen, Truk: Truk Education Department], Oct. 4, 1964; see also Thomas Gladwin, "Petrus Mailo, Chief of Moen," in Joseph B. Cassagrande, ed., *In the Company of Man* (New York: Harper & Brothers, 1960), p. 42; Frank Mahoney, "The Innovations of a Savings System on Truk," *American Anthropologist*, 62:3 (June, 1960), 465.

THE PONAPEAN CHIEFS—WITHDRAWAL [3]

The traditional political system on Ponape Island, with its duality of leaders, bears resemblance to the division of power encountered in the Samoas. Each of the five Ponapean *wehis* (districts) has its royal line of chiefs associated with the *nanmarki*, and the noble line headed by the *naniken*. Both lines consist of eleven subordinate title-holders in ranked order. The nominal head of the *wehi* is the *nanmarki* himself, but customarily the *naniken* transmitted the policy decisions attributed to the former, in a manner akin to the Polynesian "talking chief," and probably wielded the greater political power. A *wehi* is divided into *kousap* (sections), each with its own two lines of chiefs, so that a person may possess both *wehi* and *kousap* titles. In addition, the senior chiefs can award honorary titles, so that almost every adult man may have some prestigeful place in the indigenous society, even though the honorary titles do not carry any strictly ranked status.

Eligibility to become a chief depends upon inheritance and proven ability, and individuals holding titles in the *nanmarki* or *naniken* lines advance in rank upon the vacating of a higher title by death, resignation, or removal. Traditionally the holders of the two top titles are to confer together on the appointment of other leaders, and each has the right to fill the paralleling senior post upon its vacancy; in practice, the naming of new title-holders is a consultative matter. As clans are matrilineal and intermarriage between chiefly sub-clans is encouraged, father and son might hold both highest titles; even today a son's eligibility for promotion in one line may be strengthened by the father having a title in the other.

[3] Based on Fischer and Fischer, *op. cit.,* pp. 174–177; Memo of Frank Mahoney, "Homesteading in Matalanim," May 24, 1954; John Sandelmann, *Some Observations on the Problem of "Self Government" in the Trust Territory of the Pacific Islands* (Honolulu: 1953); George L. Coale, "A Study of Chieftanship, Missionary Contact, and Culture Change on Ponape" (M.A. thesis, University of Southern California: 1951); Saul H. Riesenberg, *Ponapean Political and Social Organization,* CIMA Final Report No. 15 (Washington: Office of Naval Research, 1949); William R. Bascom, "Ponape: The Cycle of Empire," *The Scientific Monthly,* 70:3 (March, 1950), 141; William R. Bascom, *Ponape: A Pacific Economy in Transition,* USCC Economic Survey No. 8 (Honolulu: 1946).

For reference to traditional political systems of Kusaie and Mokil, see Fischer and Fischer, *op. cit.;* James L. Lewis, *Kusaiean Acculturation,* CIMA Final Report No. 17 (Washington: Office of Naval Research, 1948); J. E. Weckler, *Land and Livelihood on Mokil,* CIMA Final Report No. 11, Part I (Washington: Office of Naval Research, 1949); Conrad Bentzen, *Land and Livelihood on Mokil,* CIMA Final Report No. 25, Part II (Washington: Office of Naval Research, 1949).

An absolute monarch in theory, because of his great *wau* (mana), the *nanmarki* could not deal directly with the *aramas mwal* (common people) in the administration of his office. The *naniken* served as an intermediary, interposing a moderating force, and in fact government was conducted in observance of public opinion, with royalty and nobles mediating each other's political arbitrariness. The *kousap* chief, the *kaun*, despite being a feudal vassal of the *nanmarki* and usually the leader of the most powerful lineage of the *kousap*, was appointed only after the *nanmarki* consulted the wishes of the *aramas*. The primary executive activities of the senior titles traditionally consisted of a series of reciprocal relationships between them and their subjects. As owners of the land, the former received first fruits, feasts, free labor, and other benefits and, in turn, owed obligations of defense and care of their liege subjects. These high chiefs also interpreted customary law, punished criminal behavior, and rendered decisions in civil disagreements.

Much of this political structure was weakened by the coming of the Protestant missionaries to Ponape in the mid-nineteenth century, due to the modifications they introduced, and later by the Germans when they took over governance of the island at the end of the century. Starting with the German administration, the feudal system was replaced by fee simple ownership, and the land was divided so that each man owned his farmstead. Some of the specialized functions befitting the various statuses of chieftanship were assigned to the new political institutions; the *nanmarki* appeared in public and directly managed *wehi* affairs, and under the Japanese the *naniken* became *wehi* judge. Tribute was curtailed as the high chiefs became salaried governmental officers in charge of local government; nonetheless the ceremonial life of Ponapean society continued to center around the chiefs, and they retained their influence in many aspects of their peoples' economic and social affairs. Patterns of deference and use of honorific language in addressing the high chiefs set them apart. Ponape social structure continued to legitimate leadership roles for the persons holding chiefly titles, roles which also demanded their neutrality in disputes and the abhorrence of favoritism of any kind. The prominence of their titles and the commoner's humility and unpretentiousness counterindicated the establishment of any legislature for Ponape in which the high chiefs were not granted a prominent part. If proof were needed, it was conclusively supplied by the early attempts of the Americans to structure a unicameral body, which saw mainly traditional leaders "elected" to the tentative Ponape legislature that never was authorized to assemble.

The Provisional Congress which was called "to act as constitutional assembly to express the desires of the people regarding self-government" met at Kolonia in March of 1951.[4] By ballot it decided upon a bicameral congress, with each of Ponape's five *wehis* represented by five title-holders in the Nobles' House. Four of each *wehis*' highest titles—*nanmarki, wasai, naniken,* and *nalaim*—automatically became members, and the *nanmarki* and *naniken* were directed jointly to appoint for their respective *wehi* one high ranking leader outside their lines. All four of the named high chiefs of each *wehi* were declared ineligible for election to the People's House, a disqualification not applying to the fifth title-holder, other than that he could not concurrently hold seats in both houses.

From 1951 to 1958 the high ranking chiefs of Ponape Island attended the semi-annual meetings of this congress and at first introduced a major share of the resolutions enacted. In the 1951 session, before the charter was officially ratified, it was mainly the joint resolutions originating in the Nobles' House which were adopted. At the time, the district administrator noted that "this does not indicate necessarily that the chiefs . . . forced their decisions on the People's representatives; rather that the resolutions of the chiefs were in most cases more explicit and thorough."[5] At the May 1952 meeting of the congress, there were nineteen joint resolutions in all; of these the nobles had sponsored thirteen, and twelve of their resolutions were approved. Only three which had been proposed from the People's House similarly succeeded of passage. The high commissioner expressed the hope that "this unbalanced ratio does not imply a feeling of subservience by the People's House in its relations to the Congress." The district administrator replied that the natural preponderance enjoyed by the resolutions of the Nobles' House "reflected basic Ponapean attitudes. Most Ponapeans still acknowledge the higher titles as their 'true' leaders and spokesmen even when as usually happens, these respond to the pressure of public opinion. . . . the more responsible and influential Ponapean leaders today hold high positions in the traditional system and derive much status from this fact. . . . The predominance can thus be attributed in part to a higher average

[4] Quoted in Sandelmann, *op. cit.,* p. 73.
[5] *Ibid,* p. 76.

level of political skill and in part to a feeling of confidence derived from social superiority according to native custom." [6]

As the work of the Ponape Island Congress expanded, the potential threat to their status which the Ponapean high titled chiefs saw in the legislature markedly diminished, and many of them no longer wanted to continue taking part in the new body. Membership required them to stand up and state a positive position in a manner to which they were unaccustomed. Most, having an inadequate command of English, found it difficult to deal with the business put before them in that language and awkward to have to depend upon the services of an interpreter. They were not prepared to resolve the problems brought to the new congress and were more than willing to allow the younger educated Ponapeans to tackle them, just so long as traditional rights and relations were sustained. The chiefs' dominant role in shaping the product of the congress began to wane, and their numbers attending the semiannual sessions commenced to thin. A report of the meeting held in December, 1953, refers to disagreements between the two houses over availability of guns and taxing of kerosene. At the November 1956 meeting, only three *nanmarkis* and one *naniken* answered the roll call of the Nobles' House. Of the upper house's three resolutions, only one was adopted by both houses and became a resolution of the congress; the People's House introduced six, of which four received congressional approval. In addition, the Nobles' House could not obtain concurrence of the other chamber to two of the joint resolutions advanced by the Agenda Committee. With the rise of a new political elite, trained to deal with the American administration, the high-ranking chiefs were willing to relinquish their ex officio places in the congress and let those of their number who wished to remain in the legislative halls run for office like any commoner. Paraphrasing the words of the high commissioner, the initiative to establish a unicameral legislature, abolishing the hereditary house, "had come from the hereditary nobles themselves." [7]

The new charter granted in 1958 for a district-wide legislature omits all reference to the chiefs. Persons with high titles, or in line for them, have since been elected to the congress, but they have been a minority and have received no privileged treatment. In

[6] Exchanged between HiCom and DistAd Ponape, quoted in *ibid.*, p. 78.
[7] TCOR, 22d Sess., 894th meeting, June 16, 1958, par. 42.

deference to the Outer Islands representatives, the "common language" is used. The personal discomfort of the Ponapean commoner in not addressing the chiefs in the traditional "nobles' language" is revealed by the non-titled members' jokes about it among themselves after the session. Almost everyone acknowledges that, on issues involving basic tradition, the Ponapean ranking chiefs can still muster enough support to effect the outcome of the congressional decision through reasoning with legislators from their *wehi* or by conferring honorary titles which would place the legislators under obligation. For the bulk of the matters before the congress, the high ranking chiefs have withdrawn from institutionalized participation.

THE PALAU CHIEFS—WITHERING AWAY [8]

The village constituted the original political unit of Palau and was traditionally ruled by a *klobak* of ten or more heads of the ranking clans. The highest ranking member served as village chief and was assisted as well as circumscribed by the *klobak*. The *klobak* planned the economic activities of the village, directed its affairs, and apprehended and punished lawbreakers. Five to ten villages were loosely joined to comprise a district, which had its paramount chief and district *klobak*. Position in the latter was determined by ranking clan status within the larger unit, so that some villages had no representation and the head of a low ranking clan might have little standing within a district *klobak* but appreciable power in his own village *klobak*. The district *klobak* concerned itself with warfare, maintenance of peace and order within the district, interdistrict exchanges, land disputes, breaches of custom, and other subjects of importance which defied village solution. The whole of Palau was divided into rival district confederations; the main outlines and chiefly positions of the Koror and Melekeok Confederations existing on the coming of the Spaniards were

[8] For publications treating the Palauan chiefly system, see Robert Kellogg McKnight, "Competition in Palau" (Ph.D. thesis, Ohio State University: 1960); Roland W. Force, *Leadership and Cultural Change in Palau*, Fieldiana: Anthropology, Vol. 50 (Chicago: Chicago Natural History Museum, 1960); Arthur J. Vidich, "The Political Impact of Colonial Administration" (Ph.D. thesis, Harvard University: 1952); Arthur J. Vidich, *Political Factionalism in Palau*, CIMA Final Report No. 23 (Washington: Office of Naval Research, 1949); John Useem, *Report on Palau*, CIMA Final Report No. 21 (Washington: Office of Naval Research, 1949); John Useem, "The Changing Structure of a Micronesian Society," *American Anthropologist*, 47:4 (Oct.-Dec., 1945), 567.

crystallized by the administering country's prohibition of warfare as well as other practices such as *blolobo* (institutionalized concubinage) which had facilitated adjustment of political ties. At this time the paramount chiefs of Koror and Melekeok, the two highest districts, were supreme not alone in their own districts but also in their respective confederations. Today the *Reklai* (Melekeok) and *Ibidul* (Koror) continue to be the loci of greatest traditional power in Palau.

The status of a Palauan chief was associated with claims he could make on others and was subject to demands to which he had to respond. Obedience to legitimate orders, deference, gifts and service, and the right to arbitrate personal relationships were his, but he was also required to perform his political role in a prescribed manner, make contributions commensurate with his rank in the social hierarchy, and accept responsibility for the acts of the members of his political unit against persons of other units. These rights, duties, and obligations were balanced in such a way as to minimize conflict between chiefs and others of repute in the traditional society. Excesses of the chiefs were counter-checked by religious dignitaries. As a similar check, the clans were subgrouped in consecutive pairs in opposition to each other, and villages and districts correspondingly vied for social ranking and political power. No chief could act without consultation and consensus of the other title-holders. Overall, a conception of reciprocity supplied a regulating principle for the exchange of gifts, economic goods, and services.

The introduction of Christianity by the Spaniards eliminated the shamans and removed one of the institutionalized forces opposing chiefly power as well as foreclosed the possibility of a low ranking *rubak* (male head of a kinship group) invoking religious sanctions against higher-ranking persons abusing their prerogatives. With political alliances no longer variable, the chiefs found their positions more secure but, at the same time, dependent upon cooperation with the foreign administrators. The role of paramount district chiefs changed from a symbolic to a functional one, and their theoretical powers as group heads became actual as the administrators of the Western governments assumed they commanded the right to execute freely the prerogatives of their office. The status of chief was also modified, because lineage no longer solely decided succession and the administering personnel removed recalcitrant chiefs or placed in chiefly position persons more competent to deal with the problems of introduced government, regardless of their right under tradition to the title.

Gradually the chiefs' political power became contingent on the colonial administration, and by the end of the Japanese period they were virtually stripped of all initiating functions and had become almost puppet-like figures. In the chiefs' place rose a whole new class of indigenes who derived power and position in the Palauan society through their direct association with the Japanese administration. Supplanting the district *klobak* in political importance was the *rubekul,* oriented toward dealing with the foreigner and composed of village chiefs and others with ascribed or attained status appropriate to the new duties of local government.

When the Americans came to Palau during World War II, they followed the dictum that respect for channels of indigenous authority would encourage a maximum degree of social control from within the native system. However they misconstrued this policy of indirect rule as restoring the chiefs to their former station but possessed of powers as now seen through Western eyes. Later, when there was an all-Palau government under indigenous direction—something which had never existed in pre-contact days— with chiefs in the highest posts and no longer counterbalanced by the checks of the former system, the traditional leaders gained a more important position than ever before. But many factors contributed to the erosion of the chiefs' position in the executive branch of this Palau central government and their ever narrowing role in the Palau district legislature: the chiefs' remaining base of "traditional" power was inadequate to sustain their new-found status; they demonstrated inability to cope with their expanded jurisdiction; there was a competing body of Palauans with skills which better fitted them for staffing and running a Palauan district government; and there was a basic incompatibility between American democratic concepts of free choice of political leaders and the rigid Palauan class distinctions supporting the chiefs.

The District Order establishing the first congress which met in Palau from 1947 to 1955 contains no reference to the two high chiefs or the paramount chiefs of the districts, but from the first they were afforded a place in the congressional chamber. With the granting of the new charter in 1955, they were declared full members of the Olbiil era Kelulau (Palau Congress), enjoying all powers other than voting on "resolutions" destined to become laws. According to Palau's third charter of 1963, the chiefs continue in the Palau legislature but are now stripped of all voting power and also are ineligible to hold office in the unicameral body. Commentators on the Palauan scene claim that the chiefs were retained in the new legislature because their status would benefit the legislative branch in its challenge of the executive and because some still have the ability to sway the vote of the older people in the legislative elections, especially on Babelthuap.

On the occasion of the first session of the Olbiil era Kelulau, the assistant district administrator addressed the members concerning salaries for the high chiefs:

At the time the war ended the Palau Islands were in a particularly desperate and disorganized condition. The Navy administration, recognizing the leadership and the responsibility of the High Chiefs Reklai and Ibedul for the people of Palau, placed them on the government payroll as administrative advisors. This decision was based on two facts: the recognized need of the Palau people for a focus for their loyalty and the fact that the people of Palau had no organized government of their own and no source of revenue with which to maintain these two chiefs. For this reason the government has continued to maintain the salaries of these two men, an expenditure which it considers to be only a token recognition of their great value to the Trust Territory. Now that the Olbiil era Kelulau, representing the people of the Palau District, will have revenues at its disposal, it seems only logical that they would desire to assume the responsibility of compensating these two leaders. If the Olbiil era Kelulau should determine that it has no responsibility for or to these High Chiefs, the government does not propose at this time to drop either man from its payroll. However, such a response on behalf of the Palauan people will undoubtedly be noted.[9]

The congress replied by voting each of the high chiefs $15.00 a month, the same amount provided its president. When the latter's stipend was increased in 1957, the high chiefs' monthly allotments were raised to $20.00. By 1961 all this was reversed, and by 1963, each chief, including the two high chiefs, was receiving only a token payment, semi-annually, of $5.00 for the legislative session. Equal, as distinguished from extraordinary, provision for the chiefs is now the rule, so that for fiscal year 1968, legislators and chiefs received identical per diem payments for attending sessions.

The precise quantum of power still retained by the chiefs in the

---

[9] Minutes of Ninth Session of Palau Legislature, April, 1955.

Palauan legislature is difficult to ascertain. Early in its history, congressmen who presumed to speak out without the approval of the high chiefs were reprimanded by them. Roland Force supplies several illustrations of traditional leaders' controlling the actions of the congress to maintain the status quo,[10] and the legislative records yield other evidence of their views' setting the legislature's position.[11] It is certain that the chiefs are still consulted on matters affecting Palauan custom, and congressmen report being dissuaded by the high chiefs from sponsoring legislation to eliminate specific traditional exchange and contribution obligations found vexing by the younger adults in modern-day Palau. But the chiefs do not necessarily present an undivided front. Coulter notes that the High Chief Ibedul in the mid-1950's was "eager to push innovations economically, socially, and politically, while Reklai . . . [was] conservative, and . . . [wished] to retain as many native customs as he . . . [could]." [12]

The chiefs sit to the side of the legislative chamber, chewing betel-nut, sometimes falling asleep as old men will, and many seemingly not understanding much of what is transpiring on the floor. Some take little part in floor debate; others are more aggressive. All of this is a little misleading, for before anything is brought to the legislature, in one way or another the high chiefs and some of the paramount chiefs are informed. Should there be objection, they do not hesitate to declare their views to the elected members, frequently outside the chamber, and in this way influence action on the floor. If the two high chiefs are in accord, the paramount chiefs normally follow their cue, and their combined opposition materially helps to shape the legislative outcome. Theirs remains a negating power, generally sufficient to delay if not defeat a measure when they are united, but the initiative has passed to the elected members more conversant with the activities of the government introduced by the Americans. It is thought to be only a matter of time before the chiefs' station as arbiters of Palauan traditional ways will wither to the point where they will no longer sit in the legislative halls as a matter of right.

[10] Force, *Leadership* . . . , *op. cit.*, pp. 118–119.

[11] See, for example, opposition of chiefs, at the spring, 1956, session of the Olbiil era Kelulau, to reinstituting *kabekel* (war canoe) races.

[12] John W. Coulter, *The Pacific Dependencies of the United States* (New York: Macmillan Co., 1957), p. 205.

MARSHALL ISLANDS—THE CHIEFS TRIUMPHANT [13]

In the Marshalls, traditional leadership is tied with matrilineages and intimately bound to landed tenure, and each *bwij* (lineage) of *kajur* (commoners) is led by an *alab* (senior head). At the base of the socio-political-economic pyramid are the *kajur* on the land, sharing inherited usufruct rights; at the top are the *iroij*, a noble class which receives the benefits of controlled worker production. The very apex is occupied by the paramount chief (*iroij laplap* or *iroij elap*), the ranking member of the senior ruling lineage, who traditionally owned all land and all chattels real within his jurisdiction. Above the *kajur* and close to the *iroij* were lineages with *bwirak* rank, regarded as an upper class without right of succession to the *iroij laplap*, and the *jib* ("fringes of nobility") held a place between *bwirak* and *kajur*. One or more atolls might fall under the control of a single *iroij laplap*, while other atolls were divided among a number of them. Succession usually was hereditary, and in pre-European times warfare served to transfer jurisdiction between rival *iroij*.

In the person of the *iroij laplap* resided the sacred doctrine of the stars, sea, medicine, and magic, and when he had assistants to whom he delegated part of this responsibility, their knowledge was sanctified as a corollary of his. Formerly, the *iroij* were served by the *kajur,* receiving food, manufactures, water conveyance, and military assistance. In turn the *iroij* reciprocated by furnishing relief to victims of natural disasters and maintaining inter-familial order. Buttressed by their supernatural powers, the *iroij laplap* could exact absolute obedience from their subjects under penalty of death and were the recipients of tribute, in the Radak (eastern) chain gathered by the *iroij erik* (sub-chiefs of the noble class).[14]

---

[13] For Marshall Islands, see Jack A. Tobin, *Land Tenure in the Marshall Islands*, Atoll Research Bulletin No. 11 (Washington: Pacific Science Board, National Research Council, rev. 1956), also published in *Land Tenure Patterns, Trust Territory of the Pacific Islands* (Guam, M.I.: office of the High Commissioner, 1958), pp. 1–76; Alexander Spoehr, *Majuro, A Village in the Marshall Islands*, Fieldiana: Anthropology, Vol. 39 (Chicago: Chicago Natural History Museum, 1949); Maragaret E. Chave, *Anthropological Study of Mixed Bloods in Majuro*, CIMA Final Report No. 7 (Honolulu: 1949); Leonard E. Mason, *Anthropology—Geography Study of Arno Atoll*, Atoll Research Bulletin No. 10 (Washington: Pacific Science Board, National Research Council, 1952); Leonard E. Mason, *The Economic Organization of the Marshall Islanders*, USCC Economic Survey No. 9 (Honolulu: 1947).

[14] "In the days before any of the foreign administrations came to the Marshalls, the term *iroij erik* referred only to those directly in line to succeed to the position of *iroij lablab,* whereas the Japanese very definitely applied

German administration put an end to warfare, freezing the territorial positions of the *iroij*, which added a new note of inflexibility to the social system. Since Western contact, the *iroij* have slowly been superseded, and though the Germans governed through the *iroij*, the Japanese administration was conducted in a manner designed to undermine the indigenous political system. With the development of the copra industry during the German period, tribute to the *iroij* was converted very largely into a share of the copra production, which was collected for their benefit. Japanese recognition of the *kajur* as owner of the trees and possessor of legal usufruct rights was antithetical to the concept of absolute *iroij* ownership of land. By World War II it had been determined that the *iroij laplap*, in dealing with *kajur* usage of land, no longer possessed arbitrary powers and had to act with an honest regard for the welfare of their people. This, coupled with the supplanting of the *iroij* as supreme authorities within a feudal order, led to a deterioration of the political status of the *iroij laplap*, although they retained much of their prestigeful place in the Marshallese social organization.

Today, two major social classes continue to be recognized, the *iroij* and the *kajur*, with the *bwirak* blurring into the *iroij* and the *jib* into the commoner. As an added factor, some of the persons classed as *iroij laplap* are considered to be of "tainted" blood because of descent from inter-class marriage by *kajur* and *iroij*. A century ago *"iroij laplap"* meant the "ruling chief . . . who had to have royal blood on both sides of his family. The term as applied today is that they have some royal blood, either from mother or father but inherit the large lands of the *iroij laplap*." [15]

In the Marshalls, unlike in other districts, the Americans did not deliberately structure government around the local chiefs. The reason for this distinctive treatment probably lies in the American armed forces' early entry into this area and their finding that if the political jurisdiction of the *iroij* were restored, it would not be coterminous with viable units of local government. The *iroij laplap*

the term both to people who had come to be known as *iroij in tel* (that is, royal collectors) and to *leatoktok* (title of the old-time head of the commoners, and advisors, but not of royal blood) and to others who were allowed to exercise similar powers but had no *iroij* blood." *Kumtak Jatios* v. *L. Levi* et al, Civil Action No. 1, Appellate Division of High Court, Trust Territory of Pacific Islands, decided Aug. 10, 1954, pp. 2, 3.

[15] Memo Acting DistAd Marshalls to HiCom, Oct. 17, 1960. The accuracy of this generalization as applied to both the Radak and Ralik Island chains has been challenged.

were therefore regarded as social, not as political, figures. Just like other Marshallese, they were eligible to election by secret ballot as atoll magistrates and, in addition, had seats and voting privileges on the atoll councils, "but the influence of the *iroij* varies from one area to the other dependent on the attitude of the people, the personality of the *iroij* concerned, etc." It was declared the policy of the administration that "in the final analysis it is incumbent upon the people themselves to operate the municipal councils properly and to defer to *iroij* or not, as the case may be." [16] Only on Ujelang, after the people from Eniwetok atoll were moved there to permit atomic testing on their ancestral home, did their two *iroij laplap* as a matter of hereditary right continue serving as joint magistrates.

In contrast to practices under the Japanese period, the Americans did not standardize the share of the copra proceeds to be paid the *iroij;* the amount they received in some atolls became a matter of voluntary agreement between *iroij, alab,* and *dri jerbal* (worker), much to the chagrin of the *iroij.* Concomitantly, the accountability of the *iroij* for medical expenses, as a modification of part of their traditional obligation for care of their people, commenced to be ignored by the *iroij.* The American administration held the position that the Marshallese people were becoming dissatisfied with the traditional *iroij* relationships and that its role was to protect all the Marshallese people by allowing free decisions to be reached on the *iroij* status.[17] To the *iroij,* it appeared that the Americans were encouraging the operation of the municipal councils to "destroy *iroijs'* wills and rights or take over *iroijs'* concerns." [18]

An element important to all of Micronesia has been the interposition of a new set of criteria which lies outside the traditional class systems. Medical practitioners, school teachers, pastors, and persons with knowledge of Western commerce, all English-speakers, have achieved a status from their skills and insight which competes with that derived from the old system. Spoehr in 1950 found that "in the sphere of local politics, however, formal training does not exist, nor have new standards for judging com-

[16] Memo CivAd Marshalls to HiCom, Aug. 29, 1950.
[17] See comments of HiCom, quoted in Dorothy E. Richard, *U.S. Naval Administration of the Trust Territory of the Pacific Islands* (Washington: Office of the Chief of Naval Operations, 1957), III, 1084.
[18] From a petition to 1950 UN Visiting Mission against actions of atoll councils, signed by eighteen *"iroij." Visiting Mission Report 1951,* Annex 1, p. 21 (T/Pet. 10/7).

petence developed in comparable fashion. As a result, the tendency to look to the nobility for leadership is most apparent . . . in the political field." [19] Limited in context to Majuro, this evaluation could have been applied broadside to the whole Marshalls. Since the children of leaders with ascribed status have also become members of the new professions, a sharp schism over political leadership has not developed between the two groups as the result of Westernized training.

In 1949, the Administering Authority called a meeting of *iroij laplap,* following an all-Marshalls' conference of magistrates and scribes. Of the twenty *iroij* who appeared, five had attended the magistrates' conference. At this first gathering of *iroij,* the civil administrator for the Marshalls laid before them the plans for a bicameral district-wide legislature with one house composed of hereditary paramount chiefs. By the creation of a separate chamber for the *iroij,* the administration was both indicating its "desire to support worthwhile indigenous customs" [20] and proposing to mobilize *iroij* active cooperation. In turn, the *iroij* were "alerted to the latent outlook of a new dawn for their class [with establishment of the House of Iroij]. . . . The institutionalization of their privileged status . . . injected into their group fresh vigor to resist the process of internal weakening and timely extinction. They recognize[d] in democratic practices and principles of the West efficient tools for the defense of their class interests." [21]

The original "constitution" of the Marshall Islands Congress declared the House of Iroij was to be composed "of all persons holding the position of paramount chief in accordance with the traditions, usages, and customs of the Marshallese people. The successor to a deceased or incapacitated paramount chief, recognized as that chief's proper and legal successor in accordance with Marshallese custom and tradition . . . [was to] automatically succeed to his predecessor's seat in the House of Iroij. In case of conflicting claims to paramount chieftainship, the Congress . . . [was to] establish procedure for investigating the claims and for approving the proper succession" (Art. II, Sec. 2).

In operation, much of this language was superfluous. The congress was not called upon to resolve disputes, for almost anyone with reputed claim who presented himself was allowed to sit as

---

[19] Spoehr, *op. cit.,* p. 94.
[20] See comments of HiCom, quoted in Richard, *op. cit.*
[21] Sandelmann, *op. cit.,* p. 109.

an *iroij* or as his representative. The *kajur* did nothing to correct this, according to an informant, "because the old traditions are involved and hold them back from taking necessary measures to stop it." The indeterminant composition of the House of Iroij was revealed at its very first meeting in 1950, when only eight of the twenty persons [22] who attended had also been present at the previous 1949 Conference of Iroij. The following year the total number in the House of Iroij increased to thirty-one, and thereafter it fluctuated between eighteen and twenty-eight members. At the 1956 session of the Marshallese congress, for example, fifteen *iroij laplap,* seven *iroij erik,* and six others without acknowledged status comprised the membership of the House of Iroij. In all, some sixty-seven different individuals participated in the eight meetings of the House of Iroij held between 1950 and 1958, after which a new charter creating a unicameral legislature was granted.

From the initial session of the Marshall Islands Congress, the respective rights and obligations of *iroij, alabs,* and *dri jerbals* (workers) regarding land were heatedly debated without any definitive resolution. The *iroij laplap* declaimed unequivocally that as of right they owned all the land, a claim which was sustained by a small percentage of older *kajur;* the majority of *kajur,* young and old, disagreed, stating that land was held in common. Year after year the congress adopted resolutions general to the point of ambiguity calling for respect of Marshallese customs, proper usage of land, and mutual satisfaction in the distribution of copra shares. The administration was of the opinion that many of these resolutions were forced through the congress by the *iroij* efforts to retrieve some of their waning power. Declarations on the ownership of land assumed particular importance in light of the Marshallese demands for sizeable payments by the United States for land and improvements damaged or occupied on various atolls. This litigation contributed to the reluctance of all parties to force the issue to decision. At no time did the *kajur* seek to eliminate the rights of the minority *iroij,* for the Marshallese processes of compromise and adjustment do not lend themselves to any such abrupt break with custom. Rather, maneuvering continued around the phrasing of resolutions before the congress, with charges and counter-charges of changing the terminology of measures on their drafting after

[22] The Administering Authority apparently thought the upper house of the Marshall Islands Congress would be composed of fifteen *iroij.* TCOR, 5th Sess., 17th meeting, July 11, 1949, p. 206.

passage, and even allegations of resolutions' disappearing from the final legislative record. Meanwhile, a deference to the *iroij laplap* remained, and many of the *kajur* continued to look to the *iroij* for leadership. One of the manifestations of this was the Marshallese refusal, under the instigation of the *iroij*, to accept the settlements for their land claims offered by the Administering Authority. This united position helped to hold *iroij* and *kajur* together until sizeably larger payments were forthcoming.

The high commissioner was adamant that the Marshallese congress be changed to a unicameral form. He was convinced that the House of Iroij succeeded in stopping resolutions sponsored by the House of Commoners and that its members would then turn around and, as *iroij*, ask for things to their own interest, so that the congress was not expressing the views of the Marshallese. As early as 1956, when amendments to the original charter were adopted, the high commissioner noted "that the entire original charter of the Congress needs careful examination for possible revision." [23] The *iroij* were not opposed to this, possibly because they foresaw that the mere form of the congress did not necessarily foreclose the weight of their traditional position. The staff of the high commissioner submitted a wholly new charter for the examination of the Marshallese Holdover Committee in the spring of 1958. The committee accepted it almost verbatim, including the provisions converting the congress into a unicameral body and allowing only "rightful *iroij*" to sit in the congress, but unanimously objected to denial of voting privileges to the *iroij* members. The high commissioner strongly opposed granting lifetime membership with full voting rights to the *iroij laplap*, as he did not consider that in concert with the ideals of democracy. At his instigation another meeting of the Holdover Committee was called to reconsider its decision, and a compromise was reached.

The charter draft submitted to the Marshallese congress for adoption followed the Palau model in that it did not grant the *iroij* voting rights on resolutions. But to protect them, the charter also declared that "matters affecting customary rights on land tenure, or land rights, as between Iroij, Alab, and Dri Jerbal" were outside the law-making power of the congress, and disputes thereon were "to be the province of the High Court only" (Art. VI, Sec. 1). A two-day floor fight ensued at the 1958 session, with the assistant

[23] Letter HiCom to Acting DistAd Marshalls, Nov. 21, 1956.

district administrator addressing the congress in support of the modified draft and using as arguments the advantages of Territory-wide uniformity, the necessity of compliance with the United Nations' demand for elected representation, and the democratic government to be gained through reducing the chiefs' role in all districts to one of advice and consultation. The Marshallese congress rejected the compromise, and the *iroij* emerged triumphant with both full voting rights in the unicameral body *and* maintenance of the compromise language preempting the law-making powers of the new legislature in the whole area of customary land rights. At best the administration could only take solace in the potential of the unicameral form for minimizing the powers of the *iroij* by permitting the *iroij* to be outvoted by the elected *kajur*. A number of years earlier a commentator on the Marshallese scene had concluded that, with the *iroij* once in the congress, "any reform drive is doomed to failure that aims at the abolition of the congressional House of Iroij and the reorganization of the Marshallese Council as a unicameral body." [24] His prophecy was erroneous as to structural change, but in terms of power relationships, he proved more right than wrong.

The charter directed the new congress at its first session to "determine by majority vote those who shall be admitted to membership as *iroij laplap* who shall retain membership for life" (Art. II, Sec. 5). The district administration contemplated rigidly enforcing the credentials clause "to see to it that only *iroijs* are certified and not blooded members of their families. . . ." [25] Earlier it had been anticipated that approximately thirteen would qualify, and against this small number, "the elected membership will dominate." [26] The high commissioner reported to the Trusteeship Council that the new Marshallese charter would call for about 20 per cent representation by hereditary chiefs and 80 per cent by elected congressmen. When the unicameral body first met in 1960, there were some forty *iroij* on the list for consideration! Selection of the *iroij* took a day and a half, with the vote proceeding atoll by atoll. When it was completed, nineteen *iroij* had been seated for life, and a novel principle for identifying *iroij* had been applied.

. . . some . . . are not Iroijlaplap in the strict sense of this hereditary title; although all have the duties and responsibilities of an Iroijlaplap. Each

[24] Sandelmann, *op. cit.,* p. 109.
[25] Memo Acting DistAd Marshalls to HiCom, Nov. 4, 1958.
[26] Memo Acting DistAd Marshalls to HiCom, April 15, 1958.

one has his or her own rights and can exercise such rights to execute business and independently decide important matters relating to land under that jurisdiction. . . .

In other words, the term Iroijlaplap has been given a new meaning which evolved out from long and hard debates in the Congress during the examination and certification of its permanent members. While I may disagree with the decision of the Congress, in my position, I have no choice but to be guided accordingly by the rule of the majority.[27]

The acting district administrator for the Marshalls concluded that the claims of *iroij* had become so confused over time that, to disqualify any of those seated, an anthropologist would have to make a thorough study of the entire *iroij* clans.[28] The administration acceded to the *fait accompli*.

A further embarrassment to the American administration was the fact that the Marshall Islands Congress named the Administering Authority as one of the *iroij* entitled to a seat. Lands on Majuro had long been disputed by two rival groups of claimants.[29] The administration scrupulously refrained from interfering, and from the 1950 session of the congress on, representatives of the opposing forces were seated in the House of Iroij. The decision designating the Trust Territory government as the *iroij* of the "twenty-twenty" group, one of the contestants, in effect eliminated any of the members of the group from the new congress. This drew an indignant rejection from the high commissioner, on the grounds that "the naming of the *iroij laplap*, if any, is for the people concerned to accomplish within their local customs, if they want such a title within their social organization."[30]

The new charter envisioned the termination of the practice of *iroij* representatives and supernumeraries' sitting through the legislative proceedings, and the congress was instructed that substitutes could not serve for the *iroij laplap*. Notwithstanding, as noted by the president of the congress, five of the *iroij* were not personally in the first unicameral congress but present "by their designated representatives. . . . It was within the scope of . . . [Marshallese] customs that the Iroijlaplap having been absent could logically be represented by their designated representatives. Such representa-

[27] Letter to Acting DistAd Marshalls from President of Marshall Islands Congress, Oct. 12, 1960.

[28] Memo Acting DistAd Marshalls to HiCom, Oct. 17, 1960.

[29] See Jack A. Tobin, "An Investigation of the Socio-Political Schism on Majuro Atoll," Aug. 20, 1953 (University of Hawaii Sinclair Library); also see Spoehr, *op. cit.*, pp. 84–91.

[30] Message of HiCom, Aug. 17, 1960.

tives, however, must by custom be qualified to act with full authority, and in this case, the Congress found all to be rightful heirs to the rights and prerogatives of those who were represented." Beside these representatives "there were a few guests. . . . While these people had the privilege of being heard and participating in the discussions of matters, they were not allowed the right to vote.[31]

In sum total, the form of the Marshallese congress was changed by the new charter, but the alignment of power remained undisturbed and the *iroij* class retained its vital role. Chosen as president was an elected representative who was the son of an *iroij* and *leroij,* had been a former member of the House of Iroij, and was a recognized spokesman for the *iroij.* He was backed by the *iroij laplap* seated at the congress and by "the older fellows from the northern and western atolls [who] followed the *iroij,* rather than voted of their own free will." [32] At the opening meeting of the unicameral congress, of the twelve members elected to the important Holdover Committee, two were *iroij laplap,* another two—the president of the congress and an *iroij erik*—had formerly sat in the House of Iroij, and at least three others were identified as men favorable to *iroij* interests. Thus the *iroij* faction had a clear majority on this interim committee.

The *iroij* congressmen have continued to take an active interest in the affairs of the legislature but, as a group, allow the elected representatives to exercise the lead on matters which do not affect Marshallese customs or land rights. Without recorded roll calls, it is not possible to demonstrate pro-*iroij*, anti-*iroij* divisions on measures brought to a vote, but the split between the factions in the congress persists. The question of seating additional *iroij* arose at the 1964 session of the congress; it was decided to defer action until the traditional recognition of these persons as *iroij laplap* had occurred and then to follow public opinion. The 1963 amendment to the Marshallese charter, cutting down the number of the elected representatives, increased the relative strength of the *iroij* in the congress. This change is diametrically opposite to the withering away of *iroij* influence anticipated by the Administering Authority when it first proposed a unicameral legislature for the Marshalls. But all this only reflects the general attitude of the Marshallese toward their *iroij* and the reluctance to break openly with tradition for fear this may undermine landed tenures and the security inher-

[31] Letter to Acting DistAd Marshalls from President . . . , *op. cit.*
[32] Memo Acting DistAd Marshalls to HiCom, Oct. 4, 1960.

ent in the continuation of the *iroij* institution. At the 1965 elections to the Congress of Micronesia, of the Marshalls' six-member delegation, one was an *iroij laplap,* another an *iroij erik,* and a third of *iroij* descent, the president elected at the first session of the new Marshallese legislature—tacit evidence that many Marshallese still look to their *iroij* for political leadership.

LAND AND TRADITIONAL LEADERSHIP

In these three administrative districts the distinctive interplay between the indigenous leadership and the legislative institution introduced by the Americans prompts the search for an explanation. Immediately significant, although not to be considered the efficient cause for the difference, is that the levels of chiefly participation in the district legislatures correlate positively with the importance of the chiefs' respective roles with relation to land.

In Ponape, half a century ago under the German administration, land reform gave the common people deed-holding title to their lands. Certain traditional obligations to the *nanmarki* were incorporated into these deeds, in effect continuing to recognize Ponape's stratified society, but the net result was to remove the chiefs from effective control over use of the lands. At the same time, the German government declared uncultivated lands not assigned to anyone as belonging to the district in which they were located, and available for homesteading. The Japanese regarded all lands not covered by individual title as government owned and subject to government control. All of these modifications removed the element of land from the feudal ties binding commoners to traditional leaders.[33]

Before Western contact, most of aboriginal Palau was divided into clan lands, with the public domain in the interior of the islands, the mangrove swamps, and the reefs controlled by the village *klobak* (council) or, in a few cases, by the district *klobak*. Village and district chiefs had claim to parts of the product from clan lands. Lineages within each clan were assigned rights to use land, under the control of their lineage heads, but the clan retained ultimate title. At the turn of the century, land tenure concepts began undergoing considerable change. By the Japanese period, the traditional public domain was declared to be government land. Individual land ownership concepts in Palau date back to the Ger-

[33] John L. Fischer, "Contemporary Ponape Island Land Tenure," in *Land Tenure Patterns . . . , op. cit.,* pp. 77–160.

man times, and under the Japanese many clan and lineage lands held in group ownership were divided and registered as individually owned. However, the recognition of exclusive individual titles in contradistinction to the exercise of user rights through the lineage or clan remains unclear, denoting the continuing transitional status of Palauan land tenures.[34]

In the Marshalls, the concept of *iroij* complete ownership of the land has only been modified to "one of joint ownership of land rights with the chiefs possessing certain rights and the commoners possessing other rights in the land and holding these rights as a member of a lineage in common with the other lineage members."[35] "The system of land tenure and usufruct has not changed drastically despite the acculturative forces of three different regimes and the orientation toward a cash economy."[36]

The intrinsic importance of land to the Micronesian cultures suggests that the Marshallese *iroij* had far more to protect through securing a place in the district legislature than did the Ponapean traditional leaders. This logic is supported by Palau's position more intermediary in transition from indigenous to introduced land tenure systems, and the Palauan traditional chiefs' enjoying a comparable importance in their district legislature. However, it is more accurate to regard the changes in land tenure of the three districts as but symbolic of ongoing and far more complex cultural modifications, in turn accompanied by alteration of the districts' indigenous political systems. In effect, with variances in land tenure went an erosion of the powers of the traditional leaders. For those lacking the characteristics now necessary for legitimating their presence in the new institutions having authority to make definitive political decisions, it was but to be expected that they would withdraw from the legislature.

[34] Shigeru Kaneshiro, "Land Tenure in the Palau Islands," in *ibid*, pp. 289–336.
[35] Jack A. Tobin, *op. cit.*, p. 7.
[36] *Ibid*, p. 11.

CHAPTER 6

The Ngobochei[1]—Negotiating a New District Legislature

July, 1965
FM HICOMTERPAC SAIPAN
TO DISTAD YAP

UNCLAS X REUR MEMO JUNE 25 X HEADQUARTERS WILL
ATTEMPT TO COVER ESTIMATED TRAVEL AND PER DIEM
EXPENSES FOR COMMITTEE TO FORM YAP DISTRICT—WIDE
LEGISLATURE X DR. NORMAN MELLER CMM PROF POL
SCI UH CMM AVAILABLE TO ATTEND AUGUST MEETING
MENTIONED YOUR MEMO IF HELD PRIOR AUGUST 21 X
PLS REPLY RETURN DISPATCH ON THREE QUESTIONS CLN
WHETHER POSSIBLE FOR WOLEAI MEMBER COME TO YAP
IN AUGUST CMM WHETHER COMMITTEE PLANS TO MEET
IN AUGUST CMM WHETHER COMMITTEE WISHES SERVICES
DR. MELLER . . .

July, 1965
FM DISTAD YAP
TO HICOMTERPAC SAIPAN

UNCLAS X REUR 200420Z X ABLE CMM WOLEAI DELEGATE
WILL BE IN YAP BY AUGUST 14 OR 15 X BAKER CMM
COMMITTEE WILL SCHEDULE MEETING DURING WEEK OF
16 TO 20 AUGUST X CHARLIE CMM COMMITTEE WILL
WELCOME DR. MELLER ASSISTANCE X SUGGEST DR. MELLER
ARRIVE YAP 13 AUGUST AND PLAN DEPARTURE FOR GUAM
20 AUGUST

FOR ONE WEEK in the summer of 1965, the author played
the part of an honest broker, aiding the Administering Authority's
on-going effort to establish a district-wide legislature for the Yap
administrative area. Ostensibly, indigene interest was premised
upon the desire to fall in line with the other five administrative
districts. In reality, and typical of all political maneuvering in the
Yap area, the exploratory talks were motivated by concealed drives
for power on the part of both entrenched and emergent leadership
groups, and the whole was clouded by mistrust and complicated

---

[1] The word "Ngobochei" has two connotations: one is a know-nothing,
intruding foreign meddler in local affairs; the other is the stranger in the
Yapese midst who is an intelligent guide in the management of Yapese affairs.

by the relatively primitive political forms and processes still observed in the Outer Islands of the old Yap empire. All this stemmed partially from the competition developing between persons identified with one or the other of two political institutions introduced by the United States for the governance of the four adjoining high islands of Yap, an area usually referred to collectively just as Yap, the Yap Islands, or as Yap Islands proper. Another element was the breaking away of the low islands to the east from their traditional ties with Yap and the rise of Ulithi as a potential leading force in the old Yap empire. Contributing were the disruptive influences of education, disparate population growths, and the faster pace of political change elsewhere in the Trust Territory which impinged upon this most conservative portion of Micronesia. These factors together comprised the backdrop for the negotiations, which in turn became wholly meaningful only in light of traditional government in the Yap region and its modification over time.

TRADITIONAL SOCIO-POLITICAL STRUCTURE OF YAP DISTRICT [2]

Both the peoples of Yap and those of the *Ngek* (eastern) islands, which together constituted the old Yap empire, possessed

[2] This portion is based upon a number of sources. When conflicts in content were encountered, the author attempted a reconciliation. William H. Alkire, "Cultural Adaption in the Caroline Islands," *The Journal of the Polynesian Society*, 69:1 (March, 1960), 123; William H. Alkire, *Lamotrek Atoll and Inter-Island Socioeconomic Ties*, Illinois Studies in Anthropology No. 5 (Urbana: University of Illinois Press, 1965); Edwin B. Burrows, "From Value to Ethos on Ifaluk Atoll," *Southwestern Journal of Anthropology*, 8:1 (Spring, 1952), 13; Edwin G. Burrows and Melford E. Spiro, *An Atoll Culture, Ethnography of Ifaluk in the Central Carolines*, CIMA Final Report Nos. 16 and 18 (New Haven: Human Relations Area Files, 1953); *Civil Affairs Handbook, West Caroline Islands* (Washington: Office of the Chief of Naval Operations, 1944); William A. Lessa, *The Ethnography of Ulithi Atoll*, CIMA Final Report No. 28 (Los Angeles: University of California at Los Angeles, 1950); William A. Lessa, "The Place of Ulithi in the Yap Empire," *Human Organization*, 9:1 (Spring, 1950), 16; William A. Lessa, "Ulithi and the Outer Native World," *American Anthropologist*, 52:1 (Jan.–March, 1950), 27; William A. Lessa and Marvin Spiegelman, *Ulithian Personality as Seen Through Ethnological Materials and Thematic Test Analysis*, University of California Publications in Culture and Society, Vol. 2, No. 5 (Berkeley: University of California Press, 1954), pp. 243–301; *Micronesians of Yap and Their Depopulation*, CIMA Final Report No. 24 (Cambridge, Mass.: Peabody Museum, Harvard University, 1949); Dorothy E. Richard, *U.S. Naval Administration in the Trust Territory of the Pacific Islands*, Vol. III (Washington: Office of the Chief of Naval Operations, 1957); Father Salesius, *Die Karolinen-Insel Jap* (Berlin: Wilhelm Susserot, circa 1906) [Human Relations Area Files translation]; John Sandelmann, *Some Observations on the Problem of "Self Government" in the Trust Territory of the Pacific Islands* (Honolulu: 1953); David M. Schneider, "The Kinship System and Village Organization of Yap, West Caroline Islands, Micronesia" (Ph.D. thesis, Harvard University: 1949); David M. Schneider, "Political Organization, Supernatural Sanctions and the Punishment for Incest on Yap," *American Anthropologist*, 59:5 (Oct., 1957), 791; Stanford University

a unique social organization. The empire was a composite of kin-ship system, class-caste hierarchy, and village-district organiza-tion. The two geographical sub-regions were held together by relationships that embodied political, religious, landlord-tenant, and parent-child ties. In a number of ways and to varying degrees, these bonds still play a significant part in shaping the form and processes of local government in the Yap administrative district.

Traditional Yap recognized extraordinary class distinctions, with each village originally belonging to one of nine social classes. The four [3] lowest classes comprised a serf caste, subordinate to their masters in the higher classes which may have originally been racially derived. The serf villages occupied land owned by families in the high ranking villages, and theoretically a serf family could be dispossessed if it failed to work and perform ceremonial services for its master as required by tradition. In return, the masters took a paternal interest in their serfs' welfare, so that the relationship resembled that of patron-dependent and was not synonymous with slavery. The social freedom of the serfs was restricted in many other ways to demonstrate their inferior status; for example, they were prohibited to wear combs in their hair and had to move out of the path of the free people. If exploitation occurred, a low class family could establish a new tie with another high ranking one. Class position was somewhat fluid, and ranking could change de-pending upon success at war and political maneuvering. A degree of cross-class marriage was permitted, but within a limited range, and rarely between upper and lower castes. A low caste village and its people always retained that status, although it might shift its attachment to a different high caste village. Unlike in the West-ern world where class position is correlated with levels of living, birth rates, infant mortality, life expectancy, and comparable other distinctive features, none of these relationships hold for Yap; it is in the exercise of power and the rights to special privilege that the two castes have differed.

School of Naval Administration, *Handbook of the Trust Territory* (Washing-ton: Office of the Chief of Naval Operations, 1948); John Useem, *Report on Yap and Palau,* USCC Economic Survey No. 6 (Honolulu: 1946); John Useem, "Human Resources of Micronesia," *Far Eastern Survey,* 17:1 (Jan. 14, 1948), 1; Tadao Yanaihara, *Pacific Islands Under Japanese Mandate* (Shanghai: Kelly and Walsh, Ltd., 1939).

[3] Some sources refer to a total of eight classes and to the *milingai* people (serfs) as consisting of but three classes; the Japanese tried to compress all classes into five, with the nobles as the highest, the serfs as the lowest, and three intermediate commoner classes.

A village was composed of a number of clans, each clan having up to ten households and ranked according to prestige. Men were divided into as many as six ranks within each village, primarily according to age, with the two highest of these ranks distinguished by ownership of certain status-giving land and thus attainable only in noble villages. The chief of each village (*pilung ko binau*) usually held his position by virtue of his identification with a particular plot of land which afforded chiefly powers to its owner. Low caste villages were organized in the same way as higher caste ones, with their village chiefs and lesser chiefs, village councils, magicians, and sacred places. Villages in turn were grouped into districts for political and defense purposes.

In principle, the chieftainship of a village was hereditary, probably originally passing through the female line of the highest ranking clan, but over time this was modified also to permit patrilineal succession, most commonly from father to son. The chief was afforded symbolic deference and enjoyed a well-defined role in village ceremonial life, but he had no great supervisory power except in consort with the secondary chiefs or all of the clan heads in council. However, the chief's orders once given were absolute, and the self-discipline of the village assured compliance.

During the Japanese period, the village chief's authority was greatly restricted, and since then major matters have had to be referred to district chiefs or to representatives of the Administering Authority. District chiefs (*pilung ko nug*) may come from only the two highest classes and traditionally have had high prestige. In ancestral times the responsibilities of the district chief ranged from communal matters, such as conducting war, to the details of family affairs. Much of this authority remains today, and the district chief continues to direct public policy and oversee the administration of village chiefs. Because foreigners have regarded the district chiefs as possessors of unqualified powers, they have attempted to govern Yap through the chiefs and have thereby enhanced the district chief's authority.

Yap has known no high degree of political integration. In ancient times Yap was divided into three districts, each of which was of equal rank. The Germans regrouped the villages into nine districts or *falak*, a name which apparently represents a Yapese corruption of the German *flagge*, or flag. Under the Japanese, the districts were increased to ten, under the direction of eight district chiefs, and their number some time later was expanded to ten. These geographical groupings were established for the adminis- trative convenience of the metropolitan nations, and the Yapese continued to recognize the domination of certain districts over others. Nevertheless, the districting served to establish new socio- political groupings, which are today treated as almost endemic to Yapese society.

The Yapese people are independent, anything but obsequious, unaggressive in relations with strangers, and among themselves critical of the boastful, presumptuous, and pretentious. They have neither awe of the government official nor uncritical admiration of his culture. Early American administrators were convinced that the Yapese wanted neither modern commerce nor education. When other administrative districts started leveling municipal taxes, the Yapese refused to follow suit and for a while adopted an attitude of almost passive resistance. Forewarned by the Japanese experi- ence, when the Yapese seemed to delight in resisting imposed innovations, including those patently intended for their benefit, American administrators patiently allowed time for this to work itself out. No Yapese, whether under the Germans, Japanese, or the Americans, has accepted "the promise that his destiny is to be directed by a foreign agency, either within Yap, or outside of Yap." [4] Although the Yapese have acquired a reputation for ultra- conservatism and do not lightly alter their basic patterns of living, they have shown themselves to be "eager for development and progress in political organization and in other fields as well, pro- vided it is accomplished at a pace and in a manner of their own choosing." [5] They adopt and adapt as best calculated to preserve the Yapese identity.

Two of the districts of Yap (see map p. 233) exercised suze- rainty over the low islands of the old Yap empire, which stretch some seven hundred miles to the east. With the exception of the small atoll of Ngulu (present population about forty-five), which was a satellite of Galiman (Gurror) district, all of these islands owed allegiance to Gagil, and through the island of Ulithi as an intermediary, practically all were identified with the clans of two villages in this Yapese district. Ulithi played the key role in the

[4] Quoted in Sandelmann, *op. cit.*, p. 92.
[5] *Annual Report of the High Commissioner to the Secretary of the In- terior, 1958*, p. 29.

political, landowning-kin, magic-religious ties which held the empire together. While it was subordinate to Yap, it was superior to "Woleai," the designation by which all islands to the east of Ulithi, including the atoll of Woleai, are collectively known to the Yapese and Ulithians.

Orders from the paramount chief of Gagil traveled east along a single communication channel: first to the paramount chief of Mogmog on Ulithi atoll, and then at his direction to other islands on Ulithi and externally to Fais and Sorol and also to the Woleai atoll. From Woleai the orders were next relayed to Eauripik, Faraulep, and Ifalik, which passed them on to Lamotrek, which in turn forwarded them to Elato and Satawal. Satawal then transmitted them to Puluwat, which finally sent them to Namonuito, Pulap, and Pulusuk. (These three islands and Puluwat are now administered as part of the Truk district.) This communication order was scrupulously observed, and for their part, the chiefs of the islands east of Ulithi never consulted directly with Gagil, but only through Ulithi. Ulithi derived its political power and prestige from being the intermediary between Yap and Woleai, and it relayed orders and irregularly collected tribute (*piteglitamol*) as the agent of the paramount chief in Gagil. Reflective of this, succession to the paramount chieftainship of Ulithi required formal approval from Yap. The chain of communication also identified the respective super-subordinate relationship between the islands of the old Yap empire. Within each island, administration proceeded completely independently, so that only nominal authority was actually possessed by an off-island superior.

Some of the upper caste clans of Gagil were considered owners of the lands on the islands to the east and, because of this, occupied the relation of "parents" to their Outer Island "children." Out of these ties there developed a system of periodic *sawei* (gift) exchanges, with the "children" clans from "Woleai" sending presents to Ulithi and then fleets of canoes from that atoll bringing them to Yap and returning with as many if not more gifts, which were then distributed on Ulithi and islands to the east. Should an Outer Islander visit Yap, these same relationships assured him treatment like a child of a specific clan, and any Yapese "parent" would receive corresponding care from his adult "child" if he were to travel to the Outer Islands. As "parents," the Gagil clans fed, clothed, and sheltered their "children," supervised their actions, and gave them parting gifts when they left for home; the Outer Islanders in turn owed filial respect and obedience. Ulithi enjoyed a similar *sawei* relationship with "Woleai," so that the clans of the latter were "children" of "parents" both on Ulithi and Yap.

A third form of exchange between the Outer Islands and Yap, usually via Ulithi, consisted of the presentation of offerings (*mepel*) to the head religious functionaries of Gagil. This exchange was independent of the political and *sawei* relationships. Gifts were sent regularly to propitiate the ghosts of the parent lineages on Yap, probably for the benefits which these spirits were believed to bring to the Outer Islanders. The head of the Woloi matrilineal clan of Gagil, as paramount chief, also relied upon magic to maintain his political hold over the Yap empire. From sacred places on Ulithi, his magicians could plague the Outer Islands with epidemics, typhoons, and other assorted forms of natural disaster. Conversely, white magic would assure food and fertility and could ward off calamity. Under threat of supernatural punishment, Outer Islanders journeying to Yap were required to observe many taboos in their dealings with the Yapese. The traditional socio-political ties of the two areas were thus held together by magico-religious links as well as by the economic advantages derived by all parties from various exchange relationships which complemented the islands' limited resources.

Classes and rankings also existed on the Outer Islands, so that everyone had his place, but without the sharp caste distinctions observed on Yap. The major line of cleavage, which ran between chiefs and commoners, was discernible mainly on formal occasions. The chiefs were aligned in definite order of rank, and their clans, correspondingly; clans without hereditary chiefs occupied a lower status. Within clans, lineages held positions of traditional seniority. Chiefly titles were mainly hereditary along matrilineal lines. As the people were very law-abiding, the chiefs directed their attention primarily to supervising communal undertakings and conducting external relations. On some of the islands, land-ownership districts were distinguished from political districts, with the chiefs of the latter owing their positions to their status in the chain of political authority originating on Yap. Island-wide decisions would be the prerogative of these "political" chiefs. Only with respect to relationships with Yap or the other islands in the *Ngek* (eastern) chain of communications was political authority centered in the person of a paramount chief. A council of elders, which included representatives from each kin group, normally administered village affairs. On some of the smaller islands, all of the people assembled for political meetings, although they usually allowed their senior lineage heads to speak for them. Belying the seeming aristocratic nature of the society, the prestige and authority of age afforded the older people great freedom in voicing their opinions, and this opportunity for one's views to gain expression introduced a strong element of democratic participation. To a great degree, this mildly gerontocratic socio-political system continues today in the Outer Islands.

In their relations with the Yapese, the Outer Islanders had the status of low-caste serfs. The *sawei* system may have assured their care while visiting Yap, but it also permitted them to be treated with contempt. The restrictions on dress, language, food, and social intercourse were at the very least irksome, and in truth degrading. The Outer Islanders accepted their role until the introduction of new forces caused a deterioration in the ties between the two areas. In German times, the Administering Authority supplied stores of food after disastrous typhoons on the Outer Islands, which practice undercut one of the strong *sawei* ties. Christianity was adopted far earlier on some of the Outer Islands than on Yap and freed these Outer Islanders from fear of supernatural reprisals. The Japanese administration prohibited inter-island voyages in native canoes, inhibiting the indigenes' freedom of movement, and World War II seriously interrupted the Japanese sailings. After the Americans assumed jurisdiction, the infrequent trips of naval vessels was not conducive to a resumption of periodic exchanges, and by mid-century *piteglitamol, sawei,* and *mepel* had practically stopped coming into Yap from Ulithi. The education gained in both Japanese and American schools enabled the Outer Islanders to view their ties with Yap on a more critical level and to meet the Yapese as intellectual equals. And finally, the advent of foreign power rule has been conducive to replacing Yapese suzerainty with new administrative influences and to superimposing German, then Japanese, and now American administrators over the native polities of the Outer Islanders. The foreigners have replaced the Yapese in the framework of the old organization.

The Outer Islanders acknowledged the higher rank of the Yapese, but this did not foreclose their regarding the Yapese as arrogant and dishonest and looking down upon Yapese society as torn with suspicion and dissention. For their part, the people of Gagil came to recognize only grudgingly their *sawei* obligations to care for Outer Islanders on Yap, and these obligations deteriorated to a point where they became instead a generalized Yapese responsibility. Through the new Council of Magistrates introduced by the Americans, Outer Island students attending school were provided housing in special dormitories and food was contributed from all of the districts. The Roman Catholic Church made available for the temporary shelter of Outer Island visitors a small piece of land, an area known as "Madrich," close to the American district headquarters on Yap.

For a while the Americans observed the fiction that the Council of Magistrates, because Gagil and Galiman were represented on the council, could speak for the *Ngek* islands as well. However, American ideology was incompatible with the caste basis of the old Yapese empire, and it was only a matter of time before the break from Yap would be acknowledged. The American administrators were informed by the people on the outlying islands that they desired to be relieved of their "thralldom" to Yap. As they expressed it, "We want the chance to become 'up' men and not remain dog men as the Yap chiefs want us to be." [6] The year 1951 conveniently marks the formal ending to the political ties between Yap and its empire, when the Council of Magistrates, probably at American instigation, adopted a resolution declaring that "a) servitude in all its forms is abolished; b) inhabitants of . . . [islands to east] are to be treated as equals in every respect; [and] c) the chiefs of the outlying atolls and islands are invited to join the Council of District Chiefs of Yap as equals. . . ." [7] This, of course, did not terminate any social or supernatural relationships the Outer Islanders might wish to continue.

With the slackening of Yapese bonds over the Outer Islands, Ulithi's position in relation to "Woleai" has correspondingly risen. The linkages of the traditional political organization continue to be active and important, and the social contacts between Ulithi and "Woleai" remain friendly. The islands farther east followed Ulithi's conversion to Catholicism as though the suggestion were an order. The Americans as the Administering Authority usually institute

[6] *Micronesians of Yap and Their Depopulation, op. cit.,* p. 198.
[7] Quoted in Sandelmann, *op. cit.,* p. 92.

pilot projects on Ulithi before attempting similar measures on the other islands and frequently relay policy decisions through that atoll, so the old traditional conduits of communication still hold. The placing of a junior high school on Ulithi has diverted the *Ngek* students from Yap, and "Woleai" parents are now beginning to allow their daughters to leave home for education, something they hesitated to do when advanced schooling was available only on Yap. Having enjoyed far more contact with the Americans and consequently having acquired a degree of sophistication in dealing with American political innovations, the Ulithians, as the most Christianized, educated, and acculturated of the Outer Islanders, are today in a position to expand their power to the east. In contrast to Ulithi, changes in the internal economic, political, and kinship organizations of the remaining Outer Islands have been relatively minimal, as impinging forces generated by the administering metropolitan countries have been communicated mainly through traditional channels in ways compatible to the existing culture. All this redounds to the advantage of Ulithi which, through the influence it can exert along traditional lines, can hope to weld the Outer Islands together as a potent power bloc in any district-wide Yap government and, as the leader, can hope to gain a prominence in American-introduced institutions in a way reminiscent of the glory that was Yap's in the old empire.

AMERICAN-INTRODUCED POLITICAL INSTITUTIONS

The Americans built their administrative system for the Yap Islands upon the ten political-social subdivisions left by the Japanese, naming them "municipalities" and the traditional chief of each subdivision "magistrate." The Navy administrators early encouraged designation of magistrates through elections, but much to their consternation, in the first elections the ten ranking chiefs were selected. Within the municipality, the chief-council meeting was retained, with the magistrate and the municipal secretary presiding over the attending chiefs from all the villages. Gradually, due to age or lack of familiarity with the ways of the American administration, the traditional chiefs designated others to act in their stead as magistrates, and individuals came to be elected for their popularity, integrity, and recognized abilities rather than solely for their chiefly status. However, the magistrates continued to be, if not chiefs, men of very high class. For long the function of the municipality as distinct from the village remained confused. The traditional relations within the village easily lent themselves to the performance of communal tasks, but it was "difficult for a municipal government to improve its municipality when there is no law (which gives it authority) and the people as a whole pay little attention to it." [8] Political-social domination of lower ranking municipalities by others of higher class persisted, and some villages looked not to the magistrate of their own municipality but to one from the area in which their traditional overlords resided.

To facilitate American-Yapese administrative contacts, the elected magistrates commenced meeting periodically with members of the district administration in a rather informally constituted discussion group, primarily to hear the pronouncements of the administration. Attending with the magistrates were the ten municipal secretaries, special representatives of a number of district departments, and the president and vice-president of the Fak e Pul, an organization of young Yapese. At first, only the chiefs of the senior districts spoke, but expression of views progressively broadened. This Magistrates' Council served both to provide the administration with an "advisory sounding board" and to unite all municipalities in island-wide undertakings.

Gradually, the powers and responsibilities of the council became clarified when certain functions were centralized, and starting in 1956, the council commenced operating under a "statement on organization and functions" drawn up in a series of meetings and approved by the district administrator. Magistrates were to be elected for three-year terms by secret ballot through universal suffrage, and they in turn would appoint and remove their municipal secretaries. An executive committee, composed of the president, vice-president, secretary, and treasurer of the council, represented the council and, between the monthly meetings of the council, met in an advisory and liaison capacity with the Yap district administrator. The council was empowered to appoint boards and designate committees as advisory groups, and some "thirty non-Council-member leaders and progressive citizens" sat with the magistrates and secretaries in the periodic meetings.[9] Through its treasurer, the

[8] Paper of Marnifen, read at First Trust Territory Conference on Self-Government (Truk: 1953), p. 24.
[9] Memo DistAd Yap to HiCom, "Chartering Municipalities," circa 1957, p. 3.

council levied and collected taxes, budgeting was conducted on an island-wide basis, and the council functioned as an embryonic island legislature. It also directly administered activities such as local agricultural and public works projects. Its outstanding characteristic was a desire and willingness to initiate and plan its own programs of improvements and to support them with labor, material, and funds.

When confronted with the Administering Authority's municipal chartering program, the council recommended against its institution in Yap until after "the council or an island-wide body is chartered and future needs and organization make chartering of the smaller governmental units necessary or desirable." [10] The chartering of municipalities was delayed, as well, on the ground that those first chartered would most likely be the traditionally dominant, so that caste cleavages would be bolstered. All this coincided with Trust Territory policy, for only in Truk had municipal chartering commenced prior to issuance of a charter for the district congress.

After the council appointed a chartering committee, almost a year of discussion was required for setting up a congress for Yap. Particularly troublesome was the division of authority between the new legislative body and the existing council, and the former's "detracting from the established and recognized prestige and status of the Council." [11] The charter finally agreed upon for the new congress provided for two representatives for each of Yap's ten municipalities. The chartering committee and the council were "unanimous and consistent in proposing equal representation until traditional class and rank distinctions between persons and municipalities have further decreased in local political-social-economic importance." [12] In addition to taxing and enacting resolutions "to provide for and maintain the welfare of the residents of Yap," the congress was directed to prepare an annual budget for the disbursement of revenues collected under its authority (Art. II). All would become law upon receiving the signature of the high commissioner or upon his failure to act within six months. Although unstated, the long-range plans contemplated eventual inclusion of the Outer Islands in the district political structure.

The convening of the congress in June of 1959, after the grant

[10] *Ibid.*
[11] Memo DistAd Yap to HiCom, Dec. 17, 1958.
[12] Letter of DistAd Yap to HiCom, Dec. 31, 1958.

of a charter the previous February, did not lead to any marked diminution in the power of the council and, if anything, reinforced its status. Into the new body went younger, Western-oriented men, while the council continued to be made up of older Yapese "who have the unqualified respect of the electorate, [and] are in a better position to introduce and pass on legislation than is the Yap Islands Congress." The same commentator, writing as of the end of 1962, also noted that the congressmen "introduced laws and vote the way the Council tells them to." [13] The council served as the budget committee for the congress, and prior to each spring meeting, the Executive Committee of the council prepared a budget for the following fiscal year. As an executive group, the council handled nearly all specific projects for the Yap Islands. As befitted this executive character, nominations to Yap district boards originated in the council before being submitted for approval by the congress and confirmation by the district administration.

At the end of 1962, the Yap district administrator proposed to charter the Yap Islands Council and each of the ten municipalities. The high commissioner was opposed to granting a legal basis for the council, and his staff advised him to phase out the council by forming a single municipal government for the Yap Islands, with the congress as the municipal council.[14] Faced with this conflicting advice, the high commissioner disapproved of the Yap district administrator's proposal, presumably because of Headquarter's desire to merge the traditional leadership in the council with the congress instead of strengthening the council and maintaining its identity with the Yapese chiefs. However, the high commissioner took no steps to eliminate the council.

The stumbling block to bringing traditional leaders into the congress lay in the congressional charter's prohibition against magistrates' being elected to the congress. Rather, the chiefs have continued to be part of the Yap Islands Council, and the council, to serve as a type of collective executive body for the congress. Since the chiefs have been able to direct the Yapese to work without pay upon local projects, such as road maintenance and bridge repair, the council has been able to promote "voluntary" public works as well as to administer those supported from congressional funds. Cooperating with the district administrator, the council has helped keep order and has facilitated the smooth functioning of the district

[13] Memo Assistant DistAd Yap to DistAd, circa Dec. 1962.
[14] Memo Political Affairs Officer to HiCom, Dec. 11, 1962.

administration. In its pivotal position, it has stabilized and strengthened the governments of the local municipalities. More money is
appropriated for its personnel than for that of congress. (In fiscal
year 1965, $3,680 was proposed for Yap Islands Congress salaries,
$11,752 for Yap Islands Council salaries, and $1,000 for each as
entertainment allowance.)

Over the last few years a marked rivalry has developed between
the congressmen and the members of the Yap Islands Council. The
former are mainly governmental employees,[15] younger, American-
educated, and Western-oriented. They have questioned the budget
as proposed by the council, have refused to accept the council's
recommendation for location of the new congressional building,
and have declined to finance councilmen traveling to Palau on the
problem of Palauan disorderliness on Yap. The role of the council
as a legislative committee to introduce resolutions is being resisted.
The suggestion of the district administrator to the Kanifay School
Board—that it should first present its proposed draft for a change
in the law to the Yap Islands Council because "if the Council finds
your proposal should be passed, I believe the Congress will give it
favorable consideration"—is no longer as sound advice as it once
would have been.[16]

The members of the council see their power decreasing with this
coming of age of the Yap Islands Congress. They are aware that
the administration is debating abolishing the council and reor-
ganizing local government so that a single magistrate, assisted by
a ten-man council, will serve the whole of the Yap Islands proper.
All this would be forestalled with the conversion of the Yap Islands
Congress into a district-wide legislative body entrusted with matters of district concern and no longer preoccupied with legislating
for the municipal problems of Yap. The Yap Islands Council, possibly in a new form, could re-emerge as the undisputed power
center of the Yap Islands government.

ATTEMPTS TO FORM A DISTRICT-WIDE LEGISLATURE

Until 1959, political contact between American administrators
and Outer Islanders occurred on an island by island basis; in that

---

[15] At the spring, 1965, meeting of the congress, fifteen employees from
the district administration and the agriculture, constabulary, education, public works, and public defender's departments were granted leave to attend the
Yap Islands Congress. (Yap District Memo, April 22, 1965). This represented
three-fourths of the congressional membership.

[16] Memo DistAd Yap to Kanifay School Board, March 23, 1965.

year, for the first time, a conference for the entire area was convened on Woleai. Hereditary chiefs or their representatives, accompanied by advisors and interpreters, met with the district administrator to discuss common problems pertaining to public health, education, agriculture, taxation, and field-trip operations. They tentatively agreed upon the erection of a building to accommodate Outer Islanders visiting Yap and the planting of a garden for satisfying their food needs, but these were never fully effected. Although Trust Territory plans called for repetition of these Outer Island meetings on a yearly basis, epidemics and rehabilitation efforts necessitated by natural disasters within the district caused their postponement.

At the second meeting, in 1962 on Ulithi, the conferees turned their attention to a district-wide legislature, although under very unpropitious circumstances. The Outer Islanders discovered to their chagrin that they were being subjected to a 3 per cent sales tax levied by the Yap Islands Congress on non-food items and were incensed that this had been levied without prior consultation.[17] Several chiefs, by way of emphasizing their request for the return of this money, added that should the Outer Islands decide to participate in any tax program, they would want representatives in the congress. This line of discussion prompted an invitation for observers from the Outer Islands to attend the spring 1962 meeting of the Yap Islands Congress, to which the highest ranking chief replied that "to send several observers from the Outer Islands to attend the Congress is something like sending a blind man to observe the session."[18] Background information, training in parliamentary procedure, and an understanding of the purposes of the Yap Islands Congress were all identified as prerequisites to observation tours. It was also at this 1962 conference that the district administrator proposed that the Outer Islanders consider the formation of a district-wide legislature, in which the Outer Islands would have seventeen seats in a thirty-seven-member body, a proportion to their advantage as computed upon the relative populations of the two areas at that time. The seeds for the legislature were planted, but it would take a more favorable climate for them to germinate.

[17] The Yap Islands Congress on several occasions has ignored the limits of its jurisdiction and has considered laws applicable to the whole administrative district.

[18] From notes of DistAd Yap on Outer Island Conference, Morning Sess., Jan. 9, 1962.

The 1962 conference raised a number of other matters pertinent to the organizing of a district-wide legislative body. The administration party carefully explained the function of representation, as distinguished from attendance as an observer, and offered to translate the charter of the Yap Islands Congress into Ulithian so that its provisions could be studied in the Outer Islands. The American school teacher resident on Ulithi also proposed to teach an adult class in parliamentary procedure, using *Robert's Rules of Order* and materials pertinent to the activities of the Yap Islands Congress. Probably the events of most lasting impact in drawing the Outer Islands out of their isolation were the explanation tendered at this conference on the workings of the Council of Micronesia for the whole Trust Territory and the proposal that the Outer Islanders designate a delegate to attend the council for the next two years as one of the representatives from Yap district. Previously, the Yap Islands Council had been choosing both delegates, but with one term vacant, the administration considered that the Outer Islands should be represented. The chief so named, Belarmino Hethy of Ulithi, was to be a member of the Council of Micronesia's Political Committee which, at the November 1963 meeting of the council, played a key role in the structuring of the future Congress of Micronesia. Hethy was later to be the spokesman for the Outer Islands in the 1965 negotiations for setting up a district-wide legislature for Yap.

In 1963, the Political Affairs Office at Headquarters on Saipan submitted a new congressional charter calling for Outer Islands participation, which the Yap Islands Congress approved. A representative from the office then toured the islands to the east at the request of the congress to obtain Outer Islander reaction. As was to be anticipated, the Outer Islanders would not commit themselves on the new charter other than to indicate it was unacceptable in its proposed form because they were allotted only five seats, a representation out of proportion to their population. Chief Hethy accompanied this field trip to report his observations on the work of the Council of Micronesia and, as spokesman for the paramount chief on Ulithi, to make preliminary plans for a later Outer Islands Conference at which the modification of the Yap Islands Congress charter could be discussed further. This 1963 conference never materialized, the revision of the Yap Islands Congress charter died, and here the matter rested until interest in the formation of district-wide legislature was reactivated during the preparations made for holding elections for the Congress of Micronesia in the latter part of 1964. If there ever had been a desire to establish a separate government and legislative body solely for the Outer Islands, as an alternative to joining with Yap, it was quashed at the 1964 meeting of the chiefs on Ulithi when the district administrator announced that cost precluded anything but a single district government for the whole area.

With the Congress of Micronesia's elections imminent, the Yap administrative district set up two election committees, with the members of one from the Outer Islands. After the polling, the latter committee returned with the field-trip ship to count the ballots at Colonia. At this time, informal discussions were initiated between these Outer Islanders and Yap Islands' representatives regarding the need for a district-wide legislature. Later, the principal members of this Outer Island election committee again returned to Colonia to participate in the briefing of the Yap delegation before it left for Saipan to take part in the pre-session workshop and the opening of the Congress of Micronesia. It was on this occasion that the district administrator was asked to attend a meeting between these Outer Islanders and officers and members of the Yap Islands Congress and Council. Out of the meeting emerged a formal committee "to study means of organizing the people of Yap Islands proper and the people of Outer Islands of Yap District in order to create a district-wide Legislature." [19] Four exploratory meetings, two in the Yap district center and two in the Outer Islands, were proposed. At a send-off banquet given the congressmen-elect, which the Outer Islanders attended as special guests, the keynote of the evening was expressed "in a speech dedicated to the importance of full discussion of all matters of public interest directed toward the development of a community which can work together for a better Yap district." [20]

None of the three Outer Islanders on the negotiating committee were high chiefs. Although they by themselves could not commit their respective areas, their presence signified that the paramount chiefs of the islands to the east desired these exploratory talks. Also of importance, the first Outer Island committee member, Hethy, usually represented the paramount chief from Mogmog Island of Ulithi atoll in Ulithi's dealings with the rest of the Outer Islands. This placed him at the apex of the communications and

[19] Memo DistAd Yap to HiCom, June 25, 1965.
[20] *The Rai Review,* June 23, 1965, p. 6.

super-subordinate chain of relationships which stem from Mogmog to the whole of the *Ngek* islands. Carlos Fong, a school teacher from Asor Island on Ulithi, had accompanied Hethy to Saipan as his interpreter for the Council of Micronesia and contributed the benefit of his experience gained from having lived on Yap. The third member of the negotiating committee, Chief Yalmai from Woleai, had probably been included in the original elections committee because he was fairly young in cultural terms (middle aged), recognized as intellectually quick, and experienced in dealing with Western administrators. To the negotiation sessions Yalmai brought Robert Gatelmar, a school teacher also from Woleai, who was nominally to assist him as an interpreter in English if necessary. For the Yap Islands, on the negotiating committee were Francis Luktun, Magistrate of Weloy Municipality and Secretary of the Yap Islands Council; Joachim Falmog, President of the Yap Islands Congress; and Fran Defngin, Assistant Anthropologist for the district and an accomplished polyglot able to speak Ulithian, Woleaian, and Yapese, besides Japanese and English. Luktun served as the chairman of the Yap Political Advisory Committee; the presence of Falmog and Defngin assured representation of the congress and persons knowledgeable of the administration's position. Almost as *ex officio* members, the two delegates and two assemblymen elected to the Congress of Micronesia played major roles throughout the negotiations for a district-wide legislature.

THE NEGOTIATIONS

Timing in the Trust Territory is always an approximate matter at best. Despite previous assurance to the contrary, the arrival of the field-trip ship was delayed, and Chief Hethy of Ulithi and Chief Yalmai of Woleai could not reach Yap until August 18, two days before the author's scheduled departure. Improvisation is also a necessity in the Trust Territory, and in this case it permitted a series of exploratory meetings with each of the identified groups concerned with the founding of a district-wide legislature before there was a full session of the negotiating committee. As a transitory American, the author could probe into questions so delicate that none of the parties to the negotiations would raise them, and this strategy was deliberately adopted to bring into the open all potential major stumbling blocks to the formation and functioning of a legislature for Yap. It sometimes appeared during the course of the week that this strategy might scuttle the negotiations before they even commenced. Extracts from extended field notes made during the course of the week, follow.

Morning of August 16: Met with Carlos Fong and John Rugulmar, Assemblyman to the Congress of Micronesia from Ulithi. Early in the discussions, emphasized that I considered my position to be one of raising "embarrassing" questions so as to develop a possible *modus operandi* for bringing all of the groups together. Confirmed that the Outer Islanders view entering into a political enterprise with Yap with much trepidation. The Outer Islanders consider themselves unskilled, few of them have the necessary education to "stand up" to the educated persons on Yap, the procedures of a district legislature are unknown, and they fear being "taken" should they join a district-wide legislature. Detected a great deal of suspicion concerning the motives and intentions of the Yapese.

Spent a considerable length of time explaining the possibility of commencing with limited legislative powers which could be gradually augmented as Outer Island members become more secure; partial participation and gradual step-by-step expansion; and the inclusion of protective devices such as extraordinary majority votes to adopt a measure, requiring designated subjects to run the gauntlet of two sessions, the use of local option legislation, and incorporation of provision for referendum. Kept reiterating: if the Outer Island members will determine precisely what it is they fear, it will then be possible to provide in-built protection. It is absolutely essential that they think out, talk out, work out their fears to the end that a viable legislature be structured with these in mind. If they can not do so, any legislature which might be established will prove to be only an empty shell.

They presented four problems: 1) who will carry the burden of the organizational discussions in the Outer Islands; 2) what will be the size of the district-wide legislature; 3) what should be the qualifications for members of the legislature; 4) what jurisdiction will be given to the district-wide legislature? The last was initially proposed in terms limited to taxation but was expended by the manner in which the response was phrased.

Discrete queries disclosed it is not the identity of the persons who will "sell" the district-wide legislature which is the problem, but rather a need to fix the responsibility. At the present time it remains undefined. It was agreed this constitutes primarily an administrative matter and can properly be left for the six-man negotiating committee to resolve.

The size of the legislature posed a disturbing issue. The Outer Islanders hope to receive equal representation with the Yapese—in numbers, voting strength, and importance of role to be played in the new legislature. Tentatively, each of the Outer Islands are to have at least one representative. This afforded me the opportunity to muse over the mathematics. As a minimum, seventeen or eighteen representatives would be necessary, and since some of the Outer Islands, such as Ulithi and Woleai, have disproportionately large populations, they would consider themselves entitled to more than one representative. From twenty to twenty-five representatives would be required for the Outer Islands should this formula be implemented. With the Yap Islanders having equal representation, an ungainly legislature of from forty to fifty members would result. Besides, the Yap Islands now have the predominate share of population and would probably want to have the membership of the new legislature divided proportionately between the two areas. Would the limited resources of the Yap district permit such a large legislature, with its per diem expenses, transportation costs, and salary for each member? This portion of the discussion ended with Fong and Rugulmar suggesting that possibly a twenty-member body might be the solution, with ten from the Outer Islands and an equal number from Yap. More extended consideration remains warranted.

The reference to qualifications for members was primarily one of exploration. They think the age of twenty-five too young, and thirty more in keeping with the Yap district folkways. Residence would be required, but qualified to mean island "identification" and not physical presence, i.e. a person born a Ulithian is to be treated as meeting the residence requirement even though he has not resided on that atoll for a long period of time. A woman cannot be elected from an Outer Island, but they concurred it would only be superfluous to incorporate this as a limitation in any proposed charter. I inquired about provision for the participation of Outer Island chiefs. They were generally of the opinion that many of the Outer Island chiefs are too old and inexperienced in modern ways to permit their automatically becoming members with full voting rights. On the other hand, allowing them to appear as discussants might be adopted should this prove essential to eliminating opposition from their quarter.

No hesitancy was manifest in assigning the new body jurisdiction comparable to that exercised by the other district legislatures, except for taxation. Taxation is a stumbling block. The Outer Islanders are being taxed without knowledge of the proceeds' distribution, and this has caused considerable suspicion. They want all taxes clarified and revenues allocated according to the source of collection. I pointed out that the major sources of taxation now and for the foreseeable future will be on the Yap Islands, and a policy of allocating revenues according to source of collection would be to Yapese advantage. This presented a new perspective. Left this issue with the impression that the tax levied on goods purchased by the Outer Islanders symbolizes the "trickery" which Outer Islanders believe surrounds dealings with the Yapese. This may prove to be the stumbling block over which the legislature may falter.

Languages used for legislative proceedings will present a difficult problem. Initially, at least, must anticipate translation into at least Yapese, Ulithian, and English. This will slow down proceedings until English can be used as a common language.

Pushed into the sensitive area of housing and food and confirmed that the facilities at Madrich are considered inadequate and would reflect poorly upon the status of an Outer Island legislator should he have to reside there while attending the district legislature. They responded warmly to the suggestion that, in place of receiving food by way of a gift from the Yapese, arrangements be made for Outer Island legislators to purchase all their staples. Changes of this nature would help in erasing intimations of subordinate status.

Closed the meeting with the warning that I proposed to ask similar "embarrassing" questions to all other groups and that they should discount any rumors which might arise suggesting that I was denigrating the Outer Islanders. Their response was immediate and warm: these issues ought be raised and resolved before any district-wide legislature was formed.

Afternoon of August 16: Meeting with Executive Committee of the Yap Islands Council; also attending were the two delegates to the Congress of Micronesia, the assemblyman from Yap Islands, and a few others. According to the chiefs, a mistake was originally made in chartering the Yap Islands Congress. It was intended to be a district-wide body, and the chiefs of Yap were willing then and desire now to have such a legislature.

Asked if the Yapese were prepared to treat the Outer Islanders as equals in a legislative body. Do not the Outer Islanders have lower status and are they not considered inferior to Yapese? The response was a denial. Once the relationship between the two areas meant the Outer Islanders were subordinate to the people in Gagil; this was traditional but no longer true. I shifted the approach by asking how the chief and people of Gagil would react to the Outer Islanders' receiving equal treatment. This evoked the answer that the Outer Islands are now independent of Gagil. Comparable queries produced the same response: if the people from the Outer Islands think they are being treated as inferiors, it is in their minds and is not intended by the Yapese. Upon my pointing out that the arrangements provided for Outer Islanders visiting Yap reinforce this feeling of inferiority, the reply brushed this aside: this is a matter which can be handled after the new legislature begins functioning. All responses were premised upon legal equality, and the participants either deliberately or possibly unconsciously ignored all differences of social status between Yapese and Outer Islanders.

Switched to a different area by inquiring if the Yap Islands Council was willing to accept a secondary role upon the formation of a district-wide legislature. The latter inevitably would result in downgrading the importance of the council, and the Yapese chiefs might lose some of their influence. For one thing, the legislature would then have to deal with two sets of traditional chiefs.

"Yes, we are willing to take a back seat. We are willing to become a municipal council." Now for the first time was revealed the proposal of the Yap Islands Council. The council would be reorganized to be composed of ten members, one from each of the ten municipalities. The council would then be incorporated as the Yap Island Municipality. As a group, the councilmen would exercise legislative power; as individuals, they would carry out and execute the municipal ordinances they adopted as well as all laws applicable to the Yap Islands which might be passed by the legislature. Local matters would again be returned to the council and, in effect, the ten municipalities would become boroughs, each under the control of its councilman. An ingenious proposal, but I did not know whether the administration would approve this commission form of local government. I was authorized to sound out the administration's reaction.

Inquired about representation. The reply disclosed that this had already been discussed and a formula carefully worked out. Representation would be based upon population, and both Yap and the Outer Islands would receive their proportionate shares. They had in mind a legislature of about eighteen members, ten from Yap and eight from the Outer Islands, with one representative to 379 people on Yap and one member for every 310 people on the Outer Islands.[21] Pointed out that at the moment the Yap Islands have a majority of the population but that the Outer Islands are growing at a faster rate, and in the not too distant future, use of a population formula would leave the Yap Islanders with only a minority of the membership. This contingency apparently had not been contemplated, but they did not seem to be perturbed by the possibility of Outer Island control of the district legislature.

From this it was possible to digress into a discussion of building protections into the structure and processes of a legislature and of the various forms that such protections can take. Covered much the same ground as this morning.

The potential problem of the Outer Islands chiefs' unwillingness to approve the founding of a district-wide legislature unless they can personally participate was raised, only to be met by the council's refusal to face up to this contingency until it arises. The Outer Islands chiefs ought to have confidence in their representatives, and this response closed the matter insofar as the councilmen were concerned.

In this and other matters, either because they do not wish to anticipate difficult questions or because this type of advance strategic planning is foreign to traditional ways, I was unable to engender proposals for solutions to potential problems. Possibly, with regard to the Outer Islands chiefs, they are of the opinion it is impossible for these aged gentlemen [22] to contemplate an active role in any legislature.

Morning of August 17: Meeting with representatives of Yap Islands Congress, plus all Yap delegation to the Congress of Micronesia other than assemblyman from Outer Islands. The negotiating committee does not have as firm a mandate as I was led to believe. When this six-member committee convenes, the Yap Islanders are to cover such matters as how the Outer Islanders were taxed without being members of the Yap Islands Congress. Out of this and the discussion of comparable other items may come a successful

[21] Population data in the Trust Territory are always approximate. The author therefore requested population statistics of the district administration and used the 3,982-Yap, 2,456-Outer Islands data supplied for further negotiations.

[22] A survey of thirty-five chiefs in the Outer Islands disclosed a *median* age of fifty-nine years, with one-fourth over seventy.

culmination of legislative negotiations, but much spade work remains to be done before the Outer Islanders will be mollified.

Representatives of the Yap Islands Congress confirmed there are some subject-matter areas which are solely within the prerogatives of the Yap Islands chiefs and are not considered part of the jurisdiction of the congress. For example, fishing rights and reef-land usage are not proper subjects for it to consider. This permitted discussion of means by which the jurisdiction of the new legislature could be limited or other safeguards inbuilt; developed this much in the fashion as in the previous meetings.

Although they, too, contemplate the district legislature's being apportioned upon population, unlike the council, they have not developed a formula for representation other than that the Yap Islands should receive a majority. That in the not too distant future the predominance of population will lean toward the Outer Islands has not been foreseen. They volunteered the displeasing (to them) prospect of an Outer Islands majority allocating tax revenues primarily collected on a Yap Islands' base. The discussion ended inconclusively.

Upon inquiring whether the chiefs would have to be accommodated in the new district-wide legislature, received a negative response. "The chief represents land, and the elected representatives represent the people, and there is no place for the chiefs in the legislature." Upon suggesting that the cooperation of the Outer Islands chiefs might not be obtained unless they were assured some role in the new legislature, was met with the rejoinder that if the chiefs want to take part, they should run for office. On my remonstrance that one with chiefly position would hardly run the risk of standing for office, was informed that it is impossible for a chief not to win.

Discussion next moved to the reactions which might be anticipated from the chiefs whose status and power would be implicitly threatened by the institution of a district legislature whose members were selected by secret ballot. Some of the members saw this only as a continuation of the undermining of chiefly positions which has been progressing since the American administration began. Others felt that a representative system, on its face, is not fundamentally opposed to Yapese tradition. Yapese chiefs have long used "spokesmen" to represent them. This has been adapted since German times to deal with the administrators of the metropolitan nations which have exerted jurisdiction over Yap. Today, the persons elected to the Yap Islands Congress, and those serving on the Yap Islands Council, are referred to as "chief of the white men" to differentiate them from chiefs with hereditary status chosen pursuant to Yapese custom. Under the circumstances, the mere introduction of a representational system does not appear to pose as great a threat to the position of the Yapese chief as it might seem to the outsider. True, over the long run, the people may refuse to vote as they are instructed by their chiefs, and a conflict would then emerge into the open. The legislature for the district will continue to take into account the views of the chiefs and will not lightly disregard them.

There will be no problem in cutting down the size of the present Yap Islands Congress when fewer than the present twenty can be accommodated in Yap's delegation to the new district legislature. Currently there are many people holding office in the congress who did not desire to become members but were more or less forced by their chiefs or by pressure from the people of their locale to stand for office. They would welcome the opportunity to withdraw gracefully.

A long discussion in Yapese followed my query about the relationship which today exists between Yapese and Outer Islanders. I had preceded this by an introduction stressing that equality of status in the legislature is essential for its success. As in the meeting with the Yap Islands Council members, the response almost unanimously denied that the Yapese think of the Outer Islanders as inferiors; they are not treated as inferiors; the only circumstance in which this might occur is in contact between peoples from Gagil and the Outer Islanders, with the former still remembering the super-subordinate status that once existed. In rejoinder, referred to the housing facilities at Madrich and the complaints about the provision of food for Outer Islanders temporarily on Yap. Their explanation was historical. Once Gagil had an obligation for both sheltering and feeding Outer Islanders, but now the responsibility is borne by all of the municipalities. Any inadequacies existing have nothing to do with the Yapese considering the Outer Islanders to be of lower status. Once again there was a reluctance to face the symbolic significance of Madrich and the other aspects of life surrounding Outer Islanders' residence on Yap as indicative of their status.

The Yap Islands Congress sees the new legislature as tending to district-wide matters, with Yap affairs left for a local municipal government. They had not anticipated the Yap Islands Council's being chartered as a municipal government but have no opposition to this happy solution for the growing rift they recognize developing between them and the council.

Morning of August 18: Contacted by one of the members of the Congress of Micronesia who advised me of a visitation from a member of the Yap Islands Council. Should not some people from Gagil, possibly the chiefs, sit in with the Outer Islanders during the negotiations, or possibly meet with them ahead of time to assure them that they can speak freely? Although it could not be confirmed, the impression was left that this suggestion originated in Gagil. The delicacy of the proposal was apparent: the offer might be sincerely intended to strengthen the negotiating position of the Outer Islanders by demonstrating that they should not feel constrained in any way, but it also carried the implication that without such expression, Gagil retained rights of control over the old empire. It was left to me to handle, on the grounds that if either the Outer Islanders or the chiefs of Gagil took umbrage to whichever way it was resolved, the blame could be put upon the blunderings of an American. In this way, the legislative negotiations could be saved the interjection of what otherwise could constitute an awkward issue.

Afternoon of August 18: First meeting with full Outer Islands delegation, accompanied by the assemblyman to the Congress of Micronesia from Ulithi. Opened the discussion by inquiring why the Outer Islands are now interested in a district-wide legislature when in 1963 they showed no desire to join. Response was that they were not opposed in principle to such a legislature but did not approve of the charter that was proposed at that time. They had considered themselves uneducated and also uninstructed in the manner in which the Yap Islands Congress functioned. Besides, the representation which would have been afforded—five Outer Islander members to the Yap Islanders' nineteen—was unacceptable.

Bases of representation were discussed but no formula arrived at. All that was disclosed was a desire on the part of the Outer Islanders to have a greater share in the formation of laws which are going to affect them. On the other hand, there exists a good deal of uncertainty, if not fear, about setting up a district-wide legislature. Without an extensive educational program in the Outer Islands, explaining the functions of a legislature, what it does and how it operates, and specifically what the legislature for Yap will accomplish, they do not believe full cooperation by the Outer Islands is possible. All this was tangential to the question of representation but was the closest the members came to answering my queries regarding the apportionment of a district-wide legislature.

The question of whether the chiefs are to have a place in the new legislature engendered a burst of animated discussion among the Outer Islanders. The consensus appeared to be that it is not feasible to plan a district legislature without including the chiefs. The alternative of directing their attention to running the municipal government, which is being proposed for the Yap Island chiefs, would not be an acceptable substitute. The Outer Islands traditional leaders will have to be accommodated in some way. This might be as in the Palau legislature where the chiefs are allowed to debate but not vote, and there is some sentiment for copying the Marshall Islands Congress which permits the chiefs to exercise voting rights.

The ambivalence of the Outer Islanders toward the formation of a legislature continued to crop up. Do the Outer Islands have to join a district legislature? What will happen if they turn down this bid? What is the administration's position? Suppose the process is deferred three or four years, or indefinitely, while an educational process is set up in the Outer Islands to prepare the people there for playing a full part in the legislature? More systematic observation of the Yap Islands Congress is needed, as no one from any island but Ulithi has attended and the Ulithians understood little and were unable to convey to the people back home sufficient information to put them at ease.

I responded by referring to the new tax laws just passed by the Congress of Micronesia which will provide revenue for appropriation by all of the other district legislatures, but in the case of Yap, the Outer Islands' share will be allocated at the discretion of the district administrator. This encountered a dignified rebuff. As spokesman for the Outer Islands, Chief Hethy declared they do not contemplate entering into a district-wide legislature just to benefit from money due them, nor do they expect the Yapese to opt for such a legislature for the purpose of obtaining congressionally provided funds. "What is important in building a legislature is a matter of people treating people properly and correctly and not just getting money." Pretty much my own words thrown back at me, but in a different context!

Additional meeting to be held tomorrow morning at which the Outer Islanders will put together a possible agenda for the joint negotiation session tomorrow afternoon. Suggested they familiarize themselves with the proposed charter of 1963, as this touched upon most of the matters which would have to be included in any charter, although specifics could of course be varied.

As the meeting was breaking up, one of the Outer Islands representatives volunteered the observation that the strategy of discussing the formation of the legislature with each of the groups separately may possibly have done more harm than good. He implied that more problems may have been raised than can be resolved. This permitted me to reiterate that I was not touching upon sensitive areas to hurt feelings, or exacerbate tensions, but that if there is to be a successful legislature, all members must participate as equals, and this will be furthered by the elimination of those aspects which symbolize status differences. Without an open and frank approach, the causes of insecurity will not be removed. Rather doubt that the other Outer Islands representatives look upon my presence in the negotiations with the same suspicion —tomorrow will tell.

Morning of August 19: Only Fong and Gatelmar from the Outer Islands delegation attended. Both speak English, so meeting proceeded more rapidly. Much of the ground of yesterday afternoon's meeting recovered. At their request, went over 1963 proposed charter, section by section, explaining terms and furnishing illustrations of alternative provisions which might be substituted. Remainder of morning spent in philosophical discussion of political and social change, acculturation in Yap area, and possibility of preserving indigenous ways in a modern world. Made strong pitch for the need to identify the traditional ways they desired to save and to take positive steps to do so, instead of allowing them to die with the old men.

Afternoon of August 19: Meeting with full negotiating committee around table in district headquarter's social club; assistant district commissioner and most of Yap delegation to Congress of Micronesia also in attendance. Desultory small talk, with embarrassed pauses while waiting for someone to open session. Finally President of Yap Islands Congress thanked me for holding preliminary conferences. Now did I have anything to propose? Thanked him, deliberately refrained from structuring meeting, and in effect threw burden back on him. He tried same ploy with assistant district administrator, who replied in kind. Same effort repeated again with similar parrying. For the next half hour, Yapese members presented the advantages of forming a district-wide legislature, discussing this among themselves as much as directing their comments to the Outer Islanders, while the latter listened and said nothing.

Finally, as spokesman, Chief Hethy placed on the table the position of the islands to the east. The Outer Islanders had not absolutely refused to join a district-wide legislature in 1963. They would not accept *that* proposal. They would not be here now unless some need for action was felt. The Outer Islanders are generally interested: however, they are uncertain about participating, lack qualified potential members, and are uninformed as to the advantages which would flow from belonging to a district-wide legislature now.

This encouraged a series of responses which referred to the lack of parallel acquaintance with legislative forms and procedures experienced by the Yapese when the Yap Islands Congress was first formed. The members of the Yap delegation to the Congress of Micronesia alluded to a similar situation accompanying the creation of their congress. The Outer Islands are not unique. For the advantages which can be gained from a legislature, the accomplishments of the Yap Islands Congress were paraded, including the Outer Islands' enjoying broadcasts from the radio station at Colonia, which the congress has helped fund. Taking part in a district-wide legislature will permit them to achieve Outer Islands objectives, instead of having to petition the district administrator, as is now the case. The Outer Islands delegation appeared convinced.

From this, the negotiating conference moved on to a related subject. As phrased by Chief Hethy, the Outer Islands still speak through their chiefs. How can they send representatives to a district legislature who can "speak" for the Outer Islanders until their people from the islands understand why a legislature is necessary and why representatives must come to Colonia? This pointed up the necessity for an educational program designed to acquaint the Outer Islands leaders with the workings of a legislative body and the advantages to be gained by joining in a district-wide legislature.

Discussion then ranged over a number of matters, encompassing both broad aspects of the benefit to be achieved through the Yap district's having its own legislative body and narrower considerations, such as the procedures for the enactment of bills and the operation of the legislature vis-a-vis the administration. From the afternoon session emerged five positive decisions, arrived at in the order listed:

1. There is a definite need for and there should be a district-wide legislature.

2. The Outer Islands chiefs must be educated to appreciate the reasons for establishment of such a legislature.

3. The meetings of the negotiating committee should be formalized by the keeping of records.

4. To facilitate the establishment of a district-wide legislature, the paramount chiefs of the eighteen Outer Islands should be invited to travel to Colonia a few days prior to the opening of the Yap Islands Congress in November. At that time, the members of the negotiating committee should explain the reasons for setting up a district-wide legislature and the Outer Islands visitors could be prepared for understanding the procedures of the Yap Islands Congress. Upon the convening of the congress, the chiefs should sit as observers. From this experience they ought gain some comprehension of the workings of the legislative process and of the need for expanding the legislature to include the entire district.

5. The high commissioner should be requested to loan a member from his Political Affairs staff to sit with the negotiating committee and to assist at the proposed November session.

The problem of language complicated the conduct of the meeting, as sometimes matters had to be translated from English into Yapese, and from Yapese into Ulithian, and then the reverse. The Yap Islands members carried the burden of the discussion and, typically, the Outer Islanders were very reticent. Befitting his status, Chief Hethy spoke for the latter, whereas all of the Yapese freely took part. As the discussions continued, no mark of personal subservience was demonstrated, and the members shared each others' cigarettes, lime for betel-nut chewing, and as betel-nut supplies ran low, nuts as well. By the time the meeting adjourned, a sound basis had been laid for future negotiations and good rapport established, which should carry the negotiations through the more difficult periods which lie ahead.

Morning of August 20: Meeting of negotiating committee, with outside participants present. The minutes of the previous meeting were carefully corrected so that they express the five agreements reached the previous day. The subject of representation had been suggested as one which ought to be clarified early in the negotiations, and for the opening half hour the Yap Island members spoke to this subject before the first comment was offered by the Outer Islands. I was asked what would be the approximate representation for each of the two areas if the legislature were apportioned upon population. Responded that a distribution between the two regions in the ratio of roughly about 4 to 2.5 would justify an appointment of some ten or twelve representatives for Yap to about eight from the Outer Islands. Each delegation's members then started canvassing among themselves the manner in which its share might be divided. The Yap Islanders were of the opinion that each Yap municipality must have at least one representative, which left some of the more populated municipalities on Yap with inadequate representation, unless thirteen legislators were allowed to the Yap Islands. On the other hand, the dispersion of the Outer Islands makes it difficult to combine them into representative districts for the purpose of electing a single representative. In a magnanimous gesture, the Yap Islands delegation proposed that its share be limited to twelve members and that the Outer Islands be entitled to nine, with which the Outer Islands delegation expressed satisfaction.

On the conclusion of the meeting, it was agreed that Chief Hethy, via the broadcasting station at Colonia, would explain to the people in the Outer Islands all that had been decided. He would then accompany the field-trip ship to make arrangements for the eighteen paramount chiefs of the Outer Islands to come to Yap late in October, preparatory to the next stage in setting up the district-wide legislature. The assistant district administrator would request the high commissioner for funds to finance the visit of the Outer Islands chiefs. The groundwork had been laid, and everything pointed to a successful conclusion.

THE AFTERMATH

Chief Hethy was true to his word and broadcast in Ulithian to the Outer Islands over the Yap radio station. As the representative of the paramount chief of Mogmog, he accompanied the next field-trip ship to each of the islands on the eastern run, to acquaint the people with the details of the negotiations for setting up a district-wide legislature and to alert them to send representatives to the meeting on Yap scheduled for sometime in late October. In his sessions with the chiefs of the various islands and their representatives, he shared honors with Assemblyman Rugulmar who, as Solon for the Outer Islands District, explained what had transpired at the first meeting of the Congress of Micronesia. In their wake, the two men left little eddies of action, each in its own way illustrating accommodation of the traditional leadership to the introduction of a new political institution. What is related here is the account of the succeeding deliberations of Woleai atoll, the most heavily populated of all the islands of the old Yap empire, in which Chief Yalmai, as one of the Outer Islands delegates, played a stellar role.[23]

Before Hethy left Woleai on the field-trip ship, a meeting was arranged on Utagai, traditionally the highest ranking island of the atoll. The personal attendance of most of the ranking chiefs and senior representatives from the important clans evinced the political importance ascribed to the meeting. Fittingly, it was held in the canoe house of the highest ranking village. As is proper etiquette before senior chiefs, Yalmai professed not to understand fully what had transpired on Yap, and then from his notes provided a running account of the negotiations, down to the possible formula worked out for representation in the proposed district-wide legislature.[24] Also appropriate to the role of the "white man's chief," he emphasized that no binding commitments had been reached and that further sessions would have to be held. For this purpose, each of the Outer Islands chiefs was invited to come to Yap to consider the formation of the legislature and express his wishes regarding participation. From this point on, discussion centered around who was to be sent to the October meeting and what they were to do when they reached Yap. Yalmai and his interpreter, Gatelmar, would return to Yap, accompanied by representatives from all of the other islands. Each area would "decide for itself," a phraseology which indicated that the ranking chiefs would not attend and that persons considered more qualified in the ways of Western government would be co-opted.

At this initial meeting, the matter of taxes figured prominently, and some wondered aloud whether taking part in the new legisla-

[23] For this portion of the account, the author is indebted to Dr. William H. Alkire, who was engaged in field research on Woleai at the time the events here related transpired.

[24] He computed the formula for representation at about one member for every 300 population and had worked out each island's representation, as Lamotrek one representative, etc.

ture would have as its only consequence heavier taxes for the Outer Islands. There was agreement that, unless the representatives who attended the next meeting understood everything that was transpiring, they were not to affix their signatures to any paper. Here reference was made to the previous attempt to have the Outer Islands join in the formation of a district legislature and to their refusal to commit themselves because they did not understand all the ramifications. The problem of the language to be used in the legislature figured prominently, and the view was expressed that perhaps it might be best to delay becoming part of a new body until enough people who could speak English well were graduated from school and they could be sent to sit in the legislature. No particular disagreement was voiced to the apportionment formula presented by Yalmai, nor to the aliquot allocation of representatives suggested. Rather, attention turned to how islands grouped for the naming of more than one member in the legislature should divide the representation among themselves. The balance of the session was devoted to an ungermane matter, the failure of Woleai students on Ulithi to pay the deference due by custom to the Ulithian chiefs.

A second meeting held about a week later on Woleai Island, of the atoll of the same name, was called to further consider the unresolved problem of the students' objectionable conduct on Ulithi. It was feared that the Ulithi chiefs would take offense and that this would redound to the detriment of the islands farther east. At this time it was ascertained that all of the islands had not yet chosen their representatives for the Yap conference, and it was agreed to hold a third session on Utagai to firm up plans. During the course of the Woleai meeting, one chief expressed the view that the representatives should be instructed to follow the lead of Mogmog at the Yap conference. However, others wanted more information on the founding of a district legislature before agreeing to this course of action. The meeting served to place pressure on the chiefs of the various islands to end their procrastinating. On one of the Woleai islands not converted to Christianity, the island's three supernatural functionaries met the next day to choose by divination of knots between the three candidates tentatively selected as most competent to act as representative.

The final gathering took place a week later, again on Utagai, but at another canoe shelter close to the house of a senior chief too feeble to attend the original meeting. Signifying the importance of the occasion, most of the chiefs and senior clan representatives were present. All islands had designated their representatives to go to Yap. Except for Yalmai, no chief would be sent; instead, they had selected senior men from chiefly clans or individuals who had served as "chiefs of the white man." All were fairly young by Outer Islands standards and would be comfortable in dealing with American administrators on Yap.

At the first meeting, Yalmai had been careful to state he had made the point at the Yap negotiations that, should the Outer Islands join in a district legislature, this would not constitute a bypassing of the Outer Islands chiefs. The chiefs themselves at the third gathering referred to this subject, emphasizing that sending representatives to the forthcoming Yap conference in no way reduced their authority. "We are still the chiefs." Implicit was the warning that the local political organization was not to be undermined by the structuring of any district legislature.

For the first time a problem which probably had been troubling the chiefs was openly discussed. Would not this contemplated trip parallel the old political canoe voyages and would not the Yapese expect the representatives to fulfill all of the customary obligations and behave in traditional ways? Carefully, the old *sawei* relationships were sketched for the instruction of the representatives: how they were to dress (not wear red, a color traditionally reserved for Yapese); who were their counterparts in Gagil with whom they were to associate, to whom they were to present gifts, and from whom a reciprocal gift could be anticipated; and other pertinent protocol. Some of the younger men attending protested that the legislature was a completely new organization, an American innovation, so traditional relationships should play no part. The response was a cautious "maybe," but it was best to play it safe so that the Yapese would have no occasion to become angry. Since most of Woleai is Catholic, gifts for Yap's religious functionaries could be dispensed with. And on this note, harkening back to the traditional ties and behavior patterns of the old Yapese empire, the meeting ended. Independently, one of the islands which had not adopted Christianity decided also to make a religious offering at Fais, to which it had close ties, if the field-trip ship stopped there and did not sail directly to Yap.

Via radio the Outer Islanders then heard that transportation for the representatives to Yap would be delayed. A few days later came the news that the whole undertaking would be postponed at least a half year until the spring. There were insufficient funds in the high commissioner's budget to finance the transportation and keep of so large a group of representatives. Since the revised date was set for far into the future, the subject of the Yap meeting dropped from discussion. At the end of the year, an American making a flying trip to Woleai atoll was asked what had happened to the legislative discussions on Yap and why they had been broken off. To persons familiar with the past administration of the Trust Territory, such an abrupt ending to even the best laid of plans will be recognized as not too unusual an occurrence.[25]

[25] At the end of 1967, the Yap Islands Legislature invited the Outer Islanders to attend the May, 1968, session to work out the details for a district-wide legislature (*The Rai Review*, Dec. 1, 1967, p. 1); and the upper house of the Congress of Micronesia had previously requested the high commissioner to expedite the formation of the legislature (S.R. 24 of 1967). In May, 1968, a district-wide legislature was tentatively agreed to, with the Yap Islands to be represented by twelve members, and the Outer Islands by eight.

CHAPTER 7

Antecedents to the Congress
of Micronesia

THE ANTECEDENTS to the Congress of Micronesia may be viewed from a number of vantage points, some within, and others external to, the Trust Territory. The preparing of the Micronesian people for eventual participation in a representative body of their own choosing, its jurisdiction encompassing the entire Territory, may be traced back to the founding of the district legislatures and even the precursor bodies which preceded them. More immediate, the advisory all-Territory meetings which antedated the Congress of Micronesia, by bringing together Micronesians from the several districts into cooperative activity, suggested an identity across district and cultural boundaries which eventually was to bear fruit in the nascent nationalism of the first congress. And from a third internal perspective, it was the corpus of Territorial law which provided the vehicle for the new congress' exercise of powers, so that the very evolution of Territorial law assumes significant pertinence.

Looking at the congress with a view to the influential events which occurred outside of the Trust Territory, both national and international focuses of attention appear. The indecision and ultimately the failure of the Congress of the United States to provide by statute for the organization of the Territory's government eventually shifted the responsibility for structuring the new congress onto the executive branch of the U.S. government. To a degree, though, this effort at organic drafting left its mark on the provisions engrafted into the Secretarial Order creating the Congress of Micronesia. On the international scene, the drama of establishing a Territorial legislature unfolded against the backdrop of the United Nations. Both American and Micronesian principals played their roles, sometimes improvising their lines, under the scrutiny of world attention, and there is the suggestion that the nature of the audience helped hurry the concluding act.

These various factors, although separately identifiable, jointly exerted their impact in the structuring of the Congress of Micronesia. The Secretary of Interior in 1951 by letter delegated his legislative authority over the Trust Territory to the high commissioner. The following year, in referring to this, Mr. Emil Sady, then chief of the Pacific Islands Branch of the office of Territories also stated that in the use of this power the high commissioner was to be guided by the Organic Act then being debated by the Congress of the United States. The interim before the bill's adoption was to be utilized as a trial period to test the adequacy of the governmental structure which the Federal measure proposed for the Trust Territory.[1] A decade and a number of Secretarial Orders later, after the high commissioner had materially expanded the body of Territorial law through orders of his own issuance, a presidential commission cast doubt over whether law-making power had ever been properly vested in the high commissioner. Meanwhile, the United States Congress had long since abandoned its efforts to enact organic legislation for the Territory. Mr. Sady's remarks illustrate the interrelation of the many formative influences impinging upon the establishment of the Congress of Micronesia, and that it is only in aid of their consideration that they are treated separately here.

TERRITORIAL LAW

On the creation of the trusteeship, July 18, 1947, Micronesia's existing body of law consisted of all local ordinances and proclamations, regulations, and orders of the former military government which did not conflict with the terms of the Trusteeship Agreement and Executive Order 9875, in which the President assigned the civil administration of the Trust Territory to the Secretary of the Navy. Proclamation No. 1 of the same date, announced by Admiral Louis E. Denfield coincident with his appointment as high commissioner, declared that existing customs, religious beliefs, and property right would continue to be respected and reaffirmed the continued effectiveness of the Navy's preexisting laws. This proclamation constituted the Trust Territory's first legislation. Thereafter, interim regulations prepared by the deputy high commissioner at Guam served as the "statutes of the Trust Territory." When the deputy was withdrawn from Guam and his staff combined with that of the high commissioner at Pearl Harbor, all further civil administration enactments were promulgated directly by the latter.

---

[1] Official Transcript of Proceedings—Conference of District Administrators of the Trust Territory Government, Feb. 28, 1952, p. C-1–4.

The first of the interim regulations bears the date of February 11, 1948, over six months after the Territory's transfer to civil administration under the Navy. Legislation for the basic provisions of government was delayed even further until May, due to a divergence of opinion over a number of matters, including the use of the secret ballot in elections. In all, the Navy had issued twenty-three interim regulations, grouped in four series corresponding to the date of the calendar year they bore, when the assignment to Interior's jurisdiction occurred in 1951. Under the Department of Interior, the high commissioner commenced the practice of decreeing Executive Orders for the administration of the Trust Territory. All of this body of executively declared law was systematized when the Code of the Trust Territory took effect in December of 1952. The code repealed "all proclamations, regulations, orders, and directives of the United States Military Government, all [Navy] Civil Administration Orders (except District Orders), and all Interim Regulations . . . not contained in" the code.[2] Until the Congress of Micronesia's enactment of Public Law No. 1–1—the adoption of an official flag for the Trust Territory—ushered in a new era, the Code of the Trust Territory with supplemental Executive Orders of the high commissioner served as the basic statutory law of the Territory.

Section 36 of the code declared that "subject to the supervision and direction of the Secretary of the Interior, all . . . legislative powers of government . . ." were lodged in the high commissioner. Actually, Department of Interior Order No. 2658, originally delegating the Secretary's powers over the Trust Territory to the high commissioner, expressly mentioned executive power but contained no comparable assignment of legislative authority. A new order published five years later (No. 2812) required the high commissioner to obtain secretarial approval of all new laws embodying important changes in policy, but except by implication, this failed to fill the original hiatus in the delegation of legislative authority. Little change was introduced by the new order, and few laws were submitted for the ratification of the Secretary of Interior before being put into effect. Following the recommendation of the Solomon Commission, early in 1964 the Secretary of the Interior further restricted the law-making powers of the high commissioner by mandating Secretarial consent for all additional laws and amend-

[2] Executive Order No. 32, promulgated by HiCom, Dec. 22, 1952.

ments to any existing law, except in emergencies. The net effect was to reduce the high commissioner's scope of action so that he was left with practically no legislating power without the concurrence of the Secretary of the Interior. Full turn around occurred with the convening of the Congress of Micronesia, for enactments of the congress receiving the high commissioner's signature may now become effective without need of any recourse to Washington.

PRECURSORS TO THE CONGRESS

During the Navy administration, Interim Regulation 4–48 set up a Legislative Advisory Committee, comprised of five members appointed by the high commissioner from among the heads of Territorial departments. Its responsibility was to draft regulations, process laws, and consider legislation it deemed desirable for the Trust Territory, as well as to discuss and advise the high commissioner on policy issues. The original design was to expand the committee by the addition of indigenous representatives, the number to be resolved by the committee, but with an equal number from each administrative district to be selected in a manner suggested by the district administrators and agreed to by the committee and the high commissioner. The committee was to "conduct studies, prepare plans, and recommend legislation from time to time to expand its functions to permit the steady evolution of this committee from an executive advisory group to be a true legislature representing the inhabitants of the Trust Territory, at which time the executive department representation will be discontinued." [3] Interim Regulation 3–50, amending the earlier enactment's provisions relative to the staff of the high commissioner, continued the existence of the committee. Appointed to the committee were heads of divisions handling native affairs, but the addition of indigenes never materialized.

Near the end of Naval administration, the naming of Micronesians to the committee was urged by the chief administrator of field headquarters, who recommended "that immediate steps be taken to extend the Legislative Advisory Committee . . . by the addition of two or three indigenous representatives from each administrative district, and all proposed laws and regulations involving general policy be referred to this enlarged advisory committee for an opinion prior to their promulgation, except in cases of emer-

[3] Interim Regulation 4–48, May 8, 1948, secs. 22, 23.

gency." [4] Even in 1952, when the five-member Legislative Advisory Committee had been replaced by heads of departments serving as the High Commissioner's Council, the idea of appointing indigenous inhabitants had not been relinquished, but with headquarters of High Commissioner Thomas in Honolulu, the operational obstacles could not be surmounted. As early as 1949 the United States had reported to the United Nations that the Legislative Advisory Committee was intended to be the nucleus for an independent Territory-wide legislature. However, the legislative process in the Trust Territory was not to evolve along a path paralleling that followed in English colonies, where the government officials sitting in the legislative council have been joined by unofficial members until the latter became the majority, and law-making power is transferred from administrators to the representatives of the locale. The promulgation of the Code of the Trust Territory on December 22, 1952, marked the demise of the Legislative Advisory Committee and of the conceptualized development of the Trust Territory it denoted.

Simultaneous with the tentative efforts along the direction of the English legislative council model, the Navy was also experimenting with what was to become the successful vehicle for the institution of a Territory-wide legislature, the representative advisory conference or council. This proved to be more in harmony with the American political idiom. After a few exploratory forays, the advisory council composed of indigenes became institutionalized subsequent to the Department of Interior's assuming administrative jurisdiction.

The first direct representation of Micronesians in a Territory-wide meeting took place in Guam in September of 1949, at the semi-annual conference of civil administrators, when administration personnel and two inhabitants from each district met primarily to discuss economic affairs. Unawed by the participation of the deputy high commissioner, members of Headquarters staff, civilians from the Office of the Chief of Naval Operations, and administration personnel from the districts, the appointed indigenous representatives asked assistance in fishing, boat building, the founding of additional industries, and the control of insect pests. The perennial issue of contention, the settlement of land claims,

[4] Quoted in Dorothy E. Richard, *United States Naval Administration of the Trust Territory of the Pacific Islands* (Washington: Office of the Chief of Naval Operations, 1957), III, 405.

was raised for discussion. The Micronesians were not content with a completely agricultural economy and sought Japanese technical assistance for a number of economic activities; they also requested expanded trade with Japan. In view of the opportunity for these indigenous representatives to communicate local attitudes and to pose the problems the various districts faced, the meeting stood as a prototype for the future Territorial legislature, notwithstanding the administration's disclaimer that the conference could not "in a strict sense, be considered a Territory-wide legislative body." [5]

Although "this first meeting of representatives from the entire area was highly successful" [6] and the results were described as "gratifying," [7] no comparable gathering was called until 1953. The pending shift of administrative responsibility from Navy to Interior furnishes a possible explanation for the failure to follow up earlier upon this initial conference. In July, 1953, "as one means of promoting the concept and practice of self-government among the Micronesians," two representatives from each of the then five administrative districts attended what was titled the "First Trust Territory Conference on Self Government" held on Truk. Any topic pertinent to "native social, economic, or political problems" [8] could be proposed for the agenda, but a review of the Conference Record reveals that the delegates devoted much of their time to prepared papers and responding to the questions the papers engendered. The conference served the purpose of mutually acquainting the participants with the governmental organization and the current state of affairs in the various districts. It was the intention of the American advisors to encourage more than an exchange of factual information, but when the conference chairman moved toward discussion of broader questions which dealt with Micronesians' playing a greater role in their own governance, some of those present protested that they were not empowered to express any view which might commit their areas. (Here was demonstration of willingness to facilitate the communication function of legislative bodies, but not to make recommendations, the beginning stage of the lawmaking function.) After the delegates were assured that they would be speaking as individuals and not as representatives of

[5] *3rd Annual Report of the United States to the United Nations, 1950,* p. 17.

[6] High Commissioner, Trust Territory of the Pacific Islands, *Objectives in the Administration of the Trust Territory* (Honolulu: [circa 1952]), p. 7.

[7] *3rd Annual Report . . . , op. cit.,* p. 17.

[8] Deputy HiCom to DistAds, Dec. 15, 1952.

their respective districts, the ensuing range of opinion revealed the confusion evoked by reference to self-government in the Trust Territory.

Both American advisors and Micronesian delegates contemplated periodic repetition of comparable conferences, but three years elapsed before another was called. The reason for this gap lay in the opinions behind High Commissioner Midkiff's remarks to the 1954 session of the Trusteeship Council that no significant results had been forthcoming from the Truk conference. High Commissioner Nucker amplified the previous statement by saying at the 1956 meeting that the Truk conference had been held prematurely, the delegates showed no awareness of Territory-wide problems, and that it was difficult for them to understand what was expected of them. Even the mechanical task of interpreting the different languages of the delegates had proven an arduous chore.

The step leading directly to the creation of a Territorial legislature was taken in 1956 when the high commissioner convened an inter-district conference of Micronesian leaders at Trust Territory Headquarters on Guam and reconvened the conference in 1957. As reported to the Secretary of Interior, "The popularity of the Inter-District Micronesian Conference among delegates and the Micronesians generally, led to the decision to schedule it on an annual basis. . . ." [9] More accurately, the need to structure a single, Territory-wide institution in which indigenes could play a prominent part dictated the decision, for the deliberations of the early meetings were unknown to the average Micronesian adult,[10] and even the delegates remained confused over precisely what was to be accomplished at the conferences. Rather, the week-long sessions supplied a badly needed conduit, outside the official channel of administrative communications, for Micronesian leaders to obtain a fuller comprehension of the Administering Authority's policies and objectives while at the same time the sessions afforded the administration a means for gaining a better understanding of district and local problems. Incidentally, informal discussions between the delegates in their hotel rooms at the 1956 meeting disclosed a determination to work toward setting up a "group representing the whole Territory" and the existence of a consensus of opinion that

[9] *1958 Annual Report of the High Commissioner to the Secretary of the Interior*, p. 29.
[10] This, notwithstanding the laborious translation and publication of the conference proceedings in the various district languages.

it was possible to do so without need to work toward a common Micronesian culture.[11]

The second inter-district conference in 1957 was described to the Trusteeship Council as "the outstanding event of the year." [12] The delegates discussed almost every major problem facing the Territory—political development, taxation, agriculture, shipping—and made a number of recommendations to the high commissioner. The conference demonstrably encouraged a useful exchange of views on common problems and prompted a feeling of Territorial unity. In their third meeting, in 1958, the delegates displayed growing concern for the objectives of the conference and tended to emphasize the broader aspects of the Territory's needs rather than the interests of their respective localities. It was at this meeting that the delegates voted to call themselves the "Inter-District Advisory Committee to the High Commissioner," signifying the flowering of their consultative function. Three years later, in 1961, they reconstituted themselves as the "Council of Micronesia," and at the same time, on the prompting of the high commissioner, chose one of their members as chairman. Coincident with the last change in name, the council selected *Robert's Rules of Order* to "govern all parliamentary procedures" [13] and began the practice of formally delivering resolutions and recommendations to the high commissioner upon their passage by the council. While American personnel continued to work closely with the council, the facts that the council cloaked itself with parliamentary trappings and, particularly, that the chairmanship was assumed by a Micronesian symbolized that power was shifting to the indigenous membership. This change was recognized by the district legislatures which began requesting that the council expedite action which they sought.

At first, the Saipanese delegates, with their area under Naval administration, attended only as observers; later they took part as full council members. Each district designated its two delegates for only a one-year term, but in 1959 the advisory body recommended that the districts extend the membership to two years and stagger terms so that each administrative district would be assured at least one experienced representative in attendance. Typ-

[11] From author's 1956 field notes of interview with informant just returned from attending the Inter-District Micronesian Conference.
[12] TCOR, 22d Sess., 894th meeting, June 16, 1958, par. 43.
[13] Minutes of the Sixth Inter-District Conference, 1961, p. 20.

ical of the Trust Territory's lag in implementation, by 1964 only half of the districts had modified their individual methods for selecting delegates. Further illustrating the diversity which persisted, the "popular election" of delegates reported in Trust Territory publications embraced everything from district-wide elections by universal adult suffrage, which in the Marshalls took three to five months to complete, to indirect choice through the district legislature, to the naming of a delegate by assembled island chiefs.

The staggering of members' terms was calculated to provide the continuity necessary to the performance of the body's new role as it gradually moved beyond the mere discussion of common problems and exchange of views, the obtaining of a better understanding of the Territorial administration, and the promotion of a greater realization of the community of interest existing among the islands of the Territory. By 1959 the advisory committee had a permanent subcommittee to investigate specific social problems during the legislative interim; "the report and success of the social subcommittee prompted the advisory committee to create an economic subcommittee in 1960 and a political subcommittee in 1961." [14] The last named subcommittee chose, as topics to be studied between the 1961 and 1962 sessions, municipal government, district congresses, and the Council of Micronesia itself. Through a personal tour of the Territory, supplemented by the use of questionnaires, the political subcommittee consulted with district and local officials about the possibility of the Council of Micronesia's serving as the "legislature" for the Trust Territory. While the administration contemplated setting up a Territorial legislature by 1965, it favored an intermediary stage in which representation on a proportional basis would become an incorporated feature of the council once the popular election of all delegates was attained. The subcommittee, however, recommended to the 1962 Council of Micronesia that a decision to function as a "true legislative body" may be delayed "too long" and recommended that another subcommittee be formed forthwith to review ways and means for facilitating the change-over. The work of this committee would then be followed by a constitutional convention in each district to approve the findings of the committee.[15]

Meeting for the first time within the boundaries of the Trust

[14] *Micronesian Reporter,* 13:2 (July–Aug., 1965), 16.
[15] "Report of the Political Development Subcommittee [to the 1962 Council of Micronesia]," Oct. 1, 1962, p. 3.

Territory, the council in 1962 responded favorably to its subcommittee's report, declared in favor of a Territory-wide legislature, and named what proved to be the initial drafting committee for the Congress of Micronesia. This new political development subcommittee, like its predecessor, toured the Territory, "meeting with the people, district and municipal bodies, public officials and even political parties as in the case of Saipan." [16] At a special session in March of 1963, the Council of Micronesia debated the subcommittee's preliminary proposals for the structuring of the congress and, in the form of a resolution, adopted thirty-five items, of which the bicameral nature of the congress was probably the most controversial. The council delegates, after reporting back to their constituents, convened again in November of 1963 in plenary session to reconsider and, in the main, to reaffirm their earlier decisions. The drafting of the final details of the new congressional charter then became the burden of the high commissioner and the officials of the Interior Department in Washington. At the November meeting, which was to prove to be the last before the Council of Micronesia was disbanded, Assistant Secretary of the Interior Carver pointed out the parallel between the unity of purpose achieved by the council since 1956 and that attained when the Continental Congress eased distrust between the merchants of Boston and the planters of Virginia before the adoption of the United States Constitution.

THE NATIONAL SCENE

Upon authorization by the Federal Congress, on July 18, 1947, President Truman approved the Trusteeship Agreement between the Security Council of the United Nations and the United States. It was contemplated that with the Trusteeship inaugurated by Executive Order, this would only usher in an interim administration "pending the enactment of appropriate legislation by the Congress of the United States providing for the future government . . ." of the Trust Territory.[17] Although the President declared provision for the Territory's administration to be "a responsibility which falls primarily upon the Congress," [18] the congressmen at first demurred

[16] *Saipan District Panorama*, Oct. 9, 1964, p. 1.
[17] Presidential Executive Order No. 9875, July 18, 1947.
[18] Public statement of President Truman issued on July 18, 1947. *Public Papers of the Presidents. Harry S. Truman* (Washington: Government Printing Office, 1963), p. 346. At least one commentator read the Trusteeship Agreement as imposing a duty upon Congress to enact laws for governing the Trust Territory. See Arthur L. Dean, ed., *Issues in Micronesia*, U.S. Paper No. 5 (New York: American Institute of Pacific Relations, 1947), p. 30.

and ultimately decided differently. During the interim of indecision, the President transferred administration from Navy's to Interior's auspices. The adoption of Senate Joint Resolution 6 in 1953, which temporarily continued the civil administration of the Trust Territory for only one additional year, evinced that the congressmen concerned had not despaired of enacting legislation prescribing the Territorial government. By 1954 the Congress collectively concluded that the Territory was unready for organic legislation; the 83rd Congress, through Public Law 451 renounced the endeavor and, instead, indefinitely prolonged the governance of the Trust Territory as directed by the President. This meant that the development of the legislative process in Micronesia was thereafter to be guided by the executive branch, under the scrutiny of the congressional committees charged with overseeing the region's administration and furnishing the financing for its government. Despite the failure of the early attempts at organic drafting, these efforts helped delineate the future course of legislative evolution and may properly be recorded as antecedent factors contributing to the founding of the Congress of Micronesia.

At the request of the President, in the summer of 1947, a special committee of the State Department began preparing a rough draft of an organic act for the Trust Territory. Pursuant to its terms, power to legislate for the Trust Territory was to be invested in the Congress of the United States. Upon consultation with the other interested Federal departments, there was objection to the fact that the governor (as the region's executive was to be named) was to be empowered to make directives having the force and effect of law. The State Department draft contained no provision for a Territory-wide legislative body, and this drew criticism on the ground that authorization ought be incorporated for a general legislative or advisory council, composed of indigenous representatives, to be founded by the governor when he deemed appropriate.

In House Joint Resolution 391 and Senate Joint Resolution 221, laid before the 80th Congress in 1948, note was taken of all these criticisms. Legislative power was still to be lodged in the Congress of the United States. Pending a Territorial legislature, the governor was to be invested with the temporary ability to promulgate regulations "to govern the administration and financing of the government of the Trust Territory. . . ." When the governor believed it practicable, he was to prepare a plan for holding an election by secret ballot, on the basis of universal and equal suffrage of "citizens" eighteen years of age or older, to select representatives for a Territorial legislature. This body was to have power to enact measures, not inconsistent with the proposed organic act, "concerning all matters relating to the government of the Trust Territory, including taxation and other fiscal matters and all matters on which the Governor may issue or prescribe regulations. . . ." [19] Impliedly, the initiation of legislation was to be lodged in the Territorial legislature, but the governor might recommend measures for legislative attention. Bills passed over the governor's veto were to be transmitted to the President, whose decision was to be final. Reserved to the Congress of the United States was the power to annul any enactment of the Territorial body. No form for the Territory's legislative assembly nor qualifications for its membership was prescribed; all the "details" were left to the criteria to be fixed by the governor's plan. Sustaining any fully operative legislating body was far beyond the capacity of the Territory's indigenous inhabitants in 1948. Just as evident, acceptance of general legislative responsibility for this distant area with its minescule population and unique problems would have unnecessarily burdened an overworked Congress.

Action was deferred until a congressional visit could be made to the Trust Territory. The subcommittee of the House Public Lands Committee, which undertook the journey toward the end of 1949, concluded that "until careful consideration can be given to the social patterns of the Trust Territory, and the manner in which these patterns can be adjusted to conform more closely to American democratic principles without destroying the local culture and customs, the Congress should not attempt to impose upon the inhabitants of the Trust Territory a rigid framework of government modeled on those of the United States Territories." [20] The subcommittee recommended only minimal organic legislation. About this time, the pressure behind a drive for organic legislation for American Samoa was being relieved by the prospect of Presidential transfer of jurisdiction from Navy to the Department of Interior, and the same possibility provided sufficient cause for deferring consideration of an organic law governing the Trust Territory.

Senate Bill No. 2992 of the 82nd Congress, together with its

[19] S.J.R. 221, H.J.R. 391, 80th Congress, 2d Sess. (1948), sec. 15.
[20] U.S. Congress, House, "Report to the Public Lands Committee on the Pacific" [Committee Print: 1950], p. 14.

companion House of Representatives Bill No. 7427, represents the high water mark in the move to have the U.S. Congress by formal organic legislation set the scope as well as the detail of structure and procedure for the exercise of legislative authority in the Trust Territory. It closely compares with the earlier drafts, but the new proposal added an extra element by directing the high commissioner "as soon as practicable [to] establish a Territorial Advisory Council." [21] Adumbrating the fuller delineation to be incorporated over a decade later in the Secretary of Interior's Order creating the Congress of Micronesia, the bill prescribed that "the Territorial Legislature shall have power to enact all measures for the Government of the Trust Territory, not inconsistent with the Trusteeship Agreement, this Act, and international agreements and laws and regulations of the United States in force in the Trust Territory." [22] If preferred, a bicameral body could be adopted. The general format of the veto provisions in the previous measure was retained, but in addition, an item veto was to be permitted. The bill even limited the powers of the U.S. Congress to annul laws enacted by the Territorial legislature to a period of one year from their receipt in Washington.

The varied influences which were contributing to shape the drafts of organic legislation brought before the Congress received their first legally effective expression in the Code of the Trust Territory in 1952. Department of Interior Order No. 2658 had directed the high commissioner, insofar as practicable, to make the interim regulations conform to the provisions of the draft organic act submitted to the Senate, so the antecedents for Section 43 of the code may be found on the congressional stage. As the Congress of the United States had yet to act on any authorization for a Territorial legislature, discretion dictated a slight modification when following the congressional model in the form of deferring the legislature's establishment until congressional concurrence was received.

Section 43. *Territorial Advisory Council.* The High Commissioner may establish a Territorial Advisory Council. He may, from time to time, assign to the Territorial Advisory Council such legislative authority as may be appropriate. At such time as the High Commissioner determines that the people of the Trust Territory have reached a stage of political development which would make it feasible for them to exercise legislative authority on territorial matters through a Territorial Legislature he shall draft proposed legislation for the establishment of a Territorial

[21] S.2992, 82d Congress (introduced April 9, 1952), sec. 15.
[22] *Ibid.*, sec. 17.

Legislature and transmit it to the Secretary of the Interior for his approval and submission to the Congress of the United States.

The portion prescribing congressional ratification was to prove
abortive, and the Congress of Micronesia owes its existence solely
to the executive branch. Fittingly, the Congress of Micronesia at
its first session repealed Section 43 of the code.[23]

The last significant effort to secure congressional assumption
of formal responsibility for structuring the Trust Territory's government was embodied in House of Representatives Bill No. 5381,
which was dropped into the hopper of the House of Representatives
of the 83rd Congress on May 25, 1953. Unlike the former measures, which the Congress regarded as "too elaborate and detailed,"
this draft "proposed more practical procedures." [24] In lieu of only
temporary legislative powers pending the setting up of a Territorial
legislature, the high commissioner now could prescribe all laws required for the government of the Trust Territory. Previous drafts
had directed district administrators to erect local advisory councils
and had allowed for district advisory councils composed of representatives selected by local bodies; whenever feasible, the high
commissioner was to have counseled with these district bodies
before issuing regulations. In this draft, provision for consultation
was eliminated. And finally, with one minor difference, it did no
more than echo the language already part of the Trust Territory
Code governing the creation of both the Territorial Advisory Council and Territorial legislature. The difference in the new bill implies
a little more urgency in setting up the Advisory Council than is
intimated by the code.

The 1953 draft contemplated only minimum restrictions on the
high commissioner's discretion in the area of legislative authority
and allowed him great flexibility in the development of policies
and institutions dictated by the growing political consciousness of
the Trust Territory's inhabitants. The following year, Congress gave
up the effort to erect even these modest limitations on executive
power. Nevertheless, the growth of the legislative process within
the Trust Territory has taken place within the broad outlines en-

[23] Public Law No. 1–6, Laws and Resolutions, Congress of Micronesia,
1965. The high commissioner did prepare a proposed Executive Order for
secretarial approval, but the Secretary elected to follow the pattern set by
Samoa and issue a Secretarial Order drafted in Washington.

[24] U.S. Congress, House, Report of a Special Subcommittee, House Committee on Interior and Insular Affairs, "Trust Territory of the Pacific Islands,"
84th Congress, 1st. Sess. (1954), p. 20.

visioned by this organic legislation placed before the Congress of the United States during the early years of the Territory's civil administration.

In 1961, a minor resurgence of interest in organic legislation was heralded by House of Representatives Bill No. 9278 of the 87th Congress. It mandated a unicameral legislature for Micronesia, to be chosen indirectly by district congresses. The high commissioner was to have had legislative powers matching those of the Territorial legislature, and in the event of conflict between the laws passed by the two branches, those of the high commissioner were to prevail. All of this was outside the pattern of the earlier drafts, and except possibly for the recognition of the legislature's need for the services of a legislative counsel, it exerted no effect upon the course of political development in the Trust Territory. No congressional hearings were scheduled on the bill nor did the House Committee on Interior and Insular Affairs ask for reports from the executive departments. The 89th and 90th Congresses passed without any attempt being made to reintroduce the proposal, and the whole matter of organic legislation for the Trust Territory of the Pacific Islands again sank into limbo.

THE INTERNATIONAL SETTING

Each year when the United States has appeared before the Trusteeship Council to render an accounting of its stewardship,[25] the question of the nature and pace of political development in the Trust Territory has occupied the attention of the council. As part of this scrutiny, individual representatives on the council frequently have offered recommendations on the establishment of regional congresses and a Territory-wide legislature. The delegation of the U.S.S.R. has perennially challenged the sincerity of the United States efforts, regardless of the political events of the year just concluded. Whether endeavoring to score propaganda points or motivated by a more genuine interest in the welfare of the Territory's inhabitants, the Russians have made criticisms and comments which have in part drawn attention to the lack of indigenous participation in the Trust Territory's government and, of later

[25] Because the Trust Territory of the Pacific Islands is designated a strategic trusteeship, all functions of the United Nations relating to the area are technically assigned to the Security Council. In 1949, examination of the United States' annual accounting of its administration of the Trust Territory was delegated to the Trusteeship Council. Upon completion of the annual review, the latter reports to the Security Council.

years, have sought to speed the implementation of the United States' program for introducing a Territorial legislature. In truth, a survey of the official record leaves the impression that the United States has endeavored to avoid announcing any but the most general of time tables for political change in Micronesia and, even so, has occasionally found itself temporarily embarrassed due to having outlined long-range plans, only to modify them later.

The unsuccessful endeavor to enact organic legislation for the Trust Territory caused the United States delegation to have to backtrack adroitly from its announced position. At the early meetings of the council, after House Joint Resolution No. 391 and Senate Joint Resolution No. 221 died in committee, each year the United States reported that the executive departments concerned were reviewing the draft of organic legislation for submission to Congress. In 1952 it was declared that the draft legislation had been prepared in the executive branch for congressional review but the latter had taken no action as yet; the United States was exerting every effort to promulgate an organic act, but it was for congress to make the final decision. The 1953 report of the Trusteeship Council to the Security Council noted that, in line with the former's recommendation favoring the enactment of basic legislation for the Territory, a draft of an organic law had been resubmitted to the U.S. Congress. By 1954 the United States delegation was preparing to extricate itself from the commitment, indicating it was preferable that the adoption of organic legislation be permitted to "come slowly and in response to a felt need" of the Island people,[26] and in 1955, High Commissioner Nucker stated it would be several years before suitable legislation could be enacted for Micronesia. The aim was to present such legislation by 1960, although the United States admitted it might even "take longer to produce a really satisfactory and workable organic law." [27]

At the 1957 meeting of the Trusteeship Council the high commissioner announced that he thought the time had come for an expert in the drafting of constitutional legislation to undertake exploratory inquiries within the Trust Territory with a view to sketching an organic law. The impact of this statement was counteracted, however, by the high commissioner's communication of the following year that the delegates at the 1957 Conference of Micronesian Leaders had failed to understand the need for such an act. Finally,

[26] TCOR, 14th Sess., 550th meeting, July 7, 1954, par. 35.
[27] TCOR, 16th Sess., 616th meeting, June 15, 1955, par. 63.

in 1960 the high commissioner advised the Trusteeship Council that "work was proceeding on the drafting of an organic act . . . which . . . would be submitted in due course to the United States Congress," [28] but that consultation with Micronesians was essential and "he did not think that the Micronesian elite had attained a sufficiently high level to make it possible to draw up an organic act forthwith." [29] The delegations of the other nations on the Trusteeship Council understood full well that the enactment of organic legislation would constitute the vehicle for structuring permanent political institutions at the Territorial level, so that the deferral of effort in this direction only intensified their more pointed interest in the Administering Authority's timetable for the appearance of a Territory-wide legislature.

In reply to an inquiry from the U.S.S.R. at the 1949 meeting of the Trusteeship Council, the United States stated that it had formulated no express plans for the development of legislative bodies in Micronesia. The following year the American delegate indicated it was his country's intention eventually to set up a competent legislative body for the Trust Territory; however, it was not known when it would be possible to launch even a legislative advisory body for the whole area. As early as 1949, the United States report to the United Nations referred to the Legislative Advisory Committee on the high commissioner's staff as the forerunner to a future legislative assembly, and this committee was again alluded to in the 1951 accounting before the Trusteeship Council. In the main, the council responded sympathetically to the contention of the United States that the planning for a Territorial congress would have to be delayed until problems of transport, communication, and ethnocentricity were settled, although by 1951 New Zealand was suggesting informal Territory-wide conferences of representatives elected by the various district legislatures then in existence.

At the 1955 meeting of the Trusteeship Council, the high commissioner, while stressing the need for making speed slowly, added that the United States delegation could not foresee the coming into being of a central legislative body "for some years." [30] The pace was quickened at the 1956 council meeting when the United States delegation committed itself by saying the common legislative body for the Trust Territory "would come into being in the foreseeable

[28] TCOR, 16th Sess., 1059th meeting, April 25, 1960, par. 25.
[29] *Ibid.*, par. 33.
[30] TCOR, 16th Sess., 620th meeting, June 21, 1955, par. 13.

future," and called attention to the significance of the forthcoming conference of Micronesian leaders on Guam.[31] The conversion of the advisory body to a permanent organization, meeting annually, supplied the necessary fulcrum for members of the Trusteeship Council to press for its metamorphosis into a fully representative, legislating body. When, at the 1957 meeting, High Commissioner Nucker stated it would be seven or eight years before the Territory would be able intelligently to elect individuals to serve on a Territorial Council, a fixed target date was now provided. Thereafter, renaming the leaders' conference to be an "Advisory Committee" was but the forerunner to further change, and the United States finally committed itself to establishing a Territorial legislative council by the year 1965.

On the international scene, the combined thrust of the Communist bloc and the newly emergent nations directed toward enabling all non-self-governing peoples to resolve their own political destinies inevitably placed the United States in a defensive stance in its ministrations of the Trust Territory. To a degree, the dependably negative comments of the representatives from the U.S.S.R. on the Trusteeship Council helped mitigate some of the pressure by alienating other delegates who otherwise might have approved the expression of more critical evaluations. Nevertheless, the general position of the United Nation's General Assembly—with its adoption of the Declaration on the Granting of Independence to Colonial Countries and Peoples, supplemented by the creation of the Special Committee (Committee of 24) on the Situation with Regard to Implementation of the Declaration—and the Trusteeship Council's increasingly searching examinations of political change in the Trust Territory assured an environment hostile to any prolonged delay by the United States in the creation of Territory-wide political institutions. The report of the 1961 visiting mission to Micronesia underlined the need for transforming the Council of Micronesia into a legislating body.

Once having fixed the year 1965 as the target date for setting up the Congress of Micronesia, the United States was perforce required to implement the intention, and America's friends on the Trusteeship Council urged even greater speed. Within the Territory, the recommendations of the Council of Micronesia were only firmed up in November of 1963. This left little time for negotia-

[31] TCOR, 18th Sess., 711th meeting, June 21, 1956, pars. 4, 39.

tions to resolve differences in viewpoint between the Council of Micronesia, the high commissioner, and the authorities in Washington and, thereafter, for the erection of the necessary election machinery and holding Territory-wide elections for members of the new congress. As the attention of the Trusteeship Council was fixed upon this crucial stage of the Territory's political development, every proposal of the Council of Micronesia not adopted by the Administering Authority potentially would be subject to United Nations review and might require American justification. Thus it was that international interest in a Territory-wide legislature for the Trust Territory lent strength to the position of the Council of Micronesia and directly contributed to the final structuring of the Congress of Micronesia. Time will weigh the wisdom of forcing such a representative institution of "national" character before the emergence of a "national" conscience.

CHAPTER 8

A Charter for the Congress
of Micronesia

THE PROCESS of drawing up a charter for the Congress
of Micronesia extended over a period of several years.[1] In mid-
1962, a preliminary draft, containing much of the detail of the
final Secretarial Order, was prepared in the Office of Territories
of the Department of Interior; after a series of meetings in the
Trust Territory, polishing of the completed document took place
in Washington in the fall of 1964. Even then the task was not
finished, and three amendments for clarification and to "provide
more felicitous language" [2] were made before the Congress of Micronesia first met on Saipan in the summer of 1965.

Micronesians took part throughout almost the whole of the process and received every encouragement to state their position fully.
By November 1963, when the members of the Council of Micronesia
met for a second time to debate an itemized outline of the charter,
its major provisions had been discussed with their constituents,
and council votes may properly be treated as not just based on the
personal convictions of the council membership but, on a number
of occasions, as premised upon expressions of the limited public
opinion of the districts. Nevertheless, a review of the whole drafting process leads to the conclusion that it was the hand of the administration which limned the original sketch and held the
drafting pencil firmly when fleshing out the document, refining

[1] This chapter is based upon the 1962 draft order prepared in the Office
of Territories, Department of the Interior, proposing the establishment of a
unicameral legislature; "Recommendations for Territorial Legislature," presented by the Working Committee of the Territorial Legislature Committee,
Council of Micronesia, Jan. 9, 1963; "Proceedings Council of Micronesia,
Third Session, March 19 to March 26, 1963," including Recommendation 3-
1963 of the Council of Micronesia, Special Session, March 1963; "Proceedings
Council of Micronesia, Fourth Session, November 12 to November 21, 1963,"
including Appendix A; *Report of 1964 United Nations Visiting Mission*,
Supplement No. 2 (T/1628); TCOR, 32nd Sess., 1245th–1270th meetings, May
28–June 30, 1965. Specific references thereto will be made only for materials
quoted.
[2] Letter of Director of Office of Territories to Secretary of Interior, May
25, 1965.

and rejecting a number of its sections, adding the myriad details, and covering its terms with a patina of legal jargon.

Baldly put, the operation in its totality was beyond the capacity of the Micronesian participants; most could do little more than concur with or demur to the more technical provisions. This realistic appraisal of the limited Micronesian role does not reduce its importance, nor is its significance thereby demeaned, for against the reasoning of a Presidential commission and the wishes of the administration, it was the council which opted for bicameralism. Thereafter, not even the strong unicameral persuasion of the 1964 UN Visiting Mission or the doubts of representatives on the Trusteeship Council prevented this choice from being implemented. Thus the ethnocentricity of the Trust Territory emerged triumphant, at least to the extent of safeguarding district identity and slowing down action by means of a conservative second house which was to protect traditional ways. No district-by-district plebiscite on whether or not to form a Territory-wide legislature [3] or "constitutional convention" to ratify the congressional charter [4] was ever held, but the Congress of Micronesia may quite properly be regarded as having been generally structured to accommodate the desires of the people of Micronesia. Undoubtedly, future modifications will for the most part be determined by the indigenous inhabitants themselves. Where this does not occur, just as in the original drafting, the Administering Authority will attempt to anticipate and make provision for Micronesian response, in an effort to avoid projecting on an international backdrop issues of potential controversy.

The Administering Authority approached the creation of a legislature for the Trust Territory as a collaborative and joint effort requiring a setting forth of views from many quarters, only one of which was the Council of Micronesia, albeit an important voice. The council did not meet "as a chartered convention with delegated authority from . . . [the high commissioner] to draft a legislative document. Rather it met purely in an advisory capacity. . . . [Legally,] its recommendations . . . [did] not carry any more weight than the other advisory expressions it [had] made on a variety of matters in the past." [5] At the October 1962 session of the Council

---

[3] Proposed by Delegate Santos at the Nov., 1963, meeting of the Council of Micronesia.

[4] See proposal of original political development subcommittee in its report to the 1962 meeting of the Council of Micronesia, Oct., 1, 1962, p. 3.

[5] Memorandum from Political Affairs Officer to HiCom, July 3, 1963, p. 3.

of Micronesia, the Interior Department's draft order was presented to the delegates for their consideration. A year later, at the November 1963 meeting of the council, the delegates had before them a background paper, prepared by the Political Affairs Office of the high commissioner, containing a range of proposals, many of which the council itself had advanced at a special session the previous March.

At this crucial November meeting, the council picked its way between the relatively few decisions before it: unicameralism *vs.* bicameralism, size of membership, age and residence qualifications for legislators, length of terms, and frequency of session. In some cases it non-committally adopted, "as submitted" from the background paper, sections which contemplated the council would decide between alternatives, in effect returning responsibility for making a choice to the administration. In several instances the council reinstated recommendations reached at the March meeting which the background paper had omitted or replaced. What emerged from the whole process was the demonstration of the council members' concern for those elements which related to district representation, Micronesian involvement in elections, the perquisites of legislative office, and the prospective balance of power between congress and the high commissioner, all matters of immediate personal interest or at least comprehensible to the members in personal terms. The details of more abstract nature, those relating to procedure, documentation, and comparable formalities, were left to the high commissioner and Washington to resolve. In this, the council members revealed their lack of political sophistication, for they failed to appreciate that it is by the turn of the technical phrase that the terrain of legislative battle is fixed and, not infrequently, victory or defeat predetermined.

The exchange of communications between Saipan and Washington also evidenced the existence of a basic difference of opinion between the high commissioner and the Office of Territories. Except for the high commissioner's finally counseling the acceptance of the Council of Micronesia's choice of bicameralism, the general aim of Saipan's attitude was to bulwark powers of the high commissioner and to permit him as great an area of future latitude as possible in dealing with the vagaries of the new congress. Washington tended to regard all this with a somewhat jaundiced eye and, in a number of instances, narrowed or even deleted portions of the charter designed to strengthen the position of the high commissioner vis-a-vis the congress. Sometimes the Office of Territories disclosed this variance in viewpoint in an indirect way by transferring authority for final decision to Washington rather than allowing Headquarters on Saipan to have the concluding word. Some of this divergence may be the result of the suggestions volunteered by the 1964 UN Visiting Mission after it reviewed the tentative draft of the congressional charter and, to a degree, may reflect accommodation by the Department of Interior to UN opinion rather than disagreement between Saipan and Washington.

From the foregoing discussion of contention it ought not be inferred that, to the extent Council of Micronesia proposals were amended or supplemented, all variances were resolved to the advantage of the Administering Authority. Sometimes the Micronesians would have limited themselves more than the final draft makes necessary. In order for the congress to conduct its business, the council would have required the presence of three-quarters of the membership as a quorum instead of the more normal majority. As another illustration, if the council had its way, the disqualification of office holders from serving in the new congress would have been effective from the very first election, rather than being deferred until 1968. In any event, for the symmetry of the document it was necessary to keep its provisions mutually consistent, and accordingly, many of the corrective modifications did not constitute matters of major substance.

For the most part, the Administering Authority tackled the problem of charter drafting warily, appreciating that the developing political self-consciousness within the Trust Territory and the international setting which subjected the stewardship of the United States to periodic scrutiny made the granting of any power irreversible. It was not just benevolent altruism which originally led the United States to undertake the governance of the Trust Territory, and matters of national security still dictated that caution not be thrown to the winds. Complementing this fact, by its actions, an irresponsible Micronesian congress with free-wheeling discretion could materially embarass the United States before the United Nations, even if the Micronesian thrusts through attempts at lawmaking were parried by executive veto. At the start, then, the new Congress of Micronesia would be equipped as well as hedged with all of those procedural requirements whose value had been proven by long American experience, and thereby aided while protected against itself during its formative period when its capacity was yet unproven.

UNICAMERALISM/BICAMERALISM

The legislative committee of the Council of Micronesia, comprised of one representative from each of the six administrative districts, was charged with the task of preparing a draft charter for the full council's deliberations. A three-man working subcommittee met at the Trust Territory Headquarters with the Political Affairs Office staff in the early part of January 1963. Aided by the Office of Territories' version which called for a single-house legislature, the subcommittee opted for a unicameral body. Unicameralism would expedite legislative activity, be less expensive and less complicated, and the "unicameral form is considered superior by modern political scientists." [6] Thereafter, the full legislative committee convened to discuss the report of the working committee but could not reach consensus over this structural issue. There was no recourse but to refer the question to the full Council of Micronesia for debate. The record of the council's March meeting discloses sharp clashes between the various delegations. Fundamental to the debate were two sets of conflicting factors: one—the interests of the large districts arraigned against the small—which became significant with representation based upon population in a single-house legislature; the other—the preservation of customary ways—to be achieved by the establishment of a second house, which presumably would be more conservative and would balance the radicalism of the lower house's younger membership. Some of the delegations even assumed the second house would be composed of those with traditional authority.[7] Ponape was a district faced with reconciling the advantage its larger population would afford in a unicameral body against the protection of traditionalism afforded by two houses, and its delegation chose bicameralism.

During the course of the debate on the nature of the legislature, the shift within the district legislatures from bicameralism to unicameralism was alluded to, the paucity of qualified persons to fill the posts of a bicameral body was stressed, and the general economy of a unicameral body emphasized. Against this were posited the advantages of safeguarding district interests through a second

[6] "Recommendations for Territorial Legislature," *op. cit.*, p. 1.
[7] Memorandum from Political Affairs Officer, *op. cit.*, p. 1.

chamber structured to represent the districts, of slowing down the legislative process, and protecting traditions and customs. Political reasons motivated the remarks of some as "they had to speak for bicameralism to placate the nobility at home, whose support they need[ed] in future elections." [8] The delegate from Yap, who had been a member of the working committee which proposed unicameralism, voted against it at the special session, announcing that after the 1962 meeting he had gone back to Yap and, after listening to the people there, favored a bicameral body. In the final ballot at the 1963 special session, only Truk and the Marianas supported a unicameral legislature.

The issue was again joined at the regular session of the Council of Micronesia meeting in November of 1963. The record of the proceedings indicates that the administration favored unicameralism but carefully refrained from instructing the delegates to vote against bicameralism. The Truk delegation reported later that it was the Yap delegation's switch in favor of bicameralism which was decisive on the first poll.[9] Thereafter, although the debate waxed hot and parliamentary maneuvering obfuscated the council's deliberations, bicameralism triumphed.

The delegates to the council had no assurance that the Administering Authority would accept their recommendation; therefore they offered as a second choice the adoption of a unicameral legislature with equal district representation. Their caution was unnecessary, as the high commissioner counseled the Director of the Office of Territories to honor the council's first choice. "The reasons impelling the Micronesians to favor the bicameral system are somewhat the same as those which impelled the inclusion of such a system in the American Constitution. This system has not proved to be a failure and I doubt if it will in Micronesia. The proponents of the unicameral system have, so to speak been undercut by our own forefathers." [10]

The heat of the debate at the March and November 1963 sessions of the Council of Micronesia, the closeness of the vote which adopted bicameralism, and the inclusion of an alternative countenancing the establishment of a unicameral legislature cumulatively had the untoward effect of encouraging the 1964 UN Visiting Mission to urge the adoption of the unicameral second choice, possibly

[8] *Ibid.*, p. 2.
[9] *Truk Tide*, Jan. 15, 1964, pp. 8, 9.
[10] Letter of HiCom to Director of Office of Territories, Dec. 18, 1963.

with eighteen or even twenty-four members. The report to the UN noted that "the Mission would be reluctant to concede that the elaborate institutions of federalism, with their inevitable balancing of forces and diffusion of power, are needed in a territory with a population the size of a small city." [11] Here the latent contradiction between UN sponsorship of self-government and the UN desire to direct that government's course became apparent. The Administering Authority remained undeterred, and indeed, as time was now becoming of the essence, it probably was too late to reverse a determination as fundamental as bicameralism.

Thus it was that the Congress of Micronesia was structured with two houses (Sec. 2) [12] and that the enactment of any legislative act requires the concurrence of both. Bills may originate in either house and may be amended or rejected by the other (Sec. 13), so there is no legal basis for ranking one chamber above the other. Nevertheless, in light of the debate which preceded the founding of the congress and the general process of bicameral American legislatures, from its very inception the House of Delegates, as the smaller of the two bodies, its members enjoying a term of office double that of the two-year General Assembly,[13] has conceived its role as that of the "upper house," with all the associated nuances of seniority.

At the special session of the Council of Micronesia which met in the spring of 1963, the delegates agreed that upon the expiration of one year, and if necessary at every regular session thereafter, the nature of the new congress should be re-examined. If the congress should so favor and the high commissioner approve, the body would then be converted into a unicameral legislature. Some of the interim drafts prepared after the March session omitted this proviso, but in the final Secretarial Order it re-emerged in the form of a requirement that the congress convene in joint session at its fifth regular meeting in 1969 to debate the continuation of the bicameral structure. The joint session's recommendation, to be adopted by a majority vote, is first to be submitted to the high commissioner and by him relayed to the Secretary of the Interior (Sec. 22). Despite the ability of the General Assembly to outvote the

[11] *Report of 1964 . . . , op. cit.,* par. 207.
[12] All section references are to Secretary of Interior Order No. 2882, dated Sept. 28, 1964, establishing the Congress of Micronesia. (See appendix.)
[13] Throughout this book, the two houses of the Congress of Micronesia are referred to by their original names, and not as "Senate" and "House of Representatives," the changed names requested by the first congress.

House of Delegates in a joint session, short of paralyzing stasis engendered by incapacity of the two bodies to cooperate, there is little likelihood that the Micronesians will reverse their original decision favoring bicameralism. Nevertheless, an "escape route" has been left open, and the last word remains with the Secretary of the Interior.

LAW-MAKING AND BUDGETARY POWERS

The Council of Micronesia directed relatively little attention to the scope of the legislating authority to be granted the new Territorial legislature. Probably this may be attributed to Interior's original draft order, which declared the body's legislative power would "extend to all rightful subjects of legislation, except that no such legislation may be inconsistent with (a) treaties or international agreements of the United States; (b) the laws of the United States applicable to the Trust Territory; or (c) sections 1 through 12 of the Code of the Trust Territory," the "bill of rights" sections of the code. The council would have supplemented this by allowing the congress to amend the charter by a two-thirds vote, followed by high commissioner approval, or as an alternative, by action of the Secretary on his own initiative. This was eventually resolved by Secretary of Interior Order No. 2882 limiting all amendments to the further order of the Secretary (Sec. 24). As noted by the Director of the Office of Territories, the Secretarial "Order in its major substantive provisions confers upon the Congress as much or more legislative authority and responsibility as was recommended by the Council." [14] In fact, greater law-making power resides in the Territory now than before the advent of the congress; by 1964 Secretarial Order all laws issued by the high commissioner required Secretarial approval, while congressional action now may become effective on executive approval without any referral to Washington.

In elaborating before the Trusteeship Council on the limitations placed around congressional action, the high commissioner opined there were then about six acts of the United States Congress which applied to the Territory, mainly relating to the authorization of Federal appropriations, the opportunity to obtain certain services furnished by the United States government, the transfer of funds

[14] Letter of Director of Office of Territories to Legislative Secretary, Mariana Islands District Legislature, Sept. 30, 1964, published in *Saipan District Panorama*, Oct. 9, 1964, pp. 2, 3.

of the former Island Trading Company, and the measure placing Micronesian radio operators under Federal Communications Commission licensing.[15] The treaties which conceivably might apply are more numerous but have little impact on the internal governance of the Trust Territory.[16]

The Secretarial Order eventually put into effect also prohibits the congress from imposing taxes upon United States or Trust Territory property or from discriminating in taxation between residents and non-residents. Inter-district import and export levies are proscribed, and import duties on goods brought into the Trust Territory are reserved solely to the Congress of Micronesia and the high commissioner (Sec. 3). As none of the general laws of the United States, such as criminal law, apply to the Trust Territory, "the Micronesian Congress therefore ... [has] a wide range of legislative authority, which ... [embraces] almost every matter affecting the general public, such as criminal law, business law, administrative services and public services." [17]

Denying the congress all power to amend the "bill of rights" of the Trust Territory Code drew objection from those members of the Council of Micronesia who favored direct governmental assistance to religious institutions. Section 1 of the code, as it then read, was highly specific in providing for the separation of church and state. The Micronesian contention was that the new congress, as the custodian of the legislating power for the Trust Territory, was the proper body to delineate the bill of rights to be observed within the area. In opposition was the position taken by the Interior Department that those portions of the code were based upon the authority of the Trusteeship Agreement, as well as the Charter of the United Nations and the Constitution of the United States: "If a change should have to be made, it would have to be made by the Administering Authority." [18] And so the matter rests, although a later

[15] TCOR, 32nd Sess., 1247th meeting, June 2, 1965, par. 38. Others besides those listed by the high commissioner are the Federal Disaster Act, 42 U.S.C.A. 1855-582, as amended, and the Economic Opportunity Act of 1964, P.L. 88-452, 78 Stat. 504.

[16] The United States lists 61 treaties and other international agreements which potentially have application to the Trust Territory; included are 18 concerning telecommunications and postal conventions; 10 related to security, mutual defense, or otherwise war associated; 7 dealing with aircraft and air transport; 5 consular conventions; 4 on narcotic control; 2 concerned with the South Pacific Commission; 2 providing for extradition; 2 on the international sugar agreement; and 11 miscellaneous. See *17th Annual Report of the United States to the United Nations, 1964,* Appendix A, pp. 165–169.

[17] TCOR, *op. cit.,* par. 39.

[18] "Proceedings Council of Micronesia, Fourth Session ... ," *op. cit.,* p. 22.

amendment to this section of the code may throw the whole question of governmental aid for religious institutions, particularly schools, into the domain of the courts.

One of the features of the congressional charter which prompted highly critical comments before the UN Trusteeship Council, as well as causing strong expressions of dissatisfaction among the members of the first Congress of Micronesia, was that relating to the Congress of Micronesia's curtailed control over the purse. Briefly put, the congress is to have full discretion over its own sources of funds and the manner in which they are to be used. Moneys derived from Federal appropriations are not subject to the congress' direction, so that when congress enacts legislation requiring the expenditure of funds in ways other than as Federally budgeted, it must also supply the necessary moneys (Sec. 5, as amended).[19] In addition, in the Office of Territories' draft constitution, it was declared that the high commissioner was to submit the Trust Territory budget to the new legislature for review. The Council of Micronesia's working subcommittee approved of this, reasoning that "advice of the Congress will be valuable to the High Commissioner and will develop Congress familiarity and experience in fiscal matters." [20] As finally included in the Secretarial Order creating the congress, the high commissioner is directed to present a preliminary budget plan to the congress in joint session for its review, prior to sending his annual request for Federal funds to the Secretary of the Interior. The high commissioner is also to transmit congressional recommendations not fitted into the final budget to the Secretary for his information (Sec. 5, as amended). By virtue of these provisions, "the Trust Territory . . . [will] probably have two budgets eventually, one which . . . [is] part of the United States budget, and another deriving from the revenue measures enacted by the Micronesian Congress itself, which would be separate from the Administration's budget and quite autonomous." [21] With a more adequate system of taxation, the amount that could be realized by the congress and be subject to appropriation might be as much as $2,000,000; at the inception of the con-

---

[19] It is now generally accepted that this does not prevent the congress from enacting legislation requiring funds for implementation, without appropriating such moneys. Under these circumstances, the high commissioner is not obligated to administer the act until funds are forthcoming from some source.

[20] "Recommendations for Territorial Legislature," *op. cit.*, p. 5.

[21] TCOR, *op. cit.*, par. 66.

gress it was estimated that the amount amenable to its direct control would be around $500,000 a year.

The budgetary system of the United States requires that the technical steps be instituted several years before the moneys are appropriated by the U.S. Congress and are ready for expenditure. The preliminary estimates for the fiscal year 1967, which would start on July 1, 1966, almost a year after the convening of the first Congress of Micronesia, would be prepared in April of 1965, and these estimates constitute the "preliminary budget plan" delivered to the congress on Saipan. However, final estimated figures might not be arrived at until after the congress' adjournment. Fitting the Congress of Micronesia into the United States budget process in a meaningful manner thus raised difficulties. Empowering the Congress of Micronesia to advise on an incomplete plan which would not be implemented until almost a full year later, and then only as modified by the U.S. Congress and the Administering Authority in consort, gave the Congress of Micronesia little of the power of the purse so essential to a system of government based upon the separation of powers. The 1964 visiting mission suggested that the Congress of Micronesia at least have final say on the budget as it went from the Trust Territory to Washington. Although changes might be made by the Department of Interior or by the U.S. Congress, "the Mission would hope for a conscious effort to trust the combined wisdom of the Territorial Administration and legislature. . . . No rights of the United States Government would be infringed, while the Congress of Micronesia would have an effective voice in budgetary policy." [22] Some delegations in the UN Trusteeship Council would have gone further, favoring a system under which the U.S. Congress would appropriate block grants for the administration of the Territory and the Federal funds would then be expended in accordance with the directions of the Congress of Micronesia. At this stage of political development, with the vast bulk of Territorial expenditures being funded with Federal moneys, the U.S. Congress is not favorably disposed to surrendering its prerogative of monetary control, irrespective of Territorial attitudes or international displeasure.

ELECTIONS

In the United States the traditional day for holding general Fed-

[22] *Report of 1964 . . . , op. cit.*, par. 232.

eral elections falls on the first Tuesday following the first Monday in November in even-numbered years. Although no compelling reason required the adoption of the same day in the Territory, from the outset, planning for the Secretarial Order called for biennial congressional elections also to be conducted on this day (Sec. 9). The special date of January 19, 1965, was fixed for the first general elections (Sec. 27), as insufficient time remained between the late September promulgation of the Secretarial Order and the normal November election day. It was also declared by the Secretarial Order that legislators are to be elected by secret ballot of the qualified voters of their respective districts, which required the employment of novel strategies so as not to disenfranchise the many illiterate Micronesians.

The Council of Micronesia debated spreading the election over a period of three weeks, but upon the objection of the Marshalls that the time span was too short to complete the polling, the delimitation was amended to be six months. All this was ignored in the drafting of the Secretarial Order, with its specification of a single election date, regardless of the fact that the physical dispersion of the Trust Territory precludes the holding of a Territory-wide election within even a 24-hour day. Through convenient interpretation of the order, the first election in 1965 actually commenced on December 28 and was not completed until January 27.

The Council of Micronesia voiced no objection to a provision in the draft order which declared that the franchise should be vested in resident citizens of the Trust Territory who are eighteen years of age and over. (Citizenship may be obtained by birth or naturalization.) These voter requirements were later made part of the Secretarial Order, along with a clause empowering the congress to prescribe additional qualifications; no property, language, or income limitation may ever be imposed, nor any disqualification based upon illiteracy, tribal custom, or social position, nor upon difference of race, color, ancestry, sex, or religious belief (Sec. 8). This long list mainly represents the effort of Washington to guarantee full adult suffrage and to guard against any of the Territory's caste, class, or status delineations' forming the basis of electoral discrimination.

The method for nominating candidates gave rise to considerable debate in the Council of Micronesia. The original report of the working subcommittee would have had nominations by petition requiring ten to twenty signatures, accompanied by a good-faith election fee of ten dollars. Objections stressed that the fee might prevent qualified persons from running. In lieu of this, it was variously proposed that nomination of candidates be conducted by district legislature or municipal council, or that primary elections be held. The whole nomination process caused concern in the minds of some delegates fearful that candidates might come from the nobility and rich or that the suspicions of the unsophisticated might be engendered by nomination through use of petition. More fundamentally, control of the nomination process promised leverage for influencing the electorate's vote, and some of the delegates fully grasped the political significance of the alternative nominating procedures under consideration. The delegates resolved the disagreement by an ambiguous decision to have the system of elections kept flexible to suit the conditions of each district. The Secretarial Order left the establishment of rules governing elections to the high commissioner for the first election and to the laws thereafter prescribed by the congress (Secs. 9, 27).

MEMBERS' QUALIFICATIONS, RIGHTS, AND DISABILITIES

A number of items in the congressional charter were by nature peculiarly within the ken of understanding of the council members. They could well appreciate the importance of the conditions to qualify for candidacy, the necessity of adequate compensation, and the need for supplementation of the legislative prerogatives with staff and powers of investigation.

As finally expressed in the Secretarial Order, to be eligible for election a prospective candidate has to be a citizen for at least five years, twenty-five years of age or over at the time of election, and a bona fide resident of the district from which he is elected for at least the one year preceding the election (Sec. 7). In an effort to secure persons with maturity, experience, emotional stability, and community respect, the working subcommittee of the Council of Micronesia favored a minimum age of thirty years and similarly incorporated a five-year citizenship period. The March special session of the council in 1963 lowered the age to twenty-five years for members of the General Assembly, but for the House of Delegates it increased the citizenship requirement to at least seven years and added the one-year residency. The working paper before the November council meeting assembled a range of alternatives, should the legislature be unicameral, but merely repeated the council's qualifications for candidates seeking election to a bicameral legislative body. Despite its prior action, at the November meeting the council voted in favor of setting the age for candidacy at twenty-five years.

To some members of the UN Trusteeship Council the minimum age of twenty-five for holding office seemed restrictively high in view of the fact that it was the younger generation of Micronesia which had greater opportunities for education. To at least one delegation it appeared more logical to place an age requirement at twenty-one. The Administering Authority defended the choice of the higher age on the ground that the Council of Micronesia "wished to give recognition to traditional patterns and at the same time to adapt them sufficiently to allow the younger generation to play a significant role." [23] The high commissioner also pointed out that in the Palau district, until recently, twenty-six years had been a minimum age for voting and the qualification for holding office had been even higher.

The Council of Micronesia delegates were also troubled by the effect of temporary absence from the district—as for schooling, business, and health—on a person's candidacy. Notwithstanding a vote that such absence not constitute a disqualification, the final Secretarial Order is silent. However, the normal rule that a person neither gains nor loses a residence while temporarily away from his domicile is probably broad enough to remove cause for concern. The requirement that in order to be eligible for election a person must have been a bona fide resident of the administrative district from which he is elected for at least one year directly preceding his election had as one of its consequences permitting a person to run from any one of several General Assembly districts just so long as residence within the administrative district could be proven. This gave trouble during the course of the elections held the succeeding January and was the subject of clarifying opinions from the office of the Trust Territory's Attorney General.

When the Office of Territories prepared its draft for consideration by the Council of Micronesia, it proposed disqualifying candidates who had been expelled from the legislature for giving or receiving a bribe and also those convicted of felony unless pardoned and their civil rights restored. These limitations were later folded into the Secretarial Order (Sec. 7). Prior to the convening of the Congress of Micronesia, the latter disqualification was

[23] TCOR, *op. cit.*, 1253rd meeting, par. 39.

amended so as to be applicable only to those convicted of felony before a Trust Territory court or one with the jurisdiction of a Federal court.[24] The language of this section was to play a prominent role in the challenge to the seating of Marianas Delegate Jose Cruz when the first congress convened.

The prohibition against a congressman's holding another position went through many reformulations before being finalized in the language of the Secretarial Order. The Office of Territories proposed to deny a congressman the right to accept any other public employment or to become a private employee. The working subcommittee of the Council of Micronesia was of the opinion that a legislator should not hold any other elected or appointed public office or be employed in any governmental capacity, for the new office was to be a "full time one." [25] The delegates to the Council of Micronesia believed this limitation too onerous and rephrased it so as to declare that individuals in staff positions [26] with the Administering Authority on Territorial and district levels, as well as the judiciary, were foreclosed from holding congressional office. The high commissioner's immediate preference was to further reduce this restriction so as only to disqualify those in Headquarters-staff positions and district judges. The delegates to the Council of Micronesia later concluded that employees holding top-level policy positions in the districts or at Headquarters, and (presumably) judges, should be considered ineligible for the office of congressman, although the proceedings of the Council of Micronesia for its fourth session are not a model of clarity in respect to this point.

During the last stages of the drafting process, this section underwent major revision on Saipan: ineligibilty to candidacy of judges and administrative policy makers at both the district and Headquarters level was to be effective at once, while at the 1968 elections to the congress a comparable disqualification was to be extended to persons serving as members of the district legislatures

[24] Order No. 2882, Amendment No. 1, dated June 10, 1965. As the Attorney General of the Trust Territory had already ruled that the original language of the order only disqualified persons convicted in a Trust Territory court, the effect of the amendment was to both broaden the original order and remove all ambiguity.

[25] See "Recommendations for Territorial Legislature," *op. cit.*, p. 5. Contemplated was full separation of powers between the three branches of government, and not any parliamentary form such as that advocated by Dr. Harold Seidman. *Congressional Record*, Senate, 86th Congress, 2d Sess. (Feb. 4, 1960), p. 2010.

[26] The disqualifying of persons holding "staff" positions was first written into the Truk charter of 1963; see pp. 82–83.

and to compensated officials of municipalities. The total impact would have been to encourage the emergence of a distinct body of politicians identified with the Congress of Micronesia, separate from other decision-makers in the executive and judicial branches of the Territorial government; it would also have placed the Territorial-level legislator apart from office holders functioning in district and municipal government. Conceivably, it could have had the unexpected consequence of opening a wholly new role for traditional title-holders not dependent upon governmental compensation for their livelihood.

All this was resolved by the Secretarial Order which deleted any reference to disqualification for municipal office holding. For other offices the limitation was not made effective until the 1968 elections, upon the premise that the "services of [the] most highly qualified Micronesian leaders who would be extremely valuable during [the] formative period of [the] Congress" would otherwise be lost.[27] In response to the 1964 UN Visiting Mission's comments, the provisions apply only to eligibility to serve rather than to run as a candidate for office (Sec. 11). The effect of this last change was to save an office holder from the necessity of resigning should he wish to stand for a congressional post; the decision can be deferred until his success at the polls has been determined. As a result of this sequence of amendments, Secretarial Order No. 2882 setting up the congress is not in accord with the position taken by the delegates to the Council of Micronesia and has drawn the strong objections of at least one elected member of the House of Delegates.[28] Delegates at the Trusteeship Council have also voiced the fear that by allowing current office holders to serve as congressmen, the independence of the congress as opposed to the Administering Authority might be compromised.

The prohibition against dual office holding is integrally tied to the compensation to be paid congressmen, as the remuneration of any currently held government post will be weighed by a prospective candidate against that receivable in the new legislative office. The fixing of the congressional salary also turns around the amount of work a congressman will be expected to perform, which may be partially measured by the length and frequency of congressional sessions. Little opportunity for employment outside of government

[27] Radiogram from HiCom to the Office of Territories, Sept., 1964.
[28] Letter of Delegate John O. Ngiraked to Secretary of Interior Udall, Nov. 19, 1965.

presently exists in the Trust Territory, so the delegates to the Council of Micronesia well understood the inter-relationship of all these factors as they debated their recommendations for the congress.

The Office of Territories' draft favored semi-annual congressional sessions and an annual salary of $2,080 a year. The working subcommittee of the council concurred on twice yearly sessions. However, it was of the opinion that frequent traveling would prevent congressmen from cultivating supplemental crops for subsistence. Also it believed that congressmen ought to be attractively paid, as an incentive to obtain qualified people and because of the responsibilities and the nature of the position. As an alternative to the Office of Territories' proposal, the committee suggested an annual compensation pegged on the Micronesian pay plan at C-3 level or above. This would be regarded as a very high income for a Micronesian. After debating the matter of compensation, the Council of Micronesia both at the March special session and the November 1963 regular session opposed inclusion in the charter of any express salary; instead, compensation should be fixed by law. This would leave the matter to the discretion of the high commissioner for the first sitting of the congress, and thereafter the congress would set its own pay. From the work paper prepared by the Political Affairs Office for the November meeting, it was clear that the Trust Territory administration approved of annual sessions with remuneration at a daily rate computed on a scale equivalent to proration of the Micronesian C schedule for each day the congress met and while the members were on travel status. In addition, members would be furnished travel and per diem at the standard Trust Territory government rate. Also, each member was to be allowed up to three weeks' travel following a regular session to report to his electorate. The final provisions of the Secretarial Order bowed to the philosophy of the administration on Saipan and incorporated into the congressional charter the figure of sixteen dollars per day for each day the congress is in session, while the members are in travel status to and from the provisional Headquarters and when on other official legislative business. The last embraces committee work in the interim between sessions. In addition, travel expenses and per diem at standard Trust Territory rates are to be allowed (Sec. 19). No compensation, travel, or per diem may be allowed in excess of the amount budgeted.

The 1964 UN Visiting Mission detected a tendency by the administration "to look upon representational duties as something of a temporary interruption in a member's normal and private activities," as "perhaps a nostalgic glance backward (and not the only one . . .) to the early days of the United States; a reminder of a more leisurely approach to legislation." It felt the circumstances of Micronesia were quite distinct. The work of a congressman was going to be of a full-time nature, and "the concept of working members should be reflected in the arrangements made for them, not least in the method by which they will be paid. . . . The Mission considers it would be much preferable to pay an annual salary plus the necessary allowances." To the objection that a per diem allowance might be needed to persuade members to attend sessions regularly, the mission noted that "a fixed annual salary together with an appropriate daily stipend during the Congressional session would seem adequate." [29]

The fixing of the congressional remuneration on a daily basis was consonant with the decision of the Trust Territory administration for the congress to have only one session a year, supplemented by such special sessions as might be called by the high commissioner (Sec. 12). This was unilaterally arrived at and in conflict with the Council of Micronesia's holding for semi-annual sessions, one of them each year convening at different places within the Territory.

Although some question was raised as to the thirty-day maximum length for sessions, the council did not feel it necessary to ask for a longer period because of the contemplated semi-annual meetings. As observed by the UN Visiting Mission, a thirty-day period is not an ungenerous figure, but remains an arbitrary one. The sufficiency of the thirty-day limitation has yet to be decided on the basis of experience. Presciently, in meeting the objections voiced in the Trusteeship Council that too restrictive a time had been allotted, the high commissioner replied that a special session could always be convened should the need arise. Precisely that occurred in 1965 when the first Congress of Micronesia did not complete its work within the thirty days afforded, and was repeated the following year. In retrospect, the same attitude which characterizes American state government, and has the executive branch look toward the period when the legislature is not in session as a respite from the interruption of legislative "interference," appears to have dictated

[29] *Report of 1964 . . . , op. cit.*, pars. 214–216.

the decision to hold the Congress of Micronesia to an annual session of but one month's duration.

Dating from the preparation of the draft by the Office of Territories, the congressional charter declared that the congress should be the sole judge of the election and qualifications of its members and that members would receive immunity for any speech or debate in the congress and be privileged from arrest during the sessions of the congress and in traveling to and from the sessions. Section 16 of the Secretarial Order also prescribes that the congress "shall have and exercise all the authority and attributes inherent in legislative assemblies. . . ." The high commissioner has assured the Trusteeship Council that this grant of power, together with the authorization to institute and conduct investigations, issue subpoenas, and administer oaths, enables the new congress to erect a complete committee structure and to carry on investigations in the interim between sessions.

PROTECTIONS FOR THE HIGH COMMISSIONER

From the outset, the council's working subcommittee looked with favor upon the high commissioner's being empowered to transmit communications and messages to the new legislative body. As there was no reason for the high commissioner to be other than pleased with this function, it remained in the final form of the Secretarial Order (Sec. 4). But this afforded no protection to the high commissioner should the congress refuse to follow his lead. At the November 1963 meeting, the council had before it a companion provision contained in the Office of Territories' draft which went much further, authorizing the high commissioner, with approval of the Secretary of the Interior, to promulgate legislation which had been submitted to the congress as "urgent" and which the congress had failed to pass either in its original form or amended in a manner acceptable to the high commissioner. The proceedings of this fourth session of the council indicate that some of the delegates were troubled by the potential scope of such designation and that the council voted to delete the power. Nevertheless, this provision borrowed from American Samoa's constitution remained in the redraft prepared by Saipan, but with the qualifier that the "urgent" label must be affixed no later than seven days prior to the end of the session.

As an additional measure of protection, the high commissioner also proposed that his power to promulgate laws when the congress was not in session be expressly recognized in the congressional charter. The exercise of this power would be dependent upon his finding that an emergency existed and that the public interest required such action. This ran counter to the prevailing sentiment in Washington, where Secretarial Order No. 2876 was soon drastically to limit the then currently possessed emergency law-making powers of the high commissioner. As was to be anticipated, the Department of Interior would not concur in allowing interim emergency power to remain solely subject to the discretion of the high commissioner, and this portion of the draft was deleted. The enactment of laws within the Trust Territory, consequently, is dependent upon the Congress of Micronesia's being in session, and even promulgation of "urgent" legislation by the high commissioner requires both prior referral to the congress for adoption and ratification by the Secretary of the Interior (Sec. 4). The high commissioner's legislative program constitutes but a fraction of the total work load of the congress, and except for "urgent" legislation, the latter is entirely free to accept, amend, or reject the administration's bills. Furthermore, as noted by the high commissioner before the Trusteeship Council, the conditions on the promulgation of "urgent" legislation "would seem to counter any tendency there might be to label ordinary legislative proposals as 'urgent!' " [30]

Throughout the period of firming up the congressional charter, all were agreed upon lodging veto power over the acts of the new congress in the high commissioner. This included partial vetoes over items of appropriation. When the delegates attending the November meeting of the Council of Micronesia discovered that reference to the veto had inadvertently been omitted from the draft before them, they voted to reincorporate it (at the same time eliminating retention by the high commissioner of the right to promulgate "urgent" legislation). In the council's version, the high commissioner would have but twenty days to act upon legislation, and should he fail to do so, a bill would become law without his signature. Upon his rejection, both houses by a two-thirds vote might repass the measure, and if this time he did not approve within fifteen days, the measure would be sent to the Secretary of the Interior. Again a time limit, now ninety days from receipt, was to be specified for Secretarial action; in the absence of a veto within that period, the law was to become effective. These time limits

[30] TCOR, *op. cit.*, 1247th meeting, par. 90.

were premised upon the district legislatures' long experience with delays at Trust Territory Headquarters following the forwarding of their resolutions to the high commissioner for review and approval.

The final Secretarial Order made the veto clause conform more closely to the usual practices of American legislative bodies. The high commissioner is allowed ten days within which to act upon a measure; otherwise a bill becomes law without receiving his signature. Should the congress by adjournment prevent the measure's return, the high commissioner has thirty days after the measure is presented within which to sign, and if he fails to act, the bill will be pocket vetoed (Sec. 14). The high commissioner did not favor lodging in the new congress the power to adopt measures over his veto and doubted that a repassage clause was necessary or desirable "taking a practical view of political experience and interest in Micronesia." [31] With this Washington did not agree and returned to the final Secretarial Order the language it had originally proposed, giving the congress the right to resubmit a measure disapproved by the high commissioner upon obtaining a two-thirds majority of the entire membership. Should such a bill not receive the high commissioner's signature within twenty days, he must forward it together with his comments to Secretary of the Interior. The latter must respond within ninety days or the measure dies. It was somewhat naive of the Micronesians to believe that the Secretary, like the high commissioner some years before, would willingly bind himself to act on pending legislation under the penalty of its automatically going into effect should he fail to veto it. As a compromise between the varying positions of Saipan and Washington, the Secretarial Order precludes repassage over veto at the same session of the congress in which the measure originated; thereafter, within a period of fourteen months, a vetoed bill may be reconsidered (Sec. 14), a compromise which again borrows from the constitution of American Samoa.

During the entire drafting process there was consensus that the high commissioner ought be able to call the congress into special session. Contrary to the view voiced in the Trusteeship Council that this power should also be lodged in the body itself, so that upon its own volition the congress might convene, no such position

[31] It should also be added that the high commissioner noted this was discussed with the Assistant Secretary of the Interior during his visit to the Trust Territory and was concurred in by him.

appears to have been advocated within the Trust Territory during the deliberations by the Council of Micronesia. It must be added by way of commentary that the Proceedings of the Council are little more than summary accounts, so it is impossible to ascertain whether the delegates approved of all of the conditions surrounding the holding of special sessions—namely, that the congress would be limited to consideration of matters contained in the call of the special session by the high commissioner and in his messages to the congress while in special session. The delegates to the council probably also failed to grasp the full significance of the high commissioner's authority to set the length of the special session (Sec. 12).

The original draft prepared by the Office of Territories contains one provision calculated to save the high commissioner from being pressured by members of the congress who apply for appointment to an office they have created for that purpose. The disqualification of a congressman for a new office he has established runs for one year beyond the term for which he was elected. This was retained in the Secretarial Order and eliminates one means by which congressmen might have obtained personal advantage in turn for supporting the high commissioner's programs before the congress (Sec. 20).

PROCEDURAL DETAIL

A large part of the Secretarial Order setting up the Congress of Micronesia deals with procedural detail intended to assure harmony between the two houses, the maintenance of proper records, and the following of reasonable procedures. Collectively, they promise to ease the burden of the high commissioner by insuring that minimal safeguards must be observed by the new congress. Many of the provisions also protect the congressmen themselves against questionable practices in which some of their colleagues might engage to their mutual disadvantage. Later, with the growth of organized pressure groups and the development of a more structured public opinion in the Trust Territory, these safeguards will also assist in securing a better informed public and conveying community viewpoints to the congress in time to influence the course of the congressional deliberations. More immediately, many of them are designed to hold the congressmen responsible for their official actions.

On the infrequent occasions when the two houses of the congress meet in joint session, the Speaker of the General Assembly and not the President of the House of Delegates is to preside (Sec. 2). The enacting clause of all bills is specified in *haec verba* (Sec. 13). Neither house may adjourn for more than two consecutive days, nor may either adjourn *sine die* without the concurrence of the other (Sec. 15). Every legislative act is to have but one subject, which is to be expressed in the title; no law is to be amended or revised by reference only to its title; and a bill, in order to become law, must pass two readings in each house on separate days, with the final passage originally being by majority vote "of all the members present and voting" and this vote is to be entered in the Journal (Sec. 17).[32] In this last provision both Saipan and Washington dropped their caution, for as a majority of the members comprise a quorum, the minimum vote legally necessary to pass a bill is only one more than a quarter of the total membership. This is consonant with the procedures of the Congress of the United States, but measured by that of state legislatures, with which the Congress of Micronesia might more properly be presently compared, it is highly questionable.

Sessions of the congress are to be public, and even the Committee of the Whole may not transact its business in secret session. All legislative proceedings are to be conducted in the English language, and the Journal which each house is to keep of its proceedings is similarly to be published in that language. However, notice had to be taken of those Micronesians who lack fluency in English, or otherwise the congress would be denied the participation of many persons qualified to serve as legislators but unskilled in that language. To care for this, knowledge of English is declared not to be a qualification for membership in the congress, and lacking English ability, no member may be denied the right to use his native language, while the congress is directed to provide for interpretation into English in all such cases (Sec. 17).

Should vacancies occur, the high commissioner is to call a special election, unless less than six months remains of the term. In the latter event, no special election will be held and the district administrator of the district where the vacancy arises may fill the office by appointment (Sec. 21).

[32] This section of the order was amended in 1963 by Amendment 3 to require a majority of all members.

THE UNITED NATIONS' INTERPOSITION

Throughout the whole process of limning the terms of the new charter for the Congress of Micronesia, the anticipated reaction of the United Nations was like a brooding eminence seated at the drafting table. The very act of drawing up the Secretarial Order into at least tentative form had as one of its deadlines the visit of a UN mission to the Trust Territory in 1964. At that time the mission informally recommended a number of changes designed to grant powers to the new legislative body which would assist it to develop an institutional sense of responsibility and also further the growth of Territorial consensus. For one thing, the mission regarded dubiously the section allowing the high commissioner to name the legislative counsel; the final version of the Secretarial Order continued this for only the opening session, and thereafter the congress was authorized to choose its own counsel, subject only to the high commissioner's concurrence in his competency (Sec. 23). The visiting mission looked askance at the minor proposed restrictions which would narrow the new congress' scope of power, "such as those forbidding gambling casinos, divorce or special tax inducements to corporations, which might be better left to the discretion of an assembly presumed to be responsibly constituted." [33] These, too, were deleted from the final Secretarial Order. Apparently at the visiting mission's instigation the draft was revised to require office holders to resign only after their congressional success at the polls. Later, even this was further amended so as to defer its application for the first four years of the new congress (Sec. 11).

In the main, the views of the visiting mission reflected in the Secretarial Order dealt with peripheral portions of the draft. Its critique applicable to the provision being made for compensation, budgetary powers, and other matters going to the fundamentals of the legislative process do not seem to have left any material impress upon the contents of the Secretarial Order.

The general tenor of the 1964 UN Visiting Mission's report was one of dissatisfaction with the timidity of the order creating the Congress of Micronesia. The mission "formed the opinion that the draft . . . might well meet the present wishes of most Micronesians." This, according to the mission, was not sufficient, for the legisla-

[33] *Report of 1964 . . . , op. cit.,* par. 209.

tive structure "must positively encourage the enlargement" of present views. "In a Territory where transition in some fields has been almost hectic, the pace of political advancement cannot be set by reference to the slowest or to those—the great majority in any country—who are little interested. It depends rather on the most advanced and the most active; those who will in fact be the political leaders of the new Micronesia." [34] Though some of the features of the tentative draft to which the mission objected were removed in the final form of the Secretarial Order, the basis for the mission's dissatisfaction remains. Despite its endowment with a broad scope of legislative authority, the new congress embarked upon its unknown future limited in effective powers and circumscribed in the manner in which it can demonstrate its capacity for responsible governance.

[34] *Ibid.*, par. 203.

CHAPTER 9

Apportioning the New Congress

THE IMPRINTING OF the one-man-one-vote formula on American legislatures by the United States Supreme Court, and the court's prohibition on the delimitation of legislative district boundaries designed to discriminate, have left the apportionment process in the United States garbed with an aura of disarming simplicity. Actually, the process remains highly complex, with the more general criteria of recognition for community of interest, local governmental units, natural geographic boundaries, and the practicality of maintaining constituency contact competing with the precedent of historical compromises, political party favoritism, individual member benefit, and configurations of power seeking to obtain or preserve advantages. Apportionment of the Trust Territory's new congress proved no different, evidencing that developing areas just beginning to experiment with the use of the legislative process also experience great difficulty in structuring representation premised upon any abstract standard, including that of equal population per representative. Even the fact that the apportionment was left to a single person, the high commissioner, did not mitigate the arduousness of the task.

Skewing of representation in the House of Delegates was assured by the Council of Micronesia's opting for bicameralism, with two delegates to each of the six administrative districts. All administrative districts, regardless of size, political development, resources, or economic viability were to enjoy equal treatment in this chamber of the congress. Little Yap, with a population of only 6,293, thus could play as great a role as Truk, with its 24,521 inhabitants.[1] Although not intended, from the start the composition of the General Assembly added a further note of disparity by virtue of the decision to fix its size at twenty-one members and assign five representatives to the Truk administrative district, four each to the

[1] All population statistics are from the *17th Annual Report of the United States to the United Nations, 1963*, pp. 200–203. Currently, the population of the Territory is over 90,000.

Marshalls and Ponape, three each to the Marianas and Palau, and two to Yap.

Both the size and the apportionment formula for the General Assembly were arrived at somewhat by happenstance. The 1962 draft congressional charter of the Office of Territories contemplated a twenty-one-member unicameral legislature. The original recommendations of the Council of Micronesia's working committee contained apportionment formulas for a unicameral body consisting of sixteen, eighteen, or twenty-one members. They also incorporated a minimum of two representatives from each administrative district to "maintain proper representation . . . in view of the geography of each district, population distribution, etc." [2] The working committee believed that the responsibilities might "be too big for one person from each district" and, simply put, that two heads were better than one.[3] After the Council of Micronesia at the March special session in 1963 voted in favor of bicameralism, it approved the proposal of its legislative committee that the House of Delegates be composed of twelve members, two per administrative district, and fixed on the figure of sixteen for the membership of the General Assembly. Under this plan Truk was allocated four assemblymen, the Marshalls and Ponape, three each, and the remaining districts, two.

In the interim between the two meetings of the Council of Micronesia in 1963, the Political Affairs Officer on the Saipan staff of the high commissioner, while favoring a unicameral legislature, noted that a sixteen-member body would conform roughly to population distribution, despite over-representation of the Yap district. An Assembly smaller than sixteen would introduce a serious distortion in representation based upon population, and giving some districts only one seat appeared unwise. "If we want to make it a larger body, I believe it would have to be a twenty-one member body, for no number in between would allow a fair apportionment on a population basis." [4] At this time the high commissioner still entertained "serious doubts that a bicameral body would be advisable" and supported the creation of a twenty-one-member unicam-

[2] "Recommendations for Territorial Legislature," presented by the Working Committee of the Territorial Legislative Committee, Council of Micronesia, Jan. 9, 1963, p. 2. It should be noted that the apportionment shown under the 21-member body actually added to "22," with Truk being allocated six representatives!

[3] Ibid., pp. 2, 3.

[4] Memorandum from Political Affairs Officer to HiCom, July 3, 1963, p. 1.

eral legislature apportioned as was first suggested in the Office of Territories' draft and was later to be specified in the Secretary of Interior Order No. 2882 for the General Assembly. The high commissioner added that "this apportionment conforms roughly, to the population distribution in the Trust Territory. . . . The body cannot be made smaller without distortion of representation and, I feel, a twenty-one member body would be an effective working group." [5] When the Council of Micronesia next met in November, at one stage of the proceedings the delegates voted that, if a unicameral body on a population basis were to be adopted, the number of members should be fixed at twenty-one; for a bicameral congress, a minimum of two representatives should be assigned to each administrative district in the chamber which would be premised upon population.

From all these contributing sources emerged the present size and districting of the General Assembly. In the process, a degree of malapportionment was incorporated, for the fact that Truk's delegation has only five assemblymen means that this district is underrepresented in favor of the Marianas. Ironically, it probably would have been more equitable if the original sixteen-member size had

ACTUAL AND "IDEAL" REPRESENTATION BY POPULATION, GENERAL ASSEMBLY

Administrative District	Population	Actual Representatives (21)	"Ideal" Apportionment by Population		
			21	16	26
Yap	6,293	2	2	1	2
Mariana	10,275	3	2	2	3
Palau	10,628	3	3	2	3
Marshall	18,205	4	4	3	5
Ponape	18,293	4	4	3	6
Truk	24,521	5	6	5	7
	88,215	21	21	16	26

"Ideal" apportionment determined by dividing mean district population (4,200.7) into total population of administrative district. The number of assembly men assigned as "ideal" is that which results in the least variation. (E.g., for a 21-member General Assembly, Truk is "entitled" to 5.84 seats. By allotting 6 assemblymen to Truk, the variation is +.16, whereas the actual apportionment of 5 resulted in Truk's losing −.84. Representation "due" the Marianas is only 2.45; actual apportionment of 3 seats afforded a gain of +.55.)

[5] Letter of HiCom to Director of the Office of Territories, Sept. 27, 1963.

been retained, or even if the council had agreed upon an accurately apportioned twenty-six-member assembly.

RANGE OF VARIATION, DIFFERENT–SIZED GENERAL ASSEMBLIES

Apportionment	Number of Assemblymen	Range	Difference
Actual	21	−.84 to +.55	1.39
"Ideal"	16	−.30 to +.55	.85
"Ideal"	21	−.45 to +.50	.95
"Ideal"	26	−.37 to +.61	.98

"Range" merely notes the extreme under- and over-represented administrative district for different-sized Assemblies, computed as for previous table.

It was accepted by all as axiomatic that if a bicameral congress were established, one house would be structured upon population. There were other factors so significant to the Trust Territory as to have warranted at least consideration before the apportionment of the lower chamber was fixed. As early as August of 1962, the Palau magistrates, meeting in annual conference, passed a resolution stating their confidence "that when the time comes for converting the Council [of Micronesia] into a territorial legislative body, steps will be taken to insure democratic representation in that body both on the basis of district population and ethnical groups." [6] Ethnic considerations have figured prominently in other Pacific legislatures, but it was unlikely that American practice would openly sanction its use. However, a number of other factors besides population or ethnic divisions could quite properly have been debated as prime criteria in the allocation of General Assembly constituencies. The following table indicates that if any of them had been employed, each administrative district's share of seats could have markedly varied from that mandated by the Secretarial Order.

As the United States Constitution does not automatically apply to the Trust Territory, it would not necessarily require that the standard of population be used for fixing representation in either house. The district legislatures as apportioned have failed to give full weight to the number of people residing in the larger centers, so that accepted Territorial practices would have approved of other

[6] Resolution No. 2–62, Annual Conference of Palau Magistrates, Aug. 1962.

measures. It is only that the United States is currently committed to the one-man-one-vote principle, and as Administering Authority

HYPOTHETICAL APPORTIONMENT OF 21-MEMBER GENERAL ASSEMBLY, VARIOUS CRITERIA [7]

District	Actual Apportionment	Land Area	Exports	"Self-sufficiency"
Yap	2	1	1	3
Mariana	3	6	2	1
Palau	3	6	2	2
Marshall	4	2	8	5
Ponape	4	5	4	6
Truk	5	1	4	4

it would have been hard put both at home and in replying to its international distractors not to have adopted population as the basis for at least one house of the new congress.

It will not be until 1971 that opportunity for correction of the malapportionment built into the General Assembly will occur. In that year the congress is directed to redistrict the lower house, and reapportionment is to take place every ten years thereafter. The malapportionment of the General Assembly may be righted at any of these designated times, so that Truk may eventually obtain its aliquot share of Assembly seats to which it is entitled by its relative population. However, the charter still retains the condition that each administrative district must receive at least two assemblymen, so that inherent in this proviso is the possibility that at some future date the small districts may receive even more disproportionate representation in the congress.

DISTRICTING THE TERRITORY

The high commissioner was charged with delineating the twenty-one Assembly constituencies, setting up the election machinery for

[7] Acreage, import, and export data taken from *17th Annual . . . , op. cit.*, pp. 249, 251–252. To obtain the number of assemblymen by land area, acreage was tabulated and the mean acreage per constituency computed. This mean was then divided into each administrative district's area, and the closest fit used for representation due. Representation based on dollar exports was similarly computed. "Self-sufficiency" is merely the export-import ratio for each administrative district, as follows: Ponape, 77%; Marshalls, 66.99%; Truk, 59.21%; Yap, 46.20%; Palau, 24.28%; and Marianas, 18.75%. The Mariana district with the lowest "self-sufficiency" is assigned one assemblyman as contrasted with Ponape with the highest ratio and six assemblymen.

choosing the new congressmen, and holding elections throughout the Territory, all within less than four months. Ideally, the boundaries of the districts should have been announced as soon as possible, in order to facilitate the remainder of the undertaking. Due to the difficulties encountered, over half of the period was to elapse before the high commissioner issued Special Order No. 7 on November 30, 1964, districting the Territory. To get the Herculean task underway, he requested the six district administrators to prepare apportionment plans for their respective administrative areas. Their only express guidelines were the provisions of the Secretarial Order which set the number of representatives to which each administrative area was entitled and directed that assembly districts be both "approximately equal" in population and single-member constituencies.

After consulting with magistrates of the municipalities, district legislators, and in some cases, traditional chiefs, the district administrators responded with so wide an array of proposals as to convey the impression they had conspired to attain diversity. The Marshalls advocated running candidates at large. Truk favored multi-member districting, and the Mariana district outlined not one but three tentative schemes, each embodying some form of multi-member districting. From Palau came an apportionment plan enacted gratuitously by the Palau district legislature which hewed to the single-member-district criterion but would have parcelled up the municipality of Koror, headquarters for the district. Only Ponape's initial apportionment was approved outright by the high commissioner; the second plan of the Marshalls was similarly accepted; the rest he either modified (Truk and the Marianas) or substantially revised (Palau and Yap).[8]

The Marshall Islands district administrator originally wanted to have the Marshall Islands Congress nominate candidates who would then all run at large because "consensus of opinion here is . . . [that] actual subdivision of district at this time will further delay election. . . ." [9] The high commissioner's reply noted that he understood the "special problems of Marshalls District" but that it was "imperative this election be standard with [that] of Territory." [10] From Truk came the protest that the "magistrates disfavor

---

[8] The Yap record is ambiguous, and the high commissioner's revision may have extended only to proposed districting for delegates.
[9] Communication of DistAd Marshalls to HiCom, Oct. 20, 1964.
[10] Communication of HiCom to DistAd Marshalls, Nov. 3, 1964.

the idea of subdividing the District into single member election districts. It is felt that this division will disturb their social structure, as well as create a feeling of disunity among their people. Instead they recommend that the District be divided into two [multi-membered] electoral precincts . . . ," with the Mortlocks combined with the Namoneas area of the Truk lagoon and the remaining outlying low islands combined with the Faichuk area.[11] The high commissioner's answer to this cited the Secretarial Order's mandate of single-member constituencies and "suggested" five Assembly constituencies formed by dividing each of the two locally proposed election districts into smaller segments.

Central to the whole problem of districting was the question of the recognition to be afforded municipalities, and more specifically, whether these units of local government, so carefully nurtured by the American administration, were to be split, combined in part or in whole with others, or maintained with their sense of community heightened by the retention of as many boundaries as possible. Allied to this was the question of the representation to be given the district centers. The population of each center has been swollen by the large number of persons attracted for employment either with the government or private businesses servicing the latter's needs. These are the areas which are most familiar with American-sponsored political institutions and where the greatest political acculturation has taken place. Except possibly for Koror in Palau, which in some ways tends to emphasize the status quo more than parts of Babelthuap, the district centers are also the areas which are most progressive and most desirous of political change. The high commissioner had to resolve whether to preserve their identity by keeping them as separate Assembly districts or to dilute their voting strength by joining them with areas holding to more traditional values. Complicating this decision was the uneven distribution of the Territory's population and the possibility of structuring a district so that one heavily populated area could outvote the other smaller units included in the same constituency. The opposite result could be achieved by putting two heavily populated municipalities within the same district, so that neither would receive an advantage from its voting strength.

The high commissioner's solution for Truk was to designate Moen, the municipality embracing the district headquarters, as a

[11] Communication of DistAd Truk to Assistant Commissioner for Public Affairs, Nov. 9, 1964.

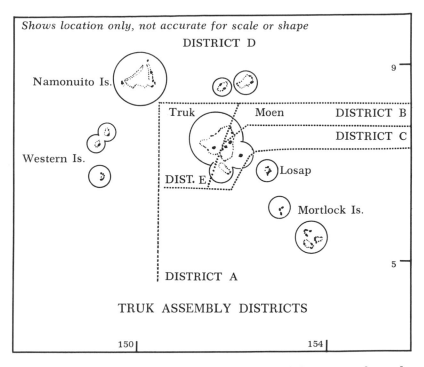

Shows location only, not accurate for scale or shape

DISTRICT D

Namonuito Is.

Western Is.

Truk — Moen   DISTRICT B

DISTRICT C

DIST. E   Losap

Mortlock Is.

DISTRICT A

TRUK ASSEMBLY DISTRICTS

150   154

separate constituency (Truk District B),[12] withdrawing it from the traditional Namoneas portion of the Truk lagoon, which became District C. He similarly spun off the distant Upper and Lower Mortlocks to form yet a third constituency, Truk District A. The Faichuk area of the Truk lagoon was designated as District E, and the outlying Halls, Namonuito, and the Western Islands were combined into a fifth, D. Except for the removal of Moen, the Faichuk and Namoneas areas, each with its distinguishing dialectical difference, were kept intact. Of necessity, municipalities had to be grouped, but the high commissioner successfully avoided splitting any and, in linking them, preserved the traditional zones of the Truk lagoon. He also prevented the Truk atoll from outvoting the outlying islands, but in doing so, he had to abandon the principle of equal representation by population.

While the Truk district sought to group municipalities in a way which would preserve customary associations, the Palau district legislature advocated the dismemberment of the municipality of

[12] By Public Law No. 2–16, Assembly (House of Representatives) districts are now numbered; for the first election each bore a letter designation.

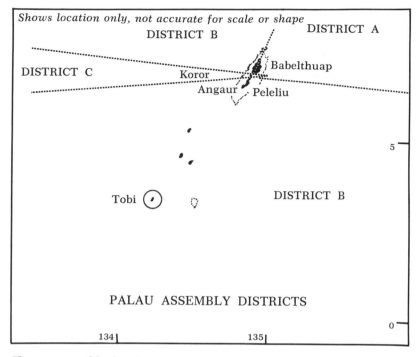

Koror ostensibly for the same reason. The Palau plan divided Koror into eleven villages, five of which it would combine with islands south of Koror from Peleliu to Tobi and the remainder join with one or the other districts cleaving Babelthuap. Again the high commissioner sympathized but demurred:

I can appreciate the fact that one of the underlying reasons may have been an attempt to follow traditional linkage of parts of Koror with parts of Babelthuap. However, the premise of a single member election district is not well served by such extreme fragmentation. Further, Koror Municipality now operates as an integral unit in the local municipal government scheme and also serves as a single electoral precinct, electing on the basis of its population, five members of the District Legislature. In population size, in geographic arrangement, it is one of the logical single member election districts. . . . [13]

With the exception of the Koror villages of Meyungs and Ngerbeched, whose inhabitants' common ties with the southern islands counseled continuance of their joinder in Palau Assembly Dis-

---

[13] Communication of HiCom to DistAd Palau, Nov. 30, 1964.

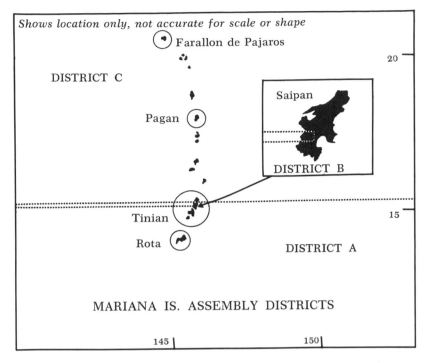

Shows location only, not accurate for scale or shape

Farallon de Pajaros

20

DISTRICT C

Saipan

Pagan

DISTRICT B

Tinian

15

Rota

DISTRICT A

MARIANA IS. ASSEMBLY DISTRICTS

145   150

trict A to swell the size of that Assembly district's population, Koror's identity as a municipality was maintained under the apportionment plan issued by the high commissioner. Other than for allocating Airrai to Palau Assembly District B (and, of course, separating Koror as Assembly District C), the high commissioner's apportionment of Palau into Districts A and B faithfully followed the boundaries of the old Koror and Melekeok Confederations.[14]

It was in the Marianas that the high commissioner faced defeat and had to divide a single municipality among the three Assembly constituencies assigned to this district. The Mariana district administration understood clearly the significance of such a decision, for the Secretary's creation of the congress had already caused opposition among the Saipanese advocating separation from the Trust Territory and union with Guam. In advancing three alternative plans, each of which bifurcated Saipan, the district administrator advised the high commissioner that "to go further in splitting the Municipality will add more to this tension." [15]

[14] Arthur J. Vidich, *Political Factionalism in Palau*, CIMA Final Report No. 23 ([Massachusetts]: 1949), p. 21.
[15] Communication from DistAd Mariana Islands to HiCom, Oct. 14, 1964.

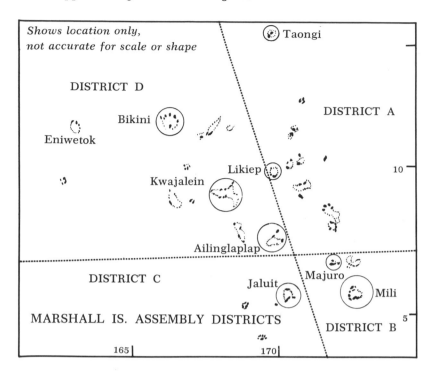

Shows location only, not accurate for scale or shape

DISTRICT D

DISTRICT A

Bikini

Eniwetok

Taongi

Likiep

Kwajalein

10

Ailinglaplap

DISTRICT C

Jaluit

Majuro

Mili

MARSHALL IS. ASSEMBLY DISTRICTS

DISTRICT B

5

165 | 170 |

MARIANA DISTRICT APPORTIONMENT PROPOSALS

PROPOSAL I	PROPOSAL II	PROPOSAL III
1 district with 2 assemblymen. Saipan and Northern Islands—pop.: 8,672 (mean: 4,336).	1 district with 2 assemblymen. Two-thirds of Chalan Kanoa Village, remainder of northern Saipan, and Northern Islands—pop.: 6,836 (mean: 3,418).	1 district with 2 assemblymen. All Saipan—pop.: 8,404 (mean: 4,202).
1 district with 1 assemblyman. Rota and Tinian—pop.: 1,603.	1 district with 1 assemblyman. One-third of Chalan Kanoa Village, southern Saipan, Tinian, and Rota—pop. 3,437.	1 district with 1 assemblyman. Rota, Tinian, and Northern Islands—pop.: 1,871.

Undaunted, the high commissioner resolved the problem frontally by dividing the municipality of Saipan into three, linking the southern portion with the islands of Tinian and Rota and the north-

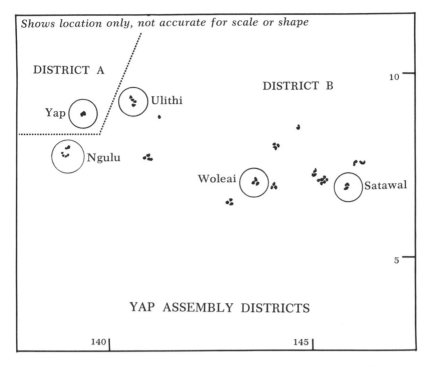

Shows location only, not accurate for scale or shape

DISTRICT A

DISTRICT B

Yap

Ulithi

Ngulu

Woleai

Satawal

10

5

YAP ASSEMBLY DISTRICTS

140

145

ernmost part with the small northern islands of the Mariana archipelago. Even more significantly, he split the most populous village on Saipan, Chalan Kanoa, with 52 per cent of the total island population, in a manner which might benefit one of the Mariana district's political parties. The fact that the average variation of the population of these three Assembly districts was but 1.2 per cent from the theoretical mean implies that, in the high commissioner's apportionment of the Mariana district, very careful attention was given to the problem of establishing districts of "approximately equal population."

Along with concern for the separate identity of local political units, there was evident interest in securing a degree of compactness, in giving due weight to geographical contiguity, and in preserving cultural and traditional groupings. All of this had to be tempered by the sheer realities of the Territory's dispersed character and the attendant inadequacies of communication and transportation. Ignoring fixed patterns for field trips not only would unnecessarily stifle any developing sense of commonality fostered by

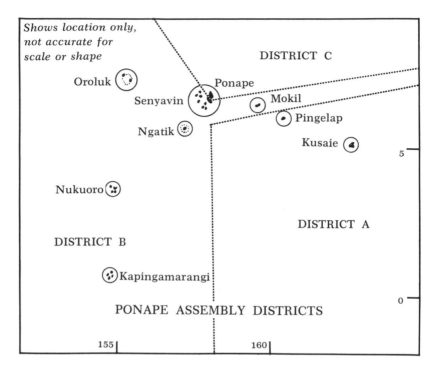

Shows location only, not accurate for scale or shape

DISTRICT C

Oroluk

Ponape

Senyavin

Mokil

Ngatik

Pingelap

Kusaie

5

Nukuoro

DISTRICT A

DISTRICT B

Kapingamarangi

PONAPE ASSEMBLY DISTRICTS

0

155   160

repeated inclusion within a single field trip but also would unduly complicate the technical conduct of what promised to be an unusually taxing election.

In the Marshalls, the geographical as well as traditional separation between the Radak and Ralik chains was acknowledged in the district's high-commissioner-approved second plan which had a line running north and south between the two; the region was then further divided "traditionally"[16] into four compact quadrants by a second bisecting line that cut horizontally roughly across its middle. The Marshall's field trips supported the logic of the district's quartering, but concealed was the fact that the plan allowed low population areas to dominate in a majority of constituencies, resulting in great disparities between the four Assembly districts.

[16] When queried as to what was "traditional" in the bisecting, east-west line which played such a prominent part in the district's second plan, an informant replied that the four resulting quadrants roughly approximated the areas which customarily would fight with each other. Chave noted that "the geographical division of the Marshall Islands is on north and south lines; the cultural division on east and west lines." Margaret E. Chave, *The Changing Position of the Mixed Bloods in the Marshall Islands*, CIMA Final Report No. 7 (Honolulu: 1949), p. 25.

The Marianas' districting also took physical contiguity into account and, in addition, reflected that Rota and Tinian have more in common with each other than with Saipan. The division adopted for the Yap administrative district placed all of the Outer Islands visited by field-trip ship in a single congressional constituency, far flung as the old Yap empire might be (see map, p. 233). For Truk it is harder to justify the combination of the Namonuito atoll to the northwest, the Hall Group to the northeast, and the Western Islands within the same Assembly district, constituting as they do distinct cultural sub-areas.[17] The only rationale is that they jointly share differences from the high islands within the Truk lagoon and each is dependent upon periodic field-trip contact.

Of necessity many factors relevant to districting had to be accommodated, and in the process the criterion of population could easily be compromised. The dimensions of the decision which had to be made are well sketched by the Ponape proposal approved by the high commissioner, which took into account "population; geographic proximity of municipalities within each election district; common interests among municipalities such as the low islands; and past and present cultural and traditional affiliations."[18]

EVALUATING THE APPORTIONMENT

With the districting of the Territory complete, so that it could be assayed in its entirety, the conclusion to be drawn is manifest: at the 1965 elections some voters were more "equal" than others, and the western half of the Trust Territory received the more favorable representation. Also, the apportionment was not politically neutral, and in some districts it pointed the pace and direction of future political change. In the Palau and Mariana districts, the fate of the parties at the polls could be partially attributed to the manner in which the Assembly constituency boundaries were drawn by the high commissioner.

None of the six administrative districts could receive delegations exactly proportionate to its share of the total Territorial population, so inevitably the voters were assured a degree of unequal representation in the General Assembly. When, in the designating of the Assembly constituencies within the boundaries of each administrative district, some constituencies were favored over others, this

[17] See John L. Fischer and Ann M. Fischer, *The Eastern Carolines* (New Haven: Human Relations Area Files, 1957), pp. 7–8.
[18] Communication from DistAd Ponape to HiCom, Oct. 8, 1964.

only compounded the disparity. The variance from equality of representation based upon population permitted by the United States Supreme Court within the states was far exceeded in the districting of the General Assembly.[19] If the equal protection clause of the U.S. Constitution were automatically to apply to the Trust Territory, there is little question but that the Assembly's apportionment would not meet with judicial confirmation.

VARIATION FROM THE ADMINISTRATIVE DISTRICT'S MEAN FOR GENERAL ASSEMBLY DISTRICTS

District	Population	Number of Assemblymen	Mean District Size	Range in Variation From Mean [20]	Average Variation [21]
Marshalls	18,205	4	4551	−44.0% to +43.1%	37.6%
Truk	24,521	5	4904	−53.4% +34.3%	27.8%
Yap	6,293	2	3146	−20.5% +20.5%	20.5%
Ponape	18,293	4	4573	− 9.2% +13.5%	6.8%
Palau	10,628	3	3543	− 1.7% + 2.1%	1.4%
Mariana	10,275	3	3425	− 1.8% + 1.5%	1.2%

Mean range, all districts, is − 1.4% to + 37.6%.
Average variation, all districts, is 15.9%.

Using the David and Eisenberg Index [22] of "the relative value of the right to vote," the vote of a person in an "under-represented" area, such as Truk District E, counts for less in the General Assembly than that of a voter in any "over-represented" area, such as Truk District D. To be precise, in this particularly extreme comparison, the "vote value" of the former is only about one-third that of the latter.[23] Assuming that the ideal apportionment will yield a

[19] See *Swann* v. *Adams*, 385 U.S. 440 (1966); *Kilgarlin* v. *Hill*, 386 U.S. 120 (1967).

[20] The range is obtained by computing the variation in population of each Assembly district from the mean in the administrative district as a whole. E.g., District C in Truk has a population of 6,185, 126.1% of the mean district of 4,904 in the Truk district.

[21] The average is computed by totalling the percentage variations from the mean Assembly district and dividing this value by the number of Assembly districts in each administrative district.

[22] The David and Eisenberg Index is $P_c = M/X$, with M the mean population for all constituencies in the chamber and X the population of a particular constituency. See Paul T. David and Ralph Eisenberg, *Devaluation of the Urban and Suburban Vote* (Charlottesville, Va.: Bureau of Public Administration, University of Virginia, Vol. 1:1961 and Vol. 2: 1962).

[23] 63.8 ÷ 183.8 or 34.1% ("vote value" from table).

"vote value" of 100, the disparity in districting the Trust Territory is shown in the following table.

"VOTE VALUE" OF GENERAL ASSEMBLY DISTRICTS

Area-District		Population	"Vote Value"
Truk	D	2,286	183.8
Yap	B	2,501	168.0
Marshall	C	2,901	144.8
Marshall	A	3,010	139.6
Mariana	B	3,362	125.0
Mariana	A	3,437	122.2
Mariana	C	3,476	120.8
Palau	C	3,481	120.7
Palau	B	3,531	119.0
Palau	A	3,616	116.2
Yap	A	3,792	110.8
Truk	B	4,115	102.1
Ponape	A	4,153	101.1
Ponape	C	4,431	94.8
Ponape	B	4,520	92.9
Ponape	D	5,189	81.0
Truk	A	5,350	78.5
Marshall	D	5,779	72.7
Truk	C	6,185	67.9
Marshall	B	6,515	64.5
Truk	E	6,585	63.8

Yap District A occupies the median position on the table with a "vote value" of 110.8. Voters in all constituencies with indices below this figure enjoyed less than average voting effectiveness. Arrangement of the twenty-one constituencies in relation to the median Assembly district reveals a geographical dispersion of representatives to the detriment of the eastern portion of the Trust Territory and, correspondingly, to the benefit of the western administrative districts. All constituencies in Yap, the Marianas, and Palau are either at or above the median.

Final evidence that the Territory's apportionment favored the western administrative districts is provided by applying the David and Eisenberg "vote value" index to both houses of the congress. This finding, of course, reflects the original structuring of the two houses, which granted equal representation in the House of Delegates to all administrative districts, regardless of population, and did not too carefully check on the mathematics of apportionment when the size of each administrative district's delegation in the General Assembly was determined. While the high commissioner is accountable for any imbalance which may be demonstrated

GENERAL ASSEMBLY DISTRICTS IN RELATION TO THE
MEDIAN "VOTE VALUE" DISTRICT

Administrative District	Number of Assembly Districts	At or Above Median		Below Median	
		Number	Per cent	Number	Per cent
Yap	2	2	100	0	0
Mariana	3	3	100	0	0
Palau	3	3	100	0	0
Marshall	4	2	50	2	50
Truk	5	1	20	4	80
Ponape	4	0	0	4	100

within an administrative district, inequalities between districts had already been assured before he took up the chore of drawing Assembly-constituency boundaries for the Trust Territory.[24]

"VOTE VALUE" OF ADMINISTRATIVE DISTRICT REPRESENTATION
IN HOUSE OF DELEGATES AND GENERAL ASSEMBLY

District	Population	Delegate "Vote Value" [25]	Assembly "Vote Value" [26]
Yap	6,293	233.6	133.5
Mariana	10,275	143.9	122.6
Palau	10,628	138.3	118.6
Marshall	18,205	80.6	92.3
Ponape	18,293	80.4	91.9
Truk	24,521	60.0	85.7

It is difficult to prove that this skewing of representation to the western districts exerted any influence upon the organization or

[24] In defense of the apportionment plan as applied to both houses, it should be noted that it scored as highly "rational" (rank correlation of .97) under Justice Clark's proposal that the apportionment for both houses, taken together, should be considered "rational" if they demonstrate a high rank correlation between population and the number of representatives enjoyed in both houses. The Clark index for each administrative district is $\frac{X}{21} + 1.75 \left(\frac{Y}{12}\right)$ where X = number of assemblymen and Y = number of delegates for the district. See concurring opinion of Justice Clark in *Baker* v. *Carr*, 369

the legislative product of the first congress. Looking solely to the Assembly, and utilizing the Dauer-Kelsay [27] approach which identifies the smaller constituencies that collectively comprise a majority —a process which simultaneously determines the minimal percentage of the population whose elected representatives comprise a legislative majority—the eleven smaller constituencies in the General Assembly enjoying majority strength (in fact, 52.4 per cent) are found to represent but two-fifths of the total population of the Territory (35,393). But this presupposes that the smaller Assembly constituencies will hold together and vote as a bloc, irrespective of their district identity. Neither general empirical data [28] nor observation of the Congress of Micronesia in action sustains the assumption. Upon organizing the General Assembly, all three elected officers were chosen from the eastern area of the Trust Territory (and so were the officers of the House of Delegates). Measures introduced by only legislators from the three eastern districts had a little greater success than those sponsored by congressmen from the West,[29] but this is inconclusive. If anything, during the session assemblymen tended more to vote with the other members of their administrative district than to choose sides along lines of constituency size.

Attention to intra-district apportionment, as distinct from cross-district comparisons, reveals that the boundaries drawn resulted in a number of extreme population disparities. Reference has already been made to the grossest of these in Truk. For the most part, the disproportions arose from the attempt to take topographical distinctions, geographical distances, economic interests, and cultural

---

U.S. 186 (1962), p. 251. It should be added that the rank correlation would not have been adversely affected if another assemblyman had been assigned to the Truk administrative district at the expense of the Mariana delegation.

[25] The mean Delegate district is 7,351 (88,215 ÷ 12). The mean is multiplied by 2 (the number of delegates per administrative district), and the product (14,702) is divided by the population of the administrative district to obtain the "vote value."

[26] The mean Assembly district is 4,200.7. "Vote value" is $P_c = MD/X$ where M represents the mean population for all constituencies, D the number of Assembly seats allocated to an administrative district, and X the population of that district.

[27] See Manning J. Dauer and Robert G. Kelsay, "Unrepresented States," *National Municipal Review*, 44:11 (Dec., 1955), 571.

[28] See Glendon Schubert and Charles Press, "Measuring Malapportionment," *American Political Science Review*, 58:2 (June, 1964), p. 305, n6.

[29] Excluding administration-proposed measures (see Chapter 14), 35.8 per cent of East-sponsored legislative measures were successful as compared with 24.8 per cent of the measures introduced solely by congressmen from the West. Measures cross-sponsored by members from the two regions had a success ratio of 36.4 per cent.

diversities into account. Sometimes these differences could be reconciled with population equivalency. In the Ponape administrative district, where an average variation of but 6.8 per cent from the mean was achieved for all four Assembly constituencies, Mokil was joined with the Sokehs areas on Ponape Island. The Mortlock, Pingelap, and other low island people who resettled in Sokehs just before World War I, after the German administration exiled the latter's original rebellious inhabitants to Palau and Yap, feel close to the Outer Islanders, while the Mokil homesteaders on Ponape Island utilize Sokehs as their headquarters. Similarly, the islands of Kusaie and Pingelap were combined into a single Assembly district, because people move readily between those two outlying areas and Kusaieans "interact" more easily with Pingelapese than with Ponapeans.

These same delineations of Assembly constituencies also potentially channel the course for future political change. Kusaieans have long expressed dissatisfaction with their inclusion within the Ponape administrative district and have desired separate, co-equal district status. The symbolism latent in the identification of their island as the principal component of Assembly Ponape District A could easily be seized upon as the first concrete move in the separatist movement. The constituency's assemblyman-elect, although himself from the small island of Pingelap, raised the question of separation at the workshop preceding the convening of the first congress and later offered a joint resolution seeking severance of Kusaie from the Ponape administrative district (AJR 16 of 1965).

The division of the Yap administrative district into two Assembly constituencies, one of which comprises the Outer Islands, clearly evinces the administration's conviction that the old Yapese empire lacks any continuing political viability. The Yap Islands chiefs were not to be afforded the opportunity of replacing the sanctions of their magicians with the maneuverings of politicians. The inhabitants of Ulithi, Woleai, and islands farther east, for the first time jointly exercising the franchise, did so without any direction from the chiefs of Gagil and stood as politically independent of the Yapese.[30] In contrast, on the Yap Islands, with both high and low caste villages in a single Assembly constituency, chiefly influence affected the electoral results.

[30] For fuller consideration of relation between the Yap Islands and Outer Islands, see Chapter 6.

By far the most immediate consequences of the high commissioner's apportionment efforts were their impact on the election contests in the two administrative districts with active political parties.[31] In both Palau and the Marianas, political parties standing for slower, evolutionary change were benefited in the General Assembly contests. In Palau, this occurred because the high commissioner proposed an essentially neutral apportionment plan, in contrast to the locally favored one, which would have aided the more "liberal" party. In the Marianas, the manner in which General Assembly constituency lines were drawn split the strength of the majority party on Saipan.

The original apportionment plan enacted by the Palau legislature, although premised upon Koror inhabitants' identification with their "home" villages, in fact constituted an outright gerrymander by splintering Koror's Progressive Party strength. The Palau legislature submitted its recommendations in the form of a bill (15–10–64), but this action was outside its legislative authority and was vetoed by the high commissioner.[32] If the Palau administrative district had been apportioned according to this bill, with a distribution of vote identical to that cast in the first congressional elections, the Liberal Party would have gained one more Palauan seat. What is more, the rival Progressive Party would have been unable to elect a single member to the General Assembly. The high commissioner's neutrality in refusing to concur in such an apportionment proposal is unquestionably defensible, but in nullifying the political advantage of the Liberal Party, he was securing for the administration a potentially more cooperative legislative delegation.

PALAU PARTY VICTORIES UNDER TWO APPORTIONMENT PLANS

	Liberal Vote Cast		Progressive Vote Cast		Independent Vote Cast	
	Legislature's Plan	High Commissioner's Plan	Legislature's Plan	High Commissioner's Plan	Legislature's Plan	High Commissioner's Plan
District A	668	813	495	439	100	0
District B	603	284	441	373	83	643
District C	287	461	388	512	630	170

Underlining indicates winning candidate.

[31] See Chapter 10 for fuller treatment of political parties in both the Marianas and Palau administrative districts.

[32] Letter of HiCom to DistAd Palau, Nov. 30, 1964.

In the Mariana administrative district, the Popular Party has assumed a bellicose stand in its drive toward splitting the Northern Marianas from the Trust Territory and joining it with Guam. The larger component of the Popular Party is Chamorro, and the seat of its strength is found in Chalan Kanoa on Saipan. The Territorial Party, by advocating Trust Territory development and deferral of Territorial dissolution, has attracted the support of many Chamorros and the larger component of the minority Carolinian population long resident on the island. The division of Saipan among three Assembly constituencies left the center of Chalan Kanoa comprising one Assembly district, which voted Popular Party, while the Territorial Party won the other two contests. As illustration of what may happen when Saipan is otherwise apportioned, in the Saipan municipal elections held a year later, the Popular Party captured all seven seats in the municipal council—an at-large contest—and nine out of eleven district commissioner posts. Since the United Nations opposes splitting the Trust Territory, as does the United States, it would have been poor judgment for the high commissioner to have sought amendment to the Secretarial Order creating the congress so as to have allowed a multi-member constituency for the Marianas, even though he would have had strong support for repudiating single-member electorates from at least half of the district administrators. Instead, trifurcating Saipan so as to place the bulk of Chalan Kanoa in separate Mariana District B gave pro-Territorial Rota and more evenly-divided Tinian a chance to tip the scales against the Popular Party in Mariana District A. The same opportunity occurred in Assembly District C. Keeping part of the pro-Territorial and heavily Carolinian precinct 4 within Mariana District B narrowed the Popular Party's predominance there. Under the circumstances, it is difficult for the impartial observer to conclude other than that the political impact of apportionment was a major factor taken into account when delineating the boundaries of the constituencies in the Marianas.[33]

In Palau and the Marianas, the standard of "approximately equal population" was applied, although an Assembly apportionment producing political consequences favorable to the administration was still forthcoming. In the Ponape district, population variation was held within the 10 per cent range while at the same

---

[33] This is denied by Trust Territory personnel who defend their decision as neutral, dividing as it did Saipan's Carolinian population (a major segment of the Territorial Party strength) among all three Assembly election districts.

time weight was given to geographical and cultural ties; nevertheless, identifying Kusaie as a separate constituency may contribute to the future dismemberment of this administrative district. In the remaining districts, so many other factors clamored for accommodation that the population criterion could not be observed. It would have been far more realistic if the Secretarial Order had expressly taken cognizance of this.[34] The logic of the U.S. Supreme Court's effort to fit the entire nation within the Procrustean one-man-one-vote criterion has been challenged, and that criterion's application to as geographically and culturally diverse an area as Micronesia is even more questionable. Physical and cultural environment placed limitations upon assigning primacy to any apportionment standard, and it was only to be expected that the political environment would be manipulated for administrative and partisan ends.

[34] As illustrative of this realistic approach, see Section 41 (ii) of the "Report of the British Guiana Constitutional Conference" held in March, 1960: "... electoral districts to be of approximately equal population except where, in the Commissioner's opinion, it is desirable to disregard equality of numbers on account of special considerations such as natural community of interest, local government areas, physical features, transport facilities and the practicability of elected members maintaining contact with electors in sparsely populated areas." *White Paper Command 998.*

CHAPTER 10

The Congressional Elections

For years we have paused at the threshold of a new epoch, unable for a moment to open that door, but aware that we must advance if we are to secure our own identity. That door is now ready for opening and that moment is approaching. . . .

As of now we can not really tell the mood of the people toward this election. However, the wind is somehow changing. People, not everyone by a long way, but enough to disturb the prevailing mood, are optimistic of the new developments. At this point we are still uncertain but expectant. This period between now [November 13, 1964] and January 19 is one of a tremendous importance. It is a period of reckoning. Like a lull before a storm, every precautions must be taken. It is an odd and baffled moment in our history. It is a moment of suspense and anticipation. One thing, however, is certain—the success of that first election and every subsequent ones will depend primarily on how well we conduct their initial preparations. This much we know, but only time will tell the eventual outcome of our efforts.[1]

THE INITIAL ELECTION for the Congress of Micronesia may be viewed from many aspects. The educated elite and the politically sophisticated, among whom would be counted the author of the quoted extract, saw the election as the opening wedge for the transfer of ever greater self-government to the Micronesians. Some transliterated this into an opportunity for immediate benefit in the form of higher Micronesian salaries and preferences for Micronesian enterprise. To most of the voters of the Territory it was akin to a sacred mystery, important but for exactly what reason they could not articulate other than in borrowed clichés. Some among them were taking part solely because of the bidding of the administration, reinforced by their traditional leaders. Not the least important of the many facets of the election was the position of the district administrator confronted with a behemoth task, certain in the knowledge that if a creditable showing were not forthcoming it would reflect adversely upon the two decades of American preparation of the indigenes for their own governance, and probably, as

[1] *Palau Post*, Nov. 13, 1964, p. 1.

well, upon his own capacity for undertaking a complex assignment.

The Administering Authority faced a number of technical problems, such as how to reconcile the need for uniformity with the flexibility essential for an election system designed to apply to an area as large as the United States. Failure to comply with those standards considered essential to free elections, or even the omission of minor details as the constructing of secure ballot boxes, would be sure to draw the attention of the Trusteeship Council and the censure of those members alert for an opportunity to challenge American sincerity. The dispersal of peoples, limited communications, and inadequate transportation facilities had to be overcome. The Secretarial Order specified that the congressional elections were to be held throughout the Territory on one day, January 19, 1965. This would require the elections to be structured in a manner never before attempted [2] and the secret ballot to be introduced to some areas yet following traditional ways of selecting leaders. Nomination of candidates would have to be encouraged and methods evolved for facilitating the processing of sponsored as well as self-nominations. The unfamiliarity of the prospective voter with the new electoral provisions would have to be rectified by a publicity campaign, and the sheer inertia of the body politic would similarly have to be counteracted. Once the rules were prescribed, a whole corps of election officers, speaking almost a dozen languages, would have to be instructed in the proper manner of running the election. And above all, these new requirements would have to be compatible with the criteria held by the Micronesians. Not to be forgotten was Yap's past intransigency and Palau's previous refusal to accept the Trusteeship Council's suggested minimum voting age, holding that people under the age of twenty-six were too immature to participate.

The solution for all of these problems was found in a general election format established through special order of the high commissioner and delegating implementation to the field. Supplementation and oversight of field decisions could be maintained in a number of ways. Opinions from the attorney general, and informal rulings from his offce, would supply interpretations of the high commissioner's order and the Secretarial Order upon which it was

[2] The high commissioner had to foreclose the pattern of one or two balloting teams visiting the Marshallese municipalities in turn, and of up to half a year being taken to elect members to the Council of Micronesia. See HiCom to DistAd Marshalls, Nov. 3, 1964.

premised. Opinions thus rendered would guide the entire Territory uniformly, whether the question be that of permitting prisoners to vote, prohibiting prospective candidates from running for two seats simultaneously, or in other ways making more clear and specific, and filling the lacunae in, the general directions of the high commissioner.

Suggestions and instructions from the high commissioner's staff to the field also served as a means by which administrative oversight might be exercised as election planning progressed in each of the six administrative districts. These instructions would not be phrased in formal authority binding upon the administrators, but they would be influential in meeting technical problems; indirectly, they would assure a degree of comparability of methods in all administrative districts. The Political Affairs Office at Headquarters well understood the importance of the election and devoted long hours to counseling the districts. Over a period of time, advice on sample ballots and techniques for sealing ballot boxes and recommendations as to what ought to be provided by way of instructions and equipment to the local election officers were all encompassed in communications from the high commissioner's staff on Saipan. Face-to-face consultation between the Headquarters' and field personnel charged with the enforcement of the congressional elections facilitated this flow of informal advice. Though not required to do so, the districts sometimes cleared with the high commissioner's office procedures and instructions drafted within the district. Serving as a controlling device which brought all details into focus, frequently requested progress reports kept the Trust Territory administration informed when deviations took place or when possible complications developed which would require further regulations from the high commissioner. These reports, the trips made by Saipan staff to the field, and the queries by the districts regarding problems arising locally all channeled to Headquarters a steady flow of information on the course of arrangements being made for the congressional elections.

The guide lines for all field preparations were embodied in Special Order No. 6 promulgated by the high commissioner. Prior to its drafting, existing district election provisions were examined to ascertain whether they could be employed as the basis for the congressional elections. The general survey revealed the absence of a body of election law and practice which could be easily adapted for such use. Truk, for example, reported it had no district election law except that in the district legislative charter, applicable only to elections for that body. The Marianas had used the Saipan municipal ordinances for electing Saipan's representatives to the Mariana Islands District Legislature. The chartered municipalities throughout the Territory followed comparable election procedures contained in their enabling grants, but in most cases these outlined procedures were too brief to serve the purpose of governing the congressional elections. District-to-district variances and the hiatuses which needed to be filled necessitated the preparation of a completely new election law which would apply uniformly throughout the Territory.

Early in the planning stage, the district administrators were circularized for regulations their staff believed ought be observed in holding the congressional elections. Once the draft of the Territorial election regulations had been completed in rough form by the Political Affairs Office, it was submitted to all district administrators with the request that it be treated as a top priority matter in order "to give prospective candidates and the people ample time to acquaint themselves with the provisions of . . . [the] proposed regulation prior to election day. . . ." [3] Meanwhile, the draft was sent to the legal office "for review and polishing up," [4] and the whole process culminated in the high commissioner's issuance of Special Order No. 6 on November 5, 1964. Incorporating recommendations gathered from many quarters, including some proposed by the Council of Micronesia when it debated the founding of a Territorial legislature, the order called for the district administrators' serving as district election commissioners, the appointment of election boards and tabulating committees, the nomination of candidates, the conduct of elections, and for recounts and appeals. Since time was of the essence, as processed by the legal office the draft could not be sent to each district for further review and comments prior to its becoming effective. However, in accordance with the guide lines expressed by the attorney general in a memorandum stating that the broad terminology of the Secretarial Order and Special Order No. 6 " . . . was intended to provide those who work with the Orders the opportunity to interpret the Orders to meet the complex situations existing in the vast Territory . . . ," [5] wide latitude was

[3] Memo of Deputy HiCom to all DistAds, Oct. 13, 1964.
[4] Memo of Political Affairs Officer to Acting Assistant Commissioner for Public Affairs, Oct. 27, 1964.
[5] Memo from Acting Attorney General to Acting Commissioner for Public Affairs, Dec. 11, 1964.

allowed each district in the application of the high commissioner's election directions.

Once these regulations governing the congressional elections were finalized and a second Special Order (No. 7) issued, designating the election districts within each of the six administrative areas of the Territory, the work of the Political Affairs Office at Headquarters was not reduced to merely reviewing and coordinating field preparations. Rather it sought to assist these field activities wherever possible. Radio programs on the new congress were prepared at Headquarters for translation and release over the district radio stations. The Liaison Office of the Trust Territory on Guam was supplied instructions for registering absentee voters, with attention to students temporarily resident in that American territory. The administration recognized the need for prompt attention, and every effort was made to expedite Saipan's handling of district election needs.

During a contest which followed the voting in the Marianas district, one of the letters exchanged which was dispatched to the Secretary of the Interior protested that "election procedure as set up in this district was in direct opposition to former elections." [6] Because of this discrepancy, the regulations propounded by the high commissioner, as supplemented by Saipan's district administrator serving as election commissioner, were challenged as not complying with Section 9 of the Secretarial Order creating the Congress of Micronesia. The author of the protest was accurate in his assessment that the regulations governing the congressional elections were not duplicated by those for holding district or local elections. Nevertheless, the protest was factually in error insofar as it referred to "direct *opposition* to former elections (emphasis added)," for much of the procedure and implementing details within the six administrative districts was based upon previous experience. Legally, the objection was unfounded as Section 27 of the Secretarial Order directed that the first general elections be held "in accordance with such regulations as may be promulgated by the High Commissioner," and for the most part every effort was made throughout the Territory to comply with this requirement.

DISTRICT ELECTION MACHINERY

The high commissioner's election regulations did not sharply

[6] Letter from Attorney G. Wilbert Grover to Secretary of Interior Udall, *circa* Feb., 1965.

differentiate between those duties which were to be performed by the district administrator as election commissioner and those which were to be assigned to his appointed district election boards. The setting up of voting precincts and of an appropriate polling place within each precinct, the overseeing of the order of names on the election ballot, and the ordering of recounts were a few of the tasks assigned to the election commissioners. Similarly, the election boards' functions were delineated with respect to the supervision and management of polling places, the actual conduct of elections, and the consideration of irregularities arising during the course of the election. Excluding these and a few other responsibilities, the bulk of the preparations remained unallocated, and it was within the discretion of each election commissioner to avail himself of his election boards' services. Most preferred to handle the election through district personnel as a normal administrative matter and, in fact, placed many of their permanent staff on the election boards. It was as acts of regular district employees, rather than as decisions of a separate board, that notices and publications concerning the elections were issued. As one of the consequences, the role played by the indigenous inhabitants in running their first election for congressmen varied markedly from district to district, with the major areas of comparability found in the staffing of the polls and the tallying of the votes.

In some districts the district administrator early called upon Micronesian political bodies to aid in preparing for the coming election. Two weeks before Secretarial Order 2882 was officially released by the Interior Department, the joint political development committees of the Yap Islands Council and the Yap Islands Congress began their deliberations on how the election might best be administered within their district. Thereafter the political committees continued to meet from time to time, while the assistant district administrator visited the Outer Islands in the Yap district to confer with local leaders there on plans for the holding of the election. The Marshall Islands District Congress and its Holdover Committee, and the chairmen of the Ponape district legislature's standing committees in the *ad hoc* capacity of a Holdover Committee, played a parallel role in their respective administrative districts. Consultations with political party leaders on Saipan and in Palau were put to the same use.

In retrospect, the ability of the election commissioner to involve his election boards in the details of election administration was closely related to their number, size, and the dispersion of their members. The high commissioner's order contemplated establishing a separate board for each election district, but some administrators named but one election board to serve all districts. For the most part these boards were too large or too scattered to function as single units administering the election. Section 5 of the election order directed that each polling place be physically supervised by at least one member of the district's election board during all hours of the election. This necessitated either the opening of the polls on different days so as to spread the use of the same personnel, if the board were to be kept small, or the creation of unwieldy, large election boards, possibly with members resident throughout the district. Forty-six members were named to the Marshallese election board; this board enjoyed a somewhat unusual composition, as it was comprised of the Marshall Islands district congressmen, each named for his respective atoll. The 13th Marshall Islands Congress was in session at Majuro when the Congress of Micronesia was announced, and the election requirements were first reviewed with the congressmen. After being appointed to the election board, they underwent a three-day orientation on the proposed election laws and procedures before returning home. The district administrator of Ponape secured both the advantage of collective advice and the service of enough members to meet the requirements of the high commissioner's Special Order. He accomplished this through the device of initially appointing only twelve persons and naming an executive committee of three on the election board to act in a liaison and advisory capacity; three weeks later, he expanded the original board to twenty-seven members, in time to enable the members of the enlarged board personally to supervise voting at all of the polls.

Special Order No. 6 disqualified any election board member from taking part in election campaigns after his appointment. The order would thus appear to have contemplated the naming of the politically neutral. Notwithstanding, in the Marshalls, where the district legislators served on the board, some candidates received active support from them. The members of the election boards in the Marianas were not appointed until the district's two political parties had forwarded the names of their nominees to the district administrator. In areas like the Marianas, where political tensions run high, such political party involvement was probably inevitable but, as a corollary, necessitated that favoritism be appropriately guarded against, as by requiring at least two persons of opposite political affiliation to be present personally at each polling place during the day of election.

In contrast to the generality of the high commissioner's order relative to political activity of election board members, it was specific in directing that board members be Trust Territory citizens entitled to vote for congressmen. Illustrative of the continuous supervision exercised by the high commissioner's office, when two Americans were added to the Marshallese election board by the district administrator, he was requested to replace them with two new appointments "at once to avoid any later challenge of [the] election proceedings." [7] There was, of course, nothing preventing American employees from serving as poll watchers along with the election board members.

REGISTRATION OF VOTERS

The high commissioner's Special Order No. 6 left to the discretion of each election commissioner the procedures for the registration of qualified voters within his district. As no previous Territory-wide registration had ever been undertaken, it was to be expected that the systems developed in the various districts would differ, as did even the registration forms. For the most part it was found impossible to insist upon advance registration as a precondition for voting, and in Ponape there was no pre-voting registration whatsoever.

Many people in the Trust Territory have lived for years in one area but regard another, possibly in a separate administrative district, as their home. Strong ties of land, family, and personal identification bind them to their "home" island. Registration was ordered because of this confused residency, with the hope that the evolving of machinery for recording residence would cause the problem to resolve itself through the recording of the voter's choice. Section 8 of the Secretarial Order creating the congress declares only that the franchise is to be vested in residents of the Trust Territory. An advisory memorandum on this section by the attorney general and on the "bona fide" district residence required of candidates (Sec. 7) added little guidance when it distinguished between " 'residence,' which is generally defined as any transient place of dwelling" and " 'bona fide residence' [which] means resi-

[7] Memo from HiCom to DistAd Marshalls, Dec. 28, 1964.

dence with domiciliary intent. . . ." [8] With advance registration, the voter would himself declare his residency, and all voting arrangements could be made accordingly. To accomplish this, the high commissioner's order allowed the election commissioners to set any procedure they preferred, so long as no one was disenfranchised. Headquarters on Saipan found no occasion to step in and reduce this grant of discretion.

In the Marianas, the services of the municipal government officers were enlisted in the registration drive, and both political parties were also pressed into service. A field trip was sent to the northern Marianas to register the several hundred potential voters residing there. In Palau, using the census as a basis, the staff of the election commissioner practically went from house to house registering the occupants. In most other areas, prospective voters had to travel to the place of registration; the forms were seldom brought to them for completion. Truk instructed its magistrates to compile lists of persons eligible to vote within their respective municipalities. The Marshalls provided for pre-election registration on only Majuro and Ebeye (the latter, part of Kwajalein atoll) and not on the outlying atolls. Long distances and scattered homes counterindicated advance registration on Ponape, so lists of voters were drawn from local census records.[9] Voters were to appear at the polling places written opposite their names on these lists.

Cut-off dates for pre-registration were announced in a number of districts and even formally extended in some, but in the end, eligible but unregistered voters appearing at the polls were allowed to cast their ballots. Except in those few places where pre-registration was vigorously enforced, as on Majuro and Ebeye in the Marshalls, registration was permitted concurrently with voting.[10] It was acknowledged by all that there had been insufficient time to institute an enforceable registration system for the first congressional elections. However, except in the few larger communities and in those between which movement is frequent, any person

[8] Memo from Acting Attorney General to Political Affairs Officer, Dec. 10, 1964.

[9] These records have a pseudo reliability, as persons changing their residences on Ponape are directed by law to notify the magistrate. In practice, not infrequently this is ignored.

[10] Early in November, the high commissioner authorized registration to be carried out on the day of election, and prior to voting, "if advance registration [is] impossible." HiCom to DistAd Marshalls, Nov., 1964. In anticipation of the second Congressional elections, advance registration was made mandatory. Sec. 8, Public Law 2–16, Congress of Micronesia.

coming to the polls is so well known that there was no need for anything but a record of his having voted.

The Political Affairs staff at Headquarters understandably took great interest in the technical arrangements for fixing the form of the ballot and for safe-keeping the ballots after the voting. A single, combined ballot was promoted for election districts with relatively few candidates, and separate ballots for each of the two house races when the choice was between a large number of candidates. Sample ballots were sent to all election commissioners. Headquarters also proposed that ballots be reproduced both in English and in the local language of the election district. This meant that administrative districts like Ponape would need employ four Micronesian languages, namely, Ponapean, Kapingamarangese, Kusaiean, and Nukuoran. Palau interpreted these suggestions in its own characteristic way by also including Japanese *kata kana* and pictoral insignia so as to accommodate illiterates and voters able to read only Japanese.

Special Order No. 6 (Sec. 1) directed the election commissioners to list all candidates in alphabetical order on the ballots for each election district. To the surprise of the uninitiated American, this had the unexpected consequence of placing all candidates in the order of their first names, rather than their last. Inferentially, this precluded ballots on which party candidates were grouped, so that it was impossible to structure the ballot to permit a single vote cast for a party to be counted for the entire party ticket.

In former elections, Palau and Truk had both employed insignia accompanying candidates' names on district election ballots. Truk decided to eliminate their use at the congressional election as it was believed that such symbols influenced the election results, apart from the candidate's personal qualifications. As one informant commented on the choice of symbols, "Breadfruit is quite appealing to the Trukese." Although there was some discussion on the part of the election staff on Palau regarding the fairness of the insignia adopted by the candidates for congressional posts, nothing obviously totemic was employed and none were ruled improper. Some of the symbols may have carried references to introduced institutions—the coconut to its user's position on the Territorial Copra Stabilization Board or the insignia of a fish to the candidate's being a Christian. In the main, the insignia served as intended, merely as a mechanism to enable illiterate voters to identify their choices upon the ballot.

Each election commissioner had the authority to devise his own absentee balloting procedures. As a degree of uniformity was advisable, Headquarters at Saipan suggested that notice be sent to residents away from their districts, advising them to apply for absentee ballots and instructing them to furnish the data necessary to prove voting eligibility. Temporary district residents were to be similarly informed of their right to absentee ballots from their home districts, and inter-district arrangements were to be made for handling absentee voting. On its part, Headquarters instructed its Liaison Office on Guam to facilitate the absentee voting of qualified students there. The response was uneven. Some districts exerted strenuous efforts to contact absent residents and to acquaint temporary residents within the district of their voting privilege in their home district. By direct correspondence between Kusaie of Ponape district and Ebeye in the Marshalls, arrangements were made to assure the franchise of the large Kusaiean population working on Ebeye. Sometimes special absentee ballots were printed. In general, all election commissioners supplied absentee ballots to persons temporarily outside their home districts for business or educational purposes. In Truk the absentee voting procedure was employed for prisoners and hospital patients unable to attend the polling place. The Marianas reported sending absentee ballots to persons who had obtained permanent-residence status on Guam. The variety of absentee balloting procedures applied and the problem presented by the large number of people at district centers who consider themselves to be permanent residents of other areas assured that a Territory-wide absentee-ballot law would be enacted for future congressional elections.

Early in the preparations for the election, Headquarters sent explicit instructions to all district administrators for the building of tamper-proof ballot boxes. Not only did the blueprints detail sturdy construction, but inner and outer locks were to be attached to prevent access by unauthorized personnel. Even prescribed was the manner in which the lid was to be sealed with masking tape after it was closed and before the exterior padlock was placed on the outside hasp. It was planned that each poll would have its own ballot box, which would facilitate the tallying of votes when the boxes were brought to a central place for counting. The durability of the boxes is attested to by their continuing to survive the rigors of rough seas and perhaps even more punishing land roadways. If for nothing else, the first congressional elections will long be remembered by the over one hundred ballot boxes which remain throughout the Trust Territory to serve local and district election needs as well as future elections for the Congress of Micronesia.

NOMINATIONS AND CANDIDACY

Soliciting views from the districts preparatory to the high commissioner's promulgation of Special Order No. 6 encouraged a number of replies pertaining to the manner in which nomination ought be processed. Given the time available and the level of election technology in the Territory, some of them were impractical, such as the suggestion from Palau for the institution of primary elections to reduce the number of candidates to three for each office. Underlying all these proposals was the joint need, on the one hand, to encourage nominations and, on the other, to incorporate some way to narrow the field of aspirants for office so that a successful candidate would represent a sizeable plurality of the voters. Other than in the provision made for party nominations, the high commissioner, in effect, ignored all district recommendations and issued election regulations based on the views expressed in the Council of Micronesia, which favored the use of nominating petitions. Nevertheless, in a number of contests, district-sponsored screening mechanisms were employed within the framework of the procedures laid down in the high commissioner's regulations.

In outlining the nomination process to be followed, Special Order No. 6 stated that nominations might be self-proposed, made by sponsors, or by political party. For the office of delegate, the five sponsors initiating the petition had to be joined by no less than fifty additional citizens all declaring that they were residents of the district and entitled to vote and that their candidate met the legal qualifications to run.

For office of assemblyman, the number of supplemental sponsors was twenty-five. Although a candidate could be self-nominated, few such nominations were filed. In the Marianas the political parties nominated all candidates, in the Palaus the bulk of the candidates were similarly proposed, and in the remaining districts most candidates' names were placed in nomination by sponsors.

The Trust Territory had experimented with a variety of procedures in choosing delegates for the Council of Micronesia, but central to most processes was the district legislature. The Marianas were atypical, with municipal bodies nominating five candidates who were voted upon on all islands but Rota for one of the Mariana district's council seats; the other council seat was allocated outright to Rota. In the Marshalls, the district congress selected ten candidates who ran at large, and the two highest vote-getters were declared elected. The Truk procedure was identical, except that a ticket of only five candidates was nominated. Palau, too, observed the five-candidate limit but consolidated the election for council delegate with the spring municipal elections. In Ponape the whole process was short-circuited by its congress' directly choosing the district's two council delegates. As was to be expected, some of the comments early forwarded to the high commissioner would have had the district legislatures continue to nominate the candidates to be voted upon.[11]

For the Congress of Micronesia elections, Ponape established committees composed of representatives chosen by the municipal councils within an Assembly district. For Assembly District B, which encompassed Mokil and other outer islands, names were forwarded to a Mokilese resident on Ponape who took part in the deliberations of the committee. Each committee made nominations for both assemblymen and delegates, and for the latter, were not restricted to candidates residing within its Assembly district. The adoption of this procedure did not discourage a few self-nominations, but at least one of these candidates later withdrew, and none was elected. In the Yap district, both the chiefs on the Yap Islands and the Outer Islands hereditary chiefs took an active part in designating candidates. Initially on the Yap Islands, nominees were chosen by "primary election meetings" in the ten unchartered municipalities, and their number was reduced by the Yap Islands Congress and Yap Islands Council. Signature of a chief as a sponsor on a nomination petition constituted the chief's commitment to aid the candidate, and this carried considerable importance in Yap.

The high commissioner's election regulations authorized political parties registered with the election commissioners to nominate candidates for office. No criteria were stated for qualifying as a party. In Palau, the election commissioner accepted the request

---

[11] There is the suspicion that nominations made by district legislatures would have permitted dominant factions within them to favor their own candidates and rule out those of their opponents.

for registration tendered by the chairman of the Progressive Party as *prima facie* proof of party existence. The president of Palau's Liberal Party accompanied his request for registration with a copy of the party's tentative charter and by-laws and reference to the fact that the party had run candidates during the previous district legislative election. Saipan's election commissioner served notice on the chairmen of both the Popular and Democratic (name later changed to Territorial) Parties that as recognized political organizations they should provide him with the names of party officers and, if possible, their by-laws. Parties had to be registered at least a week before the closing date for filing nominations in order for their candidates to be accepted. Not more than one candidate for each political office could be sponsored by a party. Both in the Marianas and Palau the parties mustered full slates for all congressional offices to be filled.

The party meetings in Palau to nominate candidates consisted primarily of caucuses of party leaders. In the Progressive Party, when some of the aspirants for office were not included on the ticket prepared by the party's policy committee, they walked out of the caucus and later ran as independents. Organization in the Marianas was more ceremonious, and delegates from the ten municipal districts (precincts) on Saipan and from Rota and Tinian assembled in formal convention to select their parties' nominees. The Popular Party is reputed to have been more democratic than its rival in allowing greater popular participation in the choosing of candidates for the party slate. As the conventions in the Marianas appeared to do little more than ratify designations already prearranged, there was more difference in form than in substance in the manner in which the parties of the two districts went about choosing their standard bearers. Only party candidates were on the Mariana district ballot; in Palau, independents stood and one succeeded in winning election.

One of the last modifications in drafting Secretarial Order No. 2882 waived the disqualification of Micronesians holding top level government posts for the first two congressional elections. The Ponape district administrator, in a memorandum sent to all district administrators, proposed that the conflict of interest inherent in the position of those executive and judicial officers also serving as congressmen, and the possible hampering effect this conflict might have on relationships between congressmen, be discussed

with potential candidates "and their candidacy not encouraged—
if not actively discouraged." [12] A memorandum from Headquarters
responded to this, arguing that the benefits to be gained from having senior government employees with training and experience in
local government take part in the formative years of the congress
outweighed the disadvantages. Although not foreclosing informal
discussions with such individuals, the memorandum stressed that
the district administrators should neither prevent nor discourage
their candidacy. The number of persons holding high administrative positions who filed as candidates evidences that little covert
sabotage of the Secretarial Order resulted.

Around district centers, no difficulty was encountered in dis-
tributing nomination forms and returning the petitions to the election commissioner for verification of the signatures affixed. In distant islands, particularly those reached at infrequent intervals by
field trip, there was insufficient time to follow this procedure. In
a few instances, as in the Hall Islands of the Truk district, residents were instructed to transmit their nominating petitions by
radio. For the most part, when residents from distant places were
nominated, petitions would be signed by persons from their areas
present at the district headquarters.[13] A nominee for the General
Assembly had to qualify only as a bona fide resident of the administrative district, but most candidates for the lower house had
at least nominal claims to residency in their putative Assembly
districts. The new procedure of nomination by petition worked to
the advantage of the Micronesians stationed close to the district
headquarters. In defense of this procedure, given the movement to
these centers of the outer-island persons most qualified to deal with
Americans and their political institutions, any other nomination
system would most likely have placed the names of the same candidates upon the ballot.

While nomination petitions were being circulated, the Attorney
General's Office ruled that a citizen could subscribe to more than
one nomination paper. This eliminated time-consuming cross-
checking by the election commissioners' staffs as they verified the
names on each petition. Post-election examination of a number of

[12] Memo of DistAd Ponape to all DistAds, Oct. 26, 1964.
[13] In the Marshalls, all candidates were nominated by action either on
Ebeye or Majuro. A radio broadcast from the latter listed the nominees and
advised the voters that, if dissatisfied, write-ins were permissible. This ex-
plains the 5 per cent write-in of all recorded votes for delegate and 4 per cent
for assemblymen in this district.

the petitions on file, some listing only subscribers' given names and with more than one obviously written by the same hand, leads to the conclusion that many names must have been accepted on faith. Given the level of political sophistication of Island life, such action was probably not ill advised and, in any event, in many cases was compensated for by multiple nominations for the same candidate. Popular Dwight Heine of the Marshalls received nine separate nominations for the Assembly and two for the House of Delegates!

Scrutiny by the election commissioner's staff also ran to the qualifications of the candidates. Residency within the administrative district had to be confirmed. The determination that the nomination of Jose Cruz should not be denied because of a felony conviction was to be the basis for a court contest and, later, for a challenge in the House of Delegates. In the Marshalls, Dr. John Kaman was disqualified as a candidate because he failed to meet the five-year Trust Territory citizenship requirement. If a candidate received nominations for both the House and the General Assembly, or for two different seats in the latter, he had to elect which to run for, which necessitated the election commissioner's communicating with the candidate. As petitions could be presented without the consent of the nominee, the election commissioners published notices of the deadline within which nominations could be refused and also tried to contact all nominees, seeking assurance that they desired to stand for election. The nomination of people absent from the Territory raised additional complications; one, in response to a radiogram inquiring if he accepted nomination, replied, "What will my people say if I refuse their nomination. What kind of a leader would I be?" The message was construed as an acceptance.[14]

Originally, it had been recommended that a deadline of around November 30 be set for filing candidates' petitions, which would have left ample time to the administration for printing the ballots and making other necessary preparations, and to the candidates for campaigning. With the high commissioner's order fixing the boundaries of the Assembly districts delayed until November 30, this time-table had to be abandoned. All that Headquarters at Saipan could do was to remind the election commissioners of their responsibility for establishing the filing date for nominations and withdrawals. Palau named December 15 as its deadline for filing and the 31st of the month for withdrawals; the Marshalls used the

[14] HiCom to DistAd Ponape, Dec., 1964. The candidate lost the election.

latter day as the filing and (presumably) withdrawal deadline; Truk settled on December 19 as the last filing date for nominations within the Truk lagoon, and the 25th for the outlying islands. Given district disparities, the need of uniformity for deadlines throughout the Territory may be questioned. Given those same differences, the relatively short time available for the circulation of nomination petitions, after the Assembly district boundaries were officially declared, supplies grounds for criticism.

With all the nominations complete and qualified, within the six administrative districts there was an average of about three candidates for each post to be filled. Of the twenty General Assembly races in which there were contests, almost half (9) were between only two contenders. Four of the six delegate elections also had only double the number of candidates for the two at-large seats. To Ponape and Truk went the dubious distinction of having so many aspirants for office as to allow each only a statistically low

STATISTICAL CHANCES OF CANDIDATES FOR ELECTION
(in percentages of 100)

	Assembly	House	Both
AVERAGE	31.3	42.8	34.7
Marianas	50.0	50.0	50.0
Yap	40.0	50.0	44.4
Palau	37.5	33.3	35.7
Marshalls	30.8	50.0	35.3
Truk	27.8	50.0	31.8
Ponape	23.5	33.3	26.1

chance of success. Three districts, D of the Marshalls and Districts A for Ponape and Truk, registered six candidates for but one legislative seat. In contrast, in one of Ponape's Assembly districts, a single candidate qualified.

Relatively early in the planning for the congressional elections, Truk district was advised that it was necessary for all nominated candidates, whose names were not subsequently withdrawn, to be placed on the ballot and voted upon, even if unopposed. The reasons underlying this were that the Secretarial Order stipulated the members of congress were to be chosen by secret ballot, and in addition, the first congressional elections were regarded as an appropriate vehicle for developing an understanding of proper voting procedures. Somehow, this instruction was not communicated widely, and Bethwel Henry of Ponape was later declared elected as an unopposed Assembly candidate. The series of events which led up to this well illustrates the workings of the nomination system on Ponape. The nominating committee proposed five candidates for Ponape General Assembly District B. One nominee quickly declined, the papers for two others did not receive the requisite number of sponsors' signatures, and on the last day for filing nominations, the fourth nominee withdrew. As Ponapeans look upon those who nominate themselves as "pushing" and few self-initiated nominations were submitted—and none for this district seat—the late withdrawal left only one candidate in the race. The election-district board met and declared Henry elected. It was not discovered that the Ponape ballot had omitted any provision for voting in District B until after the high commissioner had issued his certificate of election.

THE CAMPAIGNS

Sweeping generalizations purporting to encompass the whole of the Trust Territory are gross at best and, when relating to political activity, are highly suspect. This is due to many factors: the heterogeneity of permissible conduct within even a single administrative district, the awakening of interest in the introduced American institutions joined with a rise in political expectations, and the gradual adoption of Western forms of political action by the younger office seekers. There is good reason for believing that in some of the districts such Western-type political activity by candidates may have more harmed than aided their cause at the congressional elections, but each year the number of such candidates grows, and it is only a matter of time before the new ways are grudgingly tolerated and then become an integral part of the political mores. The Interior Department's report that "it would be a violation of traditional modesty and self-depreciation to seek support actively for public office in almost all islands of the Territory" [15] may have described the politics of 1958, but it did not as neatly fit campaigning for congressional posts on "almost all is-

[15] *11th Annual Report of the United States to the United Nations, 1958,* p. 33. As early as 1958, at a public meeting in Ponape, the first instance of active campaigning was recorded, a far cry from the Ponapean exaggerated modesty and fear of criticism for pretentiousness commented upon little more than a decade previously. See William R. Bascom, *Ponape: A Pacific Economy in Transition,* USCC Economic Survey No. 8 (Honolulu: 1946), pp. 27–31.

lands" in 1964. At succeeding congressional elections it will be even less applicable.

An additional note of caution must be sounded. Inquiries addressed to all candidates brought replies from many denying that they had engaged in campaigning. They were responding with the stereotype concept of American electioneering in mind, or as one phrased it, there were "no rallies, public debates, public addresses, luncheons, buzz sessions, campaign literature and entertainments." But this same candidate appreciated that he had actively campaigned: "My campaign was based entirely [upon] the grassroots of Marshallese politics, i.e., 'smoke-filled room' politics."

In the Trust Territory, traditional political maneuvering, at times highly involved, meets the function filled elsewhere by political parties and platforms, parades and billboards, and other aspects of aggressive electioneering. This engrafting of old processes to the new political forms is explained by the introduction of copied institutions' not always being accompanied by the processes normally associated with them in situ; customary processes then fill the hiatus so as to assure viability to the borrowed. Thus it becomes necessary to differentiate between "electioneering," or "overt campaigning" as another Marshallese candidate phrased it, and the mustering of support to influence voters in more subdued and traditional ways, the "campaigning" which is encountered in most parts of the Trust Territory. The change in political activity which is occurring in Micronesia is best epitomized as a movement from covert campaigning to overt electioneering. Of course all this confusion of terminology does not rule out the fact that some candidates for the first Congress of Micronesia did not campaign in any manner. Reported one: "I did not campaign. I did not even know that my name was on the nomination ticket but heard it over the radio. I just let it go and let the people decide for themselves who they want to elect." This Trukese candidate was elected.

The Mariana and Palau districts, each with recognized political parties and organized electioneering, polarize apart from the other four administrative districts which know no parties and in which, at most, congressional candidates engaged in individual campaigning. When the press release from the Information Office at Saipan Headquarters reported active campaigning beginning early in December and continuing to election day, "complete with rallies, motorcades, posters, handbills, speeches and hand shaking . . . carried out with the same enthusiasm and vigor of any community in the United States," [16] it was mainly referring to these two districts on the western fringes of the Trust Territory.

The formation of Palau's political parties in 1963 represented no movement of protest against objectionable practices of the administration, nor even a spontaneous coalescing of Palau's power figures to seek common cause for personal gain through the facade of party structure. Rather, the instituting of political parties nicely satisfied traditional American political norms and neatly coincided with the parallel structuring of competition traditional to Palauan life.[17] The district administrator suggested the time was ripe for the formation of parties to further self-government, and the leaders of Palau's new political elite obligingly divided themselves into the Liberal and the Progressive Parties.

At the formative meeting, the persons attending found themselves agreed on almost everything, so that their cleavage into two parties represented no ideological split but, if anything, identification of birthplace, the old Koror or Melekeok Confederation. The voters, too, favored one or the other party not so much upon the basis of platform as on their political leaders. The parties thus constituted but loose configurations around a number of individuals, without institutionalized structures or party treasuries. Expenses were met personally by the candidates and their supporters. As a consequence, the two parties' policy positions were not sharply distinguished. Both supported greater self-government, but the Liberal Party was more inclined to move faster while preserving the Palau identity from being lost in that of the Trust Territory. The Progressive Party was considered more pro-business; the Liberal Party, more critical of the administration and inclined toward restricting American entry into the Palauan economy. Progressive candidates ambiguously referred to a closer relationship with the United States in a tie resembling a British commonwealth, while Liberal Party aspirants mentioned independence for Micronesia "sometime in the future." The platform planks of the Liberal Party did not aid in erecting a distinctive party position,[18] and the Progressive Party adopted no platform for the congressional elections. The stand of each was disclosed by the tenor of party leaders' speeches and their respective stances before the public.

[16] Press Release, Information Office, Jan. 19, 1965.
[17] See Robert Kellogg McKnight, "Competition in Palau" (Ph.D. thesis, Ohio State University: 1960), pp. 98–99.
[18] "Our Pledge, Our Aim, Our Hope," 1965 Platform of the Liberal Party of Palau, *circa* Dec., 1964.

Between the Palau party candidates and independents, most campaign techniques used in the United States were duplicated short of television shows and skywriting. Because of limited resources, the campaigns were modest, but the effort was no less ambitious. The administration printing facilities were made available to candidates for publishing leaflets. Posters, pamphlets, public rallies complete with entertainment and refreshments, radio speeches, house-to-house electioneering—all were employed. Party candidates campaigned both in teams and as individuals. On the day of the election, they arranged transportation to the polls for the voters. The administration had allocated radio time on Wednesday and Sunday mornings for electioneering, with each candidate entitled to a maximum of ten minutes a day and the parties fifty minutes. While voting was on-going, the district radio maintained an all-day election schedule. Some of the campaigning was in English, most in Palauan, and even Japanese was employed for candidates' names. Candidates tended toward the "soft-sell," stressing the abilities of their party's team rather than emphasizing their own qualifications for congressional posts.

All party candidates received party assistance in their campaigning. In other administrative districts, candidates stated clubs, cooperatives, and religious groups had aided, but reference to such groups was absent in questionnaire replies from Palau. However, one candidate did indicate he had received the support of the Modekgnie, which urged its members to vote for him. The Modekgnie movement in Palau had its origins in Japanese times when it was a religious protest group, remains nativistic in appeal, and bears a vague resemblance to cargo cults found in other parts of Oceania.[19] This unsuccessful candidate was a nominee of the Liberal Party, which fact lent confirmation to the rumor that the Modekgnie movement was backing Liberal Party candidates.

Almost all that has been described about Palau in the way of party action at the congressional elections was duplicated in the Marianas, except that the Palauan endeavors appear both subdued and amateurish in comparison. The Palau congressional elections could be followed by a post-election day celebration, complete with parade, floats, and addresses by the successful candidates,

---

[19] For consideration of Modekgnie, see Arthur J. Vidich, "The Political Impact of Colonial Administration" (Ph.D. thesis, Harvard University: 1952), Chap. 10. The use of the dove insignia for the identification of candidates was undoubtedly tied to the movement.

with the chairmen of Palau's two parties jointly serving as masters of ceremony for the occasion. It is improbable that this could have been replicated on Saipan. Politics in the Marianas are highly charged emotionally and as a consequence are taken seriously. Bodily damage and injury to property as a result of political quarrels are not unknown on Saipan.

As Guam has been "the center of the Chamorro's world," [20] the Northern Mariana parties and their tendencies to political histrionics have been cast in the model of Guam's two parties. In December, 1960, when only the Popular Party existed on Guam, the Popular Party of Saipan was organized. Two months later the Northern Mariana's Progressive Party came into being, but despite its title, it had no tie with the identically named party in Palau. Later it assumed the name "Democratic Party" but never became affiliated with the Democratic Party of the United States. Finally, it called itself the "Territorial Party" because it had "the greatest respect and admiration for the Territorial Party of Guam" and also shared the same "ultimate goal" of "the highest interests of all peoples and not just those of certain partisan groups and factions. . . ." [21] All this is a far cry from a 1944 evaluation that there was no evidence "the moderate degree of political self-consciousness" developed among the Chamorros of Guam had ever spread to their cousins in the other Marianas.[22]

By 1964, the deep policy rift between the Northern Mariana parties over merger with Guam, and subsidiary differences such as free transportation on Saipan, distinguished the Mariana political organizations from the personal coterie parties of Palau. The Popular Party threatened to boycott the congressional elections in the Marianas as a protest against the founding of the Congress of Micronesia and its purpose of furthering Territorial unity. Later, it amended this position, for that course would have meant defaulting all posts to the opposition; instead, if successful, its candidates would withdraw from the congress. (Only one Popular

---

[20] Alexander Spoehr, *Saipan: The Ethnology of a War-Devastated Island*, Fieldiana: Anthropology, Vol. 41 (Chicago: Chicago Natural History Museum, 1954), p. 181.

[21] Resolution adopted by the Democratic Party, Feb., 1965. It was imperative that the name be changed as the Northern Marianas' Popular Party was openly co-operating with Guam's Democratic Party (formerly the Popular Party) in seeking union of the whole Marianas.

[22] U.S. Navy, *Civil Affairs Handbook* (Mandated Marianas Islands), OPNAV P22-8 (formerly OPNAV 50E-8) (Washington: Office of the Chief of Naval Operations, 1944), p. 79.

Party member was elected and, without incident, he accepted and retained his seat.) The candidates of both parties electioneered long and hard. There had not been organized electioneering on Rota until the first congressional elections, and both parties copied there and on Tinian the ticket appearances at public mass meetings, the posting of placards, the distribution of pamphlets, and the face-to-face campaigning which has become standard on Saipan. Only the islands north of Saipan were not visited by the candidates, and if limited transportation had not precluded, they too undoubtedly would have been engulfed in the torrent of extemporaneous political speech-making which nearly submerged the entire Marianas district.[23]

Two delegates from Ponape and the Marshalls were elected while they were in Hawaii; other successful candidates for congressional office in these two administrative districts and in Truk were absent from their electoral districts for the entire length of the campaign. It was not essential that they be present, for in Yap and the three eastern districts of the Territory electioneering was just becoming institutionalized. Because knowledge of the candidates was widely shared, it was possible for them to be elected on their reputations, aided by covert campaigning on their behalf. As expressed by one informant, "Everyone in the Marshalls knows the exact number of crimes and sins each has committed. Everyone also knows what one stands for and what one is against. Before I left for Saipan, I expressed my desire to run for the Lower House, [and] when I returned I was in."

In Truk, candidates were allotted fifteen-minute periods to broadcast over the district radio station; practically all responded with subdued, modest statements. Only two candidates complied with the request that they prepare statements to be printed in the *Truk Tide,* the district administration's weekly bulletin, "on how they feel qualified to help their fellow Micronesians." [24] Neither was successful at the polls. The experience in Ponape was comparable; several who gave "fighting speeches" on the radio and engaged in overt electioneering were defeated. It was the consensus that their approach offended and that it was believed "they thought too well of themselves." However, a "humble plea" over

---

[23] One informant estimates candidates' average public speech lasted at least thirty minutes! Their conduct was a far cry from Spoehr's statement, *circa* 1950, that for a man to campaign publicly on Saipan in his own behalf would be an unthinkable breech of modesty. Spoehr, *op. cit.,* p. 179.

[24] *Truk Tide,* Jan. 15, 1964, p. 1.

the radio was favorably received. Even in conservative Yap, several candidates distributed printed leaflets, and five candidates appeared at a rally before high school students (many of voting age), introduced themselves, and stated their platforms. All of this evidences that low key electioneering is not necessarily proscribed by traditional mores, and it may be anticipated that at future congressional elections there will be additional formulation and presentation of candidates' programs, broadcasting of laudatory statements, and use of printed materials to reach those voters who cannot be spoken to in person and to reinforce the impact of contact on those who are.

This does not mean that customary campaigning, through securing the endorsement of traditional chiefs and clan leaders who in turn influence their followers, will not still continue, or that family and friends will not discreetly champion the cause of candidates. Political aspirants will seek employment that permits them to be of assistance to potential voters and allows their capacities to become well known. Presence on field trips will bring the candidates to the attention of the inhabitants of the outer islands, even if the candidates engage in no formal electioneering. Letter writing to key friends and opinion leaders, to the latter possibly through intermediaries in the absence of close personal friendship, will enlist support in those situations where face-to-face visits are not feasible. All of these techniques played a part in shaping the vote at the first congressional elections in those more traditional areas of the Trust Territory where there was "no campaigning." As greater interest in expanding governmental services develops among the voters, and as they come to understand how their vote helps determine this, the same electioneering which is now encountered in Palau and the Marianas will gradually spread to the rest of the districts, whether or not accompanied with the formation of parties.

CONDUCT OF THE ELECTIONS

The election commissioners, through the district weekly news bulletins, radio broadcasts, and community meetings, alerted the electorate to the importance of the congressional elections and the need for compliance with election registration and voting regulations. Election board members stationed near the district headquarters were instructed in the procedures to be followed in opening and closing the polls, confirming the right of each voter to cast a ballot, rendering assistance to illiterates, safe-keeping marked ballots, and accounting for unused and spoiled ballots. The applicable directions received from Headquarter's staff on Saipan and the district election regulations were mimeographed as a supplement to this training and as preparation for the board personnel and poll watchers who could not be reached in person. Early in the election planning, voting dates were correlated with field trip schedules, and the polling places were located within the voting precincts. For each, arrangements had to be completed for providing voting booths, tables, chairs, ballot boxes, and voter registers, ballots, and necessary supplies. Licensed sellers of alcohol were warned not to furnish beverages during balloting and the police were put on notice should their protection at the polls be required. With all these preparations completed, the actual conduct of the elections fell to Micronesians scattered across the breadth of the Territory, in the main under the supervision of district personnel. As was to be expected, there were modifications and improvisations, and the polling did not always follow the letter of the regulations. But from all accounts received, the elections were administered without disturbance and accurately recorded the electorate's free choice of candidates.

Recognizing it was impossible for the elections to be held on the one day named in the Secretarial Order—January 19—given the Territory's inadequate transportation facilities and the limited time available for completing election preparations, the high commissioner expressly authorized advance elections in "romote areas" [25] and countenanced variances for others. In the Truk district, voting occurred at different places in the Hall Islands between December 28 and December 30, followed by the Mortlock and Western Islands from January 4 to January 14, while the elections within the Truk lagoon commenced on January 11, and only the balloting on Moen, seat of the district headquarters, took place on January 19. Palau, Ponape, and the Marianas started polling outlying areas early in January, as did the Marshalls. The Marshalls were unable to retrieve all of the ballot boxes and return them to Majuro for tallying until a week after the official election date had passed.[26] The elec-

[25] Memo from Acting Assistant Commissioner for Public Affairs to all DistAds, Nov. 10, 1964.

[26] In the Marshalls, district legislators returned to their home atolls on the outbound leg of the field trip which also brought the ballots and ballot boxes, supervised the elections, and delivered the sealed ballot boxes to the field-trip ship on its inbound voyage.

tions in the Outer Islands of the Yap district did not begin until January 27, a week later than the official election date, and were concluded twelve days thereafter. In short, the bulk of the Territory's population did not cast their ballots on the election date prescribed in the Secretarial Order. Nevertheless, the completion of the entire voting within the span of a little over a month represents an administrative achievement for the Trust Territory.

The same discretionary adjustments characterized application of the election regulations of the high commissioner and the district administrators. In most places, despite advance registration, any voter coming to the polls could register immediately preceding voting. The 7:00 A.M. to 7:00 P.M. polling times had to be adjusted to fit field-trip sailing schedules. Absentee voters were accommodated in numerous ways, even to setting up a special polling booth for Kusaieans on Ebeye in the Marshalls, where over a hundred qualified voters from the Ponapean district were working. Except in the Marianas district, the voters took all variations in stride without filing any formal complaints of irregularities.

In the more populated areas, voters came to fixed polling places; in some of the smaller areas, the election officials took the election boxes around from village to village, and house to house if necessary. The Palaus had little need for assisting voters at the polls due to the use of the candidates' insignia on posters and ballots, and to extensive advance voter instruction. It was reported that literacy in the local vernacular is so high in the Marshalls that it obviated the need for any voter assistance there because of inability to read the ballot; however, there is reason to discount this. In the other four districts, over an estimated 1,200 voters were aided, with "whisper" votes extensively employed in the islands between Truk atoll and the Yap Islands. However, voters no longer believed it appropriate etiquette to crawl the last thirty feet or so on all fours to whisper their preference to the administration's representative,[27] thereby exhibiting traditional deference, as occurred in some early elections under the Americans. Trust Territory employees could take temporary absences from work to ballot, and in district headquarters, where lines of voters queued before the polling booths, a goodly part of the normal three-hour maximum leave from work allowed may have been consumed in waiting.

[27] See memo of John L. Fischer, "Report of Special Investigation of Political Situation on Puluwat, May 24 to May 31, 1950" (University of Hawaii, Sinclair Library, Micro. 594), p. 5.

The Palau district reported it was impossible to land a boat on Merir Island due to rough seas, and thus the consequent disenfranchisement of eleven eligible voters. The Marianas district experienced the same difficulty on Alamagan, Sarigan, and Anatahan, all north of Saipan, and an estimated thirty-two potential voters were unable to cast ballots. On the other hand, when the Marshalls' field-trip ship could not send a boat in to pick up the ballot box from Kili, the former Bikini residents there swam the box with its load of marked ballots through the surf. The votes were later counted on Majuro, even though the registration records had to be left behind and the number of ballots in the box could not be checked against the recorded voters.

In most administrative districts the election returns were tallied at district headquarters, with the ballot boxes from the outer areas brought in and opened by the special Counting and Tallying Committees of Micronesians appointed for that purpose. In the Marianas, separate committees on Rota and Tinian counted the ballots cast in their respective areas, and the results were then added to the tallies made for Saipan. Yap had two committees, and the one named for the Outer Islands traveled with the field-trip ship carrying the ballot boxes back to Colonia and there tallied the vote.[28] At least five hundred absentee ballots [29] were included within the count of their appropriate districts. No ballot boxes were opened until January 19, so that despite the advance balloting in some areas, there was no chance for a bandwagon effect to sway the course of the voting. Final tallies were announced by January 20 in all but the Marshalls and Yap districts; in both of the latter, partial returns were released, but the final count of ballots was not completed at Majuro until January 31 and in Yap until February 10. Candidates or their representatives and numerous spectators watched the canvass of the ballots, and the district radio stations broadcast running commentaries on the contests. The final returns were both broadcast and published for distribution throughout the districts.

The conduct of the polling was uneventful, with the only un-

---

[28] In effect, Yap had two election commissions, and the one for the Outer Islands also served as their Counting and Tallying Committee.

[29] This figure of absentee ballots represents the total reported by all districts. As Ponape listed only 6 absentee ballots and had a large Kusaiean population eligible to vote absentee, the total is questionable and revised would probably approximate 600, or about 3 per cent of the vote cast at the 1965 congressional elections.

toward incident noted being in Palau, where two candidates made an attempt to instruct voters inside a polling place. Another candidate was dissuaded from campaigning with a tape recorder just outside the 100-foot neutral zone surrounding a poll. The Marshalls had to decide the right of several voters to cast ballots on Majuro, when record of their registration could not be located; this was one of the few areas in the Trust Territory where advance registration was enforced. When votes were tallied, the Marshalls also had to deal with a ballot box containing substantially more ballots than there were registration slips.

All of these incidents were minor and brought no formal objections such as the three lodged in the Marianas. One of these concerned duplication of registrations on Saipan; a bipartisan committee of four members appointed by the election commissioner investigated and found only one instance of double registration and voting, and that, in fact, had already been rectified. The protest over failure to have returns from the northernmost islands included in the final tabulations, due to rough seas preventing a landing, was rejected on a technicality turning on improper filing. The final protest concerned the qualifications of Delegate-elect Jose Cruz, and although it brought in collateral charges of alleged election irregularities on Rota, the latter protest was regarded as untimely. The basic issue could finally be resolved only by the House of Delegates itself.

THE ELECTION RESULTS [30]

In the words of President Johnson's congratulatory message to the Congress of Micronesia, "The . . . elections to the first Congress of Micronesia, with their surprisingly heavy voter turnout were an impressive demonstration of the maturity . . ." of the Micronesians.[31] A total of 25,062 persons went to the polls and cast ballots in the first congressional elections. This constituted an estimated 60.4 per cent of the eligible voters, far exceeding the turnout of "off-year" congressional elections in the United States and comparing well with that country's quadrennial presidential elections. Generally, the larger the administrative district's eligible population,

[30] The data in this section are based upon the election reports submitted by all six district administrators and the report of the high commissioner to the Office of Territories, dated March 11, 1965. In some cases, internal inconsistencies had to be resolved, but this will not materially affect any of the conclusions drawn.

[31] *The Rai Review,* July 14, 1965, p. 1.

the lower its percentage of voting (negative rank correlation of .94). The voters close to district headquarters turned out in no greater numbers than in the remaining election districts and, in a majority of cases, made a poorer showing.

VOTER TURNOUT, 1965 CONGRESSIONAL ELECTIONS

	Estimated Eligibles	Persons Voting	Percentage	Headquarters Turnout *
Yap	3,290	2,767	84.1%	75.7%
Mariana	4,104	3,356	81.8%	76.3%
Palau	4,654	3,711	79.7%	76.4%
Marshalls	8,000	4,218	52.7%	37.7%
Ponape	9,200	5,637	61.3%	61.7%
Truk	12,255	5,373	43.8%	45.7%
Total	41,503	25,062	60.4%	

* Based on estimated voters in General Assembly district encompassing district headquarters; on Saipan, District B.

Voting data for the Outer Islands in the Yap district show the phenomenally high return of 96.5 per cent of estimated eligibles. In the Truk district, the Mortlocks (64.1%) and the Halls and Western Islands (74.3%) also demonstrate that the peoples in the outlying islands went to the polls in heavier numbers than those living adjacent to the district headquarters. This finding diametrically conflicts with the commonly reported phenomena of lower voter turnout ratios for rural than for urban regions.[32] Although district headquarters areas hardly approximate an urban metropolis, it might have been expected that for somewhat comparable reasons they would have had higher voter participation among their populations. The explanation for the divergence lies mainly in two complementary factors. The smaller islands received almost hamlet by hamlet servicing, while in the more populated island groups (which include the district headquarters), voting booths were not placed in each village and as a consequence it required greater effort on the part of the voter to cast his ballot. Secondly, the relative level of political acculturation undoubtedly played a part, and in some of the outlying areas, when the district administration's

[32] Seymour M. Lipset, *Political Man* (Garden City, N.Y.: Doubleday & Co., Inc., 1960), p. 182; Robert E. Lane, *Political Life* (Glencoe, Ill.: Free Press, 1959), p. 48.

election team appeared on the scene and the polling places were set up with the sanction of the traditional leaders, all eligible persons automatically trooped to the polls to vote. In short, the composition of the Trusteeship's peoples and the manner in which elections were conducted makes summary generalizations applicable to elections elsewhere somewhat suspect when applied to the Trust Territory.

Practically all ballots cast at the congressional elections were tallied; only 172 ballots were invalidated because of improper markings. A candidate usually received the support of the area with which he or his family were identified by birth. However, the failure of several to carry their own municipalities may have been due to the tenuousness of these ties. Some candidates had been living at district headquarters for very long periods of time without any visitations "home" to renew traditional bonds. As the level of political involvement grows in the Trust Territory, accompanied with a diminution of its ethnocentricity, short of artificial cultivation of "home-town" support through electioneering, the happenstance of birthplace may be expected to decrease in importance.

Election competition in the Marianas was confined solely to party candidates; in the Palaus, beside the party nominees, two Independents ran for delegate and two for assemblyman. The almost clean-sweep of the Territorial Party in the Marianas, taking both delegate posts and two of the three Assembly seats, was not matched in the Palaus where an Independent was elected and the two parties split honors in the remaining pair of contests for each house. All but fourteen of the Territory's ninety-four candidates demonstrated creditable voting strength, arbitrarily defined as being above 10 per cent of the ballots polled. Of the twenty winning candidates in the Assembly, slightly over half (11) received majority support of their constituents, and sixteen, greater than two-fifths of the vote tallied. It was in the contests where five and six candidates ran that the vote was badly proliferated, and in Truk District A, a candidate was declared elected even though he amassed only a little over a fourth of the entire vote cast.[33] None of the Palau delegates was elected by outright majorities in the six-sided race, and in Ponape one of the two successful delegates also failed to obtain a majority tally. On the whole, though, most elected candidates represented sizable pluralities, and only four

[33] The winning candidate received 28.7 per cent; the second highest tally was 25.4 per cent.

out of the total thirty-two elected candidates received less than 44 per cent of the tallied vote.[34]

Everything considered, the first congressional elections ought to be judged a success. The turnout at the polls was very respectable, given the limited time available to prepare for the elections and the acknowledged need for greater community education regarding the new congress and its role in Territorial self-government. The nomination procedures which were followed favored those Micronesians living adjacent to district headquarters, but as they constituted a good part of the eligible educated elite, it is reasonable to conclude that the same names would have been brought forward under other possible nomination systems. The campaigns as waged in the districts ranged widely from active electioneering to covert seeking of office, but this only revealed differences in the stages and rates of the Territory's political acculturation. The elections were carried off efficiently and with little untoward incident, primarily because district headquarters personnel played a large part once administration was decentralized from Saipan to the district centers. The candidates who took their seats in the first Congress of Micronesia did so in the confidence that they were fairly chosen and represented, if not majorities, at least sizeable pluralities of their constituents.

[34] Computed as to delegates by doubling their share of votes, because an elector cast ballots for two candidates, so no candidate could receive more than 50 per cent of the total.

CHAPTER 11

The Victors and the Vanquished[1]

WHERE FREE CHOICE by balloting prevails, barring the bizarre situation of sheer random voting, no legislature constitutes a cross-section of its body politic. From the candidates brought to the attention of the electorate are selected those persons who, in the voters' opinion, best embody the qualities the electors desire in a representative. This does not posit the universality of any single or combination of attributes, but only that the voters are motivated by more than duplicating their composite self when casting ballots. Given a large enough field of candidates presenting a range of choices, the defeated candidates will be more a reflection of the electorate than those sent to the legislative halls. Thus one can identify those factors most attractive to the voter. The first elections for the Congress of Micronesia and the resultant composition of the congress only reinforce the compass of these generalizations. For their congressmen, the voters elected individuals markedly differing from the average adult inhabitant of the Trust Territory; a comparison of the victors with the vanquished demonstrates that in the main these distinctive qualities of the successful candidates were shared less widely by the defeated.

The Trust Territory voters went to the polls appreciating full well that they were taking part in an event important to the political development of the Trust Territory, regardless of how much they understood about the nature of the new governmental body. The previous Council of Micronesia and the legislatures functioning at the district level were the closest parallels with which voters were familiar, and they frequently chose as their representatives persons who had served in these American-sponsored legisla-

[1] This chapter is based upon extensive background questionnaires completed by candidates (29 of 33 elected, 41 of 62 defeated) and is supplemented by data supplied by informants and biographical material published by the Trust Territory. Incomplete data for categories are indicated by showing the number of members to which a generalization applies; if full data were available, the disparities between elected and defeated would probably be heightened. Because of the tenuousness of some data, statistical manipulations have not been attempted.

tive bodies. But they were also seeking other qualities, and the returns pointed up their preference for those more educated, those more widely-traveled, and those experienced in the affairs of Trust Territory government at the district and Territorial levels. Traditional status also attracted the voters' tally when it was coupled with ability to deal with Americans and a perception of the linkage between introduced and indigenous political institutions.

No women ran for the congress, although a few have been elected to district legislatures and *leroij* (female paramount chiefs) have sat as a matter of right in the Marshall Islands Congress. This lack of contests between male and female candidates foreclosed any opportunity to determine whether sex would be tied to success at the polls. The absence of women candidates may suggest that both sponsors and potential aspirants for congressional posts concluded that the new legislative body was basically male oriented in its requirements of absence from home. It is also likely that, because the power wielded by women in the Micronesian cultures is frequently covert and their qualification through education and participation in American-sponsored political institutions has lagged, the male prejudice in both American and Micronesian societies against women's overt leadership remained dominant.

The range of choice available to the voters was limited in ways other than the absence of women candidates, so that, in some regards, there was little or no opportunity to express a preference between alternatives. This observation applies especially to language skills. Practically all candidates spoke English,[2] as competence in English was accepted as almost a *sine qua non* for nomination. The few defeated candidates without English language abilities fared poorly, either garnering the least number of votes cast in their particular contests or placing toward the bottom of the tally. In his campaigning, one of the unsuccessful candidates in Palau attempted to offset his language deficiency by calling attention to the provisions of the Secretarial Order which would assure him an interpreter, if elected to the congress. Both of the non-English-speaking members elected hold high chiefly status and have otherwise prominently distinguished themselves in both the traditional and introduced political systems of their districts. With respect to Japanese-language-speaking skills, there is likewise little

[2] In comparison with 26.6 per cent of the population over twenty-five years of age speaking English, and 36.9 per cent over fifteen years. *17th Annual Report of the United States to the United Nations, 1964*, p. 205.

to separate the successful from the defeated candidates, for the districts vary in the percentages of their adult populations with Japanese language aptitude.[3] The findings on candidates speaking a second Micronesian language are almost equally inconclusive for similar reasons. However, in future elections this will bear further

LANGUAGE-SPEAKING ABILITIES OF
CONGRESSIONAL CANDIDATES, 1965 [4]

	Defeated (62)	Elected (33)
English	93.5%	93.9%
Japanese	66.1%	72.7%
Second Micronesian	29.0%	21.2%

scrutiny, for in the Assembly districts where languages are different from those used at district headquarters (as District A of Ponape, encompassing Kusaie and Pingelap), voters, when they had a choice, showed that they preferred House candidates with these "secondary" Micronesian language skills.

Education played an important part in attracting support for candidates. In specific contests, other factors sometimes took precedence, but on the whole the respect which is afforded an educated man in the Trust Territory stood the elected candidates in good stead. Collectively, the candidates represented a level of schooling far higher than that attained by their constituents.[5] In the eight contests where candidates who had attended college lost to others with lower educational achievements, three graduates were defeated by candidates who had not completed matriculation, as was a fourth who tallied fewer votes than a candidate who had never been enrolled in a collegiate level institution; in the other four races, candidates with some college attendance to their credit

[3] However these data do support the hypothesis that in areas adopting a new language, the legislature will evidence a larger proportion of members qualified in that language than the body politic, and also will have a larger proportion of persons skilled in the language being lost. See Norman Meller, "Bilingualism in Island Legislatures of the Pacific as an Index of Acculturation," *Sociology and Social Research*, 43:6 (July–Aug., 1959), 408.

[4] Compare the Japanese language skill of congressional candidates with that of the Trust Territory's population, with 59.8 per cent Japanese-speaking in the 25–44 years age bracket and 48.5 per cent for ages 25 and over. *Ibid.*

[5] Less than 20 per cent of the adult population has completed six years of schooling.

The same respect for education was revealed within the congress, for of the fourteen officers and standing committee chairmen, twelve had attended college or medical school; three of the four college graduates were accommodated with posts.

lost to others who had none. Significantly, the two non-English-speaking chiefs from Ponape and Truk and two candidates from royal families (*iroij*) running in the Marshalls defeated more highly educated opponents. Further revealing the importance of chiefly status, in Yap a college graduate lost to a candidate with only two years of college education but with strong chiefly backing.[6] Two of the remaining three cases may be traced to the heavy

EDUCATIONAL ACHIEVEMENT OF CONGRESSIONAL CANDIDATES, 1965

	Defeated (62)	Elected (33)
High school or equivalent [7]	*71.9%	87.9%
Some college	50.0%	66.7%
Medical/dental school	9.7%	12.1%
College graduation	6.4%	12.1%

* n = 57

ticket voting in the Marianas, and the last may also be due to the influence of organized political activity in Palau, although party loyalty there was not as persuasive as in the Marianas.

The candidates were collectively more widely traveled than their constituents, and elected candidates reported more broadening experience outside their home environment than the defeated. Much of this travel was closely tied to educational achievement, for the indigenous inhabitants of the Trust Territory must leave the region to obtain education above the secondary level.

TRAVEL REPORTED FOR CONGRESSIONAL CANDIDATES, 1965

	Defeated (62)	Elected (33)
Guam	*91.8%	100.0%
Hawaii	41.9%	72.7%
U.S. mainland	19.3%	48.5%
Other Pacific Basin Islands	†19.3%	27.3%
Japan	†14.0%	27.3%
Elsewhere	†28.1%	30.3%

* n = 61
† n = 57

[6] Compare with actions of chiefs in Outer Islands of Yap who "nominated candidates for both houses who had the most schooling and experience under the American Administration." Questionnaire response from a defeated Outer Islands candidate.

[7] As used in the table, a candidate attending a college or university, even though he did not have a diploma from a high school, was classified as high school "equivalent." Similarly, for dental and medical school graduates.

When asked by a reporter "what are the best qualifications for candidates to [the] new Congress?" Andon Amaraich, who was running for the House, replied that experience in the district legislature stands "first in importance," followed by several years in public service, which helps one to know how the government works.[8] Within his first category he might also have included membership in the Council of Micronesia and the preceding Territory-wide advisory conferences, for the voters plainly registered their preference for candidates with both forms of legislative training. Except in the Marshalls, it appeared to be of little moment whether or not a candidate was an incumbent district legislator at the time he ran for the congress; in the Marshall administrative district, only incumbents were elected to the congress. Despite its importance, prior service in a legislature per se represented but

PREVIOUS LEGISLATIVE EXPERIENCE OF CONGRESSIONAL CANDIDATES, 1965

	Defeated (62)	Elected (33)
Seat in district legislature	*60.3%	†75.0%
Seat at time of election	*31.0%	†34.4%
Ever presiding officer, district legislature	‡13.5%	†34.4%
Member Territory-wide conference	17.7%	51.5%

* n = 58, as Yap Outer Islands not in Yap Islands Congress
† n = 32, as Yap Outer Islands not in Yap Islands Congress
‡ n = 56

one factor taken into account by the voter, and in one-quarter of the contests,[9] candidates without legislative experience defeated opponents who had been members of district legislatures.

Candidate Amaraich's stress on the importance of non-legislative government experience also proved prescient. However, the voters valued some forms of governmental service and discounted others. Municipal office holding, teaching in the public schools, and association with educational administration bore no relation to victory at the polls; if anything, they were tied inversely. But candidates currently in the service of the government at district or Territorial levels, or having such past experience to their credit, were favored. Interestingly, the vehicle for personal advancement of many of the

[8] *Truk Tide*, Jan. 15, 1964, p. 8.
[9] Of the 27 contests (21 Assembly, 6 House), legislatively experienced candidates were victorious in 12, lost in 7, in 5 all candidates had served in district legislatures, and in the remaining 3 contests this factor was not pertinent.

successful candidates had been through teaching, but their immediate political saliency obtained through more distinctive forms of activity.

NON–LEGISLATIVE GOVERNMENTAL EXPERIENCE OF
CONGRESSIONAL CANDIDATES, 1965

	Defeated (62)	Elected (33)
PRESENT EMPLOYMENT		
Territory or district		
(excluding education)	38.9%	54.5%
Teaching only	21.0% [a]	9.1%
Education (including teaching)	30.6% [a]	21.2%
PRESENT OR PREVIOUS EMPLOYMENT		
Territory and district		
(excluding education)	54.8%	75.7%
Previous only	46.8%	72.7%
Present and previous education		
(including teaching)	50.0% [a]	51.5%
Teaching only	50.0% [a]	48.5%
MUNICIPAL OFFICE		
Present or previous	†63.0%	*46.9%
Within last five years	‡47.0%	*40.6%

* n = 32, excluding Outer Islands, Yap
† n = 54
‡ n = 52
[a] Does not include two teachers in parochial schools

A candidate's religious affiliation may have influenced his chances for election in some of the contests. About an equal number of Catholics (47) and Protestants (48) ran, but the 41.7 per cent success for Protestants outshadowed the smaller 27.7 per cent for Catholics. Here, cumulative data are misleading, for in the Marianas and Yap, whose inhabitants are almost all Catholic, only Catholic candidates filed nomination papers.[10] On the other hand, Catholics comprise a small part of the population in the Marshalls, but a disproportionately large number ran for the congress and all were defeated. In the remaining districts,[11] the field of candidates

[10] There is a small Protestant population in the Marianas, and in the Yap district a part of the population yet observes the indigenous religion. One candidate practices Catholicism when at home, for it is the only religion represented there, but observes another religion when outside the Trust Territory.

[11] A 1948 Navy study considered Truk and Ponape Island about divided between the two Christian religions and considered Kusaie Protestant. At that time, almost half of Palau was not identified with either religion. Stanford School of Naval Administration, *Handbook of the Trust Territory* (Washington: Office of Naval Operations, 1948), p. 197.

more closely reflected the religious composition of the electorate, and those of the Catholic faith in these contests fared relatively poorly.

RELIGIOUS AFFILIATION OF CONGRESSIONAL CANDIDATES, 1965

District	Total		Defeated		Elected	
	Cath-olic	Prot-estant	Cath-olic	Prot-estant	Cath-olic	Prot-estant
Marianas, Yap	19	0	10	0	9	0
Marshalls	4	13	4	7	0	6
Palau, Ponape, Truk	24	35	20	21	4	14

The group that stood for election was remarkably young in a region which customarily allots, at best, a limited political role to youth and which normally associates traditional leadership with at least middle-age maturity, if not old age. To qualify, candidates had to have reached a minimum age of twenty-five; a number did barely that. About one-fourth of the adult population over twenty-five [12] falls into the 25–34 age bracket; in contrast, four-sevenths of the defeated and an even larger two-thirds of the elected fitted into this category. The median ages of both the victors and the vanquished were only about thirty-three years, emphasizing the first congressional elections' accent on youth.

The congressional elections marked the emergence of a new political elite, young, American educated and trained, and in good part dependent upon government employment for a livelihood. This movement of an administrative bureaucracy into the political decision-making axis of the Territory's central government represents a process that has repetitively occurred elsewhere in the island areas of the South Seas. Writing over two decades ago, Felix Keesing noted that "practically everywhere [then excluding Micronesia], the native representative is at the same time a government employee." [13] The Trust Territory may differ in that within a few years Micronesians at the higher levels of the administrative bureaucracy must decide between their two roles, and district legislators will also be separated from Territorial solons, suggesting an institutionalizing of a path for personal political advancement

[12] *17th Annual Report . . .* , *op. cit.*, p. 204.
[13] Felix M. Keesing, *The South Seas in the Modern World* (rev. ed.; New York: John Day Co., 1945), p. 165.

from regional to Territorial post.[14] From all this there will emerge a politician type, distinct from the bureaucratic, who "love politics," [15] and the beginnings of this elite may already be detected in both the membership of the new congress and within the body of unsuccessful candidates.

THE TWO HOUSES DISTINGUISHED

On first appearances there is little to separate the members elected to the House of Delegates from those in the General Assembly. The membership of both houses derived their political prominence through acquired characteristics which prepared them for a part in the new institution patterned after the typical American legislature. Roughly three-quarters of the members of each house lived close to the district headquarters, irrespective of the legislative constituencies from which they stood, and public funds provided the major source of these legislators' incomes. Both houses were young; the median age of each was identical—thirty-three years. But closer examination reveals that the two bodies did vary in composition, and cumulatively these differences accorded the Assembly a more conservative cast.

Although the members of the two houses shared identical median ages, the *mean* age of the Assembly was older—35.3 years compared with 34.6 for the House. More important, the assembly-men's age distribution was wider (26–62 compared with only 29–45 for the House), and six of the lower house's number were forty years of age or older. This provided a strong leavening of members for the Assembly who had reached their majority during the era of the Japanese administration, while only one delegate from the House fell into this "elderly" group. Practically all the House members had grown up under the American administration, were consequently more familiar with American ways, and, incidentally, were a little more aware of the leverage afforded the legislature

---

[14] See letter of Delegate John Ngiraked to Secretary of Interior Udall, Nov. 19, 1965, protesting that the high proportion of district legislators and governmental servants in the first congress constituted "a very serious abrogation of the fundamental principles which divide the three branches [and] . . . functions in a democratic government" and requesting amendment of Secretarial Order 2882 to make these disqualifications immediately operative.

[15] The reply of one candidate to the questionnaire: "I ran for a number of reasons. . . . First, I ran for the Unity of Micronesia. . . . Second, I ran for a political-economic policy. . . . Third, I ran for an educational policy. . . . Finally, I ran for office not by default but by choice. I love politics!"

under the American political system. In contrast to the Assembly, the House membership enjoyed the advantages of superior education, wider travel—Hawaii, mainland United States, Japan, and elsewhere—and a greater command of English and Japanese, two languages which offered members the opportunity to expand their comprehension of Micronesia. All this led the delegates to be more critical of Trust Territory inadequacies and of the Administering Authority for failing to ameliorate them. The House, more so than the Assembly, was conditioned by the prior socialization of its members to propose innovations for Micronesia, and the Assembly to be more cautious in concurring with them.

A greater proportion of the House had obtained political prominence through prior membership in Territorial legislative bodies rather than through service in district legislatures or municipal offices. They were more familiar with Territory-wide political institutions and their potential policy-making and public-opinion-forming functions. This induced the delegates to seek a faster pace of change through action of the congress than the Assembly was prepared to countenance. Helping to give force to delegate action was their broader experience in running private businesses and their dependence upon private income either as sole source of support or as a supplement to their governmental salaries. They, more so than the assemblymen, personally knew the difficulties under which Micronesian business was laboring and could appreciate the advantages which would flow from building the economic infra-structure of the Territory and assuring Micronesians a larger role in the region's development. All of these factors made the House of Delegates the more radical of the two chambers.

At the convening of the first congress, the petition filed by the Popular Party of Saipan challenging the seating of Delegate-elect Jose R. Cruz had a Japanese copy attached to the English version so that "the individuals, if any, who may have some doubts as to the exact meaning of this petition may be able to refer to the Japanese text. . . ." Not only were the petitioners ill-advised in implying the members of the congress might be more at ease with a petition drafted in Japanese, but for a contest in the House of Delegates, this was particularly inappropriate. Of the two chambers, it was the more prepared to undertake its new tasks in English, and with a fuller understanding of the nuances of American political practices.

DIFFERENCES IN COMPOSITION OF TWO CHAMBERS, FIRST CONGRESS

	House (12)	Assembly (21)
Some college education	75.0%	61.9%
Language ability		
English	100.0%	90.5%
Japanese	83.3%	66.7%
Travel		
Hawaii	91.7%	66.7%
U.S. mainland	66.7%	42.8%
Japan	41.7%	19.0%
Elsewhere	66.7%	9.5%
Previous government experience		
Territorial legislative bodies	66.7%	42.8%
District legislative bodies	66.7%	76.2%
Municipal office	33.3%	52.4%
Private business activity	75.0%	33.3%

ATTITUDES TOWARD THE REPRESENTATIONAL ROLE

Addressing the students of Mindszenty School on Palau before the Congress of Micronesia was convened, Assemblyman-elect Lazarus Salii phrased the classic dilemma faced by all elected legislators:

If I know what a majority of the people think on a particular subject to be considered by the Congress, I shall be bound to act in accordance with that thinking; if I do not know what a majority of the people think on that particular subject, I shall be bound by my conscience and my best judgement as to what would be best for these people. That, after all, was the trust that was given to me on election day. If what I know to be the thinking of a majority of the people on a particular subject is contrary to what I think is good for them or is contrary to the dictates of my conscience—then I'm in a tough spot. In that case I can try to convince the people that they are wrong, although this is very difficult sometimes; if this does not work I can proceed in the following fashion: if the difference between the people and myself is on something basic and I would violate my conscience if I were to follow their thinking, then I shall follow my conscience and take my chances come next election day. But if the difference is not on something basic but represents simply a difference of opinion, then I shall be duty-bound to follow the people. It is, of course, a lot easier to say this than to always have the courage to follow it in practice.[16]

A seminal study of legislative roles in four American state

[16] Reproduced in *Saipan District Panorama*, March 19, 1965, p. 2.

legislatures [17] subjected to empirical investigation styles followed by representatives and disclosed three major role types, the "Delegate" who is the spokesman for his constituents, the "Trustee" who represents them as he, personally, believes best, and the "Politico." The last embodies an overlap of the other two, so representative types can be conceived of as occupying a continuum, with the Politico placed toward the mid-point between the two more polar positions. In numerical frequency, the Trustee type was found to dominate in each of the four states, followed by the Politico, and the fewest number of representatives interviewed said they observed the role classed as Delegate.

Responses received from the candidates elected to the Congress of Micronesia demonstrate that these representational roles apply equally as well to beginning as to established legislatures, and in the same rank order of importance, prompting the hypothesis that the roles derive from the very nature of the legislative process. At the workshop preceding the convening of the congress, the congressmen-elect were queried concerning their own and their constituents' views on representational roles. All but one assemblyman also commented upon whether role conceptions would be effected by personal or party-program promises to support a particular issue.[18] Congressmen-elect proved to be, if anything, more Trustee- and less Delegate-oriented than the average in the four state legislatures surveyed.

DISTRIBUTION OF REPRESENTATIONAL ROLE ORIENTATIONS IN CONGRESS OF MICRONESIA

Representational Role	As Sees Own Role (32 members) *	Constituents' View of Role (29 members)	4 State Legislatures
Trustee	68.7%	55.2%	63%
Politico	25.0%	13.8%	23%
Delegate	6.2%	31.0%	14%

* Does not round to 100 per cent

In seeking an explanation for the three different role orientations

[17] Wahlke, Eulau, Buchanan, and Ferguson, *The Legislative System* (New York: Wiley, 1962), pp. 267 ff.; also see "The Role of the Representative: Some Empirical Observations on the Theory of Edmund Burke," *American Political Science Review*, 53:3 (Sept., 1959), 742.

[18] However, in a few cases, replies were unresponsive to the questions asked and had to be eliminated from the analyses.

and their numerical distribution, the four-state study suggested "it is likely . . . that the representative has become less and less a Delegate and more and more a Trustee as the business of government has become more and more intricate and technical as well as less locally centered." [19] Nothing was found to substantiate this assumption that the Trustee representational role evolves with novelty or complexity of government. [20] Within the perspective of cultural relativism, quite accurately to the Micronesians, the Trust Territory government and its problems appear highly intricate and technical, simple as they may seem to an American observer. The expanding government in the Trust Territory will continue to be relatively complex, so although with greater political sophistication the Trustee's role may partially shift to that of the Politico, it is difficult to conceive of a material expansion in the number of congressmen observing a Delegate's role at the expense of the Trustee's.

The largest single group of Micronesian congressmen saw the representational role of Trustee, which they themselves follow, paralleling that expected of them by their constituents (13). This coincides with the political reality encountered in many parts of the far-flung Trust Territory where representatives tend to be chosen for their ability to face problems beyond their constituents' comprehension. Only one member viewed both his own role and that projected by his constituents as being that of a Delegate. Significantly, half of the Micronesian legislators (15 of 29) noted that their conceptualization of representation did not accord with that of their constituents. In part, this was because some congressmen adopted the role of Trustee while stating their constituents considered them a Politico or Delegate. But other congressmen voluntarily limited the scope of their own roles, taking for themselves that of Politico or even Delegate, while recognizing that their constituents expected Trustee performance from them. As reported by one Delegate:

(legislator's view of role—Delegate) "I feel that such matter should be put into full . . . [consideration before the Congress] since it is the desire

[19] Wahlke and others, *op. cit.*, p. 281.
[20] Even the State Legislative Research Project's findings on Tennessee did not bear it out, and to explain this the authors added, "it may be that 'complexity' is a function of perception, regardless of the real situation." *Ibid.*, p. 282.

of the people—the majority—for such law to be passed. I therefore will do my best . . . [to introduce and support the measure]."

(constituents' view of role—Trustee) "The voters in my district place the responsibility on me to make the wise decision. . . . they expect me to put every effort to help the people . . ."

(effect of personal or party promise) "There is no difference. . . . the voters of my district choose their representatives from those that they put their entire trust upon as their leaders."

Half of the congressmen-elect (16) concurred with the Delegate-type quoted above that neither a personal promise on their part, when they ran for office, nor a party-program pledge makes any difference in how they ought conduct themselves. However, an equal number disagreed or entirely avoided the issue by supplying non-responsive replies—it is believed deliberately. All representational role types were found divided over the moral issue inherent in the question.[21]

Throughout the coding of responses, it proved difficult to fit members' replies neatly within the trichotomous categories posited. Befitting the consensus societies of the Trust Territory, reference was made frequently to the judgement of fellow legislators as helping to resolve the dilemma of representation. Given the sense of solidarity usually engendered by membership in a legislative body and the strength of legislative norms in guiding individual action, this repeated mention of peer judgement suggests as the three major referents for the legislator his personal values, legislative norms, and constituent instructions. "Politico" thus becomes a catch-all type for the lawmaker who refuses to commit himself to observing any one of these three referents, so that he follows no single representational role.

THE TWO HOUSES TOGETHER

The members of the Congress of Micronesia stand out in bold relief against the back drop of the body politic. In an area where the overwhelming majority of the population is still engaged in subsistence economic activities and less than 7,000 people are employed for wages,[22] the congressmen form a prominent part of

[21] In view of the number of congressmen who were also district legislators, it is significant that some who felt bound by their constituents' directions specifically disclaimed similar restraint as a result of directives by their district's legislative body.

[22] 17th Annual Report . . . , op. cit., p. 264.

an emerging middle class. The legislators rank among the most highly educated and the most broadly traveled in the Trust Territory. Their experience gained through service in previous legislative bodies and their knowledge of American-introduced political institutions mark them as probably the best qualified group which could have been selected, given the vagaries of the election process, to launch the most prestigeful and potentially most powerful agency staffed by indigenes in the Trust Territory.

The fact that the new congressmen were differentiated from most of their constituents by a wide array of acquired characteristics, bespeaking the acculturation occurring in the Trust Territory as the result of Western contact, did not mean they were out of touch with the traditional mores of their people. Of the seven congressmen forty years of age or older, six held chiefly titles or were senior heads of their clans. Excluding the Marianas' Chamorro members, as chiefly titles and lineage ties no longer exist in that area, almost half of the remaining membership (at least thirteen—46.4 per cent) encompassing all of the five other administrative districts had well-recognized traditional status. Holders of chiefly titles and those in line for titles or possessing high clan status were considered good representatives, just so long as they were distinguished by more than merely ascribed criteria. In Riggs' terminology, they revealed "clect-like" characteristics,[23] sharing a geographic communalism with their constituencies, with many laying claim to traditional sources of power, but also closely identified with the processes of change taking place in the Trust Territory. In a prismatic society becoming increasingly diffracted, many congressmen, through their occupations, were introducers of change and all were essentially committed to furthering the Territorial development which was already underway. They were primarily an "institutional interest group"[24] concerned with law and order as well as modernity[25] in the articulation of political interests. However, the presence in congress of members with traditional status also meant that the congress would be kept cognizant of the customary relationships and prescribed practices which still

---

[23] Fred W. Riggs, *Administration in Developing Countries* (Boston: Houghton Mifflin Co., 1964), p. 164.

[24] See Gabriel A. Almond, "A Functional Approach to Comparative Politics," in Almond and Coleman, ed., *The Politics of the Developing Areas* (Princeton: Princeton University Press, 1960), pp. 3–64.

[25] James S. Coleman, "The Political Systems of the Developing Areas," in Almond and Coleman, *op. cit.*, p. 548.

regulate life in the Territory and assured a continuation of legislative concern for traditional matters affected by legislation.

The new members brought to the congress an element almost unique to the Trust Territory's ethnocentrism. Seventeen had been educated at the Pacific Islands Teachers Training School (PITTS) or the Pacific Islands Central School (PICS), and an additional four had attended the medical school formerly conducted by the Navy on Guam. Thus two-thirds had lived closely for protracted periods of time with Micronesians from all areas of the Territory, an experience which was to give each a sense of commonality with persons from ethnic groups besides his own. The nature of this experience and its life-long effect was well expressed by a young Yapese student a number of years ago:

When I was a child, I used to think that my father and mother were the best in the whole world. Not the world really, but Yap, for Yap was the only place I knew about. . . . Even when I came to Intermediate, I still thought that my people were the best of all. I disliked everybody but the Yapese.

When I went to PICS I still disliked the Palauans, Trukese, Saipanese, Ponapeans, and Marshallese. I always think that they are people, yes, but not as good as us Yapese. As we live and worked and played together I began to feel something in my mind. I began to forget what I have been thinking all my long life. I learned to like other people beside my own. Going to PICS cause me to get rid of that silly idea being think that my own people are the best of all. I might said that PICS changed me completely.[26]

The same breaking of Micronesian cultural boundaries was experienced by an additional three congressmen who attended the University of Hawaii without previous education at a central school in the Trust Territory, and who, through their association with students in Honolulu, developed cross-ethnic ties and a sense of kinship with other Micronesians. For many of the PITTS and PICS graduates, their further schooling in Hawaii only reinforced the feelings of unity formed earlier in the Territory. In part, this education laid the foundation for the nascent Micronesian identity, transcending the diverse cultures and peoples of the Trust Territory, which was to reveal itself at the first congress.

The members-elect attended the convening of the new congress uncertain in their powers and unfamiliar with their newly acquired

[26] *Micronesian Monthly,* July, 1952, p. 11.

status. Some thought the congress long overdue, while at least one believed it premature and that only frustration would be its result.[27] Most approached their posts expecting to formulate their own policy decisions, doing what they honestly thought best for their constituents; as a reflection of this, two-thirds categorized themselves as Trustees in their representational roles. It was accurately written of them that "they are men who almost without exception regard the future good of the Territory as more important than the immediate good of their local constituents. They are more concerned with the impression they are making on the world and on the future of their people than with the impression they make on the voters they [will] face. . . . They show a statesmanship rare in politicians anywhere, and almost incredible in people who have emerged within their own memory from a stone-age society." [28]

[27] *Truk Tide*, Jan. 15, 1964, p. 6.
[28] *Honolulu Star-Bulletin*, Aug. 18, 1966, p. A-8. Written at the close of the second, 1966, congressional session, it applies equally as well to the same men's performance after they were first sworn in as congressmen.

CHAPTER 12

Organizing the Congress

DESPITE THE SEEMING presumptuousness of the endeavor, no lesser task than that of training the congressmen-elect to run their own legislature, and incidentally sensitizing the Administering Authority's staff to the significance of the Territory's new power configuration, was undertaken during the span of the two weeks immediately preceding the convening of the first Congress of Micronesia. The high commissioner originally contemplated calling a special session in the spring of the year, shortly after the January elections, to enable the members to organize themselves as a congress. In lieu of this, under the auspices of the Institute for Technical Interchange of the University of Hawaii's East-West Center, a three-man team[1] journeyed to Saipan late in June of 1965 to equip the freshman legislators with the parliamentary knowledge and skills necessary for the functioning of the new legislative body.

Far more than the mere imparting of factual data and the furnishing of technical assistance in the drafting of legislative rules was to be attempted by the two-week workshop. The training team proposed to encourage a sense of identity sufficient to permit the congressmen to manage their own affairs. The workshop period would also afford ample opportunity for the members-elect to assay the competence, articulateness, and interest of potential officers and committee chairmen, as well as occasion for them to meet in informal caucus. These multiple objectives emphasized the importance of methodology as well as attention to content, and the necessity for in-built flexibility in both planning and day-to-day guidance of the workshop. Hindsight indicates that membership in the Council of Micronesia had already familiarized a number of the congressmen with members' strengths and weaknesses and that the training team may have underestimated the political

---

[1] The training team for the workshop consisted of Tom Dinell, then Director of the Hawaii Legislative Reference Bureau, former U.S. Congressman Thomas P. Gill, and the author.

sophistication many had gained through academia and district legislative service. For the most part, however, the pre-planning proved sound, and the success of the workshop is measured by the Congress of Micronesia's convening as scheduled on July 12, 1965, structured to undertake its historic mission.

The personality differences which typify the various cultural groups in the Trust Territory were brought into focus by the new congress. Throughout the Territory, the Palauan is viewed as aggressive, particularly when compared to Marshallese reticence which requires that one deny personal ability and publicly accept responsibility only most reluctantly. The volatile tendencies of the Chamorros from the Marianas likewise juxtapose against the gentleness of the Outer Islanders from the Yap district, just as the former's rapid acculturation contrasts with the latter's continued respect for custom. Although the individuals elected to the congress might each be somewhat atypical of the group from which he came, the workshop design had to make provision for building the confidence of the psychologically diffident so as to encourage their involvement in the congress on a par with their peers.

Parallel problems of timidity arising from Administering Authority–administered relationships also had to be anticipated. Having been governed by four nations, the Micronesians have become past masters of indirection, outwaiting disliked orders and furthering their own ends in ways not apparent to the administering metropolitan country. Frontal confrontation has tended to be abjured, and verbal agreement by the Micronesian may cloak a subtle negation unobserved by the administrator. Instead of being initiators, the Micronesians have found it far safer as well as culturally compatible to sit back and await the orders of the Administering Authority, for what they approve, they can accept, and the balance is silently ignored. Now, with a body created to exercise extensive legislating power, comprised of and serving the welfare of Micronesians, all *raison d'être* for indirect action became not just unnecessary but, together with apathy, subversive to the success of the congress itself. Active participation, indeed open challenge if that should prove to be necessary, had to become the order of the day if the new legislature, conceived of in the American concept of equality with the executive and judicial branches, was to become a viable entity. There could be no place for either personal or institutional diffidence, and the workshop took for one of its purposes the preparing of the members-elect for their new roles.

Fortunately, there existed a number of conditions peculiarly advantageous to the workshop. The English-speaking ability of all but two of the congressmen-elect enabled training to be directed at a fairly rapid pace and to encompass much more material than would have been feasible if delays for direct, multiple translation were a requisite. Several of the college graduates among the members had taken their degrees in political science, and a majority had some college education, frequently at the University of Hawaii. With the workshop staff recruited under the aegis of the university, this strengthened personal rapport and assured an informal source of feedback should the instruction fall short of its desired mark.

Also easing the burden of the workshop was the knowledge that neither legislative process nor parliamentary procedure was to be introduced into Micronesia by the Congress of Micronesia. Nevertheless, advance inquiry revealed there was no single common body of process or practice which could be lifted en bloc to the Territorial level and adopted as a unit to meet the requirements of the Secretarial Order creating the congress. The procedures of the district legislatures incline to informality and often reflect the idiosyncracies of the presiding officers. Useful as this prior conditioning to the legislative role was, it furnished at best a glimpse of the vistas of power now open to the congressmen-elect, and it had not prepared them fully to assume their new authority or to exercise it with appropriate finesse.

To fill these lacunae, in a short span the training would need cover not only how a full-fledged legislature formally functions, with all the attendant pitfalls of parliamentary maneuver, but also the rough and tumble practicalities accompanying decision-making by the legislature in action—in brief, the meaning and use of power. Somehow this had to be compressed into but a week of intensive drill and presented in a manner which would be comprehensible to persons living in a society where debate leading to a consensus is sometimes more important and far more personally satisfying than recourse to voting and tallying a majority viewpoint.

How to relate meaningfully the experience of Western-style legislatures to the cultures of Micronesia, how to do so in a manner that would help imbue the members with a sense of joint comprehension and thus contribute to the success of the congress, and how to conduct the workshop primarily through the spoken word, for this is a region whose people cannot be expected to read extensively in the English language or, indeed, any printed media? These were the problems confronted when working up the training design.

DESIGN FOR PARTICIPATION

Early in the planning, it was decided that the members-elect should be encouraged to consider themselves as integrally associated with all aspects of the training sessions, rather than just be passive objects. As a technique, involvement would spark interest and further learning. More basic, what better way to expose these solons to the full dimensions of *their* congress, a legislature for which they will be expected to furnish the motive force, than to place the workshop in their hands? This might have been best accomplished by allowing the training to take shape spontaneously, once underway on Saipan, as the queries and proposals of the individual legislators gradually lent it form. The length of time available for the workshop precluded such an approach; even with the tightest of pre-scheduling, it was already evident that whole areas of substance and procedure important to the successful launching of the congress would have to be sharply elided if not omitted. The nominating by the congressmen of a committee to which might be delegated pre-session planning chores ran afoul of the twin realities of inadequate time and spatial dispersion of the members-elect. The compromise solution of naming a few members working on Saipan for the Administering Authority to such a committee would have included a delegate from Palau and an assemblyman from Yap. This might have lent the imprimatur of congressional sanction, but it also would have entailed the risk of discrediting the whole enterprise if the committee came to be regarded as mere window-dressing.

To avoid all suspicion, it was decided to question all members-elect by mail, listing logical subject areas tentatively to be covered and soliciting replies on the priorities to be assigned, items to be dropped, and further matters to be added. The questionnaire was accompanied by a letter from the high commissioner amplifying the information earlier conveyed on the holding of the pre-session workshop and advising that the training team would rely upon the replies to the questionnaire in its planning and assembling of necessary materials.[2] The gratifying response went far to reassure the training team that its preliminary proposals would meet with the participants' satisfaction.

The questionnaire identified nine potential topics and left spaces for others to be written in. In addition to stating his priority of choices in rank order, the congressman-elect could under each topic note any special interest which he desired to have treated. About two-thirds of the replies (19) approved of all of the topics as contained in the questionnaire, and six of these volunteered additional matters. While in no case did any of the remaining ten questionnaires direct the elimination of a topic, they failed to rank all of them, thus implying lack of interest in those not marked.[3]

The members-elect wanted the workshop to give major attention to subject-matter jurisdiction of the new congress; legislative organization; legislative rules and parliamentary procedure; and Trust Territory organization, policies, income, expenditures, and funds. Subjects of less concern were education in the Trust Territory and members' qualifications and privileges. The wide scattering of additional topics which were suggested provided little further dimension for the training design; most prominent was mention of the Trust Territory's future status. On the opening day of the workshop, the training team pointedly acquainted the assembled legislators of the manner in which the questionnaire had contributed to fixing the scope and emphasis of the training program.

It was also decided that upon convening, the workshop would name a steering group for the training period. To avoid weighted representation, it was arbitrarily determined to have the steering committee composed of one member-elect from each of the six administrative districts of the Trust Territory. To this group, on the opening of the workshop, would be submitted the proposed training plan, and with its approval the workshop would then proceed. At any time the committee was to be free to modify the program. Concomitantly, this group offered a vehicle for ready feedback, enabling the training team to gain some measure of its success or

[2] Letter of HiCom to all congressmen-elect, May 7, 1965, supplementing letter of Feb. 8, 1965.

[3] Two members from each house did not return their questionnaires. As some congressmen-elect did not receive their forms until after the deadline for remailing them had expired and commented upon this when returning them late, this may furnish the explanation for the four members' failure to reply. During the ensuing workshop, all four took an active part and expressed satisfaction with its conduct and content.

failure in communicating concepts and techniques. The high commissioner's letter which carried the questionnaire to all of the congressmen-elect alerted them to the fact that such a steering group would set the content of the training program.

Finally, it was concluded that the training team's role should basically be one of prompter, providing relevant facts and positing alternatives for action, and that the congressmen-elect should be encouraged to discuss the alternatives and reach their own independent judgements. As there were bound to be some who would be culturally conditioned to refrain from expressing a viewpoint, the legislators would be divided into three discussion sections whose composition would be varied so that the membership would be rotated. Each section's deliberations would be reported to the whole assembly either by a spokesman from its ranks or by one of the team sitting with the group. Fundamental to the decision to employ sections was the hope of encouraging everyone to take an active part, so the manner of reporting conclusions and the selection of the rapporteur were of secondary importance.

The test of all this planning would come at the end of the first week when, utilizing the gamut of legislative organization and procedure sketched during the training session, two drafting committees would be chosen from their respective houses to oversee the preparation of the Rules of Procedure. Given reasonable progress, after a long weekend for drafting and two half-day sessions in the second week of the workshop for the houses to review the tentative drafts of their rules, the Congress of Micronesia would end the training session with comprehensive sets of procedural rules drawn to each house's specifications. It was crucial, then, that the drafting committees be comprised of individuals knowledgeable of legislative procedure and sensitive to the nuances of the English language. While the steering committee might serve its purpose best if its members were named because of their standing within their respective district delegations, so that the committee's satisfaction with the training design and its modification would lend endorsement, it would prove dysfunctional should status per se be the sole requisite for membership on the drafting committees. Although the training team directed that each district delegation select one of its members for the steering group, it refrained from announcing any method for determining the composition of the drafting committees. Instead, both formally and in casual conversation during the first week of the workshop, the importance of these committees' work was stressed, and the members-elect approached the formation of the drafting committees in a wholly unstructured way.

THE RESPONSE

Immediately upon the conclusion of the workshop's opening ceremonies, a recess was called so each delegation could designate its representative to the steering committee. The Marshalls caucused for about ten minutes, revealing the cleavage within its ranks between two rival factions, while the others quickly announced their choices. All six members named to the committee were delegates,[4] and all but one had served in the Council of Micronesia— the first sign that the congressmen-elect accepted the guiding role of the steering committee in the spirit intended. The agenda for the first day was then presented to the steering committee for its concurrence, and later the balance of the program was similarly reviewed. Although the training team was prepared to incorporate major modifications, the steering committee directed only minor adjustments to be made.

Each day, prior to the opening of the morning session, the training team met with the committee for feedback on the previous day's work. These sessions also offered the opportunity for clearing administrative details: hours for the commencing and closing of the daily work sessions; selection of an evening for a full-length movie; rotation of discussion group assignments; solicitation of factual questions to be answered by the administration during the second week of the workshop; and revision of the entertainment schedule originally arranged to break the rigor of the conference at a time when the plethora of social events tendered the congressmen by the people of Saipan could not be foreseen. Later, the Trust Territory administration finalized its plans for the opening day's joint session of the Congress of Micronesia, and the steering committee as spokesman for the congress met with the representative of the administration. This last was an unintended function of the committee and bridged the awkward alternative of unilateral action by the administration without consultation with the congress.

The general attitude reported was one of satisfaction with the workshop, and few responses of negative or corrective nature were

[4] Andon Amaraich, Truk; Olympio T. Borja, Marianas; Amata Kabua, Marshalls; Francis Nuuan, Yap; Bailey Olter, Ponape; Roman Tmetuchl, Palau.

forthcoming. The steering committee probably best served as a device by which formal communications to the whole congress from many sources could be informally supplemented so as to aid members-elect in understanding them. The committee never developed a distinct group identity, and there was always a fair chance that the recommendations it relayed to the training team were those from an individual member rather than the consensus of the committee, and that they may not even have emanated from the member's delegation. None of this discounts the fact that the training team's meeting with the steering committee symbolized that the workshop was the legislators' and that the team was merely assisting. Above all, the committee's existence served to forestall any possibility of the sessions' taking a direction not desired by the congress; the committee was accepted as a constraint even though it had no occasion to exercise its power.

Toward the end of the first week, each house named its drafting committee. The choice of the congress revealed a sensitivity to the significant role to be played by these formative groups. For the Assembly, each district's delegation selected a well-qualified member, six in all; [5] the smaller House of Delegates renamed only one of the members from the steering committee to serve and substituted a new member from both Palau and Truk.[6]

The drafting committees applied themselves diligently to their tasks. To each committee was assigned a member of the training team staff who served as a resource person and who explained the essential elements of the legislative rules, helped narrow down provisions to the point where the committee could make a meaningful choice, and then prepared the draft for committee inspection. This was no rubber stamp process. The rules which emerged revealed some sharp differences between the two committees; each mirrored the views of its respective house regarding the leadership role of its presiding officer and the independence of action to be allotted individual members. Combing through the details, the committee members carefully evaluated the possible results which

[5] Mitaro Danis, Truk; Dwight Heine, Marshalls; Bethwel Henry, Ponape; Juan A. Sablan, Marianas; Lazarus Salii, Palau; Luke M. Tman, Yap. The group included all four members later placed in nomination for the office of Speaker.

[6] Olympio T. Borja, Marianas; Tosiwo Nakayama, Truk; John O. Ngiraked, Palau. The last two were to be the major contestants for the office of President.

might flow from various approaches and then trimmed the final product to make it accord with what they judged to be the sentiment of their parent bodies. They did their work well, for each house accepted the bulk of its committee's original draft and, after rephrasing by the training team to secure greater technical accuracy and ease of comprehension, approved the completed work. The later caucusing of each house, and the naming of its officers-elect, served to reinforce the adoption of its rules.

THE FIRST WEEK'S TRAINING

The tentative outline of subjects for the initial week, as agreed to by the steering committee, covered:

Monday:	morning	introduction to workshop
	afternoon	subject-matter jurisdiction of congress
Tuesday:	morning	organization (structure) of a legislature
	afternoon	committees and their use
Wednesday:	morning	processing of legislative measures
	afternoon	members: qualifications, rights, limitations
Thursday:	morning	decision-making in legislative bodies
	afternoon	parliamentary procedure and legislative order
Friday:	morning	legislative staff and assistance
	afternoon	separate meetings of houses to instruct drafting of rules

The basic format normally followed for each half-day session called for an oral presentation by the training team, followed by small-group problem-solving intended to reinforce the introductory session by reiteration, to amplify through focusing attention on the running of the Congress of Micronesia, or merely to afford the opportunity for congressmen-elect to obtain explanation of matters which they had not understood but had hesitated to query in the plenary sessions. Outlines of general session presentations and small-group assignments had been sketched in detail before the team left Hawaii but were modified during the course of the week, due to insufficient time's necessitating deletions and more appropriate problems' spontaneously arising once the workshop was underway.

Both the styles and occasionally the views of the three members of the training team varied. To the training session all three brought extensive practical experience in working intimately with legislative bodies, and the easy camaraderie developed early in the workshop allowed inclusion of the teams' personal experiences as illustrations to breathe life into what too easily could have lapsed into a series of academic lectures. This lack of formality also permitted the trainers to disagree publicly, as when they were not in accord on the efficacy of Hawaii's "short form" bill as a device to ease the legislative burden. Differences of views were intentionally not concealed, for it was believed that airing them helped further the objectives of encouraging congressmen-elect to avoid rote copying of other jurisdictions' practices and discouraging uncritical acceptance of "textbook" solutions. Incidentally, this approach also assured that the gamut of trainers' personal idiosyncrasies to which the members-elect would be exposed would range from the activist to the detached and from the constitutionally suspicious to the more complacently accepting, and that the attitudes expressed regarding legislative-executive relations, legislative leadership, and comparable other matters would reflect these variances.

The opening morning of the first week's training differed slightly in approach from that of the balance of the week. It was deliberately designed for psychological impact rather than the content knowledge to be transmitted. High Commissioner Goding's remarks of welcome publicly signified not only the administration's general endorsement but also its willingness to accept the burden of the second week's training covering Trust Territory governmental structure, activities, and problems. Next, appointment of the steering committee reinforced the "working-session" formality surrounding the opening ceremonies. The congressmen-elect were then immediately assigned a workshop problem as an ice breaker, one based upon the dilemma of the representative hung on the horns of express directions of his constituents and the dictates of his own judgment. In later sessions, the small-group problem or discussion was always preceded by a general session preparation; on the first day, however, it was believed the trauma of being forced, individually, to formulate one's thoughts on representation, and then to defend them in a small group whose members were in many cases still little more than acquaintances, would start the workshop off on a level of expectancy regarding other things to come which would help carry it through some of its duller moments. It was also hoped this would early encourage all congressmen-elect to actively engage in small-group discussions.

The reaction was as expected: the members' interest was captured by the setting forth of a problem which in a vague manner had disturbed most of them. All could grasp its pertinency and grapple with its resolution. Within each of the three sections, participation was widespread and, for a Trust Territory group, spirited. When the three sections reported back, the members were informed that their problem was that of all legislators, who faced the same paradox, and that their conclusions (favoring the Trustee-Statesmen, as opposed to the Spokesman-Delegate position) in general coincided with comparable findings made in state legislatures of the United States.[7] From all appearances, this psychological emersion, the novelty for some of the "buzz" session device, and the exposure to the universality of the legislative process had the desired effect, and by the time the workshop recessed for lunch, it was obvious that it had "taken." Thereafter, despite inclement weather, distressing humidity, and at times disturbing accoustics, almost perfect attendance of the congressmen-elect served as measure of their interest in the workshop and, if not their satisfaction, at least the high anticipation [8] with which they approached each day's session.

Monday's afternoon meeting, devoted to the subject-matter jurisdiction of the Congress of Micronesia, by its very nature emphasized the limitations placed upon the powers of the congress. The Office of the Attorney General undertook to answer the questions raised, a majority of which were directed to the financial powers of the congress, its control over the budget, and the division of authority between the Territorial, district, and local levels of government. In a number of instances, members-elect differed with the interpretation placed on the applicable clauses of the Secretarial Order, in their disagreement sometimes being oblivious to the distinction between disapproval of policy and the accuracy of

[7] See pp. 284–287.

[8] Undoubtedly, interest had been whetted by the advance series of communications, and this had spread to others than the members-elect. On May 11, 1965, the Ponape District Legislature's Clerk dispatched a letter to the other districts proposing that all district legislative secretaries and clerks also participate in the forthcoming congressional workshop. This bid to take part was denied on the basis that their presence might detract from building the *esprit de corps* desired for the training.

the legal opinion being rendered. The general impression left by this session reinforced the suspicions of those members who were inclined to question the motives of the Administering Authority. As the staff from the attorney general's office gave most attention to restrictions on legislative action, while the training team's thrust was toward aiding the congress in proceeding both legally and extra-legally in accomplishing its objectives, the unintentional net effect of this session for many members was probably to align the training team "with" the congress and "against" the administration.

The outline of the first week's training, as previously sketched, fairly adequately conveys the scope of the subject matter covered each day. Insofar as possible, matters placed before the groups were oriented toward practicalities, and an effort was made to keep everything relevant to the future course of the congress. Thus Tuesday morning's discussions turned attention to a potential plan for the initial organizing of the congress, possible functions which could be undertaken during the interim between the annual legislative sessions of the congress, and the range of items which might be included in a legislative budget. On Wednesday morning, members in their small groups explored the complexities of legislative drafting and the proper usage of bills and resolutions, after the general session had considered the elements of each, the distinction between them, and the normal course of their preparation and adoption.

A full-length Hollywood movie built around the theme of morality in politics [9] was shown on Wednesday night. In addition to constituting enjoyable entertainment, it portrayed in detail the decorum and practices of the United States Senate. On Thursday morning there was a standard educational film depicting a state legislature in session [10] and a more sophisticated television print highlighting the difficulties which beset a state legislator.[11] All furnished a backdrop for the afternoon's treatment of parliamentary procedure and legislative order, and the workshop team attempted to make it meaningful through a series of role-playing presentations. As a training tool these films fully proved their worth: to the less sophisticated, the sheer pictorialization of a number of American legislatures in session and the step-by-step por-

[9] *Mr. Smith Goes to Washington.*
[10] *Legislative Process.*
[11] *The Man in the Middle.*

trayal of their procedures helped clarify matters examined orally, and for the others, the films touched upon a variety of matters for which the training week literally had insufficient time. The commendatory remarks volunteered long after the original impact should have worn off testified to the favorable impression left by the films.

By Friday afternoon, when the two houses met in separate session to instruct their drafting committees, most of the major areas applicable to parliamentary practices had been at least briefly mentioned. At this last session of the first week, a five-page check list, noting the major areas to which attention ought be given in determining the content of the rules, was distributed for the use of the members-elect. The training team carefully refrained from indicating its preferences. A team member guided each house through its consideration of the check list, served as resource person as it moved to specific decisions, and later undertook the chore of drafting that body's rules under the direction of its drafting committee. The weekend over the July 4 holiday was consumed in a series of informal meetings with the training team and the drafting committees and in the painstaking task of converting collective decisions to unambiguous, internally consistent detail.

THE SECOND WEEK'S TRAINING

Most of the burden for the second week's training fell to the staff of the Trust Territory administration. Assistant commissioners and department heads, aided by their subordinates, offered brief summaries of the administrative organization and duties of their units and answered questions put to them by the congressmen-elect. After consulting with the steering committee, the training team proposed the general format and pace for these sessions; later it arranged for revision of schedules to accommodate administrators for whom inadequate time had been allotted. Throughout the week, the team served as communication channel between members and administrators by relaying the formers' questions formulated in expectation of the latters' appearance. When not otherwise occupied, the team's rule drafting chores continued.

Tuesday morning opened with a general introduction to the administrative structure and functions of the Trust Territory and to the relation of Trust Territory Headquarters to the district administrations, followed by a visit to the offices at Headquarters and other governmental sites to familiarize all members with their location. The afternoon was devoted to financial matters. For Wednesday morning, all of community services were scheduled for treatment, but the lead-off discussion on education preempted almost the entire period, so that public health and community development had to be postponed until Friday. After an interlude on Wednesday afternoon devoted to review of the tentative rules, the plenary session on Thursday morning returned to its examination of the Trust Territory government with a session on resources and development. Here, there was only sufficient time for agriculture and fisheries, and land management and cooperatives were reassigned to the last day. On Thursday afternoon the various phases of staff services and technical administration came before the plenary session, and Trust Territory personnel policy, transportation, communications, and public works all were subjected to intensive inquiry.

Friday, the last day of the workshop, turned out to be a hodgepodge of bits and pieces, with subjects deferred from earlier in the week fitted in. On Friday morning, the attorney general was recalled to answer to a wide range of questions, replies to which impinged upon the legal limitations to the congress' jurisdiction. The administration's presentation of information on the current and proposed legislative budgets similarly waited until the last day. No time remained on Friday afternoon for confirmation of each house's legislative rules. However, this had been foreseen early in the week, so after its Wednesday afternoon session, the House of Delegates had assigned its drafting committee authority to review and ratify the final form of the House rules, while the General Assembly made arrangements to meet in caucus early on Saturday morning for the same purpose.

At the request of the administration, during the first week of the workshop the steering committee solicited the members-elect for written questions on facets of policy and administrative action which they wanted included in the general program topics suggested by the training team for the second week. Questions were delivered as they continued to trickle in during the latter half of the period. Unfortunately, some of the administration personnel appearing at the plenary sessions did not fully comprehend the nature of the new executive-legislative relationships emerging from the creation of the congress and phrased their remarks in generalities unresponsive to the specificity of the congressmen's inquiries.

Similarly dysfunctionally, some of the latter did not appreciate that the workshop's design sought to elicit information and was not intended to make the plenary training sessions a forum for debating the wisdom of administration policy or challenging individual administrator's motives.

As early as April 8, the high commissioner instituted a review of district and municipal taxes throughout the Trust Territory to determine the effect of Secretarial Order No. 2882 reserving import duties to the Congress of Micronesia. On April 15 he circularized all district administrators, soliciting proposals for possible inclusion in the administration's legislative program to be submitted to the new congress. A number of measures adopted by district legislatures had previously been disapproved by the high commissioner upon the grounds that they embraced subjects which were to be placed before the congress.[12] Nevertheless, the administration failed to utilize the opportunity afforded by the workshop to give advance notice of its legislative program, and at the plenary sessions, in replying to the questioning on future plans, some of the staff members refused to commit themselves in any way. The same hiatus applied to much of the explanation on Territorial finances furnished the workshop. When it became manifest that the administration was unprepared or unwilling to discuss its legislative program, several of the members-elect stepped into the policy vacuum by endeavoring through statements from the floor to induce the workshop to support the positions they themselves advocated.

Although the second week of the workshop succeeded in presenting a balanced coverage of the many functions performed by the Trust Territory government and the major difficulties encountered, it lacked the sense of immediacy which had distinguished the first week's proceedings. The Trust Territory staff and the congressmen were experiencing their first exposure to the emergence of a new power center in the Trust Territory, and both were yet adjusting to unaccustomed roles. The administration, in which full legislating power once resided, was still not attuned to the new relationship which presumes a degree of conflict and lack of mutuality of interest between the two branches of government. The dialogue between executive and legislature which is the hallmark of democratic government had just commenced.

[12] For example, Act 17-65 of the Tenth Session of the Truk District Legislature, disapproved in HiCom's letter to DistAd Truk, July 22, 1965.

THE RULES OF THE TWO HOUSES [13]

The decision to use the workshop as a vehicle for formulating standing rules of each house and, when the drafting committees had finished their work, to caucus for the selection of the officers and committee members called for by those rules, supplied an unusually effective unifying force for binding together the bifurcated two weeks of training. A singular goal was set, one which was real and understandable in its personal impact on all the members-elect. The congress could begin to function on its very first day, an absolute necessity if it were to complete its work within its limited 30-day session. Around this basic objective it was possible to weave an extensive body of data and opinion on legislative practices, and the coverage of topical matters during the second week only reemphasized the urgency of completing the organization of each house so as to be able to tackle substantive problems with dispatch.

Before work on drafting the rules commenced, a number of matters had to be clarified. For one thing, the Secretarial Order was ambiguous as to whether the United States congressional practice of continuing measures from the calendar of the first to the second session could be copied by the Congress of Micronesia. An opinion from the attorney general of the Trust Territory was obtained declaring that each regular session is intended to be distinct and that, except for measures reconsidered after veto, bills do not carry over from one session to another.[14] Other comparable matters similarly had to be resolved in order that the new congress' scope of discretion could be ascertained before the compass of its own rules was fixed. Of course, large areas of uncertainty will remain until judicial decisions and further rulings slowly build a corpus of law applicable to the Congress of Micronesia.

In the absence of any extensive body of parliamentary procedure followed by either the district legislatures or the Council of Micronesia, it was necessary to improvise. The training team's background prompted use of the rules of Hawaii's state legislature as a preliminary matrix. Hawaii in its Monarchial and Territorial past modeled its procedural rules on those of legislatures functioning on the mainland United States, which of course traced back ulti-

---

[13] The rules of both houses of the first Congress of Micronesia are reproduced in the "Manual of the Congress of Micronesia," published by the Office of the Legislative Counsel, Congress of Micronesia; also in U.S. Congress, House Hearings before the Sub-committee on Territorial and Insular Affairs, *Report on Pacific Affairs, 1965*, 89th Congress, 1st Sess. (1965), pp. 26–53.

[14] However, see p. 350.

mately to the British Mother of Parliaments. Now once again, like the division of cellular bodies, the legislative genes were carried forward to a brand new assembly. But following a model did not constitute rote copying, for all of the directions of the Secretarial Order had to be observed, and the Trust Territory's uniqueness also prompted many novel questions. As an example, the oath of the Micronesian legislator had to be shaped to his *sui generis* nature. As finally composed, the oath reads:

Do you solemnly swear (or affirm) that you have been duly elected and properly hold office as a member of the . . . [House of Delegates/General Assembly] of the Congress of Micronesia, that you do freely, willingly and without reservation accept the responsibilities and obligations of this high office, that you will discharge these obligations and responsibilities in a manner that will bring honor to this high body and to the people of Micronesia, that you will never use your offiice for personal pecuniary gain or aggrandizement, and that you will loyally defend the laws of the Trust Territory of the Pacific Islands and promote the well-being of all the people of Micronesia, so help you God?

For many years to come freshmen members elected to the Congress of Micronesia will probably not be conversant with the complexities of parliamentary action, so the rules were made as inclusive as possible to obviate need for reliance upon other sources. In the main, the rules of both the General Assembly and the House of Delegates read identically for processing legislative measures. This was intentional, so that legislators would have to familiarize themselves with but a single series of procedures. The variances reflect the distinctive differences of the two houses. Both sets of rules cover the organization of the respective body, officers and their duties, standing committees and special committees, methods of voting and the requisite number of votes for taking various forms of action, and the steps to be followed in the adoption of bills and resolutions. Provision is also made for the administration of each house's business affairs, the keeping of a journal, issuance of warrants and subpoenas, and the administrating of oaths to witnesses. Unlike in many jurisdictions, a wide arc of general parliamentary matters was also incorporated, and it was deemed best to include much of the detail which is usually found in manuals of legislative bodies but not reproduced in their standing orders. Thus, contained in the rules are sections specifying the format of bills, the order of contents for committee reports, the numbering system for measures designed to carry automatically reference to each amendment, and comparable other items. In lieu of joint standing orders, the rules of each chamber were dovetailed, with identical procedures governing conference committees, the setting up of joint committees by resolution or statute, and the handling of communications between the two bodies.

Both houses decided on a minimal number of officers. The president and vice-president in the House of Delegates have as their counterparts the speaker and vice-speaker in the General Assembly. Similarly, the non-member secretary and sergeant-at-arms of the House are duplicated by the General Assembly's clerk and sergeantat-arms. The Assembly added an extra officer, the legislative secretary, whose functions closely resemble those of a floor leader, and whose name was so changed at the second session of the Congress of Micronesia in 1966. This extra office owes its genesis to the recommendations of the original working committee of the Council of Micronesia, probably influenced by the practices of the Guam legislature, and owes its advocacy at the workshop to the Mariana assemblymen who were familiar with its use in the Saipan Municipal Congress.

Approximately the same provision is made in both houses for standing committees. The General Assembly divided money functions between two committees, calling one the Appropriations Committee and the other the Ways and Means Committee, while the House of Delegates assigned all financial duties to its Ways and Means Committee. The antecedents of the remaining three standing committees may be traced to the old economics, social, and political development committees of the Council of Micronesia and the district legislatures. The rules of each house prescribe that members of standing committees are appointed by the presiding officer after consultation with the members. Both houses took pains to fix the size of their committees so as to involve all members, spread the posts on key committees, and restrict the number of assignments which any one member could receive, all with a view to achieving wide district representation and precluding concentration of power in the hands of a few. Joint meetings of two committees of the same house, or of different houses, are countenanced, but final action must be taken separately by each committee. The creation of joint committees must await the enactment of a statute or the passage of an appropriate joint resolution.

The rules of both houses require that before the second (final) reading, a bill must be "experted" by the legislative counsel. Should substantive floor amendments be adopted, the measure must be reprinted in the General Assembly or in the House of Delegates if the amendments are extensive. This requirement, though meritorious in preventing ill-considered legislation, places an onerous burden upon the legislative staff, and toward the end of the first session it was found necessary to suspend this feature of the rules in order to expedite the work of the congress.

The congressional rules contain a number of novel features which might have utility for other legislatures. Except at convening and adjournment, when a temporary chaplain is appointed, the daily sessions open in the General Assembly with the members standing for a moment of silent prayer; this practice was also followed in the House, although not mandated by the rules. To forestall the high commissioner's calling a special session under circumstances which do not allow sufficient time for all administrative districts to be represented, the rules require on the opening day of a special session a quorum of at least one member from each of the six districts. The only exception recognized is when adequate notice has been given for all members to be present, so that the absence of a delegation may be attributed to willful abstention.

It is normal to require an extraordinary majority to amend the compromises engrafted into legislative rules. As there was relatively little political maneuvering attendant on the drafting of the rules for the Congress of Micronesia, there was no felt need for such protection, and as a consequence they may be modified by mere majority vote. But the rules do contain an unusual self-limiting feature which strikes a rare note of self-discipline in the enacting of legislation. Following the practice of the Congress of the United States, the Secretarial Order allows the adoption of legislation by a majority of a quorum. Conceivably, then, legislation could be enacted upon receiving the affirmative vote of four delegates and seven assemblymen out of a total membership of thirty-three! Neither house believed this would afford adequate expression of the legislative will and, by their respective rules, prohibited a bill from passing unless it receives an absolute majority vote in each house.[15]

The members-elect desired their rules to cover conflicts of interest but did not wish to offer an easy excuse for members endeavoring to escape casting a ballot on highly controversial issues. The

[15] Subsequently, Secretarial Order No. 2882 was amended to require final passage by a majority vote.

language finally adopted declares a member is not to vote when he has a "distinct, individual pecuniary interest" or when it will affect his right to a legislative seat, or in matters in which his individual conduct is involved. It remains to be seen whether this formalization of morality will be any more successful in the Congress of Micronesia than are comparable attempts in American legislatures.

Since the Monarchial period, the Hawaiian legislature has allowed the novel practice of *kanalua* (undecided) voting. A member, instead of voicing aye or no, may respond *kanalua* on a roll call or may refrain from replying to his name. Upon the completion of the roll call, his name is then recalled, and should he *kanalua* twice, the clerk records him as having voted in the affirmative. Half in jest, this procedure was described to the congressmen-elect during the workshop, and mention was made of its having once been followed by the old Marshallese bicameral congress. The members found the general idea attractive and wrote into the rules of each house the requirement that an affirmative vote be recorded when a member is present and fails to vote upon his name's being reached twice on a roll call. During the first session of the Congress of Micronesia, the House of Delegates amended its rules to have the Journal expressly state that an aye vote had been placed after such non-responding member's name.

The drafting committees of the two houses undertook their tasks attuned to the differences in the makeup of their principals. To begin with, size favored greater stratification in the Assembly, for the smaller the legislative body the more "equal" are its members. More to the point, two-thirds of the delegates had served in the Council of Micronesia and were familiar with the absence of strong leadership in that body and the attendant equality of status its members had enjoyed. This carried over into their attitude toward the House of Delegates. On the other hand, the General Assembly was of a temper to grant effective powers to its officers and to trim the rights of the individual member as necessary to bulwark such authority. Collectively, the variances in the detail of the rules corroborate this distinctive nature of the two chambers.

Whenever the House is dissatisfied with its officers, by majority vote it can remove them; in the Assembly, dismissal of an officer takes sixteen votes, the highest number required for any action of the General Assembly. A mere majority of the quorum in the House of Delegates may overturn a parliamentary ruling of its president, while the same action requires a two-thirds vote in the Assembly. In both houses the presiding officer may not be chairman of a standing committee, but only in the House is there a prohibition against its officers serving as chairmen of special or conference committees. Even to get the work of the House underway requires a larger percentage of members present (two-thirds) than in the Assembly (majority).

To the extent that the House has recognized a need for concentrating power, it has localized it in the standing committees and, more particularly, their chairmen. In the General Assembly the rules call for the presiding officer to name the chairman of each of the standing committees; in the House of Delegates, the membership of each committee chooses its own presiding officer. Despite this method for selecting committee chairmen in the House, once serving, these officers cannot be removed except by a majority vote of the total membership of the House of Delegates. When a measure is referred to committee, the House of Delegates reserves but a limited right of recall, and this to be exercised only in the latter part of the session. In contrast, in the General Assembly a measure may be removed from committee at any time and brought onto the floor with a two-thirds vote of a quorum. Finally, in any Assembly committee a majority of the members may require the chairman "to exercise his powers in the manner in which they direct"; the House rules merely allow a majority to compel the committee's presiding officer to place a measure on the agenda for committee consideration and decision.

All twelve delegates in the House are made members of the Ways and Means Committee—a device for allowing the House to have executive meetings and reach consensus without a public record being kept. (The Secretarial Order forbids closed meetings by either house in plenary session or when sitting in Committee of the Whole.) This membership of the Ways and Means Committee also assures that each delegate will take part in all decisions on taxes and governmental finances, matters pertaining to the internal organization and management of the House, and the relations of the people of Micronesia to the United States, the United Nations, and foreign countries. It avoided the risk of setting up a committee which could dominate the House and neatly disposed of the knotty problem of how to determine membership on the key committee of such a small body.

Further confirming this tendency to treat all delegates as equals,

House rules declare that delegates may actively engage in the public meetings of standing committees of which they are not members, but without right of vote. On the floor of the House, each delegate has the right to speak at least once on every motion, and not even adoption of the "previous question" can deny him this opportunity. In the Assembly, cloture can be moved after one member from each of the six delegations has had an opportunity to express his views, so that Assembly discussion may be truncated by will of the majority. Probably the zenith in this attempt to assure parity was reached in the House rules' prescription that at the beginning of each session the order for calling of the roll is to be fixed by lot, emphasizing the insignificance of even alphabetical priority.

CHOOSING UP SIDES

Size—both of chamber and of delegation—caused difficulties for the House of Delegates. The smaller the legislative body is, the less the psychological compulsion for an hierarchical organization to order its affairs. The more comparable the size of delegations, the fewer are the practical opportunities for manipulating a successful power combination. These factors, coupled with the House's lack of leaders so outstanding that support would naturally polarize in support or opposition, resulted in the delegates' being hung for a number of days before final agreement could be reached on the naming of officers. The General Assembly, larger, with delegations varying in size, and favored with a helmsman acknowledged to be competent, easily completed its organization in half a day before the congress was convened.

Long before the Saipan workshop, politicking for congressional office got underway. It mattered little that the congress was yet an amorphous body, for this vagueness fitted the leisurely, superficially indecisive maneuvering which accompanies much of the political action within the Trust Territory. Most bids for prominence, but not all, were made covertly. Starting in March of 1965, Delegate-elect John Ngiraked from Palau commenced a series of letters to all members-elect from both houses. The initial communication concerned the selection of a legislative counsel for the congress. Later letters dealt with the congress' limited budget powers and the need for funding to enable members-elect to visit their constituents. At first it looked as if this early campaign was to culminate in Ngiraked's securing the presidential post, but between the Saturday afternoon caucus which agreed upon him as president-elect and the convening of the congress the following Monday morning, enough votes had defected so as to place him in a tie with another delegate for whom a less openly aggressive campaign had been waged in a manner more in harmony with most of the Territory's political folkways. The latter was to win.

Many diverse factors influenced the members' choice between the candidates for congressional office. District representation was an element; so was personal friendship, often founded on attendance at the Pacific Islands Central School years before. Offers to trade support were tendered, and sometimes political backing turned on unexpected conditions. A prominent assemblyman-elect reported being approached on Guam, before the workshop had commenced, by Saipanese and Guamanian politicians with a promise of assistance if he would commit himself in favor of joining the Trust Territory to Guam. Another element material to decision-making proved to be the caucus rules suggested by the workshop team which narrowed opportunity for clandestine moves to gain technical advantage.

DIVISION OF OFFICER AND CHAIRMANSHIP POSTS BETWEEN EAST AND WEST

EAST

Truk	President	Vice-Speaker	
Marshalls		Speaker	H. Ways & Means
Ponape	Vice-President	Leg. Sec.	A. Education, Health, & Social Matters

WEST

Marianas	H. Resources & Development	H. Judiciary & Governmental Relations	A. Ways & Means
Palau	H. Education, Health, & Social Matters	A. Appropriations	A. Resources & Development
Yap	A. Judiciary & Governmental Relations		

When both houses were finally organized, the three administrative districts in the Eastern portion of the Trust Territory had control of all five congressional offices. The committee chairmanships were divided more evenly between the Eastern and Western regions, with the latter enjoying a numerical majority. The explanation for this distribution does not lie in the population predominance of the Eastern districts, for each district enjoys equal representation in in the House of Delegates. Any leverage in the House which could have been obtained from the Assembly's composition was lost by the Assembly's early organization during its Saturday half-day caucus.

The rules followed by the members of the General Assembly gathered in caucus, and later by the House, called for nominations to be made for each office seriatim, and then a vote by secret ballot. If no member received an absolute majority of ballots cast, the name of the candidate receiving the fewest votes was to be struck and the process continued. The General Assembly caucus also followed this in selecting the chairmen for all five Assembly standing committees. These caucus rules forestalled the common practice in the Trust Territory of election by plurality. As one of the Palau assemblymen did not attend the Saturday meeting due to religious convictions,[16] to secure finality of decision it was tacitly understood in the General Assembly caucus that the requisite vote for election would need be a majority of the total membership.

Neither the General Assembly nor the House of Delegates had a slate-maker who put together a "package" of posts in an effort to secure majority support. Perhaps this is a function of more sophisticated legislatures in which positions of power are more prized; the lack of any Territory-wide party or organized political faction undoubtedly contributed; the caucus rules calling for one election at a time and requiring all decisions to go to majority vote may have discouraged "ticket" formation—all of these explanations suggest hypotheses for further exploration in other developing areas of the world just beginning to experiment with the legislative process. If any of the members played the role of "king-maker" it was Truk's Assemblyman Petrus Mailo who helped engineer the selection of Tosiwo Nakayama from Truk as the president of the House of Delegates.

The Assembly caucus from the start assured fairness in its deliberations by having its temporary chairman drawn by lot. The

---

[16] The absence of this member from the Assembly caucus and of his co-religionist from the delegates' caucus was later to start the erroneous rumor in Palau that this failure to attend caused the Palauan candidates for presiding officer in both houses to lose the nomination.

honor of opening the caucus fell to Mitaro Danis of Truk; upon the election of Dwight Heine as speaker-elect, Danis surrendered the chair to him. Auspicious as this beginning was for Danis, it was to be his only post, for though his name was later placed in nomination for three different offices, he was not successful in any of the contests. Initially the House of Delegates' caucus proceeded informally without a chairman and little evident leadership. When on Saturday afternoon John Ngiraked was finally chosen as president-elect, he assumed the chair for the balance of the day. Thereafter, while the stalemate over the presidential election dragged on, Amata Kabua of the Marshalls by mutual agreement served as chairman of the caucus until the deadlock was broken.

Other than for the posts of speaker and vice-speaker there was little to show pre-caucus negotiation for the purpose of mustering support in the Assembly. Many nominations appeared to be made on the spur of the moment, seemingly stimulated by the person named having just previously placed another in nomination. For the speakership, factions had coalesced behind Dwight Heine of the Marshalls and Lazarus Salii from Palau. The former's long prominence in Territorial politics gave him a decided advantage, and Salii's first canvass of nine votes to Heine's ten (the remaining tally was cast for Bethwel Henry) was proof of Salii's capacity as a political campaigner. Upon the second balloting, Heine emerged victorious with an absolute majority of twelve votes. Throughout the balloting, while all were seated around the long table of the conference room, in typical Marshallese modesty, Heine remained with his head in his hands and kept his head bowed through the spontaneous applause which signaled his win and the recount of ballots taken to assure the accuracy of the tally. Only after a further pause did he finally admit his election and accept congratulations.

There was a tacit agreement among a number of delegations to support Chief Petrus Mailo for the vice-speakership, because of his sagacity as an elder statesman and acknowledged status among the Carolinians. After he and Juan Sablan of the Marianas were nominated, Salii's name was added, to all appearance without any prior commitment to this course of action. The count of votes showed Petrus leading with nine ballots, Salii with six, and Sablan, four. (Heine, as chairman, did not vote.) When Sablan's name was removed from the run-off pursuant to the caucus rules, Salii an-

nounced his desire to withdraw so that the vote for Mailo would
be unanimous. The rules made no provision for this alternative,
and it was only after lengthy discussion that the caucus authorized
this innovation.

The choice of Bethwel Henry from Ponape for legislative secretary of the Assembly was by an absolute majority of thirteen votes,
as was Salii's election to the chairmanship of the Assembly's Ways
and Means Committee. Juan Sablan's designation as chairman of
the Appropriations Committee next followed by acclaim, as everyone present was in accord that his previous long experience with
Territorial accounting practices made him the logical occupant of
the post. When Jacob Sawaichi of Palau received only ten ballots
for chairmanship of the Resources and Development Committee,
there was an unexpected problem as the two lowest candidates
were tied; Heine, as chairman, then broke the impasse by publicly
casting his vote in Sawaichi's favor. The run-off tally for chairmanship of the Assembly's Education, Health, and Social Matters
Committee found Drs. Henry Samuel of the Marshalls and Olter
Paul from Ponape with ten and nine votes, respectively; the split in
the Marshalls' delegation was possibly revealed when Heine, a
Marshallese, then cast his vote for Dr. Paul. Heine's vote could also
be explained as a desire to register the priority of Territory-wide
solidarity over district loyalty. The resulting draw was broken by
the pulling of lots, which Dr. Paul won. The balloting for chairmanship of the remaining Assembly Judiciary and Governmental Relations Committe gave a majority of twelve votes to Luke Tman from
the Yap district.

The caucus rules called for each member, before the caucus
broke up, to submit the names of the two committees on which he
desired to serve, and the speaker-elect would later attempt to work
out committee assignments satisfactory to all. In lieu of this, and
after a short recess for the delegations to meet, committee preferences were delivered to the speaker-elect and all names were written down. It was discovered that the choices closely fitted the
billets to be filled, and few members had to be reassigned. Committee posts were thus quickly and amicably distributed. Yap's
delegation held the chairmanship of the Judiciary and Governmental Relations Committee, but a waiver of the prohibition against
a chairman's sitting on another committee allowed that district to
also have seats on both the Appropriations and the Ways and
Means Committees. The standing rules adopted for the Assembly

made provision for such a contingency, so it was only necessary to refer to them. Finally, following the lead of the House of Delegates' caucus, ascertained by a phone call to the latter, the General Assembly caucus decided to hire a temporary clerk and employ a policeman as temporary sergeant-at-arms. Its work completed, the caucus disbanded.

In all, during the course of the Assembly caucus, twenty-three nominations were made for the eight Assembly posts. One-third of the assemblymen (7) were not placed in nomination for any office; roughly another third of the assemblymen (8) received only a single nomination, and of their number Heine, Mailo, and Tman were elected; the remaining six amassed a total of fifteen multiple nominations, and all of them but one succeeded in gaining some office. On several occasions two assemblymen from a single delegation were nominated for the same post, but the final run-off elections in all contests were between assemblymen from different districts. Based on the number of members in a delegation, Palau's assemblymen garnered the most nominations and the largest number of Assembly posts. Although Truk and the Marshalls captured the two highest Assembly offices, in relation to the size of its delegation, Truk fared poorly, and this fact may have added impetus to the drive to unseat Palau's John Ngiraked as president-elect of the House of Delegates and replace him with Tosiwo Nakayama of Truk.

The House caucus devoted all of Saturday morning to exploring ways of staffing the body with a secretary and sergeant-at-arms. The compromise finally reached was to appoint a temporary secretary from the Headquarters' Political Affairs Office and detail a policeman as sergeant-at-arms until advertisements could be placed for permanent staff. When on Saturday afternoon the caucus settled down to the task of balloting for the post of president, each delegate secretly wrote his nomination on a slip of paper. On the slips being counted, it was found that Ngiraked led, followed by Bailey Olter of Ponape and Tosiwo Nakayama, in that order. The exact tally each received was not announced, but the spread of nomination ballots was five for Ngiraked, four for Olter and two for Nakayama. The record remains unclear as to what happened next, but upon the elimination of Nakayama as "low man," balloting apparently gave six votes to Ngiraked and five to Olter. Although this was only a majority of the caucus, the support of the absent Palau delegate when the House of Delegates organized the following Monday would presumably assure fellow Palauan Ngiraked an absolute majority. A comparable contest for the vice-presidency eliminated Amata Kabua on the first round and resulted in the election of Tosiwo Nakayama with six votes to the five received by Olympio Borja of the Marianas. As at this time the Marianas district reputedly was aligned with Palau, the vice-presidential vote revealed a configuration of forces distinct from that which had elected Ngiraked. The final ballot was for chairman of the House Ways and Means Committee, on which all delegates sit, and after Borja's name was dropped on the first round, Kabua was elected with seven votes to Olter's four. This tally for Marshallese Delegate Kabua represented the largest vote gained during the entire balloting. Under the rules of the House, each of the other three committees elects its own chairman.

Once the delegates had noted their committee preferences, it was necessary for Ngiraked to obtain their concurrence to shift them into secondary and tertiary choices in order to comply with the House rules prohibiting more than one member from the same district on any but the Ways and Means Committee. The distribution of members among the committees was accomplished without rancor, and on voice vote all but the House Judiciary and Governmental Relations Committee agreed upon their chairmen. A series of secret ballots showed this four-member committee divided between Olter, Andon Amaraich of Truk, and Jose Cruz of the Marianas, the latter with two tallies. Pursuant to the House rules, this left the decision to Ngiraked as president, who also was a member of the committee, and he deferred his selection until Monday when it was assumed his election would become official. He was never to announce his choice, for over the weekend his coalition of backers for the presidency broke.

Stories differ on who shifted loyalties. The popularly accredited account is that alignments were originally along an East-West axis and that the Marianas delegation split, and the defector joined the three Eastern districts—the Marshalls, Ponape, and Truk—in refusing to name Ngiraked as president. As all balloting was secret, it is neither possible to confirm nor refute this. There is probably some credence to the widely circulated rumor that the delegations from the Eastern districts took umbrage at the boasting by some members from the smaller districts of the West—the Marianas, Yap, and Palau—about how they "had put it all over" the former. Another factor may have been the unpopularity of Palauans in the

Territory. The Carolinian residents on Saipan have close ties with the Truk district, and reputedly this large component of the Marianas Territorial Party put strong pressure on their two delegates to shift support from Ngiraked to Nakayama. Chief Petrus Mailo from the Assembly was reported to have urged delegates to back his fellow Truk congressman, Nakayama. Whatever the cause and whatever the means employed, when the House of Delegates convened on Monday and disqualified Jose R. Cruz, the motion to name Ngiraked as president was defeated by a vote of six to five.

The forces opposed to Ngiraked had agreed on no substitute candidate, so except for the hearing on the challenge to seating Delegate Cruz, the House marked time. When the caucus resumed on Tuesday, with Cruz now seated, balloting for the presidency gave Nakayama seven votes to Ngiraked's five. The most creditable interpretation of this final tally is that the Mariana delegation divided its allegiance and one of its members joined the Eastern districts, now voting as a bloc.

The following day, when the House of Delegates convened, Borja of the Marianas moved both that Nakayama be elected president and later that Olter be chosen as vice-president. The first motion carried by a secret vote of seven to five and the latter by an even larger tally of nine to three. Committee assignments and chairmen posts apparently stood as agreed to on Saturday, and no one voiced the objection that the entire caucus agreement might be void. The next day's Journal carried a listing of committee chairmen; Borja was named as chairman of the Resources and Development Committee as agreed to at the Saturday caucus, and the contested chairmanship for the Judiciary and Governmental Relations Committee was shown as being held by Jose Cruz, also of the Marianas. Election of Olter to the vice-presidency disqualified him for the chairmanship of the latter committee, so that Cruz was next in line.

Only half of the total membership were nominated as potential candidates for the three elected offices filled by House vote, and the contests mainly turned around but four congressmen from as many districts. With the House finally organized, five districts shared the six officer and chairmanship posts, with the Marianas gaining two and Yap none.

In retrospect, a review of both houses in caucus points up their similarity in delaying coming to grips with and resolving the hard decisions inherent in choosing officers. Characteristically, deferral was achieved by turning attention elsewhere. The members of the General Assembly debated long and earnestly over the question of whether, in Saipan's humid climate, just shirt and tie, or also coat, were the appropriate garb for Monday morning's opening session and the afternoon's joint meeting. The House of Delegates' caucus consumed even more time on the question of obtaining a staff for the House. Both may have merely been forms of preliminary sparring, but in the light of the attention given to the style of address and to the legislative staff when the rules of the two houses were drafted, there is the suspicion that formality and patronage *were* of more immediate importance for some congressmen-elect than the business of organizing the two chambers.

CHAPTER 13

The First Congress at Work

A BEGINNING LEGISLATURE is usually characterized by formalism, in good part to compensate for its members' lack of experience with the legislative process and with the wielding of power. This equally applied to the new Congress of Micronesia, for from the opening days of the workshop, the members-elect displayed keen interest in how the congress could be run in a "proper" way and prestigeful manner. Formalism was equated with the manifestation of the recently granted legislative authority, just as it probably was unconsciously associated with important traditional events within the Micronesian cultures.

The importance of the new body required that it be equipped with all the trappings appropriate to its dignity. Long before its convening, the administration devoted arduous hours to ordering all of the furbishings which would help convey the impression to member and spectator alike that here was a legislature properly prepared to undertake its responsibilities. Absent was comparable attention to the structuring of those services essential for running a legislative body or articulating the executive with the legislative branches in a manner which would facilitate the exercise of power by the freshman congressmen. The preparatory efforts of the executive only further illustrated that the ceremonial life of a new legislature tends to be external to much of its process, and the first Congress of Micronesia proved to be no exception.

During the caucuses which marked the termination of the workshop, and on a number of occasions subsequently, the matter of fitting garb occupied the concern of the congressmen. It represented a matter particularly pertinent to a people going through rapid acculturation and identifying Western dress—including coats, white shirts, and ties—with that culture's institutions. The joint session of the opening day, the taking of group pictures, and the later meetings with the high commissioner on official and social occasions caused protracted debate about dress. As one member remarked, if a group picture of the congress were taken with the members shown in shirt sleeves, the constituents would not think of the congress as "amounting to much." Another side of formalism, nicely combining Micronesian patterns with Western modes of expression, was to be found in the holding of banquets. The ceremonial furnishing of food constitutes an integral part of Micronesian life. During the course of the workshop and the ensuing session of congress, the banquets at the club at Trust Territory Headquarters and those given by the various communities on Saipan had in common the elements of traditional "feasts," as indeed they were referred to in the appreciative remarks entered in the journals.

The members of both houses approached the first session unfamiliar with the limitations within which they were operating, as fixed both by the restrictions of Secretarial Order No. 2882 and by the rules they had adopted governing their own conduct. Their actions during caucuses demonstrated their individual abilities in the rudiments of parliamentary maneuver, mainly gained through service with district legislatures and the Council of Micronesia, and this experience was their mainstay throughout the session. The lack of a sufficiently trained and numerous staff made impossible the observance of the safeguards built into the rules to protect the members against the mounting legislative pressures. The absence of strong leadership from within or without, complicated by the members' lack of comprehension of their own powers and concomitant duties, all contributed to an inevitable drift, ending in a log jam with unfinished business piled up as adjournment neared. The slowness of the administration in submitting its desired legislation and in presenting the Territorial budget for review only further compounded confusion. The wonder is that the congress succeeded as well as it did in winnowing out the pork barrel measures premised upon campaign promises made solely to attract voters and the idiosyncratic proposals reflecting political naïveté, and in producing a record sound enough to permit its becoming the foundation for further congressional sessions.

Literally the whole congress was learning: the clerks, how to keep track of measures; the duplicating staff, how to develop systems for coping with the mountain of paper engendered by a legislature in action; the committee chairmen, how to order their committees' work loads and bring matters to decision; the members, how to cooperate with their colleagues from other districts in moving favorable measures to passage and defeating those they opposed; and the officers, the hard lesson of adapting Micronesian indirection to the more demanding style of the new political institution. The American administration was also learning a new role of working with a co-equal, composed solely of Micronesians, which now had the destiny of the Territory within its grasp.

Opening day went off much as scheduled, with a little of the awkwardness which accompanies the first night of a play and the members sometimes stumbling over their script and missing cues. The high commissioner called the House of Delegates to order; the deputy high commissioner performed the same function in the General Assembly. After the provisional adoption of the rules drafted during the workshop, the presiding officers named at the Saturday caucuses were elected temporarily to chair their houses. The Assembly's Committee on Credentials found the high commissioner's certification of assemblymen's elections in order, and after a roll call of all members, the Mariana district judge, designated by the chief justice, administered the oath prescribed by the rules. This was followed by the rules' being made permanent and, upon motion, election of the slate of officers agreed upon at the caucus. So well coordinated were these actions in the Assembly that an incipient attempt to put other officers in nomination had no chance of materializing. (These dissident members later claimed that they misunderstood the caucus procedure and that the agreement applied only to the naming of temporary officers.) After the offering of prayer, the General Assembly by committee advised the high commissioner and the House of Delegates it was organized, passed four resolutions of appreciation, and received the Speaker's announcement of committee appointments, here again ratifying caucus action. The General Assembly then recessed, to reconvene in joint session with the House of Delegates to hear the high commissioner's "State of the Territory" address and the speeches of visiting dignitaries from Washington.

The organizing of the House of Delegates did not take place with the despatch of the General Assembly. The filing of a formal protest by the Popular Party of Saipan against the seating of Delegate-elect Jose R. Cruz, after both the Mariana district court and the high court of the Trust Territory ruled they lacked jurisdiction to consider it, caused the House Credentials Committee to recommend that his seating be deferred until his credentials could be further examined. After the swearing in of the remaining members and the drawing of lots to start staggering each delegation's terms of office, the House was unable to agree on its permanent organization.[1] The temporary chairman continued to preside until the election contest was resolved on the second legislative day and permanent officers elected on the third.

Challenge to the seating of an elected member is a "sordid business" [2] at best, but this contest in the House was especially taxing as it turned on both legal technicalities and broader moral issues. Section 7 of Secretarial Order No. 2882 disqualifies any person convicted of a felony from sitting as a congressman, unless he is pardoned and his civil rights restored. This was interpreted in the Trust Territory and by the Interior Department as not applying to convictions in state courts of the United States, and by an amendment to the order promulgated after the congressional elections, the section was modified so as expressly to limit its span to convictions before U.S. Federal and Trust Territory courts. The contest proffered proof of Mr. Cruz's felony conviction by a state court, alleged his lack of moral qualifications to sit, and also claimed election irregularities in the Marianas, although no evidence was submitted on the latter. Throughout, the committee handled the contest as a quasi-judicial hearing, allowing the attorneys for both the petitioners and Mr. Cruz to present arguments and take exceptions to each other's positions and ruling with judicial mien. In recommending the seating of Delegate-elect Cruz, the committee reported it "was reluctant, although sufficient evidence might exist for doing so, to go behind the wishes of a majority of the electorate and refuse to seat the member-elect in question." It emphasized that the disposition of the case in no way denied the authority of the House of Delegates to be the sole judge of the qualifications of its members. "The Committee's recommendation is based, in large measure upon the urgent need to get the House of Delegates organized and at work, and to promote cooperation and harmony at the outset of the convening of the First Session of the Congress of Micronesia." [3]

At this juncture the Administering Authority had reason to question the nature of this "cooperation and harmony," for the first

[1] See p. 318 ff.
[2] Robert R. Robbins, " 'Be it Enacted': The New Legislative Branch," *Micronesian Reporter*, 13:2 (July–Aug., 1965), 19.
[3] Journal of House of Delegates, First Session, Congress of Micronesia, July 13, 1965, p. 1.

working day in each house saw the cumulative introduction of twelve bills and four joint resolutions, practically all aimed at restricting the administration's jurisdiction or obtaining greater benefits for Micronesians at the expense of the Administering Authority. Later events were to show that only two of these measures would be enacted, and one was an innocuous resolution of appreciation to the University of Hawaii.[4]

PHYSICAL AND STAFF ARRANGEMENTS

Saipan is declared to be only the Provisional Headquarters of the Trust Territory, and it was to be expected that the new congress would meet in "provisional" quarters. The community club at the top of Capitol Hill on Mount Tagpochau was borrowed for the purpose. This represented the best that could be arranged under the circumstances but meant the two dining areas of the club, separated by movable wall panels, would be pressed into service as the legislative chambers, and that the "back-room staff" of eight to ten persons would be crowded into a workroom of but sixteen by twenty-four feet, there to compete for space with mimeograph machines, collating tables, desks, stacked supplies, and an embryonic "bill room" holding copies of all measures and reports duplicated for the congress. The congress itself shared the use of these facilities with the Toppa-Tappi Club [5] (which during the month-long session continued to serve dinners several times a week), just as the congress' legislative counsel jointly occupied the office of the club's manager with the latter. All this bears relation to the total administration of the Trust Territory, for the Territory has become so used to temporizing with makeshift facilities that, rather than caviling, the congressmen accepted these quarters as the administration sincerely intended them, the best of those available for the new Congress of Micronesia.[6]

The high commissioner's staff ordered the fittings for each chamber many months in advance so that they could be shipped to Saipan and be ready for the convening of the congress. Each member enjoyed the luxury of a padded swivel chair, a small table

[4] Joint Resolution 1–38, Laws and Resolutions, Congress of Micronesia.

[5] The name "Toppa-Tappi" appears in no congressional publication, as this corruption of a Saipanese geographical designation (top of Mt. Tagpochau) carries a highly immoral connotation in Marshallese.

[6] Separate quarters were erected for the second session of the congress, utilizing prefabricated structures formerly used by the Naval Technical Training Unit.

serving as his desk, and an individual microphone which not only amplified his remarks for his colleagues' benefit but also fed into a tape recording system. Later these same tapes could be edited and spliced and then played over district radio stations for the edification of the people of the Trust Territory. Each presiding officer sat on a raised dais, flanked by Trust Territory and United States flags, and a rostrum was available for the use of guests addressing the chamber. An individual name plate mounted on a block of Palauan ironwood adorned each desk, as gifts of the high commissioner. Each desk was also bedecked with a small Trust Territory flag. Personnel from the Headquarter's staff worked long hours setting up all of the equipment and laying the temporary wiring for the sound system, preparatory to the convening of the congress.

The responsibility for staffing the congress was never as well defined as that for handling the physical arrangements to accommodate it. This may be partly attributed to the lack of success in both houses' quest for staff aids; contributing to it was the ambiguity of the position of the legislative counsel. The caucuses assumed their respective houses' ability to hire a "permanent" secretary or clerk and sergeant-at-arms and enlisted the aid of temporary staff from the Political Affairs Office of the high commissioner, the six districts' political affairs officers brought to Saipan to assist the new congress, and the Mariana Islands District Police Department. What started as a stop-gap arrangement was perpetuated for the balance of the session, and as secretary of the House, clerk of the Assembly, and assistants to both, all remained on in the service of the two houses. Competent staff in the Territory is hard to come by, and without resolution of whether the posts were to be filled on a year-round basis and whether their occupants were to be on the Micronesian pay plan and enjoy the benefits associated with that status, it proved impossible to attract qualified local applicants. In addition, the posts could become patronage plums for Saipan, given the shortage of housing on the island, which would discourage any non-Saipanese from applying. Under the circumstances, the easiest way out of the dilemma was to continue with the temporary staff and to recognize the sergeant-at-arms as "permanent"—for the duration of the session.

During the pre-session workshop, five high school trainees aided in typing and errand running, and this group became the core of the congress' "work-room" crew. Besides their typing, proof-reading, duplicating, and collating chores, they doubled as bill clerks and congressional pages. One secretary was placed in charge of this group and of the typists (their number sometimes down to one) borrowed from the administration. This total work crew, which never exceeded ten at any one time, kept five loaned typewriters, two mimeograph machines, and one spirit duplicator busy while consuming 377 reams of paper, fifty dozen stencils, and 425 file folders. Despite their yeoman work, duplication remained bottle-necked throughout the whole session.

Pursuant to Section 23 of Secretarial Order No. 2882, the high commissioner appointed Dr. Robert R. Robbins, Professor of Government and Chairman of the Department of Government at Tufts University, as legislative counsel of the first session of the congress. The structuring of the Guam Congress under its Organic Act had shown the value of a trained counsel to assist that neophyte legislative body. Although neither the Secretarial Order nor the rules of either house so specified, the work of the House secretary and Assembly clerk gradually came to fall within his purview, and in addition he assumed over-all supervision of the work-room and its duplicating crew. The district political affairs officers assisting the congress also received guidance from him. By sheer necessity, a unified staff under the direction of the legislative counsel gradually emerged.

The Secretarial Order also called for the congress by joint resolution during the course of the first session to nominate a legislative counsel of its own choosing to serve for the second session of the congress and the interim. Long before the convening of the congress, attorneys practicing on Guam and Saipan were promoted for the post, and in weighing the merits of the contenders, the new congress underwent its baptizement in the exercise of patronage power. A special committee of the General Assembly and the Ways and Means Committee of the House turned back a drive spearheaded by the Mariana delegation for a candidate it sponsored and selected Kaleb Udui, the first (and, at that time, only) Micronesian from the Trust Territory to have received a law degree. With this symbolic nomination of one of the Trust Territory's own for the congress' first permanent officer, and given the problems of recruiting personnel for a thirty-day legislative session, the odds favor institutionalizing the staffing pattern set by the 1965 congress. This will see a year-round nuclear staff maintained under the legislative counsel filling the key posts of both houses during the congressional session, with their numbers supplemented by temporary employees hired just for the period the congressmen meet on Saipan.

Indirectly, the congress is mandated by the Secretarial Order to provide interpreters for members lacking fluency in English (Sec. 17(f)). At the first session, the two assemblymen requiring this assistance chose their own interpreters, and these aides accompanied them to Saipan at governmental expense. This personal relationship facilitated the interpreting process as well as speeding legislative action. Simultaneous translation was not undertaken; rather, the interpreters reviewed legislation with their principals before each daily session and kept them advised of the gist of action as it took place on the floor. Should these members wish to speak, they communicated their views to the interpreters who then rephrased them for the Assembly, elaborating as necessary. With increase of facility in English, there will be less need of personal interpreters. However, as the congress grows in prominence, with the consequence that more Micronesians give evidence before congressional committees, staff personnel who can translate written materials and interpret for witnesses in all of the Micronesian languages may become a necessity. The first session saw the beginning of this need, when the testimony of Chamorro-speakers from Saipan had to be translated by delegates from the Marianas who, incidentally, held positions hostile to that supported by the witnesses.

The session opened with no advance preparation for record keeping or for the mechanical handling of congressional materials. Through trial and error, as the session progressed the staff learned to systematize its work. Check-off sheets for noting both congressional and staff action on each bill and resolution, and attendance and roll-call lists early appeared. Before the session closed, a legislative style manual had been developed which set forth both forms and procedures guiding the drafting, reproduction, numbering, transmittal, and final disposition of congressional measures. Needed was a status table or history, periodically reissued, to keep congressmen, administration, and interested citizens informed of each measure's progress. Efforts in this direction toward the close of the session were abandoned under the pressure of competing congressional work, and even the records maintained by the secretariats of the two houses became out of date as posting fell behind. Out of the somewhat traumatic experience of learning-by-doing, a background of expertise was shaped which was to stand future congresses in good stead.

By their contents, the journals of each house disclose the difficulties encountered when attempting to maintain, with untrained personnel, a record of the actions of a congress. Neither staff nor members were prepared to speed the administrative machinery of running the houses; the journals disclose a lapse of as much as four days from the adoption of a measure in one house until its delivery to the second. But most of the time the journals did not consistently report this or any other data except for the votes taken on questions before each house. Passage of measures on first and second readings as well as voting on motions was carefully noted, although lost sight of was the *raison d'être* for the distinctive forms of voting. Voice-votes recorded in the Journal might be accompanied with numerical tallies, while roll calls, whether required by the Secretarial Order or pursuant to the standing rules, appear only as summary counts without indication of how each member cast his vote. Early in the session, members carefully scanned each day's Journal, correcting its contents to insure accuracy. As the work of the session grew more congested, they willingly deferred the reading of the Journal, and by the end of the session the preparation of the Journal fell too far behind for even the gesture of formal waiver. Reference to these journals, particularly those for the closing days of the session, at times leaves one puzzled as to exactly what did occur, but this may only reflect the last days' confusion.[7] The wonder is that the journals of both houses, being only summary accounts of action taken and not verbatim records, managed to preserve as much detail as they did.

COMMITTEES

The first congress made use of standing committees, special committees, conference committees, and even assigned measures to interim committees. Special committees treated administrative problems associated with staffing, amendment of the rules, and substantive matters. A number of the Assembly standing committees divided themselves into subcommittees along subject-matter lines, each reporting informally to the full committee and the latter

[7] See exchange of letters between Delegate Ngiraked and HiCom, turning in part on the House Journal's failure to register legislative intent regarding the use of funds appropriated for interim purposes. Letter of HiCom to Delegate Ngiraked, Feb. 7, 1966; letter of Ngiraked to HiCom, Feb. 14, 1966.

then deliberating and preparing a report. The House Ways and Means Committee, consisting as it did of all twelve delegates, also bifurcated itself into two subcommittees, but in the main, action was by the whole committee, which adversely affected the ability of the House to dispose of the variety of legislative business before it. The composition of the House Ways and Means Committee allowed executive sessions in which all delegates could participate, circumventing the Secretarial Order which prohibited closed meetings of the houses; otherwise, the committee's unwieldy size was dysfunctional. Not only were all appropriation and tax measures referred to this committee but also many of the time-consuming "hot" issues, and this volume of work so bogged down the House that on a number of important measures it had no alternative other than to respond to Assembly initiative by either accepting or rejecting the latter's position in toto. The General Assembly's division of money matters between its Appropriations and Ways and Means Committees proved to be far more efficient.

The standing committees were slow in organizing and setting to work, in part evidencing the need for their members to establish operating procedures and their chairmen to arrange committee calendars. Contributing was the delay in drafting and duplicating measures for the membership of both houses and the administration's being unprepared to offer its legislative program at the opening of the congress. Working sessions of standing committees commenced about the fifth official day, the first public hearing waited until the beginning of the session's second week, and for the whole of the first two weeks relatively little committee work was undertaken. At the end of this period it was obvious that an intensive series of committee meetings would need be instituted if the work mounting in committee was to be disposed of before adjournment. Starting in August, the General Assembly commenced sitting at night, reserving the full day for committee sessions; the House, with its smaller size and lack of overlapping committee membership, could recess for its Ways and Means Committee to meet or to divide up into its three other standing committees.

Practically all bills and resolutions received committee scrutiny in at least one house. A few, upon introduction, were allocated initially to two committees. Following the same pattern, a petition by members of the district medical staffs alleging "serious grievance" was assigned to a House standing committee for investigation and report. The petition was finally disposed of by reference to an interim committee for further study.

Handicapping the committees was the paucity of staff to help them in their chores. The district political affairs officers, when not engaged in session work, aided as best they could, but sorely needed was continuous assistance in maintaining committee records, scheduling meetings and contacting prospective witnesses, keeping notes of decisions reached at committee session, writing reports, and in comparable other ways facilitating the committees' deliberations. Practically all responsibility fell upon the committee chairmen; in some committees the load was too heavy, and measures died due to inability to find time to consider them. The legislative counsel and the Attorney General's Office drafted committee reports on the more technical subjects and prepared committee amendments, but their services, too, were thinly spread, and committee chairmen frequently were dependent upon their own efforts. It ought also be added that a few chairmen entertained exaggerated ideas of their roles and the assistance to which they were entitled, out of all proportion to the resources of the Territory, and failed to apply themselves fully to their tasks, so that the quality of committee review and the caliber of committee reports suffered accordingly.

Normally the chairmen of committees orally announced the scheduled meeting of their committees prior to the adjournment of each day's general session. Hearings designed to encourage public presentation of viewpoints were announced over the Saipan district radio. Written notices might be distributed to all members of a chamber notifying of forthcoming committee sessions, be they public, regular, or sometimes even executive meetings. Conflict in the timing of Assembly committee meetings quickly materialized, and an attempt was made to divide each working day among the committees so as to eliminate overlapping. Rationality of the planning notwithstanding, the work load of the committees fitted no preconceived scheme, and in the absence of strong leadership to enforce it, the master scheduling soon was ignored.

Committee chairmen approached their tasks as mere amanuenses of their respective houses and by progress reports compiled a journal of their committees' actions. They soon discovered that each house was interested primarily in committee recommendation on the matters before it and not in accounts of how each committee was ordering its own affairs. The nature of reports tabled changed accordingly. A summary review of all reports reveals their marked unevenness: some are complete with statements of pertinent facts, the nature of the "urgency" if the bill happened to be so classified, the legislative purpose to be accomplished, and the committee recommendations; others consist of little more than a statement that the committee approves of the enactment of the proposed measure. The committees were normally lax in noting their reasons for favoring a measure, so that they failed to acquaint their parent body with an understanding of the issues inherent in adopting or rejecting the legislation before it. The reports are of even less aid in enabling an administrator or judge to ascertain the probable congressional intent. The House of Delegates was more inclined to abbreviate reports than was the Assembly. Committees usually returned a number of measures to their chamber in one report, with no necessary subject-matter relation between the measures so joined together. Frequently, committees suggested amendments for greater clarity and consistency, to correct grammatical inadequacies, and to include technical detail but very rarely added major substantive changes or made massive revisions in the drafts before them. These written committee reports were almost always accompanied with revised drafts incorporating the amendments recommended, so that until the later days of the session the members had a completely redrafted measure before them when voting to accept the committee's report. At first both did not identify their reports through a numbering system, but they later corrected this failure.

The committees were unsure of their powers and of their appropriate role. As committees they tended to regard themselves as arbiters, with their non-involved members serving in quasi-judicial capacity, and not as parties to the process of instituting change. They hesitated to apply their screening powers rigorously. Measures were returned to their sponsors with the request to submit improved versions at the next session of congress or to consult further with the administration. The committees badly needed background information and technical advice, but lacking experience to develop such knowledge or unwilling to call upon the administration, they were swayed by the advocacy of one or several members presumably informed upon the subject. At meetings to which the public was invited, the lack of procedural format for giving testimony led proponents of a measure to harangue the audience on the need for the desired legislation, so that legislative shaping of public opinion loomed large in the functions of such meetings even though not intended by the majority of the committee or its chairman.

The members appeared to share a sense of guilt if they failed to examine extensively all measures assigned to their committee, some on the premise that the adequacy of the committee was to be measured by the number of measures returned for floor consideration. Reporting a bill out demonstrated the committee's efficiency, but allowing a "bad" bill to slip through questioned the competency of the committee's entire membership. Unless consensus developed quickly within the committee, the typical reaction was to procrastinate, hesitating to choose either alternative. When it became necessary to act, the members fell to arguing among themselves, so that decisions tended to be unduly delayed. In part because of this, only one-third of the House measures received written reports of any kind from the committees to which they were assigned, and toward the end of the session, the House of Delegates discharged a number of measures from committee so that they might receive floor debate. Comparable action in the General Assembly was quashed by one member's objecting to another's motion to bring out a measure from committee by threatening to follow suit, and thus to throw everything onto the floor. The Assembly was more willing than the House to accept its committees' determinations to "ice box" measures.

Neither by training nor staffing were the committees of the first congress equipped to cope with the diverse questions confronting them. Many of the problems had baffled the administration for years; some required expenditures of larger sums than the congress had access to, which meant that at best congress could only request the administration to give the problems heed when shaping the next year's Federal budget. The legislators eliminated the patently impractical and suspiciously examined all measures affording limited local advantage. Referral to the administration or to an interim committee for study and report served the purpose of side-tracking without offending the sponsors. The committees thus in fact served as cathartic agents, both for the general public and the congress' own membership. On occasion they helped structure the Territory's limited opinion through committee hearings and reports which received radio and multi-district coverage in the districts' weekly bulletins. Little was proposed in committee; committees mainly sought to dispose, and their parent body felt no compunction in refusing to follow their recommendations. Just as the committees were mastering their new roles, so both chambers were adjusting to their relations with them.

ACTION ON THE FLOOR

As was to be expected, both the members and the staff of the new legislature had to learn to cope with the orderly legislative business as contemplated by the rules. Sometimes measures received erroneous numbers, so that duplications had to be corrected and measures redesignated. Several times members from one house signed measures intended for the other, making it necessary for the clerks or the backroom staff to correct the error before duplication. A few members took umbrage when their names were omitted or placed in incorrect order as sponsors, being fearful that the corrected version would not be reported on the radio and they would not receive credit back home. Finally, the clerks had to warn the members about the necessity of signing bills carefully so as to preclude further repetition of this type of objection.

Members adopted forms of debate which they had found successful in district legislatures or the Council of Micronesia, or possibly on the stump while electioneering. The response of their fellow members tested the transferability. During the session it was noticeable that some members adapted well to the requirements of the physical and human dimensions of the new environment, while others, sometimes to their own detriment, retained their previously learned styles of deportment.

This was not a legislature ignorant of parliamentary methods. However, experience in the Council of Micronesia or district legislature was not sufficient preparation for the complex procedures and measures now faced, and each day of the congress was literally a training session in the intricacies of a full-fledged legislature at work. Thus, each house had to develop systems for handling measures passed by the other and transferred to it for enactment. The house of origin had to learn how to take in stride the amendments attached by the second house and, if it did not concur, how to use the device of a conference committee to iron out the areas of disagreement. Unfamiliarity of the members with the courtesies associated with bicameralism resulted in the enactment of single-house resolutions applicable to both houses of the congress. It also manifested itself in failure to honor the priority of a measure already passed by the other house and now awaiting action along with its companion measure in the latter's house of origin.

The development of chamber solidarity was early disclosed by the members of the House of Delegates' voting unanimously for the seating of Delegate Cruz, even though his disqualification might have resulted in a different presiding officer's being chosen. Toward the latter part of the session, when Cruz, as publisher of the *Micronesian Times*, editorially attacked the competency of the congressional staff, both houses rose en masse to its defense in the form of privileged statements delivered on the floor.

The officers of both houses appreciated that some of the members would encounter trouble in the application of the rules and took pains to make sure all understood the procedures being followed. Thus, in the General Assembly, when for the first time an amendment was offered to an amendment on the floor, the speaker stopped the proceedings, asked "Does everyone understand what we are doing?" and then allowed a few minutes for the members to recall that the series of motions would have to be voted on in reverse order until the original measure was before them. Gradually, the members became adept in applying the house rules and just as skilled in suspending them. They early grasped the necessity for specifying the rule to be waived and found that it was normally easy to obtain concurrence, just so long as the measure concerned was not highly controversial. Due to the lag in duplication, the requirement that a measure be reprinted after amendment on the floor and prior to final passage was often laid aside. Usually, neither the procedure in the House of Delegates nor that observed in the General Assembly was overly technical, and rarely was objection raised on some minor point of the rules. Towards the end of the session, various rules were suspended to speed the process of final enactment, and sometimes action was taken without such waiver or any complaint about the violation. At the conclusion of the general session, measures were being passed through two readings in one house on the same day, on the questionable informal ruling of the attorney general that Secretarial Order No. 2882 only mandated a two days' lapse in the passage of a bill through *both* houses.

Members of both houses became proficient in referring measures to committee to gain time or hoping to dispose of them. The journals also record that some measures were killed on their first reading, voted down on their second reading, or despatched more delicately but just as effectively by being tabled indefinitely. Even sending a measure back to its house of origin as a means to defeat it is recorded in the Journal.[8] The versatility of some of the members in maneuvering within the rules of their chamber, and the gullibility of their colleagues, is well illustrated by the by-play on Delegate Resolution No. 31 which originally favored a 50 per cent increase in the Micronesian pay plan. As this large an increment would have cost over $1,650,000, or close to 10 per cent of the total Federal budget for the Trust Territory, the resolution was recommitted to committee in an effort to defeat it. Notwithstanding, it later was withdrawn from committee and again placed upon the calendar, whereupon the same delegate who had moved to re-refer it then sponsored an amendment materially jumping the benefits. The authors of the resolution supported the revision as being in line with their purpose, only then to find that the resolution as amended was soundly defeated on the floor. Later, the opponents relented, reconsidered the vote, reduced the rate of increase to a figure considered to be more within reason, and then allowed the resolution to pass. The whole operation was consummated with great finesse and revealed the ease with which some members were able to outflank their colleagues.

The manner in which a committee report should be handled upon being submitted to its respective house caused difficulty both in the General Assembly and in the House of Delegates. Finally it was determined that the committee report could be accepted without thereby signifying approval of its contents. Also, reports could be amended on the floor of the chamber so as to incorporate the language approved by the membership, even though the amendment did not necessarily express the views of the committee. It was not unusual in the House of Delegates for a committee to offer its report and the House then to reject its recommendations. The receipt of a report only placed a measure before the body, and as each delegate appeared to consider that he, and not the House committees, should chart the course of action, far more discussion and

[8] D.B. 11, Journal of the General Assembly, First Session, Congress of Micronesia, Aug. 10, 1965.

modification of measures occurred in the House than in the Assembly.

The amendments presented in both houses indicate that the members were troubled by language problems and, in the desire to be overly careful in the expression of their ideas in English, would quibble over the appropriate wordage, even when there was no legally significant difference. The rules directed review of all measures by the legislative counsel before final passage, and this would have obviated all inadequacies caused by members' unfamiliarity with the nuances of the English language. Earlier in the session this review was enforced, but the rule was gradually abandoned as work piled up on his desk, and toward the last of the session it became a dead letter.

The rules of both houses prohibited members' voting when there was a conflict of interest. During the contest over the seating of Delegate-elect Cruz, he was excused as an interested party. The vote on Delegate Resolution No. 20 caused some members to claim conflict of interest as the grounds for abstaining, but so large was their number that the president directed the secretary to call upon all members to record their votes.[9] Assembly Bill No. 3, when before the General Assembly, was amended so as to allow the congressmen, in addition to the district legislators already specified in the bill, to be consulted on the district budgets before they are sent to the high commissioner. An amendment to delete congressional participation was offered by a delegate from Palau who also served as speaker for that district's legislature. His position was supported by another assemblyman who was the speaker of the Truk district legislature, and by others. A solon who was not a member of any district legislature pointed out the possible conflict of interest and recommended that all assemblymen who were also members of district legislatures should refrain from voting on the amendment. His objection was held ill-founded upon the premise that those congressmen who happened to be members of the district legislatures had no personal interest or benefit to be gained from the motion before the General Assembly and therefore were not within the prohibition of the conflict rule.

Throughout the whole session of the congress, there was a noticeable tendency for the members to suggest what ought to be

---

[9] Journal of the House of Delegates, *op. cit.*, Aug. 4, 1965. D.R. 20 called for the suspension of the charter for the Micronesian Hotel Corporation.

done by way of procedure without taking the appropriate steps to put their proposals into motion. The fact that neither house formally selected a member as majority floor leader encouraged such inconclusive volunteering to continue. The legislative secretary of the General Assembly performed many of the duties of a floorman in keeping the action of the Assembly moving but without policy responsibility for the body's adoption of any set program. The chairman of each committee bore the burden of presenting his committee's reports, and either he or the lead-off sponsor of the measure reported upon would likewise carry the brunt of working toward achieving a measure's final passage. In this situation, the role of the legislative secretary was limited to eliminating parliamentary snags, aiding the presiding officer in assuring that the rules were followed (as by noting that a motion died for want of a second or that the request for a roll call had to be supported by three members), and raising questions when amendments from the floor were ambiguous or did not appear to be responsive to the matter at issue. Because of the inclusion of the legislative secretary within the structure of the General Assembly, and in part because of the distinctive nature of the two houses' membership, the floor leadership was more efficient in the Assembly than in the House, where several members attempted unofficially to assist the House president.

It was to be expected that in a first session some defensible measures would be "lost" and never pass second reading. Also, in the excitement of the fast-paced floor action, the incongruity of directing the clerks to redesignate one measure as another (as a Delegate Resolution's becoming a Delegate Joint Resolution) was apt to be ignored. Finally, with the seemingly inevitable pressure that builds up in every legislature before adjournment, it could be anticipated that the presiding officers of both houses would come to wink at minor violations of the rules in order to complete as much of the unfinished work as possible before the end of the thirty-day session. But despite all of the flaws to be found in the records, and the members' inadequacies which they mirrored, the total impression is one of invaluable experience gained for the conducting of future sessions of the congress. Despite the occasional awkwardness of floor action, the haggling over minescule points, and the reluctance of the House of Delegates to surrender discretion to a body smaller than its total membership, the members in both House and Assembly mastered their house rules and learned effectively to support or oppose the legislation in which they were interested, a good measure of success.[10]

Throughout the session there was a slight note of play acting. In other legislatures, this arises out of the members' being so involved in the machinations of the legislative body that the game for the game's sake becomes more important than the substantive issue around which the play takes place. In the Congress of Micronesia the element of unreality mainly stemmed from the members' still being unaccustomed to their newly granted powers and to their chambers' procedures. Some adopted distinctive roles appropriate to the ploys of gamesmanship which set them apart from their colleagues. When the congress came to a close, in the last minutes of the one-day special session extension, the president of the House of Delegates specifically singled out several members to whom he wished to extend his appreciation. With tongue in cheek, he commended one for his constant abstaining when a measure was put before the House to a vote, another for his consistent putting of points of information at the very time the vote was being taken, a third for his ability to utilize the House rules and his determination to uphold them when they were not being religiously followed, and a fourth for his outstanding performance on the floor in making the House laugh when debate grew heated. The Congress of Micronesia in its floor action thus takes its place alongside American legislative bodies where the same idiosyncratic practices may also be observed.

LEADERSHIP STYLES

Many of the members elected to the Congress of Micronesia were or had previously been officers of district legislatures. Relatively few of them sought to obtain comparable position in the Congress of Micronesia, nor did they push themselves to the forefront during the flow of debate upon the legislative floor. To the extent their leadership was expressed, it probably was most potent in influencing the decisions of their own delegation. Members from the same administrative district in the Assembly were inclined toward voting en bloc. This was less evident in the House of Delegates,

[10] This contrasts with the experience of the indigenous members of Papua–New Guinea's House of Assembly, a legislative body established for the other remaining Trusteeship one year earlier than the Congress of Micronesia. See Norman Meller, *Papers on the Papua–New Guinea House of Assembly*, New Guinea Research Bulletin No. 22 (Canberra: Australia National University, 1968).

where the two members from Palau would openly disagree in debate over the merits of legislation as, less often, would members in some of the other delegations.

The delegates to the Council of Micronesia had learned the efficacy of "talk under the coconut trees," and this practice of discussion outside of the legislative halls was carried over to the congress. All during the two weeks of the pre-session workshop, informal cross-district meetings and delegation caucuses occurred. Conferences of the Mariana Islands delegation preceded the workshop and continued throughout the month-long congressional session. Some members of a delegation might not take part in its caucus, as when party cleavages or personal cliques excluded a member. The Mariana Islands delegation imposed upon itself a "gag" rule which required both its assemblymen and delegates to work in their respective bodies for the measures approved by caucus majority. The Palau delegation, though meeting frequently in informal sessions, found variances in the views of its members so strong that it could seldom agree upon a united stand. In that delegation, the wounds opened by the election campaign had yet to heal, in contrast to the Marianas delegation, where all but one member bore the endorsement of the same political party.

In the Truk delegation, the policies followed were shaped by an exchange of views in which many of the younger members played prominent roles. Chief Petrus served as spokesman of the consensus. In the meetings of the Marshall Islands congressmen, Amata Kabua is reported to have played a key role in setting the course followed by many of its members. The Yap solons seemed reluctant to commit themselves individually on major issues until after the delegation had a chance to meet; Delegate Francis Nuuan probably was its dominant figure. Finally, it becomes more tenuous to identify Ponape's most influential member. Delegate Olter and Assemblyman Henry worked closely together and in the main divided the leadership of the Ponape group between them. Because of Chief Petrus' role as nominal leader of the Truk delegation in the Assembly, the members from Palau and Yap paid close attention to his comments. Truk's five-man bloc in the Assembly constituted almost half of the majority vote necessary for that body to take final action, and small delegations like Yap or Palau could maneuver with assurance only with foreknowledge of the way in which the Truk members proposed to move.

The discussions outside of the chambers lessened the need for clarifying explanation upon the floor when a measure was called for consideration upon its merits. The fact that the House of Delegates had greater floor debate in part revealed an inability to reach agreements in these extracurricular meetings. However, much of the final disposition of measures before the House was arranged outside of that body by its elected officers' meeting with a few other key delegates, so that a measure's chances of success or failure were fairly well known before it came to a final vote. The Marianas House delegation never fully appreciated this, and its members would argue at length on the floor, only to have the House vote down its measures.

Many of the members in the House of Delegates were personally acquainted with each other through education at the Pacific Islands Central School or in Hawaii, and a number had served together in the Council of Micronesia.[11] This affected their behavior toward each other in the House and facilitated their overcoming district cleavages. The two delegates from the Marianas were not members of the "club," and this could be sensed in the conduct of the House. To a lesser degree the same inner clique existed in the General Assembly, and personal friendship, common intellectual interest, and mutual prior participation in Territorial activity brought members together across district delegation boundaries. However, leadership shifted with the subject matter, and the same individuals might not occupy similarly dominant positions irrespective of the measures debated. The officers of the General Assembly supplied a degree of direction in keeping the Assembly administration functioning, the rules observed, and the calendar of work cleared. There was little in the way of binding commitment reached outside of the legislative halls to limit the free-wheeling nature of the debate in which most members engaged within the chamber.

The cultures of Micronesia do not adapt readily to authoritative forms of leadership, and it was not to be expected that these would be encountered in the congress. Rather, leadership as exercised by the officers of the two houses was subdued in style and indirect in nature. Generally, the direction they gave was pointed more toward furthering the work of the chambers than to favoring or opposing the policy inherent in the matters before their bodies. The

[11] Delegate Nuuan from Yap reported, "Almost every member of Congress knew and had worked with as many as half of the total Congress members. In the House of Delegates I knew and had either worked with or went to school with ten of the members." *The Rai Review,* Aug. 18, 1965, p. 8.

House, consisting as it did of members who distrusted power exerted by others and who regarded each delegate as equal, had as its president a person of gentle mannerisms who fitted the role expected of him. Tosiwo Nakayama was willing to serve as one of a peer group and issued few commands channeling the course of the House's deliberation. When, about half-way through the session, the need to expedite the business of the congress was voiced, his reaction was typically to announce he would meet with the committee chairmen to see whether some way to speed the work of the House could be achieved. But all this cloaked both competency and resiliency, and when it appeared that points of order were being made to break the train of a speaker's argument and to disturb him in his delivery on the floor, he firmly gave short shrift to such dilatory tactics.

In comparison with the House, Dwight Heine as the speaker of the General Assembly played a more dominant part, although his actions were as unobtrusive as those of the president of the House of Delegates. He diplomatically refrained from forcing his decisions on the Assembly and hesitated to rule in ways that would give offense. He would almost invite floor discussion before putting a matter to a vote, and the awkward silences separating the comments of members on the floor encouraged others to rise and fill the gap. At the beginning of the session, after suggesting the manner in which the Assembly might meet, he recessed the body to enable the members "to think it over." He was not panicked by objections from the floor, but, rather than abruptly truncating them, took advantage of distracting elements to achieve his ends. Thus, when an assemblyman protested the referral of a measure to one committee and proposed that it be sent to another, the comment by a second member that the measure was of a nature that would permit its being sent to either was allowed by the speaker to pass as an adequate reply, and he proceeded to ask for "any other announcement."

The speaker's greatest strength probably lay in his ability to work behind the scenes in reconciling disagreements. Two members who were not speaking to each other found themselves together to their mutual surprise drinking soda pop during a recess; the speaker had asked each to join him without knowledge of the other. Committee chairmen were requested to agree upon committee schedules so they would not conflict, and if necessary the speaker met with the chairmen to accomplish that purpose. When measures on second reading ran into objections which could be resolved by informal discussion, he would call a recess so that the parties could get together. A member slowing Assembly action by taking an inordinate amount of time upon the floor in seemingly needless detail was admonished indirectly through the speaker's requesting the leading man in that member's constituency to bring pressure to bear upon the assemblyman to curtail his "enthusiasm."

Probably the best example of the speaker's style of leadership was his handling of the joint resolution designed to stampede the congress into accepting one of the candidates for legislative counsel. "Somehow," after the joint resolution nominating that candidate was introduced, it never was sent to printing. By the time this was finally discovered and another copy had been duplicated (A.J.R. 15), the speaker had carefully planted the seed for assigning the matter to a special committee. When it was suggested from the floor that the choice of a legislative counsel be made the responsibility of a select committee, the speaker immediately treated this as a motion and asked for a show of hands for its adoption. At this time, at least one member on each delegation favored the particular candidate. The speaker side-tracked a supplemental proposal for the delegations to name members to the special committee, on the ground that the motion had already been agreed to, and then appointed six uncommitted individuals. Upon the report of the special commitee, another candidate was selected for the post of legislative counsel.

Vice-Speaker Petrus of the General Assembly assumed the chair toward the last days of the session and demonstrated the contrast in the degree to which a show of direction may be exercised by the presiding officer. The illness of the speaker was feigned, unbeknown to the membership, and had been arranged between the speaker and the vice-speaker to expedite the flow of work on the Assembly floor. Chief Petrus had led the Truk legislature as its first speaker, and his knowledge of parliamentary procedure dated back to the chartering of Moen municipality when, as magistrate, he received private briefing sessions prior to the administration's granting of the charter.[12] His mannerisms while presiding were businesslike, and members were reluctant to stand up and request

[12] Chief Petrus is "aggressively intelligent in a culture wherein it is a virtue to be dull and stupid—although protesting the while his own stupidity." From Thomas Gladwin, "Petrus Mailo, Chief of Moen," in Joseph B. Casagrande, ed., *In the Company of Man* (New York: Harper & Bros., 1960), p. 56. See also pp. 121–122, *supra*.

the floor for prolonged debate. In no way did he stop any member from discussing the merits of a measure, but he led the members to understand, as one later expressed it, that "no funny business" would be tolerated.

Chief Petrus does not speak English, but this was no great obstacle as prior to the sitting he had been briefed on the backlog outstanding by the legislative secretary, the legislative clerk, and his interpreter. The smooth working relationship with the legislative secretary and the clerk of the Assembly which had been established by the speaker for handling floor action assisted the vice-speaker. On the few times he required prompting on parliamentary rulings, these were supplied by the legislative secretary, sometimes by signal rather than by the latter taking the floor to make a statement. The vice-speaker might also ask the clerk to check on a matter in question, which would give the legislative secretary time to advise the chair. If a measure seemed to be engendering unnecessary floor discussion, Chief Petrus would call a recess and walk among the members, remarking that they ought to wind up the debate; in this way he projected himself into the course of legislative floor action more directly than was the wont of the speaker. Because comments in English from the floor had to be translated, the vice-speaker's remarks were sometimes not exactly apropos to the course of debate, but when it came to matters of parliamentary procedure, his rulings were proper.

One onlooker, recalling this situation commented, "I sort of wondered why the members acted passively when the chief was presiding." One of the contributing reasons was respect for Chief Petrus' age, his sagacity, and his acknowledged status. Another was apprehension that assemblymen by their actions might embarrass him before the American and Guamanian visitors present. It was almost as if a tacit understanding had been reached that no complicated parliamentary maneuvers would be undertaken while the chief was presiding.

With the work of the General Assembly speeded and a number of measures disposed of, the speaker recovered from his indisposition and returned to the chamber. His more diplomatic and soft-spoken style on the podium differed from that of the more brusque vice-speaker, just as it did from that of the more permissive president of the House of Delegates. In a non-Micronesian assemblage, any of the three styles of leadership might have led to chaos; given the roles of the respective presiding officers, their actions were highly appropriate for a Micronesian legislature for which indirection and inoffensiveness are the hallmarks of competence.

THE CONTRIBUTION OF THE ADMINISTRATION

The convening of the first Congress of Micronesia offered the administration an unequaled opportunity to aid the congress in coming to grips with the many policy problems facing it. The relationship would have to be treated delicately, for many members regarded the powers granted to the congress as niggardly, due to the congress' limited control over finances and the restriction to a thirty-day, annual session. Congressmen would be suspicious of anything that could be interpreted as an effort to control their decisions. But the first congress was woefully deficient in policy leadership, and the assistance of the administration, diplomatically tendered, could have gone far to help fill the vacuum. The sincerest of intentions on the part of the congressmen could not compensate for their lack of expertise in the range of subjects with which they had to grapple nor substitute for the skill of the trained legislator in handling matters beyond his immediate ken of understanding. Unfortunately, these very inadequacies helped to widen the gulf between legislator and administrator, rather than bring the two closer together.

The administration had long adopted a defensive stance in its presentations before the United Nations and the United States Congress. The best picture possible was always painted of Trust Territory conditions and deficiencies were only grudgingly conceded. Now power was being turned over to the Micronesians, and the administration was committed to transferring even more. In the offing was a general challenge to the administration's stewardship and a more immediate threat to every insecure American on the high commissioner's staff. Each time a Micronesian congressman posed a question or scored a point, it exacerbated the defensiveness. The Congress of Micronesia was occasion for the administration's first real exposure to searching legislative oversight by indigenes, far more intensive and extensive than that at the hands of the Council of Micronesia. Just as the Micronesian legislator looked suspiciously upon the administration's dealings with the congress, so did the high commissioner's staff cautiously examine all inquiries pertinent to congressional affairs. This was the normal irritation between the governed and the governors, but compounded by the friction endemic to American executive-legislative relations.

The Secretarial Order reserved to the high commissioner the right to submit legislation and, if labeled "urgent," empowered him to put it into effect unilaterally should the congress not concur. The prospective termination of import and export taxes decreed by the Secretarial Order, and the obvious need for delineating the jurisdiction and responsibilities of the three levels of government in the Trust Territory, assured the high commissioner's recommending a series of major legislative measures to the first congress. As early as the opening of the pre-congress workshop, congress voiced its request for advance information on Territorial income and expenditure, the moneys available for running the first congress, and the prospective Territorial budget. Had the administration announced its legislative program in advance of the convening of the congress, or even revealed it on the opening day, the congress could have had major matters before it from the start, and this would have gone far toward filling the vacuum the first congress faced and have set the committees briskly off on their assignments. Instead, the "State of the Territory" address delivered at the joint session marking the beginning of the congress contained only the most general references to the administration's plans. Almost a third of the session elapsed before the high commissioner at joint session delivered the budget for review and the essential tax legislation to support his financial proposals. Measures were still being introduced at the request of the administration when the three-quarter point of the session had been reached.

As member-initiated legislative measures poured in, many of them impliedly if not openly critical of the administration, the defensive sensitivity of the staff at Headquarters heightened. They tried to ascertain what action was being taken on these and other measures before the committees, only to find that the congress had little information on committee plans for calling up the measures assigned to them. The ambiguity of the first legislative counsel's position became apparent as the staff officers at Headquarters looked to him to keep them advised of committee meetings and hearings on measures affecting their agencies. Of course it was an impossible chore, and to those persons who wished to believe the worst of the congress, the absence of advance scheduling only proved the body's ineptitude, if not scheming obfuscation.

The committees, on their part, early indicated selectivity in their hearings, requesting the presence of some administration personnel and pointedly omitting to ask others. The Assembly Appropriations Committee, in reviewing the Territorial budget. announced a week-long schedule of "conferences" with named department heads, adding that "all such conferences will be by invitation" and that upon completion of the conferences, invitations for summary statements would be issued to the assistant commissioners to whom these department heads reported. To the administration, here was proof that the committees were seizing the opportunity to settle grudges and show up the failings of American personnel. When some administrative departments communicated to the congressional leadership through the legislative counsel that it was the high commissioner who would name the persons to represent the various departments, the leadership made it clear that the decision rested with the congress. The tempest blew over, but the gulf between the congress and the executive departments remained, resembling more the civic textbook's account of classical separation of powers than the close working relationship which develops between an executive and legislature knowledgeable that the work of government can be furthered only by the effective cooperation of the two branches of government.

The members of the congress had to learn the dimensions of their legislative roles, including those which dealt with the executive branch. The speaker, at the beginning of the second week of the congress, gently admonished the assemblymen that they should tender the high commissioner the courtesy of giving him notice before calling on him, just as the Assembly was extended the same treatment by the high commissioner. The executive branch may have been just as inexperienced in working with a legislature, but at least it was so organized as to have permitted it to take the initiative in bringing the two major branches of government closer together. Instead, as the session approached, the administration found itself unprepared, without final agreement on budget or legislative program. Unable to ease the anticipated problems of the new congress by such cooperative action as advance notice of the high commissioner's legislative program, the executive branch held the congress at arm's length while the proposed legislation was being finalized. The aloofness of the administration allowed it to declare to the world that it exerted no undue influence on the deliberations of the congress. What is omitted in such a statement is that thereby the actions of the congress were hindered and the necessary adaptation of the members to their new roles slowed.

END-OF-THE-SESSION LOG JAM

The last minute rush attendant upon adjournment is a common phenomenon in many legislative bodies. Sheer volume of work, outside pressures impinging upon the legislature, one house jockeying for advantage against the other so as to tie the fate of a measure in its possession with that of a measure reposing in the custody of the other house, and comparable trading within a single chamber all contribute to the building of a log jam as the end of the session draws near. Finding the "key log" to break the impasse, and hurriedly opening the channels of action before the mounting desire of the fatigued members to have done with it all and return to their homes stampedes them to adjournment, constitute a major task of the legislative leadership. The same last minute rush accompanied the concluding days of the first session of the Congress of Micronesia but, except for the delay in the budget measures, primarily for different reasons. There was little outside of the congress in the way of demand for passage or defeat of measures, and there were few "tying" maneuvers within or between the chambers. Most of the administration-sponsored bills would have been enacted if the congress could have called them up for passage. The explanation for the rush lay more in inexperience and human deficiencies than in political machinations. The staff was unable to duplicate materials with enough despatch, the committees were slow to complete the scrutiny and refinement of the measures referred to them, and the formal leadership was unprepared to assign priorities and concentrate upon those issues which it believed most warranted the congress' attention. As the time for adjournment approached, the volume of business on the floor of each house mounted while the members attempted to bring even more measures out from committee. Not only did there remain insufficient time to dispose of it all, but not until long after adjournment was it possible to determine with precision exactly what had transpired during the last hectic hours preceding the congress' close.

One-third of the session passed before the first Assembly bill (A.B. 3) cleared the Assembly, and over half the session before any measure originating in the House of Delegates reached the Assembly. Some of the assemblymen quickly appreciated that at its first session the congress would be hard put to dispose of even a small work load and, as early as the twelfth day of the general session, advocated the adoption of a cut-off date for the introduction of new measures. Nothing came of this effort. The House established the unrealistic terminal date of August 5 for all but urgent matters, and even this was sometimes ignored.

As ever more measures were sponsored and the committees gradually filtered them out, the need for pre-planning the flow of legislative business became apparent with the end of the session drawing near. The last few days found on the floor of each house a large number of complex measures demanding careful study, and the members were unwilling to rely upon their committees' recommendations and hesitant to commit themselves without possessing the knowledge adequate for personal decision-making. Neither the leadership nor any informal groupings were so organized as to be able to pull all the threads of policy together to prevent the threatening debacle. With the last day upon them, chairmen of committees and sponsors of individual measures vied for the floor to push measures to a vote. Spokesmen for the administration lobbied to save administration-sponsored bills from defeat. In the resulting confusion, the limited time available to the congress was dissipated in a number of unproductive ways, such as bills' being put to a first reading in their house of origin. The secretary of the House and the clerk of the Assembly attempted to keep account of the action on the floor, but most members lost track of what had been passed and what was still pending.

It was only after adjournment that the staff could trace down all of the measures and separate out the adopted floor amendments from those which had been defeated. The pressure of that last day is revealed in the legislative history which reported the fate of each measure. The Congress of Micronesia is recorded as having passed on the final day of the general session a majority of all the bills and a third of all joint resolutions enacted during the entire first general session.

THE SPECIAL SESSION AND THE BUDGET

In view of the congress' inability to agree on the Territorial budget and failure to make provision for its own expenses, the high commissioner had little alternative but to allow the congress to remain in session; this he did through his power to summon the congress into special session. The high commissioner's call was for but one extra day, and the congress resumed where it had left off the previous day in the consideration of the money measures before it. When the conference committee reached a compromise, the houses quickly adjourned after concurring in the passage of two appropriation measures and a joint resolution, the latter extending the life of the election regulations promulgated by the high commissioner for the first congressional elections. From this special session was derived a precedent which may see the congress treated as a continuing body, at least for the period between biennial elections, for in fact the special session consisted of nothing more than a prolongation of the first general session. The length of one day for a special session did not allow for the minimum two-day reading of bills mandated for the passage of laws by Secretarial Order No. 2882, so the measures enacted were those which had already received a first reading at the general session. The actions of the congress, of the high commissioner in signing the bills, and of the administration's staff in countenancing the expenditures authorized by the legislation, all demonstrate that no measures died on midnight of the thirtieth day of the general session. This prolonged life cannot be justified unless the congress is accorded the status of a continuing body.

Another precedent also emerged out of this special session, for the Congress of Micronesia refused to appropriate the Territorial funds to be realized from the taxes it had just enacted and in effect also repudiated the high commissioner's budget proposals. In accordance with Secretarial Order No. 2882, the high commissioner had, before sending it to the Department of the Interior, submitted to the Congress of Micronesia his preliminary Federal budget for fiscal year 1967, drawn within the $17,500,000 ceiling set by the United States Congress. Also presented to the Micronesian legislators were budget plans for the appropriation by them of the revenues to be raised from Territorial taxes, estimated at $480,000 for fiscal year 1967 but a much smaller sum for the then current fiscal year 1966. The high commissioner also stated at the joint session on July 20 that he would request the Federal Congress to increase the Trust Territory's appropriation ceiling, so as to step up the pace of Territorial capital improvements and expand governmental services. The members had no objection to such augmentation of Federal appropriations, but they were not inclined to concur with the high commissioner on the manner in which local revenues ought be expended, nor could the two houses agree on the modifications to be recommended for the Federal budget for fiscal year 1967.

From the days of the pre-session workshop, the members-elect had disputed the high commissioner's interpretation that Secretarial Order No. 2882 did not transfer to the congress control over the approximately $1,000,000 received annually from air transportation fares and other Territorial service fees which he was placing in a revolving fund managed by the administration. When he presented the Federal budget for fiscal 1967 to the congress in the form of summary departmental requests, without justifications or monetary breakdowns, the members, bent on carefully scrutinizing the budgetary details, were further antagonized. After consultations with the Territorial Director of Budget and Finance and other members of the administration, the Assembly Appropriations Committee did amass enough "back up materials" to make a report on the fiscal year 1967 budget, adding that $410,000 more ought to be expended to supplement the funds to be appropriated in the Federal budget. Before making these recommendations, the committee had solicited the suggestions of all assemblymen and incorporated many of them in its report. The House Ways and Means Committee also turned to studying the fiscal 1967 budget but, unlike the Assembly, did not prepare specific probes, and its analysis ran to more general principles of administrative philosophy and stressed the inadequacy of the budget estimates in meeting Territorial requirements. The two houses were never able to narrow the gap between their separate approaches, and the resulting impasse over the budgeting of Federal and Territorial funds necessitated the special session.

For almost four hours during the one-day extra session the ten-member conference committee debated the high commissioner's budgets, devoting most of its time to his estimates for Federal expenditures. Personality conflicts exacerbated the differences of the positions taken by the two houses. Allocation of funds for local capital improvements among the six administrative districts was proposed as a means of ending the stalemate, but this "pork barrel" solution failed to break the deadlock. When the conference was completely bogged down, a legal opinion was obtained that the congress could refuse to appropriate any local revenues beyond those necessary to meet its own costs. This furnished a viable compromise between the poles of "all or nothing," and the conference committee agreed upon a $96,562 supplement for the current year's legislative budget (FY 1966) and a fiscal year 1967 appropriation of $145,000 to run the congress. No report was ever made by the conference committee on the high commissioner's estimates for the Federal fiscal 1967 budget, so although the conference committee was satisfied with the House Ways and Means Committee's general statement of principles, it never was adopted as the formal recommendation of the congress to the high commissioner and the Secretary of the Interior.

The rationale offered by the conference committee for only appropriating its own expenses was that the congress should wait until the productivity of the new tax bills was established before prospectively allocating any other local revenues. It was also obvious that this tactic would enable the Congress of Micronesia to supplement funds made available by the Federal government, rather than having the Federal appropriations premised partially upon the already determined apportionment of local revenues. To a congress already annoyed by the high commissioner's delay in communicating his budget estimates and further irritated by the manner of their presentation when they were submitted,[13] this prospect of turning the tables on the administration was readily accepted. No real harm would be done, for at the next regular session in 1966 the revenues already collected as well as those anticipated for fiscal year 1967 could always be appropriated. Here was a vista of power, and in a quarter where the members thought of themselves as weakest. In rejecting the administration's budget proposals, the congress had flaunted its independence, and also flirted delightedly with irresponsibility, knowing that it was leaving financial matters in a state of confusion just to see how the administration would respond. In doing so, the congress paradoxically had come of age as a co-equal branch of the Territorial government.

[13] Still remaining is ". . . the difficult problem of devising some procedure by which the Congress of Micronesia can participate more directly and more influentially in formation of the annual budgets and allocation of funds made available by the Congress of the United States." Closing Statement of HiCom to United Nations Trusteeship Council, June 15, 1967, Trust Territory Press Release, 129:67 [undated], p. 5.

CHAPTER 14

The Congressional Effort
and Its Impact

ANY METROPOLITAN POWER today must regard with a degree of trepidation that period in the planned development of its colonies when political power is being transferred from the hands of its own personnel to those of the administered. The past was within its control, the future is a promise of maturing expectations, but the present is fraught only with uncertainty. The popular selection of local officials may elevate the demogogue, the unqualified, the irresponsible. Full authority is not yet the colony's, so the mother country remains responsible for the course of normal government and is blamed for not complying with every voiced demand. So, too, might the first elections to the Congress of Micronesia have brought to the fore totally incompetent indigenous leaders or those bent upon obtaining the impossible, and with the session concluded, the United States might have found itself confronted with chaos in the Territorial government and discredited before the world. The high commissioner and his staff must have felt immeasurably relieved when the Congress of Micronesia adjourned on August 11, 1965, and they had their first chance to view the totality of the congressional product.

LEGISLATIVE INPUT

In all, 204 bills, joint resolutions, and single house resolutions were sponsored at the first congress. Almost two-thirds of these measures were resolutions—70 joint and 57 single house resolutions. A number of reasons contributed to the employment of the resolution form, in addition to its use as an expression of the congress' appreciation, commendation, and felicitation. The members understood that they had no ability to allocate Federal funds, and Territorial moneys which could finance administrative action had yet to be collected and, in any event, would be limited in amount. Recognizing that they did not grasp all the ramifications surrounding most programmatic changes they sought and lacking effective fiscal powers, many of the members deliberately introduced resolutions rather than bills. They were political realists and sensed that, even though a resolution might not have the force of law, the administration would give heed to these expressions of legislative views and aspirations. A resolution could not be vetoed and would appear permanently upon the record as an accomplishment of the first congress. Besides, members were familiar with resolutions from service in the predecessor Council of Micronesia and also in district legislatures, and some were not yet too sure about the distinction between the different legal forms.[1] For all of these reasons, an analysis of the first congress' input must treat resolutions right along with bills.

The congressmen were far more inclined to obtain advantages for their constituents than to place burdens upon them. Four times as many measures proposed benefits or services from government for residents of the Trust Territory as imposed greater obligations on them. Tax legislation figured prominently among the latter. This ratio is reduced to three to one if those measures with which the government must also comply are included, such as displaying the Trust Territory flag in an approved manner. Half of this legislation classed as more "onerous" owes its origin to the request of the administration!

As was to be expected, the expanded governmental services and benefits desired ranged widely, from setting up a procedure for claims against the Trust Territory to granting more scholarships. Some measures, such as the bill proclaiming Micronesia Day which impliedly promised a holiday for governmental employees or overtime pay for working, furnished indirect advantages. Nineteen measures requested public works expenditures, some specific, others for classes of projects. Thirteen would have lent greater support to Micronesian endeavor, as by Micronesian preferences in governmental bidding or easier access to Guam. An almost equal number of measures sought reclassification, raises in classification, or generally higher compensation for governmental employees.

Practically all members approached their new roles imbued with the purpose of legislating for the Territory as a whole. As a consequence, there was relatively little effort to single out an administrative district or a local area for congressional attention. In all, only ten measures carry reference to named districts or part of a district in a way pertinent to future action of government, and of

[1] See p. 94 ff.

these, two were administration measures applying to Kwajalein. Five of the ten refer to the Marianas, with four calling for capital improvements. More fitting to the climate of the congress was the equal treatment accorded all districts by eleven measures, such as those calling for representation of each district on congressional committees or Territorial boards and establishing a named office or a service in all districts. Consonant with this were the several measures setting Territorial standards or authorization but allowing local option for their application. The bill empowering each district to opt for a jury system nicely balanced congressional interest in Territory-wide matters with allowance for local variances.

A number of measures were oriented toward the congress, the administration of its affairs, expansion of its powers, and enhancement of its status. The largest component of this group was concerned with the running of the congress, its annual appropriations, the election of its members, the acquiring of a meeting site, and the selection of its legislative counsel. Eight measures proposed the creation of interim committees or called special sessions to conduct studies or undertake designated work. If the two resolutions requesting the high commissioner to negotiate with the East-West Center of the University of Hawaii to facilitate training of congressmen in Hawaii are added, the total is increased to ten. Almost equal in number (11) were the measures which would enlarge the scope of the congress, be it through amendments to the Organic Act so as to permit semi-annual sessions, requirement of congressional confirmation of appointments to top Trust Territory posts, attendance of congressmen at the meetings of the Trusteeship Council of the United Nations and budget hearings of the United States Congress, or mere consultation of the high commissioner with the Territorial congress before foreign business might be undertaken in the Trust Territory. The remaining portion of this group directly or indirectly contributed to the status of the congress through commemorating the date of its convening by a national holiday, changing the names of the houses so as to coincide with those of the Federal Congress, or issuing special identification for congressmen.

Examples of measures revealing development of a greater Trust Territory identity, if not nascent nationalism, abound: adopting a Territorial flag to be called "the national emblem of Micronesia"; [2]

[2] Assembly Committee Report No. 1, July 20, 1965.

making July 12, Micronesia Day, a "national" holiday; proposing that two Micronesians be chosen by the congress to "represent the Congress at the annual meeting of the Trusteeship Council"; requesting diplomatic passports for congressmen; seeking a Junior College of Micronesia as a single educational center for the Territory to compensate for that lost when the Pacific Islands Central School was replaced by separate district high schools; founding a Territory-wide agricultural exhibit; directing vessels bringing cargo for the Trust Territory to bypass Guam; and requiring all Trust Territory vessels to fly the Territorial flag. The enactment of an Organic Act, as advocated by a delegate resolution, also would have afforded an acknowledged status to the Territory.

Allied to these measures were a plethora of resolutions giving Micronesians preference in bidding for or handling Trust Territory business (5), restricting the entry of non-Micronesian businesses or employees (6), and otherwise favoring the activities of Territorial citizens. Several resolutions requested cancellation of the charter granted to a non-Micronesian-owned company. Bills which would have required congressional confirmation for Trust Territory department heads and district legislative advice on local appointments may have had as their hidden purpose the securing of governmental posts for Micronesians, an objective more openly revealed in another measure. Of course not all measures were compatible with the development of Trust Territory "nationalism" or greater self-identity, but those that were not were greatly in the minority and their authors may not have even recognized the incompatibility.

A few of the measures contained an undercurrent of anti-American sentiment, such as those calling for a more restricted leave policy and mandatory rotation of United States personnel or for a tax on non-Micronesian salaries. However, most of these can also be explained as reflecting anti-administration feeling, which tended to be more manifest in measures criticizing on-going programs and advancing proposals for their modification. At least nine measures were expressly aimed at greater Micronesian control over the high commissioner's administration of the Trust Territory, for the most part by requiring his prior consultation with the congress, district legislatures, or both. Given the long period that the people of Micronesia have been governed by outsiders, undoubtedly there were other measures covertly calculated to reduce the administration's discretion or to afford Micronesians greater powers of control, but this was not patent from their reading.

A review of the sponsorship of measures at the first congress reveals the political dynamism of the Mariana delegation.[3] The Mariana members not only came to the congress with a partial program already prepared in draft form, but they also obviously attempted to capitalize on the potential momentum to be gained by the early introduction of measures in a legislative body unsure of its procedures and consisting of many members who by cultural conditioning were reluctant to play an overt role in initiating or

SPONSORSHIP OF NON-ADMINISTRATION MEASURES, BY DISTRICT

District	Measures Sponsored *	Initial Sponsor	Percentage
Mariana	117	107	91.1
Marshalls	23	15	65.2
Palau	31	18	58.1
Ponape	23	15	65.2
Truk	11	4	36.4
Yap	31	12	38.7

* Totals more than 171 due to multi-district sponsorship.

leading action. During the first half of the session, Mariana legislators affixed their names to four-fifths of all the measures which they were to author at the first congress. By the time of adjournment, they stood accountable for over two-thirds of all the non-administration measures and, of these, were the first-named sponsor, normally signifying initiator, on almost all. The magnitude of the Mariana delegation's role was so great that the members of no other single delegation signed their names to even one-fifth of the measures. This predominance was generally manifested whatever the form of the legislative measure and whichever the house of congress.

Another demonstration of the Mariana Islands members' political sophistication is supplied by their complementary activity across legislative chamber lines. Among different measures initi-

[3] This analysis of sponsorship data is computed upon the 171 measures remaining after there were excluded the twelve organizing resolutions for which a procedure was prearranged and the twenty-one administration bills which by convention received introduction by a single, designated member.

ated by congressmen themselves, there were fourteen House of Delegate bills with companion measures in the General Assembly and eight joint resolutions found in both houses.[4] This total should also be augmented by another fifteen comparable resolutions corresponding in content but varying in form. In this latter group, failure to concur exactly often reflects originally inadequate drafting; as presented to the secretary of the House or clerk of the Assembly they were identical, but from their form it was impossible to ascertain whether they were intended to be single house or

SPONSORSHIP OF NON-ADMINISTRATION MEASURES, BY FORM AND DISTRICT

District	22 H.B.	34 A.B.	21 H.J.R.	49 A.J.R.	35 H.R.	10 A.R.
Mariana	17	18	9	34	35	4
Marshalls	0	5	5	6	2	5
Palau	4	10	5	7	4	1
Ponape	3	4	7	6	3	0
Truk	0	3	5	3	0	0
Yap	2	4	10	4	11	0

joint resolutions. Corrective drafting by the staff in conforming these resolutions to both the requirements of the standing rules and the hurriedly ascertained intent of the lead author resulted in their taking diverse final forms. Of this total of thirty-seven companion measures, twenty-two received sponsorship from delegations of the same district in both houses. In another ten, the single district sponsorship found in one chamber was included within the multi-district authorship for the companion measure in the other chamber. For all but three of these thirty-two companion measures, the first persons named in both houses were from the same administrative district, proof that a mechanism existed for delegation cooperation between the two legislative chambers. In most cases [5] this statement can be more appropriately rephrased so as to limit its application to the Mariana delegation, for Marianas' sponsor-

---

[4] Note that this does not include the ten administration-sponsored proposals for which companion bills were introduced in both houses. An eleventh administration bill in the Assembly had no duplicate in the House.

[5] Not only in the Marianas, as see the sponsors of *Delegate* Joint Resolution No. 7, as printed, including the incongruous signature of *Assemblyman* Olter Paul, in addition to those of the two Ponapean delegates; subsequently, Assemblyman Paul was leadoff sponsor on companion Assembly Joint Resolution No. 34.

ship on one or both of each companion set accounted for 92 per cent and 81 per cent, respectively, of these thirty-seven non-administration bills and resolutions.

At the pre-session workshop, the question of joint versus single authorship of measures was discussed, but the drafting committees did not propose that any limitation on multi-member sponsorship be incorporated into either house's rules. The congress quickly adopted multiple authorship of measures into its unwritten procedures; less than a third of all non-administration measures bore the signature of only one member, and this proportion roughly applies as well to bills, joint resolutions, and single house resolutions when each is considered separately. The delegates proved to be twice as willing as the assemblymen to sign another member's measures and also more ready to cross delegation lines. However, the various combinations revealed by the multiple sponsorship suggest the existence of divisions within congressional delegations, sheer legislative inexperience, and most likely, a combination of both.

SINGLE- AND MULTIPLE-MEMBER SPONSORSHIP OF NON-ADMINISTRATION MEASURES

	H.B.	A.B.	H.J.R.	A.J.R.	H.R.	A.R.
Single sponsors	3	12	6	20	6	8
Two or more sponsors, same district	15	17	4	22	16	2
Two or more sponsors, different districts	4	5	11	7	13	0

In the Assembly, not one bill or resolution was introduced by all members of an administrative district; the House of Delegate's tally of thirty-five measures bearing the signatures of both members of a district's delegation is almost wholly attributable to the joint action of the Mariana delegates on thirty-three. The most convincing explanation for this lack of intra-delegation cooperation (other than the contribution of party cleavages in the Mariana Assembly delegation and in the Palau delegations of both houses) lies in the members' inexperience with the process of the new congress as well as their unfamiliarity with the various dimensions of their new legislative role. As a result, cooperative activity within each administrative district's delegation developed on an *ad hoc* basis.

In addition to inexperience, the paucity of *inter*-district co-sponsorship serves as an indicator of the cultural variances which divide the Trust Territory. Less than one-fourth of all measures and barely a third (40) of the multi-sponsored measures bore the signatures of members from two or more districts. With the atypical Mariana district delegation excluded, this number further shrinks to but ten measures jointly offered in either house by members from delegations of at least two districts.[6] The Congress of Micronesia was too new and its powers still too untried to allay the mutual uneasiness latent in the dealings of the people from one island group with those of another. Such display of overt cooperation awaited proof that the stratagem of joint authorship is so associated with the greater possibility of a measure's success in the congress that legislators will actively enlist others' open support, and thus evidence early endorsement for their proposals. The Mariana delegation obviously gave some credence to the efficacy of cross-district sponsorship, and to a degree the new congress proved it right.

NON-ADMINISTRATION MEASURES INTRODUCED AND
ENACTED, BY NUMBER OF SPONSORS & DISTRICT

	Single-Member Sponsor		Multi-Member, Single-District Sponsor		Multi-District Sponsor	
	Intro-duced	Passed	Intro-duced	Passed	Intro-duced	Passed
Bills	15	2	32	0	9	4
Joint Resolutions	26	6	26	9	18	6
Single-House Resolutions	14	9	18	8	13	4
Totals:	55	17(30.9%)	76	17(22.4%)	40	14(35.0%)

Totals— ⟵————131/34 (26.0%) ————⟶
Introduced/Passed

⟵————116/31 (26.7%)————⟶

Upon adjournment and the resolution of the confusion attendant on the last few days of the congress, it was found that a greater proportion of measures of multi-district authorship succeeded in passage (35.0 per cent) than those of one or more members from a single district (26.0 per cent).[7] Although it cannot be determined whether the attractiveness of a measure secured it cross-district support or the reverse, one or both explanations appear related to its more favorable treatment by the congress. Less significance can be assigned to the fact that single-member initiation of measures enjoyed a little more success (30.9 per cent) than multi-member sponsorship (26.7 per cent), regardless of whether the latter was from one or more districts.

The Mariana members were the first-named authors, as well as co-sponsors, on more adopted measures than the members of any other delegation, but this constitutes a somewhat dubious accolade. Under relative standards of effectiveness, the Marianas' performance was not outstanding; the degree of success varies with the specific comparison employed.

The Mariana delegation, particularly in the House of Delegates, approached the congress with more political sophistication than the rest and tended to equate this with a personal responsibility for the political tutelage of the members from the other districts. As Chamorros, they came from a relatively more acculturated ethnic group whose mores now encourage aggressive conduct and thus facilitated their active role in the new congress. Despite their joint sponsorship of some measures with the members of other delegations, they mainly tried to push measures through to passage without the bargaining necessary to reaching agreement in a collegial body unhindered in its decision-making processes. The resultant statistics mirror all this, both in the volume of measures introduced by the Mariana members and their relative degree of success.

Contrasting with the Chamorros of the Mariana district are the self-effacing Trukese, who characteristically display traits of dependence and submission rather than aggressiveness, certain that show of initiative and public attention may lead to trouble. A priori it would be expected that the Truk delegation's performance in the first congress would be muted, at least in the authorship of legislative measures, and this is confirmed by the data previously recounted. Despite being the largest delegation, congressmen from Truk proposed the fewest number of measures—either by them-

[6] Cooperative sponsorship by members from three or more delegations, even with the Marianas included, accounted for a minuscule 10 per cent of the 171 legislator-initiated measures.

[7] Two-district and three-or-more-district sponsored measures had identical ratios of success.

INDICES OF LEGISLATIVE EFFECTIVENESS ADJUSTED FOR COMPANION MEASURES *

	One-District Sponsorship			District of First-Named Sponsor			Any-District Sponsor		
	Introduced	Passed	Percentage	Introduced	Passed	Percentage	Introduced	Passed	Percentage
Marianas	79	18	22.8	88	24	27.3	101	30	29.7
Marshalls	13	8	61.5	15	10	66.7	22	14	63.6
Palau	12	3	33.3	18	4	22.2	31	8	25.8
Ponape	7	2	28.6	14	4	28.6	22	7	31.8
Truk	4	0	–0–	4	1	25.0	11	6	54.5
Yap	7	3	42.8	11	5	45.4	29	10	34.5

* Adjusted to remove from the total of the "introduced" column half of all companion bills and joint resolutions with the same district sponsors in both houses. (Still included are joint resolutions with parallel single-house resolutions in the other house, as a delegation might have wished to work for the passage of both.)

selves, with others, or as initiator—and on those few occasions when they did join with others, they enjoyed a higher index of effectiveness. Here, again, delegation sponsorship of legislation correlates with district political acculturation.

The mores of the Marshall and of the Ponape districts also do not take kindly to the extrovert political type, nor to formally organized and arrogant political behavior. The pattern of legislative sponsorship observed by the delegations from these two districts corresponds fairly closely with that of Truk, in sharp contradistinction to the Mariana congressmen, again suggesting the potential utility of quantifying legislative sponsorship for distinguishing differences of political acculturation. From all this it would be expected that Yapese conservatism would have been revealed by a smaller number of measures sponsored than even that of Truk, but this did not prove to be the case; rather, the Yapese congressmen affixed their signatures to measures on a scale comparable to the members from the Marshalls and Ponape. Even more perplexing is the Palau delegation, for the competitive nature of both Palauan personality and society, and the adjustment of the Paluan culture to Western political institutions and processes, should have been evidenced by a volume of sponsorship somewhere midway between the extremes of the Mariana and Truk delegations. Instead, the conduct of the Palauan congressmen was not distinguishable from that of the other delegations which bunch toward the "Truk pole." The explanation for this lies in the conscious tactic of the Palau congressmen to refrain from publicly authoring many measures at the first congress, a decision quite in conformity with Palauan traditional ways of adopting guiding strategies in advance of embarking upon a political course of action.[8] Thus only the sponsorship of measures by the Yap delegation remains incongruous with what might have been anticipated *a priori* from each district's general cultural attitude toward political participation.

THE LEGISLATIVE OUTPUT

Behavioral studies of American legislatures identify at least five major factors shaping the legislative process and product: the structural composition of the legislature itself, executive-legislative relationships, the individualized contribution of the legislator,

[8] Robert Kellogg McKnight, "Competition in Palau" (Ph.D. thesis, Ohio State University: 1960), pp. 86–96.

group pressure, and constituency forces.[9] Each of these really is but a convenient designation for a bundle of many "sub-factors" encompassed under a single appropriate heading, as "group" includes political party and pressure activities of organized congeries as well as other less formal groupings. Usually it is difficult to pinpoint the effect of a single factor, and recourse is frequently made to statistical analysis of legislative roll calls in the effort to apply precision measurements. The failure of the Micronesian congressional journals to record each member's vote forecloses their use for this purpose. By way of compensation, there is less need to rely upon roll call statistics, for fewer factors molded the actions of the congress, and the impact of most was patently evident.

No Territory-wide party exists in Micronesia, so the control exerted by any organized party activity could at most be observed only in the actions of the Mariana and Palau delegations. Some legislative measures representing party stands were introduced by members from Palau, and the inability of the delegation in either house to present a unified front was partly because of the party schism which split it. However, this division also partially corresponded with the differences in personality and political socialization of some of the delegation's members and, given the weakness of the party movement in Palau, may more safely be attributed to them. On the other hand, the cohesion displayed by the Mariana Territorial Party members during the whole of the congress surmounted personal idiosyncrasies, and this party's influence was manifest in the many Marianas measures embodying its platform pledges, the joint sponsorship of measures in the same house, and the initiation of companion measures in both houses by the Mariana district congressmen. The failure of all three of the assemblymen in the Mariana delegation to join in the initiation of a single measure may be traced to the cleavage between parties.[10] With regard to party pressure exerted from outside the chambers, the necessity for extra police protection arising from a massing of Mariana Popular Party supporters in the back of the House of Delegates, during the party's protest to the seating of Delegate

[9] See Norman Meller, "Legislative Behavior Research," *Western Political Quarterly*, 13:1 (March, 1960), 131, and " 'Legislative Behavior Research' Revisited," *Western Political Quarterly*, 18:4 (Dec., 1965), 776.

[10] Only one measure, A.B. No. 40, was sponsored across Mariana political party lines, but not even this by all three assemblymen from the Mariana Islands district.

Cruz, forcefully brought home to the congress the relation of party position to the organizing of the House. There is nothing to indicate that this show of party strength swayed the findings and recommendations of the Credentials Committee or the confirming action of the House, but it most certainly made everyone involved more careful in observance of all the technicalities. Less material results flowed from the effort of Saipan's local officials affiliated with the Popular Party in supporting the high commissioner's awarding of a charter for hotel building over the objections of the Territorial Party; their stand notwithstanding, the position of the Territorial Party members in the House triumphed and the House adopted Delegate Resolution No. 20 (R. 1–26) requesting the high commissioner to suspend the charter and solicit public bids for the undertaking.

Organized group activity was also just developing in the Trust Territory, and for all practical purposes any effective pressure placed on the congress came from congressmen who were leading members of such incipient groups, rather than from outsiders forcing their views upon the congress.[11] As school teachers, health personnel, and government employees, the congressmen could bespeak their fellow workers' needs as their own. Under the circumstances, a lobbyist for an organization of Trust Territory employees asking for revision of the Micronesian Title and Pay Plan would have been superfluous. Spokesmen for a few Saipanese economic organizations testified at committee meetings; this had an aura of window dressing, providing a backdrop to show the other congressmen that the Mariana members were supported in their positions by their constituents. If the Carolinians living on Saipan are treated in the category of a pressure group, it should be noted that, through informal contacts with members, they lobbied for organizing the House of Delegates in a manner which would favor the Trukese delegate as president. This cannot very well be classified as constituency pressure, for none of the residents on Saipan were electors of any of the delegates from the other districts whom they were importuning. But by far the most observable and effective lobbying, if such it be called, was that of the administration.

The relationship between the congress and the Administering Authority's staff was the second most important factor in shaping

[11] Expressing this in more technical terms, with practically no interest aggregation in the body politic, the congress assumed the representative function of such interest articulation and aggregation as occurred.

final congressional action—sometimes because the position of the administration was accepted in toto; occasionally because the congress consciously took a tack opposite to that outlined by the administration, so that the latter remained potent in a negative way by inversely suggesting the course of congressional conduct; and most significantly, because the administration's background data supplied the members with material upon which many of the congressional decisions were premised. The administration staff came before committees both in open and closed meetings and was repeatedly contacted less formally for advice and required information. The high commissioner submitted twenty-one of the seventy-seven bills introduced in the first congress, and his staff worked arduously for their passage. Some of administration measures adopted were only delivered to the congress within the last week before adjournment. Nine of the fifteen bills enacted were administration measures; excluding those measures which had companions, only two separate bills favored by the administration were killed by the congress. Although the Territorial legislature also failed to follow the high commissioner's recommendations on appropriating local revenues, the record of success for the administration is impressive.[12]

The Council of Micronesia advocated bicameralism upon the premise that the House of Delegates would be more concerned than the General Assembly with the protection of the traditional elements of Micronesian life. Once the congress was in session however, it was quickly evident that the House looked upon itself neither as a conserver of custom nor as a bastion of conservatism. It revealed itself as the more flamboyant of the two chambers, the one more willing to countenance major innovations. The Assembly proved to be the more cautious body, inclined more to ask for Administration studies upon which laws could be based in the future than to push for the immediate enactment of measures. The words of Assemblyman Tman in the closing day's Journal, "It is better that we chart our course carefully. . . . We must not make hasty decisions," [13] could more fittingly have been uttered on the convening of the General Assembly as the guiding principle for the session.

[12] As only two bills bore "urgent" designations, the administration's success cannot be attributed to the congress' truckling to the inevitable.

[13] Journal of the General Assembly, First Session, Congress of Micronesia, Aug. 10, 1965.

The one case of protection for traditional ways recorded in the first congress was instigated by the Assembly and not the House of Delegates. Assembly Bill No. 23, an "urgent" measure, in delineating the responsibilities of the various levels of government would have repealed Section 44 of the Code of the Trust Territory. This section in part allows the continuation of "local political institutions, systems, or customs insofar as they are in consonance with the Trusteeship Agreement and the laws of the Trust Territory." The Assembly Judiciary and Governmental Relations Committee to which the bill was referred reported that "the committee does not feel sufficiently certain that the traditional and customary forms of political institutions and organizations in Micronesia are adequately protected under the provisions of the proposed measure." [14] It therefore recommended that the section be retained, and the Assembly adopted the amendment. The House followed the lead of the Assembly.

The most potent factor in shaping the congress' legislative output was the congressman himself—his preconditioning as he grew to his present estate and its contribution to the attitudes and opinions he currently held on the rate and direction of advisable change for the Territory, his familiarity with parliamentary procedure and the intricacies of the legislative process, and his abilities to interact with his colleagues in ways conducive to arriving at decisions. With minimal political party and group pressures upon the congress and with the bulk of their constituents little informed of what they were doing during the course of the congressional session, let alone what the congress could accomplish, the members functioned mainly as free agents, acting in ways they considered best for the Territory, and incidentally sometimes for themselves.

The congressmen understood the contribution of education to personal advancement, for most owed their own political prominence to educational achievement. From their governmental service, they knew intimately the strengths and weaknesses of the administration. They were in accord that Micronesians should assume responsibility for their own governance but disagreed on when and the manner in which this was to occur. In their ignorance of the complex supportive data necessary for resolving the issues before them, and in the absence of countervailing assistance

[14] Assembly Committee Report No. 6, July 30, 1965.

from outside sources, they had no recourse but to rely upon the administration for counsel. In those areas in which they could depend upon personal knowledge, they felt competent to act and did not hesitate to do so. The cautious among them remained hesitant; those who were hypercritical of the administration pushed for major changes. As the session advanced, both compromised their positions, but the cautious had the advantage, for without their concurrence the status quo would be maintained. The consensus reached normally leaned toward the conservative and, at least for the first session, showed a willingness to hold with the administration and obtain further grounding before supporting any major revision directed against it. The actions of the first congress were mainly the expressions of the members themselves, reflecting the hopes and fears and futures of the citizens of the Trust Territory, tempered by the reality of decision-making under conditions of inadequate knowledge and in a strange and new environment.

The Congress of Micronesia adopted one-third (69) of all measures considered at the first general session and its one day extension; eliminating the more or less routine resolutions of appreciation and those addressed to organizing the congress, this fraction reduces to less than one-fourth (47). In this final tally, only two measures [15] patently proposed to extend greater Micronesian control over the Americans' administration of the Trust Territory, and for the moment the effort came to nought. Assembly Bill No. 2, which would have required district administrators to present their preliminary budgets to their district legislatures for review and recommendation prior to submission to the high commissioner, was vetoed on the technicality that at this stage "of the United States budgetary process as it applies to the Trust Territory . . . [it] is still wholly an administrative matter and that budget materials are privileged information for use of the Executive Branch." [16] This bill hardly constituted a call for revolutionary change, far reaching as its effects might prove to be, for the members knew

[15] Resolutions 1–24 (D.R. 4) and 1–33 (A.J.R. 11)—the former requesting the high commissioner to place one member from each district on the Copra Stabilization Board and the latter asking the high commissioner to study the feasibility of establishing a Civil Service Commission—may have had the same intent.

[16] Robert R. Robbins, " 'Be it Enacted': The New Legislative Branch," *Micronesian Reporter*, 13:2 (July–Aug., 1965), p. 22.

that district budget review had already been practiced in the Truk district and its institution in the Marianas had been halted only at the direction of the high commissioner. The other bill which did not receive the high commissioner's approval, Delegate Bill No. 14, would have had immediate impact upon the entry of non-Micronesian economic interests into the Trust Territory, requiring prior consultation with both congress and concerned district legislatures before chartering, and would have insured indigenous participation in foreign economic enterprise in Micronesia. The high commissioner held that this exceeded the congress' authority and, moreover, that chartering was by nature executive.[17] Debatable as these grounds for disapproval may be, it was accepted by all that the latter bill would have cut deeply into the high commissioner's discretion in charting the economic development of the Territory. Both of these "executive control" measures which succeeded of passage, only to be vetoed, would have permitted Micronesians to slow up innovation and opt for retention of the status quo, a type of legislation which the cautiously inclined congressmen could support.

The administration encountered more difficulty in working with the House of Delegates than with the General Assembly. Of the eight adopted companion measures which were introduced at administration request, five originated in the Assembly, while only three of the delegate bills passed. The Assembly trial by jury bill had no mate in the House; the latter body followed the Assembly's lead in enacting this executive-proposed measure. Subsequent to the Assembly's adoption of the administration bills for regulating hotel operations (A.B. 27) and for keeping the peace (A.B. 30), the House killed both the Assembly's and its own duplicate measures. The refusal to enact these bills and the amendments made to three of the other bills which were passed reveal the congress was not just "rubber-stamping" the administration's requests. In those areas in which it felt competent, the congress did not hesitate to adopt its own views in preference to those of the administration. Import rates were modified (D.B. 18); customary political institutions were protected, unilateral power to charter district governments was withheld from the high commissioner, and disqualifications for holding district legislative office were lightened (A.B. 23); and the

[17] *Ibid.*

qualifications for jury service were varied from those the high commissioner supported (A.B. 44).[18] Some of the amendments, such as that precluding the high commissioner from chartering districts until he informs the congress of the procedural legislation he proposes to submit for effectuating this development, represented maneuvering for power. The first congress was willing to concur in most of the administration-favored legislation; as the congress becomes more knowledgeable about the legislation before it and more secure in its own judgment, the administration is certain to experience far more critical scrutiny of its legislation and greater restraint in its acceptance.

The largest component of the legislative output sought more "extensive and rapid economic and social betterment for the people of the Trust Territory. . . ." [19] Through resolutions the houses went on record as requesting expansion of the public health services (R. 1–41), speeding up the Homestead Program (R. 1–22), increasing electric power and water services (Rs. 1–30 and 1–34), developing roads (R. 1–32), improving harbors and channels (R. 1–40), considering the hard-surfacing of airfields (R. 1–35), and bringing shipping directly into the Trust Territory, eliminating transshipment at Guam (Rs. 1–15, 1–27, 1–29, and 1–43). The review and updating of the Micronesian Title and Pay Plan requested in Resolution No. 1–39 presumably would be followed by raises such as those detailed in Resolution No. 1–48. The expansion of the outlet for Micronesian products on Guam (R. 1–49) and the awarding of future contracts for copra exporting to Micronesian companies (R. 1–42) spoke even more pointedly to economic development than did the resolutions looking to the improvement of the Territory's economic infra-structure. Some of these were repetitions of resolutions adopted at sessions of the Council of Micronesia and were calculated to warm the hearts of the congressmen's constituents.

As was to be expected, the congressmen did not ignore their own needs or their own status. Resolutions passed by the House of Delegates requested the high commissioner to provide members of congress with special personal and vehicular identification (R. 1–47) and diplomatic passports (R. 1–46). The high commissioner

---

[18] The item veto of Public Law No. 1–3 of 1965 represents no executive disagreement with an amendment incorporated into an administration bill, but correction of a technical error contained in the original draft.
[19] Robbins, *op. cit.*

concurred in the congress' selection of a legislative counsel and also signed the bill appropriating the lump sum of $145,000 for the operational costs of the congress during fiscal year 1967. The high commissioner vetoed a $900 item for subsistence to Saipanese congressmen but otherwise approved the $96,562 supplement to the congress' fiscal year 1966 budget. Besides making a modest sum available for interim travel allowances, the bill allocated "not to exceed $400" to each member for "office expenses," $97.50 for "land transportation," and $25 for "official representation," excepting in the last that the presiding officer of each house could draw up to $500. The balance of the supplemental budget was for meeting the costs of the congress' first session not covered by the money earmarked in the Territory's Federal budget and for committee expenses and a possible special session during the legislative interim. The high commissioner declared the subsistence allowance for Saipanese congressmen violative of Secretarial Order No. 2882 because it would have supplied per diem to congressmen who were not in a travel status.

The high commissioner found Resolution No. 1–31 (D.R. 5) ineffective in that it neglected to furnish funds to finance its request for him to send congressmen to Hawaii to observe that state's legislature in session. Resolution No. 1–51 adopted by the Assembly (A.R. 10) attempted to avoid this fatal hiatus by appropriating $10,000 when it authorized the speaker to appoint a six-member interim committee "to make decisions on administrative and staffing problems and other matters as described by the Speaker." The administration took the position that a resolution alone was insufficient to make a valid appropriation, but funds were considered appropriated for the purpose by the supplemental budget bill.

New legislatures tend toward the ceremonial in procedure as well as in product, and the Congress of Micronesia proved no exception. As the legislators are still unfamiliar with the scope and application of their recently acquired powers, their attention turns to matters of a formalistic nature, and political symbolism ranks high in legislative activity. The first bill (Public Law 1–1) and the first joint resolution (R. 1–18) to be enacted by the congress well illustrate this phenomenon.

Resolution No. 4 adopted at the 1961 session of the Council of Micronesia promoted a flag contest. The following year, from each district's two best designs the council chose as the official flag of the Territory the entry drawn by Gonzalo Santos of the Mariana

Islands. The decision of the council was approved by the high commissioner on October 4, 1962, and the flag was put into use throughout the Territory. As his last unilateral legislative act prior to the transfer of lawmaking power to the Congress of Micronesia, the high commissioner by Executive Order 100 amended the Code of the Trust Territory to require all locally registered vessels to fly the Trust Territory flag. Disregarding this long history of almost three years' acceptance, the Congress of Micronesia enacted Public Law 1–1 describing the flag and specifying its display. In the words of the Assembly Committee on Judiciary and Governmental Relations, ". . . it would be more desirable and appropriate for this body, the Congress of Micronesia, to validate by its legislative action the decision of the former Council of Micronesia [which had advisory powers] by officially adopting the described flag as the national emblem of Micronesia." [20] The flag bill was the first to pass the General Assembly, then the House of Delegates, and to be sent to the high commissioner for signature. Assembly Joint Resolution No. 14 became the first resolution to be enacted by both houses. This, too, was formalistic in nature, requesting the Secretary of the Interior to amend his Order No. 2882 so that the House of Delegates would be designated the "Senate" and the General Assembly the "House of Representatives," analogous to the Congress of the United States. The contents of neither measure extend or adjust governmental services, add or reduce sanctions, vary relationships between private persons, or otherwise achieve a substantive purpose; both point to formal and not power ends. Their greatest immediate achievement was as acts of political symbolism to contribute to the status of the congress.

THE LEGISLATIVE IMPACT

The enactment of legislation may be the most salient legislative activity, but hardly measures its sum total. This particularly holds true for the initial session of the Congress of Micronesia, for although the bills that it passed and resolutions it adopted have, like stones thrown into a pond commenced stirring ever-expanding circles of impact, the other functions served by the congress cumulatively will have an even greater influence on the course of Territorial political development.

Institution building is a slow process, one that cannot be encom-

---

[20] Assembly Committee Report No. 1, July 20, 1965.

passed within a single meeting of a legislative body. To be sure, organizing the congress and keeping it running was a creditable feat and greatly eased the operations of the next, and of all future, sessions. But the establishment of the congress as a viable institution will not be assured until it is part of the warp and woof of a Trust Territory political system, and it is in forming such an all-Territory system that the congress promises to make its major contribution. District legislatures have come to be part of their respective districts' political life while, concomitantly, they have given previously dispersed islands and groups of islands a sense of unity. When the initial session of the congress was successfully concluded, it had been demonstrated that representatives from every administrative district of the Territory could meet together and collectively direct the application of legislative authority uniformly throughout Micronesia.[21] In this, the Congress of Micronesia has given promise of realizing for the Territory what the district legislatures are bringing about in their more restricted spheres.

The role of the legislature as a vehicle for building political integration is lost sight of in those countries whose legislatures have long since been merged into a single tapestry of government. In the Trust Territory, whose capacity as a separate polity has yet to be determined, the Congress of Micronesia represents the sole all-Micronesian agency for achieving that purpose. This, then, highlights the significance of the convening of the first congress and of its product. As phrased by Assemblyman Tman, "If we had passed but only one good piece of legislation for the people of Micronesia, we have accomplished something unprecedented in our history." [22] By allowing members from all districts of the Territory to work in consort toward a common end, the congress helped to dispel inter-district suspicion, something which the Council of Micronesia never succeeded in doing. The mere presence of the congress had a cohesive effect by bringing effectively to the attention of the Chamorros on Saipan the facts that the people of other districts are not "savages" and that the Saipanese politician is not necessarily superior. In individual terms, out of this meeting grew a personal sense of solidarity: "There are individual as well as district differ-

[21] In anticipation of the convening of the congress, the high commissioner vetoed a number of district legislative proposals which would have provided piecemeal solutions to Territory-wide problems.
[22] Journal of the General Assembly, op. cit.

ences, that is true, but that is not enough to offset the prevailing feeling of brotherhood." [23] In collective terms, from the congress there emerged the beginning of a Micronesian "self." Just as the British Parliament helped foster and form a public opinion which ended the dissociation of that country's parts, so the Congress of Micronesia, by bringing together the people from the districts, helped blend distinctions in common political action.

The effort to secure Micronesian unity was embodied in many forms of congressional action. It was manifest in the attempt to restrict the entry of non-Micronesian businesses into the Trust Territory. Interest in the founding of a Junior College of Micronesia, the designation of Micronesia Day, and the adoption of a Territorial flag all serve as expressions of this groping toward a Micronesian "identity."

Viewed against the backdrop of history, the flag bill already referred to takes on added significance, for it would not have received unanimous approval fifteen years previously. Under Navy administration, a contest in the Trust Territory for the design of a Micronesian flag ended in a tie vote, and the matter then was allowed to die quietly. The Marshallese had not submitted an entry, and their Flag Committee reluctantly agreed to participate in the judging, and this only after questioning the value of adopting a Territorial flag. In its statement registering disapproval, the committee added, "It is our desire and we believe their [the people of the Marshall Islands] desire that no 'third' flag should ever be displayed beside the old Glory and the flag of the United Nations. To unify the Trust Territory, it is their belief that a nation, such as the United States should 'embrace' it altogether. The difference is a great barrier toward unification. Without something greater, something stronger, something that each cultural group looks up to, a mere flag won't unify the people of the Trust Territory." [24]

Much has transpired in the intervening period, and it was summed up in the Congress of Micronesia. In the congress all of the people of the Trust Territory could now find a unifying purpose, and the flag was but its symbol. A second DC-4 airplane was

[23] Delegate Nuuan, "Impressions of the Congress of Micronesia," *The Rai Review*, Aug. 18, 1965, p. 8.
[24] Quoted in Dorothy E. Richard, *U.S. Naval Administration in the Trust Territory of the Pacific Islands* (Washington: Office of the Chief of Naval Operations, 1957), III, 380–382. Similarly, the first petition received by a U.N. Visiting Mission was from the people of Rota who protested the use of a Trust Territory flag. *1951 U.N. Visiting Mission Report*, par. 15.

acquired by the Trust Territory at the end of 1965, and it was only fitting that it be named the "Congress of Micronesia" and be welcomed ceremoniously by each district's congressional delegation as it traversed the flight routes across the Territory. When the plane reached the last district headquarters, on Palau, appropriately it was met with the Micronesian "national anthem," " 'Tis Here We Are Pledging." [25]

Another valuable contribution made by the Congress of Micronesia was as an information conduit between the high commissioner and the people of the Trust Territory. The Council of Micronesia had its greatest utility as a communication medium, short circuiting the customary administrative channels. This function continued to be served by the congress, and through the very formal means of printing legislative measures and publishing committee reports, the more personal questioning at committee hearings and members' statements of views, and the highly informal contact of business and social occasions, there was transferred to the staff at the provisional Headquarters on Saipan much of the background data essential for its administration of the affairs of Territorial government. Previous to the congress' convening, the election of the congressmen and the issues of their campaigns had already alerted the administration to modifications desired in governmental policies and the reasons advanced for wanting them. In turn, the high commissioner and his staff could use their access to the congress as a means for conveying to the members' electorates the plans of the administration and the steps necessary for effecting them.

The congressmen fully understood the role of the new congress in facilitating communications. In a public address given before coming to Saipan, Assemblyman Salii stated, "Probably the most important function of the Congress is that it creates a forum for discussion between the people of Micronesia and the Administering Authority, a forum through which the thinking and desires of the Micronesians can be made known to the High Commissioner, the Department of the Interior, and, ultimately, to the Congress and President of the United States." [26] A number of delegations held meetings at their district headquarters to allow constituents an opportunity to offer suggestions on what should be considered at the forthcoming congress. In Palau a special session of the Palau

[25] Press Release, Information Office, March 14, 1966.
[26] Reproduced in *Saipan District Panorama*, March 19, 1965, p. 1.

district legislature was called for this purpose. Congressmen also individually encouraged citizens to contact them, and when the legislators arrived in Saipan for the workshop prior to the convening of the congress, they were primed with matters to bring up before the appropriate administrative departments or embody in a bill or resolution for more formal presentation to the administration.

Much of what transpired on Saipan during the month-long congressional session was transmitted back to the districts by word of mouth. Taped records of the daily sessions were edited and played over the district radio stations, but this could only convey a fraction of all that transpired. The Marshallese "roving reporter" who brought back interviews with Marshallese congressmen and his own transcribed comments to broadcast over the district education department's station on Majuro added a note of color, and his explanations furthered comprehension. The press releases from Headquarters, which were reproduced in the weekly bulletins published in each district, also helped to highlight the major activities of the congress as well as the addresses of the high commissioner and the positions the administration expressed in its contacts with the congress. But the bulk of informal communications remained unreported, and it was only as the congressmen themselves spoke with people in their districts after returning home that some of these informal transactions and discussions gradually filtered in garbled fashion throughout the areas.

A related function served by the congress was the exercise of supervision over the high commissioner's administration of the Territorial government. Armed with legislating power, the congress could direct the course of the Territory's conduct, although admittedly the limitations on its fiscal powers severely curtailed the scope of this congressional activity. Its first formal step in the direction of controlling non-Micronesian investment policy was met with a veto, and the House of Delegate's request to halt the Micronesian Hotel Corporation's operations on Saipan came to nought, but the administration is now sure to observe extreme caution in admitting further non-Micronesian economic enterprise into the Trust Territory. The letter of the House committee chairman requesting the high commissioner to suspend hotel operations pending congressional hearings [27] undoubtedly will have a reverse counterpart in future sessions, when clearance is sought by the ad-

[27] *Micronesian Times*, Aug. 12, 1965, p. 1.

ministration in advance of the expression of a formal congressional authorization. The Micronesian Medical Officers' petition to the congress brought the medical program of the Trust Territory before congressional review and subjected it to potential interim scrutiny. In demarking the various levels of government in the Trust Territory and their respective responsibilities, the congress served notice on the high commissioner he was not to be afforded *carte blanche* power in the chartering of district governments. The Assembly Appropriations Committee examined the operations of all Headquarters' agencies in its review of the fiscal year 1967 budget, and this form of administrative inquiry by congress may lead to congressional direction over executive action, a covert direction which may never have written embodiment in either committee report or legislative bill. Even less visible will be that type of supervision which subtly occurs through individual contact between congressman and executive when the former protests a policy or objects to inefficiency of administrative personnel. At the very first session of the congress, members from at least two district delegations called on the high commissioner to request removal of allegedly incompetent American administrators in their districts. Armed with legislating power, the new congress is now able to exercise administrative oversight in ways never before attempted by Micronesians in the Trust Territory.

Already the impact of the first congress is being manifest in diverse ways throughout the Trust Territory. The establishment of the congress and its attendant elections have encouraged wider political involvement of the Territory's residents and stimulated greater interest in government at district and local levels. Political party activity was spurred to new heights in the Marianas and Palau districts for the congressional elections, and this has continued to grow. The municipal elections held in Metalanim on Ponape shortly after the conclusion of the congressional contests saw aggressive electioneering for municipal posts and the largest voter turnout ever recorded. The Outer Island effort to instigate the formation of a Yap district legislature stems from their people's participation in the congressional elections [28] and their chiefs' realization that Outer Island isolation is no longer feasible as the Trust Territory becomes a closely knit unit.

It is probably at the district legislative level that the immediate

[28] See Chap. 6.

effects of the congress have been most pronounced. In the Trust Territory, political sophistication normally has been introduced downward, so that the methods and techniques employed in the district government have spilled over to the conduct of municipal government, rather than the reverse. Now it is the procedures of the new congress which are beginning to shape the operations of the district legislatures. Coming back to their districts with wider horizons and having experienced the utility of following a full set of parliamentary rules, district legislators who served in the congress have instituted revision in their district legislative procedures, and at least one has closely used the congressional rules as a model. After the promulgation of Secretarial Order No. 2882, the Mariana district legislature amended its charter also to provide for the appointment of a legislative counsel. Some returning congressmen have been overheard instructing their district colleagues in the wider conception of the role and duties of a representative which they gained from attendance at the first congress. Both at regular and special sessions of district legislatures throughout the Territory, change of district tax laws has taken place as necessitated by the revenue measures passed by the congress, and the addition of the jury to each district's judicial system has been debated and in some cases already approved. Facing all of the district legislatures is the date of December 31, 1968, when, pursuant to the decision of the Congress of Micronesia in enacting Public Law 1–6, some of their members may no longer be eligible for legislative posts.

Administration at the Territorial level of government also reflects the influence of congressional activity. Upon the expiration of the current contract, prompted by Resolution No. 1–42, the Copra Stabilization Board awarded the marketing of the Territory's copra for the first time to a Micronesian firm formed by representatives from all six administrative districts.[29] A complete restudy of the Micronesian Title and Pay Plan was instituted, followed by the appointment of a five-member task force to develop proposals for a Micronesian Civil Service Act, all in line with resolutions adopted at the first session of the congress. Direct shipment of cargo to Trust Territory ports was found feasible by the high commissioner, "and every possible effort consistent with port capabilities [has

[29] The comparable Micronesian bid for the Territory's petroleum needs was unsuccessful, but later, in consort with an American airline, a contract was entered into to operate the Trust Territory's air transportation.

been directed by the high commissioner to] be extended to carry
. . ." out the applicable congressional resolutions.[30] The appointment of a sanitary engineer on the public health staff of the Trust
Territory was a partial answer to Resolution No. 1–41 calling for
improvement and expansion of the public health services. The
wide use of the resolution form as the means through which the
congress spoke may have been legally deficient to compel action,
but the political implications were clear and the administration
responded accordingly. From the high commissioner level down to
the farthest outlying municipality, the first congress of Micronesia has left an indelible mark, a base point from which the course
of the Trust Territory's political future will be measured.

[30] Letter of Assistant Commissioner Public Affairs to Legislative Counsel,
October 26, 1965.

CHAPTER 15

The Political Future

FOUR METROPOLITAN COUNTRIES have governed the region encompassed within the Trust Territory of the Pacific Islands, and until recently, the island peoples have had little part in determining the nature of that governance. During this period of colonial status they have suffered, through no choice of their own, the devastation of total war and the dangers of atomic testing.[1] Micronesia Day, commemorating the convening of the first Congress of Micronesia, signifies the opening of a new era and that the people of the Trust Territory, through their congress, now possess the means by which to begin shaping their own political future. What this will be yet remains problematical, but the alternatives are relatively few and the range of decision promises to narrow as economic ties with the United States continue to strengthen.

The exploitation of Micronesia's resources has furnished none of its four colonial powers with great wealth. The Japanese did show a profit from the phosphate on Angaur, bauxite on Ponape, commercial fisheries, and copra, but hidden subsidies and the expenses of administration probably turned it into a net loss. The islands have been an economic liability to the United States since American armed forces occupied them during World War II. The cost has been modest, however, compared to the worth of the advantages which the United States has enjoyed. Greater parity between benefit and burden is promised in the immediate years ahead.

From the period of Navy administration, when many Territorial expenses were not itemized and reported separately from those incurred for naval operations, until 1963, annual Federal appropriations ranged from $4.3 to $6.3 million. This was barely sufficient to provide minimal basic services. The "niggardly" nature [2] of this financial outlay may be measured against the estimate

---

[1] Early in the Trusteeship, the Trukese petitioned the United Nations to have the next war somewhere other than Truk, and the Marshallese requested the United States to test its atomic might some place other than the Marshalls.

[2] Harold J. Wiens, *Pacific Island Bastions of the United States* (Princeton: D. van Nostrand Co., Inc., 1962), p. 105.

made at about the time the Interior Department assumed jurisdiction of the Trust Territory that it would cost this amount just to maintain adequate surface and air transportation for the Territory, excluding capital investment and depreciation.[3] When in July, 1962, the ceiling for Federal appropriations was increased to $17.5 million, in the words of President Kennedy, "the Congress . . . [of the United States had] taken the first step toward providing the means whereby a new and vital phase of development may be instituted." [4] The accelerated social and economic programs which were instituted with these moneys, supplemented by the impact of opening up of the area for American capital investments, promise to be dwarfed by the next stage of development, when the greatly augmented funds under the new $35 million ceilings authorized by the Congress are appropriated annually.

The larger the expenditures of Federal funds within the Trust Territory, the more its peoples become dependent upon the United States for their increased standard of living and governmental services which the Territory's limited resources cannot support. As the process continues, it becomes ever more probable that upon the termination of the Trusteeship, the people of Micronesia will opt for ties of some form with the United States. However, if this does not occur in the immediate future, the choice may prove embarrassing to the United States. The advent of the Congress of Micronesia has added a new element to the scene, a capacity to posit and weigh the advantages of alternatives, and the people of the Trust Territory, under the guidance of their congress, may choose a political status which the United States is unprepared to honor.

COLONIAL POLICY VACUUM

The United States does not regard itself as a colonial power and, consistently, has neither a colonial service nor a colonial policy. This of course has not prevented it from acquiring vast possessions on the North American continent and widely scattered island holdings overseas. For the former, territorial status was but a temporary stage to statehood, which appropriately matched the outward movement of America's people. This promise of eventual integration into the Union was abandoned by the twentieth century with

[3] See James B. Shahan, "American Colonial Administration in the Western Pacific" (Ph.D. thesis, Ohio State University: 1950), p. 273.
[4] *Annual Report of the High Commissioner to the Secretary of the Interior, 1963*, p. 1.

the acquisition of the island areas in the Pacific and Caribbean after the war with Spain. The granting of statehood to Hawaii and Alaska despite their lack of continental contiguity has not revived the former doctrine, and the attitude of "apathetic paternalism with strategic considerations,"[5] which Congress has assumed toward most of the nation's insular possessions, has not contributed any indication of what the United States policy is to be for the smaller dependent islands in the Pacific. This hiatus might have been filled by a colonial corps adhering to some evolving plan for political development dictated by a professional ethic, but this, too, is lacking. The nearest the United States ever came to establishing a colonial office has been the Division of Territories and Island Possessions (now Office of Territories) in the Department of the Interior, and it has distinguished itself by contributing to a "policy vacuum."[6] As a result, the programmatic objectives of the United States administration have been pragmatic, fostering adaptation to life's problems as they are, rather than setting final goals and then moving in a planned, coherent way to their achievement. In the Trust Territory this meant that the administrators followed neither wholly "idealistic" nor wholly "realistic" objectives,[7] but left the local inhabitants to work out their own social and political destiny.

Traditionally, American political interest in the Pacific Basin has surged and ebbed, with the rise in interest tied to war. The Spanish-American conflict was the occasion for acquiring Hawaii and Guam, the former on its own volition. The United States quarreled with Japan over the use of Yap at the end of World War I. Okinawa and the bulk of Micronesia fell to the military control of the United States by the end of World War II. The value for future strategic purposes of Micronesia's deep water lagoons, which allowed the building of logistic supply bases in forward areas, gave rise to the dispute between the Interior, Navy, and State Departments over annexation, a disagreement which was partially resolved by first placing the former Mandate under Trusteeship and then the Trusteeship under civilian administration. Once the poignancy of war abated and the islands no longer remained a storm

[5] Garth N. Jones, "Administration of the Trust Territory of the Pacific Islands" (Ph.D. thesis, University of Utah: 1954), p. 62.

[6] See Thomas R. Adam, *Western Interests in the Pacific Realm* (New York: Random House, 1967), p. 169.

[7] See G. P. Murdock, *Social Organization and Government in Micronesia,* CIMA Final Report No. 19 [Washington: Office of Naval Research, 1949], Part III, pp. 4, 5.

center, the Pacific again slipped from public attention, and in Oberdofer's colorful language, the Trust Territory became "an orphan child." [8]

One of the advantages claimed for the imperialistic system of holding colonies was that it did not cast them adrift, leaving them dependent on uncertain world markets, but linked their economic development to that of the mother country. Lacking any pretensions about such a system, the United States accordingly has not moved to tie the economies of all its island possessions closely with its own, and in the case of the Trust Territory has even failed to afford the special custom arrangements for access of Territorial products to the United States which apply to the other insular possessions. For fiscal year 1967, only about 7 per cent of the region's exports were destined for America.

The natural economic leanings of the Trust Territory are toward Japan, the major purchaser of the islands' copra and supplier of many of the products the Micronesians consume. Japan, in turn, has been desirous of reestablishing closer relations with the Trust Territory severed by World War II, and here Japanese interest in unrestricted economic access runs counter to the military-strategic importance of the region to the United States. The Navy still retains a veto over any foreign national visiting the Trust Territory and disapproves of the institution of unrestricted tourist travel from Japan. Unvoiced is the fear that allowing Japanese economic entry would preclude raising a bar against similar Iron Curtain country access because of Article 8 of the Trusteeship Agreement, requiring "most favored nation" treatment to the nationals and companies of all members of the United Nations. The Trust Territory thus floats free of economic integration with the United States, although it is dependent upon heavy Federal expenditures for everything materially above a subsistence existence, and is unable to form associations with other nations to facilitate mutually advantageous trade relations and exploit the Territory's limited resources. Writing two decades ago, John Embree foresaw accurately that Micronesia faced two fundamental types of problems, one political and the other economic, and that "before any real economic development can take place political questions must be answered." [9]

[8] Don Oberdofer, "America's Neglected Colonial Paradise," *Saturday Evening Post*, 237 (Feb. 29, 1964), 29.
[9] John F. Embree, "Micronesia: The Navy and Democracy," *Far Eastern Survey*, 15:11 (June 5, 1946), 164.

With nothing but the vaguest of goals, namely, that the political, economic, social, and educational advancement of the people of the Trust Territory should be promoted, every short-run policy in the Territory may be challenged upon the basis of disagreement over long-run objectives. Investment policy in the Trust Territory is intimately related to the possibility of the area's swinging completely into the American or the Japanese economic orbit. American administrators cannot conduct themselves as conscientious trainers, as counterparts preparing Micronesians for their new roles, if the future remains unknown. It is of little assistance to posit that the Micronesians are being made ready for "self-government," for of itself this carries no blueprint for action. During the two decades of American administration, the Micronesians have been gradually equipped with the education and the institutions necessary for them to make their own political decisions. Otherwise, the period has been mainly one of stasis, but this is shortly coming to a close as the Trust Territory, under pressure from the United Nations, prepares for a plebiscite to record its choice of a political future. Inevitably this will force the Congress of the United States to turn its attention from such relatively minor matters as whether the high commissioner and his deputy should be called "Governor" and "Lieutenant Governor" to "make these officers' titles commensurate with their authority as administering agents"; [10] the United States will have to declare more basic policy, such as that the change of title signifies Congressional intent that these officials are to serve as the chief administrative officers of a Federal "territory," with the latter term employed in its American constitutional sense.

ALTERNATIVES FOR THE FUTURE

The creation of the Congress of Micronesia reopened an old quarrel in the United Nations. Was the United States prepared to allow the Micronesians to choose independence, or were they to be restricted to only greater self-governance? Would the United States go on record declaring "that the Trust Territory of the Pacific Islands would never, for any reason, be annexed to the United States?" [11] This challenge was prompted by the language con-

---

[10] U.S. Congress, House, Committee on Interior and Insular Affairs, *Report on H.R. 17505 of the 89th Congress*, 89th Congress, 2d Sess. (1966), p. 4.
[11] TCOR, 32d Sess. 1248th meeting, June 3, 1965, pars. 78, 79; 1253rd meeting, June 10, 1965, pars. 53, 54.

tained in Secretarial Order No. 2882 setting up the Congress of Micronesia, which referred only to the United States' having "undertaken to promote self-government in the Trust Territory of the Pacific Islands," without any mention of independence for the Micronesians. However, the *antecedents* of the quarrel are old and relate back to events of twenty years before, which still cause the U.S.S.R. to distrust American intentions in Micronesia and which will have particular pertinency as the time approaches for terminating the Trusteeship.

In the Atlantic Charter, the United States pledged it would "seek no aggrandizement, territorial or otherwise." By the Cairo Declaration issued by Roosevelt, Churchill, and Chiang Kai-shek in 1943, the signators declared they "coveted no gain for themselves and had no thought of territorial expansion." In the summer of 1945, President Roosevelt was still asserting that "there is not one piece of territory or one thing of monetary value that we want out of this war." [12] But at the Cairo meeting it was also stated that Japan would be stripped of all the Pacific islands "which she had seized and occupied since the beginning of the first World War in 1914," and this was reiterated at Potsdam in July of 1945.[13] The United States viewed Japan as having lost legal sovereignty when she fortified Micronesia in violation of the terms of the League of Nations Agreement and had no intention of surrendering either the physical or legal right to the control of these islands to Japan or any other country.

With the United Nations treated as the successor to the League of Nations, the subterfuge adopted was that of having the former Japanese South Seas Mandate assigned to the United States under terms which enabled the latter to maintain hegemony by military force. Outright annexation as urged by the military was forestalled by both the State Department and Interior's championing a trusteeship, and military control was further curtailed when the House of Representatives' Public Lands Committee forced a transfer to civil government under the Department of Interior after the Trust Territory of the Pacific Islands was formally established. Nevertheless, by inventing the "strategic Trusteeship" and letting

[12] Roy E. James, "The Trust Territory of the Pacific Islands," in Rupert Emerson, *et al.*, *America's Pacific Dependencies* (New York: American Institute of Pacific Relations, 1949), p. 119.
[13] Dorothy E. Richard, *U.S. Naval Administration of the Trust Territory of the Pacific Islands* (Washington: Office of the Chief of Naval Operations, 1957), III, 3.

it be known that the Trusteeship Agreement would be withdrawn if the Security Council of the United Nations did not approve its terms, the United States saved for its military services the right to erect fortifications, to station armed forces in the former Japanese Mandate, and, most importantly, to close part or all of the region for security reasons. The last safeguard allows the United States unilaterally to decide the extent to which the generally applicable trusteeship functions can be exercised in Micronesia. The Trusteeship Agreement also differed from those made for the other ten original trusteeships by giving the United States preferential treatment in commercial and economic matters, a concession dictated by the special considerations of the area. All of this has led to the strategic Trusteeship's being referred to as a "somewhat bastard and contradictory" conception, and as a "union of doubtful legitimacy between the ideal of colonial trusteeship and the practical needs and objectives of foreign policies of Great Powers. . . ." [14] "Great Powers" might be less charitably rephrased to read "the United States," as the Trust Territory of the Pacific Islands constitutes the only strategic Trusteeship in the world.

At the San Francisco Conference, the U.S.S.R. and Nationalist China strongly supported the goal of "full national independence" for all dependent peoples, a position to which the United States among other nations took exception as not necessarily being practical or desirable. The sections of the United Nations Charter concerned with non-self-governing peoples, and with trusteeships in particular, embody the compromise reached: Article 73, which applies to all such peoples, carries no reference to "independence" but only to development of "self-government" for dependent peoples; Article 76 specifically relates to trusteeships, and in it the basic objectives of the trusteeship system are declared to include "progressive development towards self-government *or* independence" (emphasis added). It was therefore to be expected that exception would be taken when the United States submitted to the United Nations' Security Council a draft of the Trusteeship Agreement for the former Japanese Mandate which only proposed the goal of "self-government." In line with the objection of the representative of the U.S.S.R., to the phrase "promote the development of the inhabitants of the Trust Territory toward self-government" was added the words "or independence as may be appropriate to the par-

14 Hugh McDonald, ed., *Trusteeship in the Pacific* (Sydney: Angus and Robertson, 1949), p. 54.

ticular circumstances of the Trust Territory and its peoples and the freely expressed wishes of the peoples concerned." The United States qualifiedly concurred with the amendment, accepting the principle of independence but recording its opposition "to the thought that it could possibly be achieved within any foreseeable future in this case." [15]

Another amendment to the original draft of the Trusteeship Agreement also bears materially on the future political status of the indigenous inhabitants of the Trust Territory. The United States had proposed that as Administering Authority it should have full powers of administration, legislation, and jurisdiction over the Territory "as an integral part of the United States," language which found its antecedents in the provision made for class "C" mandates of the League of Nations, under which Japan originally governed the area. According to United States Ambassador Austin this did not imply sovereignty over the area. At the request of the U.S.S.R., these words were deleted, but in agreeing to this modification the United States representative "affirmed" for the record that the United States' authority was not to be considered in any way lessened. The high commissioner later declared "that the islands can be made, if the United States so desires, as much a part of the U.S. territory as if they had been annexed outright." [16]

All this supplied the background for the challenge raised twenty years later by Mr. Fotin of the U.S.S.R. at the Trusteeship Council. Was this failure to refer to "independence" in Secretarial Order No. 2882 establishing the Congress of Micronesia an oversight or a deliberate violation of the United Nations Charter and the Trusteeship Agreement? The reply of the United States representative assured the Soviet Union that America was committed to the promotion of self-government *or* independence for Micronesia and that there was no hidden meaning behind the omission.[17] But was this what is known in the psychological novel as a Freudian slip?

The range of future political statuses theoretically open to the Trust Territory may be graphically portrayed by a grid concentrating attention on two factors, geographic components and the nature of the new political entity to be formed (see p. 388). Of course, to delineate some of these alternatives is but to reject them.

[15] See Richard, *op. cit.*, pp. 41, 42.
[16] Trust Territory of the Pacific Islands, *Basic Information* (Honolulu: 1951), pp. 43, 44.
[17] TCOR, 1248th meeting, *op. cit.*

POLITICAL FUTURE OF TRUST TERRITORY

	LARGER THAN PRESENT TRUST TERRITORY	TRUST TERRITORY KEPT INVIOLATE	TRUST TERRITORY DIVIDED: PARTS
SOVEREIGN NATION	with Gilberts, Nauru	independent unit	Carolines & Marshalls, or smaller segments (possibly combined with Gilberts, etc.)
"FREELY ASSOCIATED STATE"	with Gilberts, Nauru	Trust Territory as a unit	Carolines & Marshalls, or smaller segments (possibly combined with Gilberts, etc.)
INTEGRATED WITH MAJOR POWER *			
Possession	Samoa and Trust Territory	Trust Territory as a unit	Carolines & Marshalls, or smaller segments
Territory	Guam and Trust Territory	Trust Territory as a unit	Guam and Marianas; Carolines & Marshalls, or smaller segments
Commonwealth	Guam and Trust Territory	Trust Territory as a unit	Guam and Marianas; Carolines & Marshalls, or smaller segments
"Higher Status"		Trust Territory as a unit	Carolines & Marshalls, or smaller segments
Statehood	Guam and Trust Territory; Hawaii, Guam, and Trust Territory	Trust Territory as a unit	Marshalls and Hawaii
MAINTENANCE OF TRUSTEESHIP			
Administrative union	Guam and Trust Territory; Samoa and Trust Territory		Guam and Marianas
Direct administration by U.N.		Trust Territory as a unit	Carolines & Marshalls

* The United States is used only as an example; categories would be different for joinder with another nation.

Thus it is possible to conceive of the Trust Territory as integrated into the United States by being combined with American Samoa as a single possession, but all evaluations of this status would stress its negative features and the absence of any compensatory advantages. The same difficulties of administration would apply to continued maintenance of the Trusteeship, but with an administrative union established between the Trust Territory and American Samoa.

Limited resources, minuscule population, physical dispersion, ethnic diversity, and almost insuperable communication and transportation difficulties make contemplation of complete independence for the Trust Territory as a sovereign nation something of an academic enterprise. Combination with the Gilbertese of the Gilbert and Ellice Island Colony to the south of the Marshalls would to a minor degree augment the area and population of the proposed entity, but this would also compound the remaining difficulties which would face the new nation. Joinder with Nauru, just below the equator and west of the Gilberts, would add essential resources, but large as that tiny country's annual income from phosphate will be, it would be rapidly dissipated if spread across the entire area of the Trust Territory of the Pacific Islands. The British have intimated they might welcome relinquishing the economic drain of administering the Gilbert Islands, which are populated by Micronesians, as is Nauru; there is no indication whatsoever that the Nauruans, who only recently forced the termination of their Trusteeship, would even discuss amalgamation under conditions which would have them paying the costs of running the government but constituting only a tiny fraction of the new entity's population. Conceivably, also, the Trust Territory could be split along major ethnic lines to form a number of sovereign nations. The Carolines would constitute one, presumably including Ponape, Truk, Yap, and the Palaus; disregarding ethnic differences, Kusaie, the Marshalls, and the Gilberts would be another. But if it is not feasible to treat the Territory as a viable single polity, it becomes even more tenuous to contemplate the area split into component parts, any or all of them independent countries. All of this is probably moot, for long ago the high commissioner gave notice that so long as the Trust Territory is a strategic area, it is inappropriate to think in terms of complete independence.[18]

The South Pacific saw Western Samoa become a separate nation

[18] TCOR, 14th Sess., 552nd meeting, July 8, 1954, par. 18.

under the guidance of New Zealand in 1962, but termination of this Trusteeship has been accompanied by massive financial assistance, the seconding of key personnel, and the continuance of military defense and foreign relations responsibilities for its former ward. Should some comparable status of "freely associated state" be projected for the Trust Territory—whether with its present geographical boundaries preserved intact, as an entity augmented by other island groups, or divided into two or more parts along ethnic lines—this would meet most of the disabilities of independence as a wholly sovereign nation. "As a freely associated state, Micronesia could have unfettered control of its own affairs, including whatever protection was desired for its land and customs, while ensuring the outside assistance without which it could not exist." [19] Micronesia's strategic position would make this arrangement attractive to a major power and could be availed of both in the form of permission for the maintenance of military bases and in agreement to foreclose other nation's access to the area. Its major disadvantage lies in the uncertainties of international relations; if the United States were to occupy a different stance in the Pacific, such a "freely associated state" might find itself no longer courted and, as a result, unassisted by outside aid.

Strong separatist tendencies exist among the Chamorros, possibly encouraged by the splitting of administration between the Navy and Interior Departments, and placing Saipan and then all of the Marianas under the former. More likely, as the most culturally advanced in the Trust Territory, they have seen their economic future as speeded by separating from the Territory and joining with Guam. Whatever the cause, Saipanese and Guamanians through resolutions of their respective legislative bodies have long gone on record as favoring the reintegration of the Northern Marianas with Guam. The logic of common language and religion, traditions and customs, and intermarriage supports this union. However, the United Nations' response has been to disapprove of the partial dismemberment of the Trust Territory and to favor the resolution of its political future as a single unit. Meanwhile, Mariana district lawmakers continue to visit Guam's legislature, and the latter's solons, to travel to Saipan to meet with the Mariana Islands District Legislature and the Saipan municipal council. A Marianas Legislative Conference open to all Trust Territory legisla-

[19] *1964 U.N. Visiting Mission Report*, par. 297.

tors, hopes "to show the lawmakers of the Trust Territory what Guam has to offer as the center of social and economic development." [20] Today, the political parties of the Marianas district are divided over this issue, with the Popular Party supporting immediate integration with Guam and the Territorial Party advocating postponement of the question until further advancement of the Trust Territory. On Guam, there is bipartisan support for bringing the separated archipelago under one jurisdictional roof. Guam's political leaders have advocated the political consolidation of the whole Trust Territory with Guam but, finding the first Congress of Micronesia cool to the proposal, espouse Marianas' reintegration as the first step. They see an expanded Guam eventually as part of a "commonwealth" of Micronesia and, someday, the fifty-first state of the Union.

The non-Chamorro peoples of the Trust Territory as yet do not look particularly favorably upon any form of union with Guam, knowing that the Chamorros tend to regard the Carolinian residents on Saipan and the inhabitants in the rest of the Trust Territory as "less civilized." Palauans resident on Guam occupy a position somewhat resembling that of Negroes in northern American cities, with little social interaction occurring between the two ethnic groups. The Carolinians remember the favored positions that the Chamorros held in Micronesia under the Germans and Japanese and that the friction between the Chamorro minorities and the local inhabitants in the Carolines caused the former to welcome resettlement to the Northern Marianas after the Americans took control and commenced ministering equally to every ethnic group. Simultaneous with the consolidation of the Marianas, the other major ethnic groups in Micronesia may opt for joinder with the United States, but as a separate territory or possession, or possibly as more than one with boundaries of each coterminous with ethnic cleavages. The choice between territory or possession status may turn on whether traditional rights, particularly to land, may be preserved as a territory or, following Samoa's precedent, only as a possession.

A decade ago, Emil Sady broached the federation of the Trust Territory with Guam and the association of the entire region with the United States as a commonwealth, like Puerto Rico.[21] This

---

[20] *Guam Daily News*, April 6, 1968, p. 1.

[21] Emil J. Sady, *The United Nations and Dependent Peoples* (Washington: Brookings, 1951), p. 201.

appears to provide an attractive alternative between statehood and independence, the historical terminal goals of United States possessions. It would allow the continuation of a Micronesian identity, while keeping the region amenable to control of the United States. Presumably, it would be associated with special benefits, akin to the tax treatment now enjoyed by Puerto Rico, so that economic, social, and political advancement could continue at a pace compatible with the various cultures of Micronesia. It could even be accompanied with United States citizenship and free access to the mainland of the United States for all wishing to emigrate. Unfortunately, in the example chosen, Puerto Rico's phenomenal development has carried with it only the demonstration that commonwealth is a way station along the path to determination of its final political status. Already there are strong statehood and independence movements active within that Caribbean island; withdraw its favorable Federal tax exemptions and the issue would be immediately joined, and commonwealth would lose its current attraction to Puerto Ricans. Eventually, if American constitutional history is observed, Puerto Rico must become either free, in fulfillment of its Latin-American heritage, or an equal state of the Union.

Short of statehood but "higher" than commonwealth, a status might be evolved modeled on that of the Cook Islands, which enjoy complete internal autonomy. No New Zealand law is applicable within the Cooks unless made so by the Island government. The Maoris of the Cook Islands continue to be citizens of New Zealand, with the right of unlimited ingress and egress; once outside of the Cooks, its residents observe New Zealand laws like other citizens of that nation. This "higher" integrated status would go far to provide both the benefits and protections desired by Micronesians, while satisfying the United States' strategic interests in the Trust Territory. Assuming that this "higher status" may be constitutionally erected, perhaps it is too much to expect that the Congress of the United States would voluntarily commit itself to supplying funds without conditions and enacting laws that could have no effect within the present Trust Territory without the consent of that area's peoples. This is one of the possibilities theoretically open to the Micronesians which, should it be chosen, might prove embarrassingly difficult for the United States to deny.

From Hawaii comes the suggestion that all of the American-administered islands of the Pacific be incorporated within the State of Hawaii to form a greater Pacific State. This would not only resolve the future of the Trust Territory but also that of American Samoa and Guam. Just as tourism is becoming the mainstay of Hawaii's economy, so would it form the backbone of a more durable economy for the others. The ties which would emerge would indirectly contribute the means for resolving some of the problems now facing the Pacific, as the lack of a logical base for air transportation. The main virtue of this suggestion lies in its integrating all the regions into the United States, so that as constituent parts of a state they would enjoy the full political participation denied them as territories, possessions, or even as a Pacific commonwealth. The administrative problems posed would be enormous, but not insurmountable; the cultural and political difficulties would be less amenable to resolution. The areas' cultures are diverse, their rates of development disparate, and for a long period of time such a jointure would remain artificial. Local autonomy in forms as yet unknown to state practices would need to be invented to accommodate the vast differences endemic to the areas encompassed as well as permit the delegation of discretion essential to govern such a far-flung region. The large Federal expenditures now made in the Western Pacific would have to be continued in the form of Federal subsidies, since Hawaii's resources could not underwrite the $75 to $100 million annual burden now borne by the national government for all three island regions.

The enormity of this statehood proposal almost overwhelms its plausibility, but the simplicity of a single solution to the futures of all three American-controlled Pacific areas has already attracted wide attention. Guam and the Trust Territory each have greater population than the minimum requirement for statehood set forth in the Northwest Ordinance; however, separate statehood for them and Samoa, individually or combined, is ruled out by size if not other factors. During the Spanish period, the Marianas and nominally the rest of Micronesia under Spanish jurisdiction were administered through the governor of the Philippines; the Germans during their era in the Pacific finally attached their Micronesian holdings to German New Guinea so that they were supervised by way of the latter's imperial governor. Tying the Trust Territory to a larger political unit such as Hawaii would only constitute a repetition of history, but this time with the material difference of Micronesians as equals in their own governance.

From possession to statehood, all statuses are premised upon integration in some way with the United States. Such relationships coincide with American policy, for it is believed that the United States has "had a consistent goal from the start and that has not gone beyond holding out self-government under the American flag as a goal." [22] But what if the Micronesians should seek annexation by a nation other than the United States? Under present circumstances, this would be Japan, for in addition to symbiotic economic ties, some Micronesians' nostalgic memories of life under the Mandate, before military preparations for World War II destroyed civilian normalcy, might lead them to favor return to Japan. Most expressions of Micronesians have not been so inclined, but should such feeling grow, it would probably evoke a sympathetic irredentism in Japan. The United States would be hard put to stop such a movement. Nevertheless, given the bitter internecine quarrel between the Federal departments, which almost saw the Trust Territory annexed outright at the end of the war, and the opinion which still holds that the neutrality of the old Mandate remains essential to American national security, it is unlikely that the United States would countenance any other nation's exercising jurisdiction over the Trust Territory. Palau is too close to the Philippines, Indonesia, Australia, and the Malay peninsula for American military planners to forego its future use as a military staging zone, or to allow its occupancy by another nation to neutralize Guam. The same outflanking problem holds true for other areas in the Carolines and the Northern Marianas; in addition the latter will probably be developed as a forward air base when the United States withdraws from Okinawa, while the Marshalls still remain central to development of American missile defense, if no longer important for atomic testing. Given Micronesian choice of another nation, the United States would consider it had no alternative other than to exercise its reserved power under Article 15 of the Trusteeship Agreement, which allows it to veto any alteration or termination of the agreement.

If permitted the opportunity to opt for continuing the Trusteeship, many Micronesians would accept it as a means for delaying a definitive decision on the Territory's future status. To some the ideal solution would be for the United Nations itself to assume direct administration, this premised upon the belief that pressure

---

[22] Paper presented by Dr. Robert R. Robbins, "Trust Territory of the Pacific Islands—The Development of a Polity," at the New England Political Science Association Meeting, April 1967, p. 16.

emanating from the U.N. to end the Trusteeship would abate once the region was no longer under American jurisdiction. Continuation of the Trusteeship for a reasonable period into the future, or even some modification in the trusteeship relationship, is not an impossibility in this world of realpolitik, but that such a change will consist of the United Nations' becoming the Administering Authority appears highly improbable. More likely, although not currently being seriously considered, would be the joining of the Trust Territory in an administrative union.

Article 9 of the Trusteeship Agreement permits the United States "to constitute the Trust Territory into a customs, fiscal, or administrative union or federation with other territories under United States jurisdiction and to establish common services between such territories and the Trust Territory where such measures are not inconsistent with the basic objectives of the International Trusteeship System and with the terms of . . ." the agreement. If America were to follow the example set by Australia in its joint ministration of the Trusteeship of New Guinea with the Australian Territory of Papua, the Trust Territory of the Pacific Islands could be brought together with Guam. Although the United States would continue to remain accountable for the Territory's stewardship, such a joinder would grant the Micronesians greater powers of self-governance and postpone any definitive step until they are more politically acculturated. It presents no final solution, primarily because Guam's status as an unincorporated territory of the United States places it in an uncertain position, but this should make it all the more attractive to those opinion leaders of the Trust Territory who incline toward a temporary solution which can be reviewed in the future rather than a permanent resolution that would force irrevocable action now. Safeguards against exploiting the Trust Territory to the advantage of the Guamanians and mechanisms by which Guamanians as United States citizens [23] and the inhabitants of the Trust Territory share a joint "administrative federation" could be evolved. In view of Guam's relative internal autonomy, Australian experience in administering Papua-New Guinea would provide limited parallels, and many technical obstacles would have to be overcome for such administrative union to be implemented. Greater administrative cooperation between

[23] Papuans are citizens of Australia; New Guineans are not. However, unlike Guamanians who may freely travel to the United States, Papuans have no greater access to Australia than do New Guineans.

Guam and the Trust Territory may be anticipated, and their chief executives have already taken steps to that end, but it is unlikely that Carolinian and Marshallese attitudes toward Guamanians would favor the closer ties requisite to administrative union. In any event, the pace of political change has so quickened that the time for incremental steps such as administrative union has now probably passed.

Political union with other Pacific areas under a loose form of confederation, possibly with the South Pacific Commission re-vamped to achieve this end, may be regarded as a supplement to aid the viability of some of the alternative statuses discussed for Micronesia. Geographically, climatically, and economically, as well as in patterns of land use, forms of social demoralization due to rapid acculturation, and the assumption of ever greater powers of control over their own political conduct, the South Pacific pre-sents a high degree of regional uniformity. The South Pacific Com-mission was designed to facilitate collaboration in promoting the indigenous peoples' economic and social welfare among the powers which have dependent territories in the Pacific. Presently, Aus-tralia, France, New Zealand, the United Kingdom, the United States, and Western Samoa are members of the commission. The admission of Western Samoa and, prospectively, Tonga has modi-fied the commission's character from that of a body composed solely of states administering dependent territories. The representatives of the indigenous inhabitants who attend the South Pacific Con-ferences of the commission have expressed dissatisfaction with the commission's concentration on consultation and research limited to economic, health, and social matters, and there is strong senti-ment to expand its attention to include political activities and to allow the Pacific territories a share in commission decision-making. In light of their mutuality of interest, it may not be too visionary to think of the smaller areas of the South Pacific linked together in a common front on regional problems and cooperating to utilize their limited resources to best advantage. However, this is not to contemplate the formation of an independent federation, with Micronesia as a component state. The same lack of resources, com-pounded by commonality of economic endeavor, causes most of the South Pacific, like the Trust Territory, to rely upon outside assistance, so that Micronesia's ties with some world power under any future status would not be obviated.

Trusteeship for Micronesia only postponed the reckoning which must eventually be made between the United Nations' policies of self-determination and the United States' concern for its own security. As events are shaping up, the course finally followed by the Micronesians may not be incompatible with either. However, the growth of an articulate, educated, political elite in Micronesia will cause this issue to be resolved to the Micronesians' benefit, any views of the United Nations or the United States to the contrary. Already, through the Congress of Micronesia, they have given notice that, for the "privilege" of being able to "declare all or any part of the islands a closed area within which it can unilaterally determine the extent to which the general applicable activity of a Trusteeship may be exercised," the United States should be prepared to provide adequate outlays of funds for Micronesian development, and that the U.S. Congress has not met this obligation.[24] This is no appeal to humanitarian principles, although it was in their name that the United States undertook responsibility for the administration of the Trust Territory; rather, this is the language of the political realist, and it is in these terms that the Micronesians will resolve their political future.

STRAWS IN THE WIND

It is always hazardous to predict the future, but there are many signs which intimate Micronesia's retaining its American ties when the Trusteeship is terminated. As epitomized in a press interview by the first Speaker of the General Assembly of the Congress of Micronesia, "We have American ideas. . . . All our education is American; the tools of government with which we work are American." [25] The form of the relationship between the two has yet to be firmed, whether it be annexation as an American possession, a commonwealth in conjunction with or separate from Guam, an integral part of the State of Hawaii, or some new arrangement still to be conceived. But the indications for this end to the Trusteeship reach back into the early acceptance of American responsibility for the ministration of the area.

In 1950 the first petition received by a United Nations Visiting Mission to Micronesia stated that the people of Rota were "entirely satisfied with the administration of the United States of America and request[ed] that the flag of that nation continue to be flown

[24] House of Delegates Committee Report No. 20, First Congress of Micronesia, Aug. 8, 1965.

[25] *Honolulu Star-Bulletin,* July 17, 1965, p. B-1.

on ..." the island. The U.N. mission noted that the petition reflected the disinclination encountered elsewhere in the Territory to weaken in any way the Micronesians' relationship with the United States.[26] Similarly, an early petition delivered by the chiefs of the Yap Islands to the Congressional party which visited them in 1949 retains significance, although it must be evaluated against the Yapese known trenchant to maneuver their administrators to the end of preserving Yapese identity:

During Spanish came to this island our parents told us to see these people and see what they had and what kind of living they had, something like that. If they have good living and good things, we going change our system and be friends with them. Soon they went away from this island, and Germany come. Same thing our parents told us—you have to see these people and if you think they are good people and do good things you can be friends with them. Soon the Germans went home. Japanese came in to get our islands. Our parents told us again. ... This is a promise. You work with these people and go to school with these people but do not change our custom and be Japanese, because these people are poor and we do not want to be people of Japan. We have to wait for another country—England or America. Soon the World war Two began. Some of us prayed for American people to get our island. Finally the American came to our island. Now we are glad, because our parents told us and we remember the promise we had with our parents. So now is the time to change—to drop the bad customs and pick up the good customs and get new customs and be friends with you people, and work with you. Even today we pray in church or in another religion for you Americans to stay with us forever.[27]

The Marshallese also as early as 1950, through their Flag Committee, expressed the belief "that the people of the Marshall Islands hope some day the Trust Territory will become a part of the United States." [28] Although, in a petition to the visiting mission in 1953, the Marshallese voiced their fear of any attempt to merge them "culturally or otherwise" with the other peoples of the Trust Territory with the resultant loss of their own individuality, these two positions of the Marshallese were not inconsistent. The Micronesians

[26] *1951 U.N. Visiting Mission Report*, par. 15.

[27] In 1952 Yap file, Political Affairs Office, Headquarters, Saipan. Following this recital, the chiefs asked for "some things that we need to help us build our island." High on the list was a separate administrative status for Yap, which at the time was being administered through Palau. Parenthetically, it may be added for those who are familiar with Yapese stone money, the first request was: "We want to know the way to get some money on this island. We know how to make and use our own money, but it is difficult to know how to make American money. We don't want to use just the old custom. We want to build our island up."

[28] Richard, *op. cit.*, p. 381.

are becoming unified by reason of the United States administration, and each ethnic group looks to America as its protection against being indiscriminately "lumped together with other groups of Micronesian peoples as one people." [29] In a continued association with the United States lies protection.

The recent actions of the Yapese supply another illustration of this desire for closer ties with the United States as a means of forestalling undesired change. In November of 1965, the American Ambassador to the United Nations Trusteeship Council and a Congressional group visiting Yap were presented with a petition adopted by the Yap Islands Congress and endorsed by the Yap Islands Council. The petition first stated that the political determination of the remaining three trusteeships is bound to be made in the near future and "the people of the Trust Territory of the Pacific Islands may be forced by world pressure to make a decision, the consequences of which we may not be ready to accept, and that whatever that may be it is going to have permanent effect upon the inhabitants of these islands." It then requested "that the question of the future political status of the Trust Territory . . . be set aside until such time as the people of these islands feel ready to make that decision, provided that:

1. The Trust Territory of the Pacific Islands be released from the United Nations Trusteeship Council supervision and be placed under the direct supervision of the United States of America, preferably under the Administration of the Department of the Interior.

2. That being placed under the United States supervision, a form of political association with the United States shall be worked out whereby we will retain our Congress with an executor appointed by the President of the United States of America.

3. The United States of America shall agree to enlarge the present annual Trust Territory budget and to fully develop the islands economy with due consideration to the total development of political and social welfare of these islands." [30]

The Trukese were more specific than the Yapese in pointing the direction of political development they desired. Resolution 9–64 of the 1964 Truk district legislature recommended to the Council of Micronesia that it take the necessary action for the Trust Territory to become a commonwealth of the United States. As originally in-

[29] *1953 United Nations Visiting Mission Report*, par. 23.
[30] Transcript, Yap Islands Congress, Second Special Session, Nov. 19, 1965, p. 22.

troduced at the initiation of Chief Petrus and the Moen Municipal Council, the resolution sought Federal territorial status, but the Political Committee of the Truk legislature amended it, and the whole legislature concurred in the change.

The people of the Marianas would move faster and farther in cementing their ties with the United States than any of the other Micronesians. In 1950, the Saipan legislature delivered a petition to the United Nations Visiting Mission stating that the Northern Marianas hoped to be incorporated into the United States either as a possession or as a territory, "preferably as a territory," and to attain American citizenship.[31] Fifteen years later the Mariana Islands District Legislature was still memorializing the grant of United States citizenship, but now for all the inhabitants of the Trust Territory. The Chamorros are in the forefront in demanding change of the Trust Territory's political status, and for most of them there can be no alternative but integration with the United States.

STATUS COMMISSION AND THE CONGRESS

As a rule, the solons in the Congress of Micronesia are unwilling to express themselves as unequivocally as the district legislators from the Marianas or even from Truk or Yap. During the congressional campaigns of 1965, a few of the candidates advocated joining the United States as a territory, others looked toward an eventual status suggesting commonwealth or independence, and most neither publicly nor probably privately committed themselves on the issue. For one thing, it fits Micronesian mores not to take an exposed position until after first ascertaining the direction of the achievable consensus. For another, many Micronesian leaders are admittedly ambivalent. They favor political development of Micronesia yet would prefer somehow to preserve the cultural identity of their own and each of the region's other ethnic groups. They recognize that the emergence of a Micronesian "self" is facilitative of the former and destructive of the latter and fully comprehend that the feasible alternatives open to them in setting permanent political goals for the Trust Territory inevitably will modify, if not destroy, their individual cultures. The leaders were startled by the greatly accelerated development program and the lightening of security restrictions in the Trust Territory adopted pursuant to the

[31] Richard, *op. cit.*, pp. 1075–1076.

policy set by the National Security Council in 1962, and they resent the apparent motive underlying the Administering Authority's actions since then, namely, to have the Trusteeship terminated as quickly as possible to the advantage of the United States. They are appreciative of the augmented flow of Federal money into Micronesia and welcome the youthful enthusiasm of the Peace Corps volunteers, who are moving to outlying islands on which American administrators have never resided. All this they regard as pointing them along a single course, hurrying them to permanent affiliation with the United States before they can be confident in their choice.

Few if any of the Territorial legislators have seen the classified portions of the Solomon Report of 1963, but it is no secret that it recommends an early plebiscite. They know that the high commissioner told the Trusteeship Council in 1966 that "the point is moving perceptibly closer when we [the Administering Authority] will stand aside and say to the Micronesians, 'Now where do you want to go from here? The choice is yours.'" [32] What is feared is that this will occur before each of the alternatives has been thoroughly explored and the people of the Trust Territory are able to make a meaningful decision. All this was summed up before the Trusteeship Council in 1965 by Delegate-elect Bailey Olter, as advisor to the United States Delegation:

Three weeks ago I toured my district with my fellow Congressmen from Ponape District. In every place we visited, we concluded our meetings by asking the people their future political preference. Given several alternatives, the people invariably insisted that they wished to remain under the present system until they are ready in terms of educational standards, economic stability, political sophistication and social maturity and responsibility. The Micronesians are cautious and are reluctant to gamble for the price of uncertainty. When we are ready to accept the responsibilities and are aware of the implications and consequences of committing ourselves to whatever political status we prefer, we will ask for it. [33]

At the first session of the Congress of Micronesia, the House of Delegates turned down a bid for organic legislation for the Trust Territory, as it also did at its second session. Resolutions calling for closer ties or special relations with the United States met similar defeat at the latter session. However, in this 1966 term the congress petitioned the President of the United States "to establish a

---

[32] *Honolulu Star-Bulletin*, June 30, 1966, p. D-7.
[33] Quoted from *The Rai Revue*, Aug. 4, 1965, p. 4; précised in TCOR, 32d Sess., 1246th meeting, June 2, 1965, par. 18.

commission to consult the people of Micronesia to ascertain their wishes and views, and to study and critically assess the political alternatives open to Micronesia. . . ." [34] A year passed while the Departments of State, Defense, and Interior deliberated upon the terms of the resolution to be introduced into the United States Congress providing for setting up a status commission. Rumor has it that underlying this delay was the State Department's protest against contemplating a tie of the Trust Territory with the United States unless a concrete political change were offered, such as incorporated territorial status.

At its 1967 session, the Congress of Micronesia again took action. Now it established its own status commission, composed of six Micronesian congressmen, to study the future political alternatives of the Trust Territory and to help educate the people of Micronesia to understand the significance of their choices.[35] Here was both protection against hasty resolution and recognition that the basic economic and social decisions currently to be made waited upon the shaping of the Territory's political future. Shortly after the Congress of Micronesia adjourned, the President of the United States sent a communication to the U.S. Congress asking for the adoption of a joint resolution setting up a Federal status commission for the Trust Territory. This was in line with the original petition of the Congress of Micronesia and not necessarily antithetical to its subsequent action. However, in contradiction to the Micronesians' desire to frame the terms and then study the various alternatives carefully, the draft of the joint resolution accompanying the President's message called for the people of the Trust Territory "freely to express their wishes as soon as possible, and not later than June 30, 1972, on the future status of the Trust Territory." [36] A date has now been proposed for the termination of the Trusteeship, and regardless of whether the U.S. Congress will approve, in the Trusteeship Council the United States will be pressed to abide by this date set by the President.

---

[34] House Joint Resolution No. 47, *Laws and Resolutions,* Congress of Micronesia, 1966.

[35] Senate Joint Resolution No. 25, *Laws and Resolutions,* Congress of Micronesia, 1967.

[36] President's letter dated Aug. 21, 1967; *Weekly Compilation of Presidential Documents,* 3:34 (Aug. 28, 1967), 1190. For the President's power to act unilaterally, see "Executive Authority Concerning the Future Political Status of the Trust Territory of the Pacific Islands," *Michigan Law Review,* 66:6 (April, 1968), 1277.

As this manuscript goes to press, the U.S. House of Representatives has yet to act upon the President's request, while the Micronesian status commission has commenced studying the range of alternatives open to the Trust Territory. To a sub-committee of the U.S. Senate visiting Saipan early in 1968, the Micronesian solons courteously rejected the proffer of seating Micronesian legislators on the Federal study body but offered to cooperate with it when created. The members of the Micronesian status commission wanted no entanglements which might restrict their freedom of maneuver. They know that there are three parties to the termination of the Trusteeship, and that while the United States may hold a veto, so does the United Nations. To convince the members of the United Nations to ignore the precedent of all previous nine trusteeships and to accept some form of integration of Micronesia with the United States requires such overwhelming Micronesian support as to drown all criticism that the choice was not freely made. This places the Micronesian in a central position as to the alteration of the Trust Territory's status, and at this stage, it is the Micronesian solon who controls the political destiny of the Trust Territory.

Traditionally the United States has relied upon the legislature as the vehicle through which to develop the political capabilities of the peoples in its territories. Long before they have been deemed competent to choose their own chief executive or judges, they have begun exercising legislative power through their locally elected representatives. The legislature has been the forum in which to debate each incremental step toward self-government and to activate public opinion in its support. Already in the Trust Territory, the district legislatures have commenced shaping the course of political development within their respective jurisdictions. The Congress of Micronesia is now assuming this same role for the whole of the Trust Territory. On the founding of the congress, the President of the United Nations Trusteeship Council, Frank Corner of New Zealand, prophetically forecast: "Through the establishment of the Congress of Micronesia . . . the people of Micronesia will be able to get to grips with the essential question of what sort of people they wish to be and what sort of Micronesia they wish to create. Then they will be able to go on to mark out an ordered path towards the future political status which they alone can choose." [37]

[37] Quoted in *Saipan District Panorama*, Oct. 23, 1964, p. 1.

Contents

Congress of Micronesia

SECRETARY OF THE INTERIOR ORDER NO. 2882

Subject: Legislative Authority for the Congress of Micronesia, Trust Territory of the Pacific Islands.

Whereas, pursuant to the Trusteeship Agreement between the United States and the Security Council of the United Nations, the United States has undertaken to promote self-government in the Trust Territory of the Pacific Islands; and

Whereas, in 1956 the High Commissioner of the Trust Territory created an Inter-District Advisory Committee composed of Trust Territory citizens to assist in the development of programs and policies for the area; and

Whereas, the Inter-District Advisory Committee in 1961 was reconstituted as the Council of Micronesia, selecting its own chairman; and

Whereas, the deliberations of the Council of Micronesia have been of a uniformly high order; and

Whereas, the Council of Micronesia has recommended the establishment of a legislature for the Trust Territory of the Pacific Islands to be known as the Congress of Micronesia;

Now, therefore, there is hereby created the Congress of Micronesia, as set forth in the following order:

Section 1. *Purpose.* The purpose of this Order is to grant certain legislative authority to the Congress of Micronesia in the Trust Territory of the Pacific Islands, to delimit its membership, duties, and procedures, and to define its relationships to other branches of the Government of the Trust Territory of the Pacific Islands.

Section 2. *Organization.* The Legislature of the Trust Territory of the Pacific Islands shall be known as the "Congress of Micronesia" and shall consist of two Houses, the House of Delegates and the General Assembly. The two Houses shall sit separately except as otherwise provided herein.

When the Congress shall convene, each House shall organize by the election of one of its number as presiding officer and such presiding officer shall be designated by the title of "President of the House of Delegates" or "Speaker of the General Assembly", as the case may be. When the Congress meets in joint session, the Speaker of the General Assembly shall preside.

Section 3. *Legislative Power.* The legislative power of the Congress of Micronesia shall extend to all rightful subjects of legislation, except that no legislation may be inconsistent with

(a) treaties or international agreements of the United States;

(b) laws of the United States applicable to the Trust Territory;

(c) Executive Orders of the President of the United States and orders of the Secretary of the Interior; or

(d) sections 1 through 12 of the Code of the Trust Territory.

No law shall be passed by the Congress imposing any tax upon property of the United States or property of the Trust Territory of the Pacific Islands; nor shall the property of non-residents be taxed at a higher rate than the property of residents. No import or export levies shall be imposed on goods transported between or among the Districts of the Trust Territory, as described in Section 39 of the Code of the Trust Territory, or any political subdivision thereof, and the levy of duties on goods imported into the Trust Territory is hereby reserved to the Congress of Micronesia and the High Commissioner.

Section 4. *Powers of the High Commissioner.* At the opening of a legislative session and at any time thereafter the High Commissioner may submit to the Congress and recommend the enactment of legislation.

In the event that the High Commissioner has submitted to the Congress proposed legislation which he has designated as urgent, and the Congress has failed to pass the same in its original form or an amended form acceptable to the High Commissioner at the session at which it was submitted, the High Commissioner may himself, with the approval of the Secretary of the Interior, promulgate such legislation as law: *Provided,* That such designation as urgent shall be made no later than seven days prior to the end of the session.

Section 5. *Budget.* Prior to his final submission of the annual budget of the Trust Territory to the Secretary of the Interior, the High Commissioner shall submit a preliminary budget plan to the Congress of Micronesia in joint session for its review and recommendations. The High Commissioner shall adopt such recommendations of the Congress as he may deem appropriate, but he shall transmit to the Secretary of the Interior all recommendations he has not adopted. Legislation enacted by the Congress of Micronesia requiring the expenditure of funds other than as budgeted shall include revenue measures to provide the needed funds.

Section 6. *Membership.* For the purpose of representation in the Congress, the Trust Territory is divided into six Districts as described in Section 39 of the Code of the Trust Territory.

The House of Delegates shall consist of twelve members, who shall be known as "Delegates," of which each District shall elect two.

The General Assembly shall consist of twenty-one members, who shall be known as "Assemblymen," and who shall be elected from each District as follows:

In the Mariana Islands District, three;

In the Marshall Islands District, four;

In the Palau District, three;

In the Ponape District, four;

In the Truk District, five;

In the Yap District, two.

Each of the six Administrative Districts shall be subdivided initially into single member election districts of approximately equal population, in such manner as the High Commissioner shall determine, and each such election district shall elect one of the Assemblymen to which the Administrative District is entitled. Future subdivisions shall be established by law.

Election districts shall be reapportioned every 10 years on the basis of population, but each District (as described in Section 39 of the Trust Territory Code), shall be entitled to at least two Assemblymen regardless of population. The first such reapportionment shall be made in 1971.

Section 7. *Qualification of Legislators.* In order to be eligible to election as a member of the Congress a person shall:

(a) be a citizen of the Trust Territory for at least five years;

(b) have attained the age of twenty-five years at the time of his election; and

(c) have been a bona fide resident of the District (as described in Section 39 of the Code of the Trust Territory), from which he is elected for at least one year next preceding his election.

No person who has been expelled from the Congress for giving or receiving a bribe or for being an accessory thereto, and no person who has been convicted of a felony, shall sit in the Congress, unless the person so convicted has been pardoned and has had restored to him his civil rights.

Section 8. *Franchise.* The franchise shall be vested in residents of the Trust Territory who are citizens of the Trust Territory and eighteen years of age or over. Additional qualifications may be prescribed by the Congress: *Provided,* That no property, language, or income qualification shall ever be imposed or required of any voter, nor shall any discrimination in qualification be made or based upon literacy, tribal custom, or social position, nor upon difference in race, color, ancestry, sex, or religious belief.

Section 9. *General elections.* General elections shall be held biennially in each even numbered year on the first Tuesday following the first Monday in November. All elections shall be held in accordance with such procedures as this order and the laws of the Trust Territory may prescribe. Legislators shall be chosen by secret ballot of the qualified electors of their respective districts.

Section 10. *Term of office.* Each Delegate shall hold office for a term of four years: *Provided,* That of the Delegates elected at the first general election, one from each District shall hold office for two years only, and the determination of which Delegate shall serve the short term shall be made by drawing lots.

Assemblymen shall each hold office for a term of two years.

The terms of all members of the Congress shall commence at noon on the third day of January following their election, except as otherwise provided by law.

Section 11. *Disqualification of government officers and employees.* No person holding a position as a Department Head or Assistant Department Head in the Headquarters of the Trust Territory Government, as a Department Head or Assistant Department Head in a District Administration, as a District Administrator or Assistant District Administrator, or as a Judge, and no person serving as a member of a District Legislature, shall be eligible to serve as a member of the Congress while holding said position: *Provided,* That this disqualification shall not become effective until the third general election to the Congress.

The High Commissioner shall permit any employee of the Government of the Trust Territory to be accorded leave without pay, for a period not to exceed 30 days prior to and including the day of the general election, for the purpose of seeking election to the Congress.

No member of the Congress shall, while on official legislative business, receive any other compensation from the Government of the Trust Territory or any political subdivision thereof.

Section 12. *Legislative sessions.* There shall be a regular session of the Congress held in each year beginning on the second Monday of July and continuing for not to exceed 30 consecutive calendar days. Each such regular session shall be held at the seat of the Government of the Trust Territory.

The High Commissioner may call special sessions for such period of time and at such time and place, as in his opinion the public interest may require. No legislation shall be considered at any special session other than that specified in the call therefor or in any special message by the High Commissioner to the Congress while in such session.

Section 13. *Enacting clause.* The enacting clause of all bills shall be: "Be it enacted by the Congress of Micronesia," and no law shall be enacted except by bill. Bills may originate in either House, and may be amended or altered or rejected by the other.

Section 14. *Veto by the High Commissioner.* Every bill passed by the Congress shall, before it becomes a law, be presented to the High Commissioner. If the High Commissioner approves the bill, he shall sign it. If the High Commissioner disapproves the bill, he shall, except as hereinafter provided, return it, with his objections, to the Congress within ten consecutive calendar days after it shall have been presented to him. If the High Commissioner does not return the bill within such period, it shall be a law in like manner as if he had signed it, unless the Congress by adjournment prevents its return, in which case it shall be a law if signed by the High Commissioner within thirty days after it shall have been presented to him; otherwise it shall not be a law.

Not later than 14 months after a bill has been vetoed by the High Commissioner, it may be passed over his veto by a two-thirds majority of the entire membership of each House but may not be so repassed at the same session at which originally passed. A bill so repassed shall be re-presented to the High Commissioner for his approval. If he does not approve it within 20 days, he shall send it together with his comment thereon to the Secretary of the Interior. Within 90 days after its receipt by him, the Secretary of the Interior shall either approve or disapprove the bill. If he approves it, it shall become a law; otherwise it shall not.

If any bill presented to the High Commissioner shall contain several items of appropriation of money, he may object to one or more of such items, or any part or parts thereof, while approving the other items or parts of the bill. In such case he shall append to the bill, at the time of signing it, a statement of the item or items, part or parts thereof, to which he objects, and the item or items, part or parts thereof, so objected to shall have the effect of being vetoed.

Section 15. *Adjournment.* Neither House may adjourn for more than two consecutive days nor may either House adjourn *sine die* without the concurrence of the other House.

Section 16. *Publication of laws.* The High Commissioner shall make provision for publishing laws and resolutions within 30 days after the close of each session and for their distribution to public officials and sale to the public.

Section 17. *Procedure.*

(a) *Quorum.* A majority of the members of each House shall constitute a quorum of such House for the transaction of business. A smaller number may adjourn from day to day and may compel the attendance of absent members in such manner and under such penalties as each House may provide.

(b) *Reading of bills—Passage.* A bill in order to become a law shall pass two readings in each House, on separate days, the final passage of which in each House shall be by a majority vote of all the members present and voting, which vote shall be entered upon the journal.

(c) *Title.* Every legislative act shall embrace but one subject and matters properly connected therewith, which subject shall be expressed in the title; but if any subject shall be embraced in an act which shall not be expressed in the title, such an act shall be void only as to so much thereof as shall not be embraced in the title.

(d) *Certification of bills from one House to the other.* Every bill when passed by the House in which it originated, or in which amendments thereto shall have originated, shall immediately be certified by the presiding officer and sent to the other House for consideration.

(e) *Amendment and revisions by reference.* No law shall be amended or revised by reference to its title only; but in such case the act, as revised, or section or subsection as amended, shall be re-enacted and published at full length.

(f) *Language.* All legislative proceedings shall be conducted in the English language: *Provided,* That knowledge of the English language shall not be a qualification for membership in the Congress. Nothing herein shall limit the right of a member to use his native language if he lacks fluency in English, and the Congress shall provide for interpretation into English in such cases.

(g) *Journal.* Each House shall keep a journal of its proceedings, and publish the same in English.

(h) *Public sessions.* The business of the Congress, and of the Committee of the Whole, shall be transacted openly and not in secret session.

(i) *Procedural authority.* The Congress shall be the sole judge of the elections and qualifications of its members, shall have and exercise all the authority and attributes inherent in legislative assemblies, and shall have the power to institute and conduct investigations, issue subpoenas to witnesses and other parties concerned, and administer oaths.

Section 18. *Immunity.* No member of the Congress of Micronesia shall be held to answer before any tribunal other than the Congress for any speech or debate in the Congress, and the members shall in all cases, except treason, felony, or breach of the peace, be privileged from arrest during their attendance at the sessions of the Congress and in going to and from the same.

Section 19. *Compensation.* Each member of the Congress shall be paid $16 for each day the Congress is in session, regular or special. Each member shall also be paid $16 for each day during which he is engaged in official legislative business, when the Congress is not in session. Compensation at this daily rate shall be paid for each day the member is in a travel status to and from each session or while on other official legislative business. Travel shall be performed by the most expeditious and direct means. Compensation shall be paid for days when travel is delayed for reasons beyond the control of the member. Travel shall be arranged by the Trust Territory Government by the most direct and expeditious means, and travel expenses and per diem at the standard Trust Territory Government rates shall be allowed: *Provided,* That compensation, travel, and per diem shall not be allowed in excess of such amount as may be budgeted therefor.

Section 20. *Appointment to new offices.* No member of the Congress shall, during the term for which he was elected or during the year following the expiration of the term for which he was elected, be appointed to any office which was created by the Congress during such term.

Section 21. *Vacancies.* Whenever, prior to six months before the date of the next general election, a vacancy occurs, the High Commissioner shall call a special election to fill such vacancy. In case of a vacancy occurring within six months of the next general election, no special election shall be held and the District Administrator of the District wherein such vacancy arises may fill such vacancy by appointment.

Section 22. *Conversion into a unicameral body.* At its fifth regular session following the effective date of this order, the Congress shall convene in joint session to consider whether the bicameral legislature should be continued, or whether the legislature should be converted into a unicameral body. The final recommendation to the High Commissioner shall be adopted by a majority vote, and the recommendation shall be submitted to the High Commissioner and by him to the Secretary of the Interior.

Section 23. *Legislative Counsel.* Prior to the first regular session of the Congress of Micronesia, the High Commissioner shall designate a legislative counsel to assist and advise the Congress during that session. During the course of the first session, and biennially thereafter, the Congress may by joint resolution nominate a legislative counsel of its own choosing to serve the Congress during and between subsequent sessions, subject only to the High Commissioner's concurrence in the competency of the designated legislative counsel. Compensation for the legislative counsel shall be budgeted by the High Commissioner at a grade level equivalent to that of the highest grade Assistant Attorney General of the Trust Territory. The High Commissioner shall also make budgetary provision for such supporting staff for the legislative counsel as the Congress may request by joint resolution, and as the High Commissioner may deem necessary.

Section 24. *Amendment.* This order may be amended only by further order of the Secretary of the Interior. The Congress may, during any regular session, by a two-thirds majority vote of the membership of each House, recommend to the High Commissioner the amendment of any part of this order. The High Commissioner shall transmit such recommendation, together with his own recommendations thereon, to the Secretary of the Interior.

Section 25. *Existing laws.* All laws and regulations of the Trust Territory not inconsistent with the provisions of this order shall continue in effect until modified or repealed by competent authority.

Section 26. *Temporary extension of export and import duties.* Notwithstanding any other provision of this order, any District or municipal import and export duties in effect upon signature of this order may continue in effect until July 1, 1965, unless sooner reduced or repealed by the District Legislature or municipality concerned: *Provided,* That no such District or municipal import or export duty may be increased above its rate as of the date of signature of this order.

Section 27. *Effective date.* The provisions of this order shall become effective upon signature, with the first general elections to the Congress of Micronesia to be held on Tuesday, January 19, 1965, in accordance with such regulations as may be promulgated by the High Commissioner therefore: *Provided,* That subsequent general elections shall be held as provided in Section 9 of this order: *Provided, further,* That the terms of members elected to the first Congress of Micronesia shall commence February 16, 1965.

Section 28. *Prior orders.* Section 3 of Order No. 2876 is superseded, effective July 12, 1965, or effective on the date the Congress of Micronesia meets in special session, whichever first occurs. Provisions of other prior orders of the Department of the Interior, insofar as they are inconsistent with the provisions of this order, are hereby superseded.

/s/ STEWART L. UDALL
Secretary of the Interior
September 28, 1964

AMENDMENT NO. 1 TO ORDER NO. 2882

Subject: Legislative Authority for the Congress of Micronesia, Trust Territory of the Pacific Islands.

Whereas, on September 28, 1964, the Secretary of the Interior promulgated Secretarial Order No. 2882 creating the Congress of Micronesia and granting legislative authority thereto; and

Whereas, the said Order No. 2882 in Section 3 reserved to the Congress of Micronesia and the High Commissioner the levy of duties on goods imported into the Trust Territory; and

Whereas, Section 26 of the said Order No. 2882 temporarily extended until July 1, 1965, District and municipal import and export duties in effect on September 28, 1964; and

Whereas, such date of July 1, 1965, will not afford the Congress of Micronesia an opportunity to act prior to the expiration of District or municipal import or export levies; and

Whereas, certain revisions in Sections 5, 6 and 7 are also desirable so as to clarify the appropriation and legislative authority of the Congress of Micronesia and the apportionment of members among the several districts of the Trust Territory and the language relating to the qualifications of members;

Now, therefore, Secretarial Order No. 2882 is amended in the following particulars, the amendments to become effective July 1, 1965:

1. Section 26 of the said Order No. 2882 is hereby amended to read as follows:

"Section 26. *Temporary extension of export and import duties.* Notwithstanding any other provision of this order, any District or municipal import and export duties in effect upon signature of this order may continue in effect until October 1, 1965, unless sooner reduced or repealed by the District Legislature or municipality concerned; *Provided,* That no such District or municipal import or export duty may be increased above its rate as of the date of signature of this order."

2. Section 5 of the said Order No. 2882 is hereby amended to read as follows:

"Section 5. *Budget.* Money bills enacted by the Congress of Micronesia shall not provide for the appropriation of funds in excess of such amounts as are available from revenues raised pursuant to the tax laws and other revenue laws of the Trust Territory. Prior to his final submission to the Secretary of the Interior of requests for Federal funds necessary for the support of governmental functions in the Trust Territory, the High Commissioner shall prepare a preliminary budget plan. He shall submit such plan to the Congress of Micronesia in joint session for its review and recommendations with respect to such portions as relate to expenditures of funds proposed to be appropriated by the Congress of the United States. With respect to such portions of the preliminary budget plan, the High Commissioner shall adopt such recommendations of the Congress as he may deem appropriate, but he shall transmit to the Secretary of the Interior all recommendations he has not adopted."

3. The final paragraph of Section 6 of the said Order No. 2882 is hereby amended to read as follows:

"Election districts shall be reapportioned every 10 years on the basis of population, but each District (as described in Section 39 of the Trust Territory Code), shall be entitled to at least two Assemblymen. The first such reapportionment shall be made in 1971."

4. The final paragraph of Section 7 of the said Order No. 2882 is hereby amended to read as follows:

"No person who has been expelled from the Congress for giving or receiving a bribe or for being an accessory thereto, and no person who has been convicted of a felony by any court of the Trust Territory or any court with the jurisdiction of a district court of the United States, shall sit in the Congress unless the person so convicted has been pardoned and has had restored to him his civil rights."

/s/ JOHN A. CARVER, JR.
Acting Secretary of the Interior
June 10, 1965

AMENDMENT NO. 2 TO ORDER NO. 2882

Whereas, on September 28, 1964, the Secretary of the Interior promulgated Secretarial Order No. 2882 creating the Congress of Micronesia and granting legislative authority thereto; and

Whereas, Section 24 of the said Order No. 2882 provides that the Congress may recommend amendments to the Secretary of the Interior by a two-thirds majority vote of the membership of each House; and

Whereas, the Congress of Micronesia adopted Resolution No. 1–18 requesting that the "House of Delegates" be redesignated "Senate" and the "General Assembly" be redesignated "House of Representatives"; and

Whereas, revision of section 23 of the said Order No. 2882 is also desirable to clarify provisions relating to the compensation of the Legislative Counsel;

Now, therefore, Secretarial Order No. 2882 is amended in the following particulars, the amendments to become effective July 1, 1966:

1. Beginning July 1, 1966, the House of Delegates is redesignated the Senate and the General Assembly is redesignated the House of Representatives and wherever they appear in Order No. 2882 and Amendment No. 1 to Order No. 2882, the words "House of Delegates" and "General Assembly" shall be read as "Senate" and "House of Representatives," respectively, and the words "Delegates" and "Assemblymen" shall be read as "Senators" and "Representatives," respectively. This amendment shall not be so construed as to affect the seniority of any member of the Congress of Micronesia nor otherwise to affect the organization of the Congress of Micronesia.

2. Section 23 of the said Order No. 2882, as amended, is hereby amended to read as follows:

Section 23. *Legislative Counsel.* The Congress of Micronesia may by joint resolution nominate a legislative counsel of its own choosing to serve the Congress during and between sessions, subject only to the High Commissioner's concurrence in the competency of the designated legislative counsel. Salary for the legislative counsel shall be budgeted by the High Commissioner at a level comparable to the United States GS 12 level including those periodic step increases which would be available if the position were in fact a GS 12 position. Personnel benefits for the legislative counsel, including, but not necessarily limited to, annual and sick leave, shall be provided by the Congress of Micronesia: *Provided,* That such personnel benefits do not exceed those provided United States Government employees in the Trust Territory. The Congress of Micronesia may make budgetary provision for such supporting staff for the legislative counsel and the legislature as it may deem necessary.

/s/ STEWART L. UDALL
Secretary of the Interior
June 28, 1966

AMENDMENT NO. 3 TO ORDER NO. 2882

Subject: Legislative authority for the Congress of Micronesia, Trust Territory of the Pacific Islands.

Whereas, on September 23, 1964, the Secretary of Interior promulgated Secretarial Order No. 2882 creating the Congress of Micronesia and granting legislative authority thereto; and

Whereas, Section 24 of the said Order No. 2882 provides that the Congress may recommend amendments to the Secretary of the Interior by a two-thirds majority vote of the membership of each House; and

Whereas, the Congress of Micronesia adopted Senate Joint Resolution No. 43 requesting that Order No. 2882 be amended so as to require the passage of bills by the majority votes of all members of each House; and

Whereas, provision needs to be made for the conduct of biennial elections in the event a natural disaster or other Act of God should prevent balloting on the appointed day; and

Whereas, a further clarification of the appropriation power of the Congress appears to be desirable;

Now, therefore, Secretarial Order No. 2882 is amended in the following particulars, the amendment to become effective immediately:

1. Section 17(b) of the said Order No. 2882 is hereby amended to read as follows:

"Section 17(b). *Reading of bills—Passage.* A bill in order to become a law shall pass two readings in each House, on separate days, the final passage of which in each House shall be by a majority vote of all the members of each House, which vote shall be entered upon the journal."

2. Section 9 of said Order No. 2882 is hereby amended to read as follows:

"Section 9. *General elections.* General elections shall be held biennially in each even-numbered year on the first Tuesday following the first Monday in November: *Provided,* That in the event of a natural disaster or other Act of God, the effect of which precludes holding the election on the foregoing date, the High Commissioner, with the approval of the Secretary of the Interior, may proclaim a later election date in the affected election district or districts. All elections shall be held in accordance with such procedures as this order and the laws of the Trust Territory may prescribe. Legislators shall be chosen by secret ballot of the qualified electors of their respective district."

3. Section 5 of the said Order No. 2882 is hereby amended to read as follows:

"Section 5. *Budget.* Money bills enacted by the Congress of Micronesia shall not provide for the appropriation of funds in excess of such amount as are available from revenues raised pursuant to the tax laws and other revenue laws of the Trust Territory: *Provided,* That income derive from the provision of air and sea transportation services; reimbursements from public works sales and services; and income from the operation of water, power, sewerage and communications services shall be applied against the costs of providing those services and shall not be considered to be revenues within the meaning of this order. Prior to his final submission to the Secretary of the Interior of requests for Federal funds necessary for the support of governmental functions in the Trust Territory, the High Commissioner shall prepare a preliminary budget plan. He shall submit such plan to the Congress of Micronesia in joint session for its review and recommendations with respect to such portions as relate to expenditures of funds proposed to be appropriated by the Congress of the United States. With respect to such portions of the preliminary budget plan, the High Commissioner shall adopt such recommendations of the Congress as he may deem appropriate, but he shall transmit to the Secretary of the Interior all recommendations he has not adopted."

/s/ STEWART L. UDALL
Secretary of the Interior
July 29, 1967

Charters of District Legislatures

CHARTER OF THE
MARIANA ISLANDS DISTRICT LEGISLATURE
1963

PREAMBLE

Whereas, the people of Mariana Islands District of the Trust Territory of the Pacific Islands have expressed their desire for representation in the government of their district; and

Whereas, they selected and entrusted delegates to meet together in a Legislative Convention to draft a Charter for the establishment of a District Legislature; and

Whereas, the Congress of the United States of America has agreed by ratification on July 18, 1947, of the Trusteeship Agreement between the United States and the United Nations Security Council to promote the development of the Trust Territory of the Pacific Islands toward self-government;

Now, therefore, I, M. W. Goding, High Commissioner of the Trust Territory of the Pacific Islands, do hereby charter the people of Mariana Islands District to assemble a Legislature of their elected representatives to be known as the Mariana Islands District Legislature to assist in the government of the District in accordance with the laws of the Trust Territory of the Pacific Islands, and the provisions of this Charter.

ARTICLE I

Section 1. The legislative powers of Mariana Islands District herein granted by the High Commissioner of the Trust Territory of the Pacific Islands shall be vested in a unicameral house to be known as the Mariana Islands District Legislature.

Section 2. The Mariana Islands District Legislature, hereinafter referred to as the Legislature, shall be composed of sixteen (16) Representatives chosen every three years by the electors of the Mariana Islands District.

Section 3. There shall be four electoral precincts, as follows: The island of Rota; the island of Tinian; the island of Saipan; the islands north of Saipan. Apportionment of Representatives shall be as follows: Rota shall have three (3) Representatives; Tinian shall have one (1) Representative; Saipan shall have eleven (11) Representatives; the Northern Mariana Islands shall have one (1) Representative. If new municipalities are created the number of precincts and the apportionment of Representatives shall be changed by amendment to this Charter.

Section 4. Reapportionment on a population basis shall take place every five years, beginning in 1965. Regardless of population change, Rota shall have a minimum of three (3) Representatives; Tinian shall have a minimum of one (1) Representative; and the islands north of Saipan shall have a minimum of one (1) Representative.

Section 5. To be eligible for election or appointment, a person must be a citizen of the Trust Territory of the Pacific Islands, be a resident of his electoral precinct for a period of not less than two years immediately preceding his election, must be twenty-five (25) years of age or over; and must not be a convicted felon currently serving a sentence for that felony.

Section 6. No person may sit in the Legislature who holds an elective office in a municipal government or who holds a judicial office.

Section 7. Where a Representative is unable to perform the duties of his office due to physical or mental disability or death or who resigns or is impeached by the Legislature, another shall be appointed to fill the remainder of the term by the Chief Executive of his municipality. In the event a representative-elect is unable to assume office, there shall be a special election in his electoral precinct in order to choose another in his place.

Section 8. Election of Representatives shall be by secret ballot, and the Legislature shall set the time of election by law. Municipalities shall enact ordinances prescribing the manner and places of election, although the Legislature may change them at any time by law.

Section 9. The Legislature alone shall determine the qualifications of its members. The Legislature may by an affirmative three-fourths vote of its members impeach any member.

Section 10. Election of Representatives to the first Legislature shall be held within ninety (90) days of the approval of this Charter by the High Commissioner of the Trust Territory of the Pacific Islands.

Section 11. Communications and draft bills may be transmitted to the Legislature by the District Administrator for consideration by it.

Section 12. Municipal Ordinances shall have the full force and effect of law insofar as they are not in conflict with any law promulgated under provisions of this Charter. District Laws shall have the full force and effect of law insofar as they are not in conflict with the Trust Territory Code or Executive Orders of the High Commissioner.

Section 13. Qualifications of electors shall be as follows: Each shall be eighteen (18) years of age or over; a citizen of the Trust Territory of the Pacific Islands; have been a resident of his electoral precinct for a period of at least one year immediately preceding the election; not be serving a criminal sentence at the time of the election and be of sound mind.

ARTICLE II

Section 1. The Legislature shall convene twice a year in regular session on the first Monday of February and the first Monday in August. The first Legislature shall be convened at a date set by the District Administrator. The District Administrator may convene the Legislature into special session, whose proceedings shall be confined to the subjects stated in the District Administrator's convening call.

Section 2. The Legislature shall be considered as being continuously in session from the date convened, but no session of the Legislature shall exceed twenty (20) days. Sunday and holidays shall not be counted, otherwise, each day of the week shall be counted as one.

Section 3. At the first Legislature the District Administrator shall act as chairman and examine the credentials of each Representative-elect prior to convening the Legislature. Credentials shall be in the form of a statement from the Chief Executive of the municipalities presenting and authenticating the vote. There shall be an oath of office which the Chairman shall administer to each member individually. The Legislature shall then elect from its members a chairman who shall be called President. The Legislature may elect other officers as it desires.

Section 4. The Legislature, by a majority vote of its members, shall establish rules of procedure.

Section 5. Each member of the Legislature shall have one vote. An affirmative vote of a majority of the members present and voting, shall be required to pass a bill. Three-fourths of the members of the Legislature shall constitute a quorum.

Section 6. Any member may introduce a bill. Each bill introduced shall be read in its entirety before the Legislature two times on different days, before a vote shall be taken.

Section 7. Upon passage of a bill by the Legislature it shall be signed by the President of the Legislature and shall be called an Act of the Mariana Islands District Legislature.

Section 8. Each bill shall have an enacting clause as follows: Be it enacted by the Legislature of the Mariana Islands District, that, etc.

Section 9. Each enrolled bill shall be submitted to the District Administrator for approval. If he approves, he shall sign the bill and transmit it to the High Commissioner. If the High Commissioner takes no action within thirty (30) days after receiving the bill, it shall become law. If a bill is disapproved by the District Administrator, it must be done within fifteen (15) days after he receives it, otherwise it shall be considered approved. Bills disapproved by the District Administrator shall be returned to the Legislature with his objections. By a two-thirds affirmative vote the Legislature may submit the vetoed bill directly to the High Commissioner notifying the District Administrator of this action, and the High Commissioner shall take action within thirty (30) days after receiving the bill. If he does not, the bill shall be considered approved and shall become law. All approved bills shall be known as District Laws of the Mariana Islands District.

Section 10. The Legislature shall keep a journal of its proceedings and publish the same. Every enactment of the Legislature and the vote on any question shall be entered in the journal.

Section 11. The Members of the Legislature shall, in all cases except treason, felony or breach of the peace, be privileged from arrest during their attendance at the Legislature and going to and returning from the same. No member shall be held to answer before any tribunal other than the Legislature itself for any speech or debate in the Legislature.

ARTICLE III

Section 1. There shall be four standing committees—Hold-over, Political, Social, and Economic. Chairmen and members of the Political,

Social and Economic Committees shall be appointed by the President. The Chairmen shall, with the President, Secretary and District Treasurer constitute the Hold-over Committee. It shall meet as required when the Legislature is not in session to handle necessary matters. It shall also meet in advance of the regular sessions to plan an agenda for the Legislature. Agenda items as well as individual bills of members shall be given to the appropriate standing committee by the President for consideration. Items shall be reported out by the committees to the Legislature in written form as draft bills, resolutions, or recommendations.

Section 2. There shall be a Secretary who shall be appointed by the President with the approval of the Legislature. The duties of this office shall require that the Secretary be a full-time employee and he shall receive an annual salary with the amount to be decided by the Legislature. The person serving as Secretary shall remain in the position as long as his performance is satisfactory and shall not be subject to elections of the Legislature.

ARTICLE IV

Section 1. The Legislature shall have the power to levy and provide for the collection of taxes and fees.

ARTICLE V

Section 1. Compensation of the members of the Legislature and its employees shall be established by law.

ARTICLE VI

Section 1. Appropriation and expenditure of revenues produced under the authority of District Laws or whose allocation is the responsibility of the Legislature, shall be in accordance with the budget of the Legislature which shall be established by law.

ARTICLE VII

Section 1. Amendments to this Charter may be made upon an affirmative vote of three-fourths (¾) of the members of the Legislature and approved by the District Administrator and the High Commissioner, or by the High Commissioner on his own initiative. No amendments shall be made which shall deprive any municipality of its representation in the Legislature.

Given under my hand and seal this 7th day of January 1963 at Saipan, Mariana Islands.

/s/ M. W. GODING
High Commissioner
Trust Territory of the Pacific Islands

CONSTITUTION OF THE
CONGRESS OF THE MARSHALL ISLANDS

(Kwelok eo Elap)
1949
United States Navy—Governor of the Marshall Islands
Proclamation No. 1–1949

To the people of the Marshall Islands:

I, Cecil B. Gill, Captain, United States Navy, and Governor of the Marshall Islands, Trust Territory of the Pacific Islands, do hereby proclaim as follows:

ARTICLE I

The Congress of the Marshall Islands is hereby established as an advisory body to the Civil Administrator of the Marshall Islands District, to express the will of the Marshallese people on matters affecting the laws and government of the Marshall Islands.

ARTICLE II. COMPOSITION

Section 1. The Congress shall be composed of two Houses, designated as the House of Iroij and the House of Assembly, respectively.

Section 2. The House of Iroij shall be composed of all persons holding the position of paramount chief in accordance with the traditions, usages, and customs of the Marshallese people. The successor to a deceased or incapacitated paramount chief, recognized as that chief's proper and legal successor in accordance with Marshallese custom and tradition, shall automatically succeed to his predecessor's seat in the House of Iroij. In case of conflicting claims to paramount chieftainship, the Congress shall establish procedure for investigating the claims and for approving the proper succession.

Section 3. The House of Assembly shall be composed of a representative or representatives, of each municipality of the Marshall Islands District, each duly selected by the people of his municipality in accordance with established procedures. Each municipality shall have at least one representative; larger municipalities shall have additional representatives in proportion to their population, the exact number to be determined by a fixed ratio, to be set by the Congress from time to time and approved by the Civil Administrator.

Section 4. In case a member of the House of Iroij is elected to sit in the House of Assembly he shall be entitled to one vote only and that vote shall be cast in the House of Assembly.

ARTICLE III. CONVENING AND ADJOURNING

Section 1. The Congress shall convene each year on the fourth day of the month of July; unless the fourth day is a Sunday in which case the Congress shall convene on the fifth day, at the Civil Administration headquarters at Majuro, and at such other times and places as the Civil Administrator of the Marshall Islands District or the Congress itself may designate.

Section 2. When convened, the Congress shall continue in session until adjourned by common consent of both Houses. The Houses may recess, but not adjourn, independently. The Congress shall inform the Civil Administrator of the date of its adjournment.

ARTICLE IV. PROCEDURE

Section 1. Each House shall prescribe its own rules of procedure.

Section 2. At regular sessions of the Congress matters for consideration may be presented by members of either House, and by the Civil Administrator. A procedure shall be established whereby, insofar as possible, important items of the agenda shall be made known to members of the Congress prior to the convening of the Congress, to enable members to determine the consensus of their people on those matters.

Section 3. Upon calling the Congress into special session, the Civil Administrator shall prepare and deliver to a joint session of both Houses a written agenda of matters recommended for consideration. Additional topics for consideration may be added to the agenda by members of either House.

Section 4. The Congress may make recommendations in writing in the form of Resolutions to the Civil Administrator of the Marshall Islands District, passed by a majority of both Houses on any or all matters relating to the administration of the Marshall Islands. These matters may include, but are not limited to: local taxation, expenditure of local revenues, civil and criminal law, and regulation of shipping and commerce.

ARTICLE V. GENERAL PROVISIONS

Section 1. Compensation, and allowances for travel and subsistence of members of the Congress of the Marshall Islands during sessions of the Congress, will be as provided for by a Resolution or Resolutions passed by the Congress and approved by the Civil Administrator of the Marshall Islands District.

ARTICLE VI. EFFECTIVE DATE

This proclamation will become operative in each island or part thereof of the Marshall Islands on the date of its first publication.

Given under my hand at N.O.B. Kwajalein, M.I. this 17th day of November 1949.

/s/ CECIL B. GILL
Captain, United States Navy
Governor of the Marshall Islands
Trust Territory of the Pacific Islands

CONSTITUTION OF THE
MARSHALL ISLANDS CONGRESS
1958

Whereas, the Constitution which on the 17th of November 1949 established the Congress of the Marshall Islands as a body advisory to the Administration was executed to enable the Marshallese people to express their will in the government of their islands at a time when they had little or no knowledge of democratic processes of government; and

Whereas, that Congress, which has functioned continuously in accordance with its Constitution since that date, now expresses the desire of the Marshallese People for a more effective Constitution and a greater representation in their government;

Now, therefore, I, Delmas H. Nucker, High Commissioner of the Trust Territory of the Pacific Islands, having full confidence in the abilities of these people to exercise greater powers of government under our laws and provisions of this Constitution do hereby grant the Congress of the Marshall Islands those powers and authorities hereinafter set forth in accordance with the provisions hereof.

ARTICLE I. ORGANIZATION

Section 1. The Congress shall be constituted of a single assembly to be known as the Congress of the Marshall Islands.

ARTICLE II. MEMBERSHIP

Section 1. The membership of the Congress shall be composed of the Iroij Laplap and an elected Representative or Representatives from each of the Municipalities of the Marshall Islands Districts, who shall be known as Congressmen.

Section 2. Each Municipality shall be represented by at least one Representative. Municipalities having a population of more than 250, as determined by the last official census, shall elect one Representative for each 250 residents and one for any excess in population over an even multiple of 250.

Section 3. Representatives shall be elected to serve a term of two years.

Section 4. In order to qualify for membership in the Congress a candidate must be a citizen of the Trust Territory, at least twenty-five years of age and a resident of the Marshall Islands District for the five years immediately preceding his election.

Section 5. At the first session after this Constitution becomes effective, the Congress shall determine by majority vote those who shall be admitted to membership as Iroij Laplap who shall retain membership for life. Upon the death of an Iroij Laplap member, his heir may be admitted to membership upon majority vote of the Congress.

Section 6. Upon the election of a Representative, the Scribe of the Municipality from which he is elected shall forward to the Congress prior to the opening of the first session thereafter, a statement certifying the election and eligibility of the Representative. Certification of newly elected Representatives shall be reviewed by the Secretary of the Congress at the first meeting of each session and a Representative may be denied membership if disapproved by majority vote of the Congress, provided, that no duly elected and certified Representative may be denied admission as a member except for failure to qualify. No person may take the place of or be a substitute for a duly certified Representative to the Congress.

Section 7. In the event of the death or incapacitating illness of an elected Representative, the Council of the Municipality from which he was elected shall elect a successor to serve the remainder of his unexpired term and the successor shall be duly certified and admitted as provided in Section 6 of this Article.

Section 8. Congressmen may receive compensation or allowances for travel and subsistence involved in attending a session of Congress.

ARTICLE III. VOTING

Section 1. All duly qualified members of the Congress shall have equal rights to cast their vote. A duly qualified member acting as chairman shall not cast a vote except in the event of a tie vote of the voting members.

Section 2. The Secretary shall maintain a record of all votes cast which shall be made a part of the permanent records of the session.

ARTICLE IV. OFFICERS

Section 1. As the first order of business at each session, a duly admitted member, thirty years of age or more, shall be elected as President of the Congress to serve during that session and at the openings of the succeeding session until his successor is elected. In the event a President is not returned to Congress, the Vice-President, Secretary, or an elected Chairman, in that order, shall preside until a new President is elected. It shall be the duty of the President to preside at all meetings, to appoint officers and committees as herein provided and as provided in duly adopted rules of procedure, and to discharge such other duties as may be required of him by action of Congress.

Section 2. A duly admitted member, thirty years of age or more shall be elected at the first meeting of each session as Vice-President of the Congress to serve during that session and until his successor is elected.

Section 3. A Secretary and a Treasurer shall be appointed by the President with the approval of a majority vote of the Congress to serve such term and under such conditions as may be provided by majority vote of the Congress.

Section 4. A committee of twelve, to be known as the Hold-Over Committee, shall be appointed by the President at the close of each session to act until the close of the next succeeding session, which committee shall be empowered to complete the business of the past session of Congress and to prepare for the business of the next succeeding session. The Hold-Over Committee will not be empowered to initiate new issues except in the event of emergency that may result in jeopardy or catastrophe to the Marshallese people in which case they may act with the full authority of the Congress except that they shall not appropriate funds or expend funds except for the purpose for which they were duly appropriated by Congress. Appointments to the Hold-Over Committee shall not become effective until approved by the Congress.

ARTICLE V. MEETINGS

Section 1. The Congress shall convene during the month of August on a date set by the Hold-Over Committee.

Section 2. The Congress shall be adjourned by majority vote of the members.

Section 3. A quorum of two-thirds of the members shall be required to transact business.

ARTICLE VI. POWERS

Section 1. By Resolution, approved by the High Commissioner the Congress shall have the power to enact laws for the Marshall Islands District in accordance with Section 20, Trust Territory Code, amended, except those which are directly related to matters affecting customary rights on Land Tenure, or Land Rights, as between Iroij, Alab and Dri Jerbal, such disputes to be the province of the High Court only.

Section 2. Resolutions approved by the High Commissioner shall become effective when promulgated or as otherwise provided: Resolutions not approved or disapproved or otherwise acted upon by the High Commissioner within 180 days of the acceptance of an English translation thereof by the District Administrator shall become effective upon promulgation or as otherwise provided, except, that no act of the Congress amending or abrogating any provision of the Code of the Trust Territory, an Executive Order of the High Commissioner or a District Order shall become effective until approved by the High Commissioner.

Section 3. By Resolution, the Congress shall have the power to levy and collect taxes not in contravention to provisions of the Code of the Trust Territory, as amended, and to maintain and disburse funds as provided by Budget Resolution approved by the District Administrator, notwithstanding the provisions of Section 2 of this Article.

Section 4. The District Administrator shall cause each Resolution accorded the force and effect of law as provided herein to be promulgated as provided by law.

Section 5. Any Resolution accorded the force and effect of law shall control over any municipal ordinance.

Section 6. The Congress shall establish its own rules of procedure except as herein provided.

Section 7. The Treasurer shall maintain full records of all tax assessments, collections, and the appropriation and disbursement of funds. Fiscal and other records of the Congress shall be made available for audit by order of the Congress or the District Administrator upon demand. Funds shall be deposited with the Treasurer who shall be responsible for their care and disbursement in accordance with law; no disbursements shall be made except as authorized herein.

Section 8. Acts of Congress not having the force and effect of law may be addressed to the District Administrator or other persons within the District as Representations without reference to the High Commissioner.

ARTICLE VII. AMENDMENTS

Section 1. All Provisions of this Constitution shall remain in effect until amended by Resolution passed by two-third vote of the Congress or by Order of the High Commissioner.

ARTICLE VIII. EFFECTIVE DATE

Section 1. This Constitution of the Congress of the Marshall Islands shall become effective when adopted by majority vote of the Congress and approval of the High Commissioner.

Section 2. Upon approval of this Constitution by the High Commissioner, all provisions of the Constitution of the Congress of the Marshall Islands, otherwise known as Proclamation No. 1–49, given under the hand of the Governor of the Marshall Islands on the 17th day of November 1949, are hereby abrogated and terminated.

The foregoing has been approved by the Marshall Islands Congress. This Constitution will become effective at the next Session of the Congress. Dated 1st day of November 1958, at Majuro, Marshall Islands.

/s/ ATLAN ANIEN   /s/ AISEIA DAVID
/s/ ROBERT REIMERS   /s/ REWA SAMUEL
/s/ AJIDRIK BIEN   /s/ MIKE MADDISON
/s/ CARL DOMNICK   /s/ ABIJAI JOKLUR
/s/ ISAAC K. LANWI   /s/ KABUA KABUA
/s/ AMATA KABUA

Approved this 8th day of December 1958.

/s/ D. H. NUCKER
High Commissioner
Trust Territory of the Pacific Islands

PALAU COUNCIL
1948

Palau District Order No. 3–48

To the people of the Palau Islands:

ARTICLE I. FUNCTIONS

On July 1, 1948, a Palau Administrative Council shall be formed with the following functions:

Membership
  (1) High Chief of the Southern Palaus.
  (2) High Chief of the Northern Palaus.
  (3) Advisor to the Political Department.
  (4) Advisor for Legal.
  (5) Advisor for Finance.
  (6) Advisor for Public Safety.
  (7) Advisor for Labor and Agriculture.

(8) Advisor for Education.
(9) Advisor for Statistics.
(10) Advisor for Commerce.
(11) Advisor for Public Works.
(12) Advisor for Public Health.
(13) Advisor for Lands.
(14) Advisor for Administration.
(15) Such other members as the Civil Administrator may appoint.

The function of the Palau Council is purely advisory to the Civil Administrator. They will submit conclusions and recommendations on any matter submitted to them by the Civil Administrator. They are encouraged to originate and submit to the Civil Administrator any matters relative to Civil Administration. In other words, the Council is to keep its fingers on the pulse of the people and so inform the Civil Administrator on public opinion. The council may originate desired legislation and submit to the Palau Congress via Civil Administrator.

Sessions. The Palau Council shall be subject to call of the Civil Administrator. No dates for regular sessions will be set until such times as the need for them is indicated. Any member of the Council may request to the Civil Administrator that the Council be called into session, stating their reasons thereof.

Given under my hand this 17th day of June 1948.

/s/ C. M. HARDISON
Commander, U.S. Navy
Civil Administrator, Palau District

PALAU CONGRESS
1948

Palau District Order No. 4–48

To the people of the Palau Islands:

The composition, function and duties of the Palau Congress are as follows:

ARTICLE I. COMPOSITION

The Palau Congress shall be composed of the magistrate of each municipality and elected members from each municipality as follows:
One (1) member for 0 to 199 population.
Two (2) members for 200 to 499 population.
Three (3) members for 500 and over population.
The members must be indigenous to the municipality they represent, and will be elected for a term of two (2) years. In case of vacancy brought about by death or illness of a member, a special election will be held in the municipality concerned to fill the vacancy.

ARTICLE II. SESSIONS

The Palau Congress shall meet once a year, on the first Monday in

April and shall remain in session until the business before it is finished or a three-fourths majority vote adjourns it. The Congress can be called into extra session by the Civil Administrator and in such event, it will remain in session as long as the Civil Administrator deems it necessary.

ARTICLE III. FUNCTIONS

The function of the Palau Council is purely advisory to the Civil Ad-Administrator. It will be the duty of the Palau Congress to submit opinions and recommendations upon any matter brought before it by the Civil Administrator. The members of Congress may submit matters for opinion and recommendations to the assembled Congress.

The rules of procedure for the Congress will be published separately. This order effective 1 July 1948.

Given under my hand this 18th day of June 1948.

/s/ C. M. HARDISON
Commander, U.S. Navy
Civil Administrator, Palau District

PALAU DISTRICT ORDER NO. 1–49
1949

To the people of the Western Caroline Islands:

ARTICLE I. RULES FOR THE ELECTION OF CONGRESSMEN

1. Election of congressmen will be held by the municipality concerned within 10 days after the termination of Congress.
2. Elections will be conducted by an electoral assembly.
3. The Chief and the Magistrate (or Clerk, in municipalities where the Chief is Magistrate,) are charged with the proper conduct of elections.
4. Three days prior to the election day the Magistrate of the Municipality will publish the time and place of the electoral assembly.
5. All persons eligible to vote, except those physically unable, are urged to leave their daily tasks and be present at the electoral assembly.
6. An electoral assembly is duly and legally constituted if a majority of the electors are present.
7. The Chairman of the electoral assembly will be furnished by the Clerk of the Municipality concerned, a roster or registration list of eligible voters.
8. The Chairman of the electoral assembly will register the electors participating in the electoral assembly and make a report to the Civil Administration. This report will contain the following: Number of voters eligible to vote, number of voters present, names of nominees, number of votes cast for each nominee, name of person or persons elected.
9. It is prohibited to hold an election without the permission, in each case, of the Civil Administration.

10. Members of Congress will be elected from each municipality of the Palaus in the ratio of:

One member for up to 199 population.

Two members for 200 to 499 population.

Three members for 500 and above.

11. The Magistrate of a Municipality will automatically become a member of Congress over and above the ratio as shown in paragraph 10.

12. Each Palauan 26 years of age or older is hereby qualified to vote for or to be elected as a member of Congress except that:

(a) Persons must vote in the municipality where they maintain their legal residence.

(b) Persons elected must be legal residents of the municipality concerned.

(c) Persons imprisoned are hereby disqualified for the length of their term of imprisonment.

(d) Persons under probation are hereby disqualified for the length of their term of probation.

13. Members of Congress will be elected for a term of office of two years from the date of election.

14. If there is a session of Congress convened at the expiration of any Congressman's term of office the date of the new election will be postponed until the Congress has adjourned and the member will retain all his rights and prerogatives as a member of Congress until the postponed election can be held.

15. Each municipality is authorized to pay to its Congressmen an allowance of not more than $1.00 per day each day Congress is in session.

ARTICLE II. RULES FOR THE CONDUCT OF CONGRESSMEN

1. Congressmen shall attend all sessions of Congress.

2. Upon receiving notification of the convening of Congress, Congressmen shall be punctual in arriving on the date set.

3. In the case of temporary illness or other circumstances which would prevent a member from attending Congress, it is directed that the Civil Administrator be informed as soon as possible.

4. In the case of permanent illness or inability of a member to attend Congress, Civil Administrator will appoint a member to fill the unexpired term of office of the Congressman concerned or until an election can be held.

5. The President of the Congress will be elected at the beginning of each annual meeting of Congress. If a special session of Congress is called the President of the last regular session will preside. The President of the last regular session will preside at the opening of the new Congress and will, as the first matter of business before the Congress, hold the election of the new President of Congress. The President of the Congress may be reelected.

6. The President of the Congress is charged with the following:

(a) He will open and close the sessions.

(b) He will moderate the discussions.

(c) He will appoint the Secretary of Congress; said Secretary will not be a member of Congress.

(d) He will keep order in the Congress. In this duty he is empowered to order the removal of any person who will not keep order; he may order the spectators cleared from the Congress if they do not keep order.

(e) He may, with the consent of the Congress, limit the discussion on matters brought before the Congress, or, he may declare out of order, discussion which has no bearing on the matter before the Congress.

(f) He may summon such advisors as he deems necessary for advice or explanation of matters before the Congress. He may not disregard a request from the Congressman for summoning of such advisors.

(g) He may not submit any opinions or enter into the discussion of the matter before the Congress except to introduce said matter for discussion.

(h) He may not vote on any matter before the Congress except to break a tie vote.

(i) If a motion to introduce new matter for discussion is brought to the floor while another matter is already under discussion, he will not close such discussion without the consent of the Congress.

(j) He will present the record of the business of the Congress to the Civil Administrator.

7. If the President is unable to sit as President a new President will be elected, for the time being.

8. The Secretary of the Congress is charged with the following:

(a) He will keep the record of the proceedings. In this duty he is allowed to appoint assistants as he deems necessary.

(b) He will call the roll at each session.

(c) He will record the results of all voting of the Congress and enter them in the proceedings.

(d) He will assign a serial number to all matters introduced into the Congress. Such serial numbers will show the number of the documents and the year and session of the Congress. This may be in the form of the following examples: 1–48, regular session, or; 12–48, 2nd special session.

9. All matters to be brought before the attention of Congress, whether introduced by the Civil Administrator or a member of the Congress, will be submitted to the President of the Congress on the first day of the Congress or as soon thereafter as may be practicable. The President of the Congress will then give them to the Secretary of the Congress to be numbered and placed on the agenda for discussion. All bills must be placed on the agenda except as otherwise ordered by the Civil Administrator.

10. All bills submitted to the Congress will be forwarded to the Civil Administrator with the record of the voting and discussion.

11. Each Congressman will cast his own vote and all votes will be counted equally.

12. The Civil Administrator may close Congress at any time.

13. Sessions of the Congress are open to the public.

14. Congress is empowered only to render opinions and make recommendations to the Civil Administrator.

15. The Civil Administrator is not required to follow the opinions and recommendations of the Congress; however, he will, in all cases, take account of such opinions and recommendations.

16. Recommendations once approved by the Congress and the Civil Administrator will then become effective upon publication and posting of the various municipalities.

17. The Civil Administrator reserves the right to modify, change, or retract any of the rules in this order at any time.

ARTICLE III

The rules given in Article I, Section 12, shall apply to elections, for municipal officials or to any issue that requires a vote in the municipality.

District Order No. 8–48 is hereby cancelled.

Given under my hand at Koror, Palau Islands, this 12th day of January 1949.

/s/ C. M. HARDISON
Commander, U.S. Navy
Civil Administrator, Palau Islands

CHARTER OF THE
OLBIIL ERA KELULAU ERA BELAU
1955

Whereas, the Palau Congress was inaugurated on July 4, 1947, under the authority of the Military Government of the United States of America to act as a body of advisors to the Military Government of the Palau District; and

Whereas, the Palau Congress has met annually in regular sessions since its inauguration; and

Whereas, the people of the Palau District of the Trust Territory of the Pacific Islands have stated their desire for representation in the government of their district; and

Whereas, the Congress of the United States of America has agreed by ratification on July 18, 1947, of the Trusteeship Agreement between the United States and the United Nations Security Council to promote the development of the inhabitants of the Trust Territory of the Pacific Islands toward self-government;

Now, therefore, I, Delmas H. Nucker, Deputy High Commissioner of the Trust Territory of the Pacific Islands, do hereby charter the people of the Palau District of the Trust Territory of the Pacific Islands to convene a Congress which shall be known as the Olbiil Era Kelulau Era Belau, hereinafter referred to in this document as the Olbiil Era Kelulau, to advise the District Administrator, and otherwise aid in the government of their District as hereinafter provided.

ARTICLE I. MEMBERSHIP

Section 1. The Olbiil Era Kelulau shall be composed of the two High Chiefs of North and South Palau, and of the magistrate, the recognized paramount hereditary chief, and the duly elected representative or representatives of each municipality of the Palau District, these elected representatives to be hereinafter referred to as Chadal Olbiil.

Section 2. The secretary of each municipality shall certify each newly elected or appointed member of the Olbiil Era Kelulau from his municipality for eligibility and shall so inform the secretary of the Olbiil Era Kelulau prior to the opening of each session of that body.

Section 3. Members of the Olbiil Era Kelulau may receive compensations and allowances for travel and subsistence as may be determined by each municipality.

ARTICLE II. REPRESENTATION IN CHADAL OLBIIL

Section 1. Each municipality shall hold elections for Chadal Olbiil at least every two years.

Section 2. Each municipality shall elect one but not more than five Chadal Olbiil provided, that if the population as determined by the last official census preceding election is less than 200 it shall elect one Chadal Olbiil; that if the population exceeds 199 but not 499 it shall elect two Chadal Olbiil; and that if the municipal population exceeds 499 it shall elect one additional Chadal Olbiil for each additional 500 population or fraction thereof.

Section 3. Any citizen of the Trust Territory is eligible for membership in the Chadal Olbiil, regardless of sex, provided that he has attained the age of twenty-six years prior to the date of election; and that he has been a resident of the Palau District for more than three years prior to the date of election; and that he has been a resident of the municipality which he is to represent for the year immediately preceding his election; and that he has been elected by vote of the electorate of that municipality; and that he continue to be a permanent resident of the municipal district from which he was elected for the period of his term in office.

Section 4. An Chadal Olbiil shall serve for a term of two years following the date of his election, unless he is removed from office as hereinafter provided, or until such a time as his successor is elected or appointed.

ARTICLE III. OFFICERS

Section 1. A member of the Olbiil Era Kelulau shall be elected president, to be known as Bedul Olbiil, by majority vote of that body at the beginning of each April session. He shall serve until the qualification of his successor, unless he is removed from office or dies in office, in which case a new president shall be elected to complete his term.

Section 2. The Bedul Olbiil shall be assisted by a secretary, whom he shall appoint with the approval of the Olbiil Era Kelulau.

Section 3. The Bedul Olbiil, shall be assisted by a body of advisors to be known as Tebechelel Olbiil; he shall appoint the Tebechelel Olbiil with the approval of the Olbiil Era Kelulau.

ARTICLE IV. MEMBERSHIP VACANCIES

Section 1. Upon the death or ineligibility of a duly elected Chadal Olbiil, a substitute shall be appointed by the municipal council to represent the municipality for the remainder of the term of office so vacated.

Section 2. In the event that a duly elected Chadal Olbiil or a magistrate is unable to attend a session of the Olbiil Era Kelulau, a substitute may be appointed by the municipal council to represent the municipality for that session.

Section 3. An Chadal Olbiil may be removed for cause by the District Administrator or by petition of two-thirds of the electorate of his municipality and a substitute shall be appointed by his municipal council to fill the unexpired term in office.

Section 4. After certification by their municipal secretary, appointees to the Olbiil Era Kelulau under the provisions of Sections 1, 2, and 3 of this Article shall in all ways be considered members of the Olbiil Era Kelulau with all of the powers of those whom they are appointed to replace.

Section 5. In the event that the paramount hereditary chief of a municipality or either of the two High Chiefs is unable to attend a session of Olbiil Era Kelulau, he may designate a substitute who shall have all the powers that he himself could exercise if present. In cases where a paramount chief is unable to confer such appointment, his chief's council may act in his stead. The council will certify such appointment and will so inform the secretary of the Olbiil Era Kelulau prior to the opening of its next session.

ARTICLE V. POWERS

Section 1. The Olbiil Era Kelulau shall have the power of resolution upon any subject, including but not limited to those herein specifically mentioned.

Section 2. The Olbiil Era Kelulau shall determine its own rules and procedures, provided that they do not contravene any provisions of this charter, and may choose any officers or employees it deems desirable in addition to those herein provided.

Section 3. The Olbiil Era Kelulau is hereby empowered to receive and administer real and personal property, including that which was formerly acquired or held by the Congress authorized and existing pursuant to District Order 1–49.

Section 4. The Olbiil Era Kelulau shall have the power by resolution to levy and provide for the collection of taxes and fees.

Section 5. The Olbiil Era Kelulau shall have the power to disburse funds in accordance with resolutions.

ARTICLE VI. MEETINGS

Section 1. The Olbiil Era Kelulau shall meet as a single body, convened in regular session during April and October at dates to be fixed by that body prior to the close of the previous session.

Section 2. The Olbiil Era Kelulau may be convened in special session by the Bedul Olbiil or by petition of one-third of its membership.

Section 3. Any session of the Olbiil Era Kelulau shall be adjourned by majority vote.

Section 4. A quorum to do business shall consist of two-thirds of the Chadal Olbiil and two-thirds of the membership not eligible to vote on resolutions.

ARTICLE VII. VOTING

Section 1. All members of the Olbiil Era Kelulau shall have equal rights and privileges, except as hereinafter provided.

Section 2. All members of the Olbiil Era Kelulau shall have the right to propose resolutions and to vote on all matters except resolutions. The Chadal Olbiil alone shall have the right to vote on resolutions, each Chadal Olbiil having a single vote. Magistrates, paramount hereditary chiefs, and the two High Chiefs of North and South Palau may vote on resolutions only if they are also elected Chadal Olbiil.

Section 3. Any matter, in order to be expressed as a resolution of the Olbiil Era Kelulau, shall require a two-thirds majority vote of the Chadal Olbiil present and voting.

Section 4. The secretary of the Olbiil Era Kelulau shall maintain a record of all sessions of that body and forward a copy thereof in Palauan or in English as the body may determine, to the District Administrator.

Section 5. Resolutions adopted by the Olbiil Era Kelulau shall be signed by the Bedul Olbiil and the secretary and submitted to the District Administrator.

Section 6. Resolutions will be approved or disapproved by the High Commissioner within a period of one hundred and eighty days from the date of acceptance by the District Administrator of an English translation thereof; if the High Commissioner fails to approve or disapprove any resolution before the expiration of the one hundred and eighty day period, the resolution shall be considered approved, providing it does not conflict with any provision of the Trust Territory Code or an existing District Order.

Section 7. The District Administrator shall cause to be filed with the Clerk of Courts of the Palau District a copy of each resolution accorded the force and effect of law together with copies of all action thereon.

Section 8. Any resolution so approved or considered approved in accordance with Section 6 above, shall have control over any municipal enactment.

Section 9. Questions may be submitted to the Bedul Olbiil by the District Administrator for consideration by the Olbiil Era Kelulau.

ARTICLE VIII. AMENDMENTS

Section 1. All provisions of this charter shall continue in force until amended by resolution of the Olbiil Era Kelulau or by order of the High Commissioner.

ARTICLE IX. EFFECTIVE DATE

Section 1. The effective date of this charter shall be the 5th day of January 1955.

Section 2. Approval is hereby granted for a District Order rescinding Palau District Order 1–49 effective on the same date as this charter.

Given under My Hand and Seal this 5th Day of January, 1955.

/s/ DELMAS H. NUCKER
Deputy High Commissioner of the
Trust Territory of the Pacific Islands

CHARTER OF THE
PALAU DISTRICT LEGISLATURE
1963

PREAMBLE

Whereas, the Olbiil Era Kelulau Era Belau was established under the provisions of the Charter granted January 5, 1955 by the High Commissioner of the Trust Territory of the Pacific Islands, in order to provide a representative legislative body for the people of Palau District; and

Whereas, the elected representatives of Palau District, meeting as the Olbiil Era Kelulau Era Belau, pursuant to the terms of that Charter, on April 9, 1963 by unanimous vote requested that the Charter be replaced by a revised one, provisions of which they recommended;

Now, therefore, I, M. W. GODING, High Commissioner of the Trust Territory of the Pacific Islands, hereby rescind the Charter of January 5, 1955 and grant to the people of Palau District this present Charter, giving them the right, in accordance with its provisions, to participate, through the Palau Legislature in the government of Palau District. The Palau Legislature is the successor in all respects and in every way, and in accordance with this Charter, to the Olbiil Era Kelulau Era Belau.

ARTICLE I

Section 1. The legislative powers of the Palau District herein granted by the High Commissioner of the Trust Territory of the Pacific Islands shall be vested in a single house to be known as the Palau Legislature.

Section 2. The Palau Legislature, hereinafter referred to as the Legislature, shall be composed of twenty-eight (28) legislators elected every four years by the electors of the Palau District, the Aibedul and the Reklai and the recognized paramount hereditary chief of each municipality. Only elected members may vote and hold office in this body.

Section 3. The first elections for legislators under the newly amended charter shall be held within two months after the approval of this amendment.

ARTICLE II

Section 1. There shall be sixteen electoral precincts, as follows: Aimeliik, Airai, Angaur, Kayangel, Koror, Melekeiok, Ngaraard, Ngarhelong, Ngardmau, Ngaremlengui, Ngatpang, Nghesar, Ngiwal, Peleliu, Sonsorol and Tobi.

Apportionment of legislators shall be as follows:

There shall be five legislators elected at large;

Koror shall have five legislators;

Ngaraard, Ngarhelong, and Peleliu shall each have two legislators;

Aimeliik, Airai, Angaur, Kayangel, Melekeiok, Ngardmau, Ngaremlengui, Ngatpang, Nghesar, Ngiwal, Sonsorol and Tobi shall each have one legislator.

Section 2. Reapportionment on a population basis shall take place every ten years, beginning in 1970. Regardless of population change, each municipality shall be guaranteed at least one legislator.

Section 3. To be eligible for election or appointment, a person must be a citizen of the Trust Territory of the Pacific Islands, have resided in Palau for a three-year period immediately preceding his election, be a resident of his electoral precinct for a period of not less than one year immediately preceding his election, must be twenty-five (25) years of age or over; and must never have been convicted of a felony.

Section 4. Where a legislator is unable to perform the duties of his office due to physical or mental disability or death or who resigns or is impeached by the Legislature, another shall be appointed to fill the remainder of the term by the Chief Executive of his municipality who shall select the replacement from a list of three persons nominated by the Municipal Council. In the event a legislator-elect, other than an at-large, is unable to assume office, there shall be a special election in his electoral precinct in order to chcose another in his place. In the case of an at-large legislator who is unable to assume office or who is unable to attend a session of the Legislature, a substitute shall be appointed by the District Administrator from the roster of candidates in the preceding general election.

ARTICLE III

Section 1. No person may sit in the Legislature who holds an elective public office in a municipal government.

Section 2. The Legislature alone shall determine the qualifications of its members. The Legislature may by an affirmative three-fourths vote of its members impeach any member. A legislator may be recalled by a majority vote of the registered electors in his precinct.

Section 3. Qualifications of electors shall be as follows: Each shall be eighteen (18) years of age or over; a citizen of the Trust Territory of the Pacific Islands; has been a resident of his electoral precinct for a period of at least six months immediately preceding the election; not be serving a criminal sentence at the time of the election.

ARTICLE IV

Section 1. The Legislature shall convene twice a year in regular session on the first Tuesday of April and the first Tuesday in October if possible. The District Administrator may convene the Legislature into special session, whose proceedings shall be confined to the subjects stated in the District Administrator's convening call. The Legislature may also be convened by petition of one-third of its members.

Section 2. Each legislator shall present credentials which shall be in the form of a statement from the Chief Executive of his municipality authenticating his election. There shall be an oath of office which the Speaker shall administer to each elected member individually. The Legislature shall organize annually at the beginning of each April Session selecting a Speaker and Vice-Speaker.

Section 3. The Legislature, by a majority vote of its members, shall establish standing rules of procedure.

Section 4. An affirmative vote of a majority of the members present shall be required to pass a measure. Three-fourths of the members of the Legislature shall constitute a quorum.

Section 5. Any member may introduce a measure. Measures introduced shall be read before the Legislature two times on different days, before a vote may be taken.

Section 6. Communications and draft measures may be transmitted to the Legislature by the District Administrator for consideration by it.

Section 7. Upon passage of a measure by the Legislature it shall be signed by the Speaker.

Section 8. Each bill shall have an enacting clause as follows: Be it enacted by the Palau Legislature, that, etc.

Section 9. Each act shall be submitted to the District Administrator. If he approves the act he shall sign it and transmit it promptly to the High Commissioner. If the High Commissioner takes no action within sixty (60) days after receipt, it shall become law. If the District Administrator takes no action within twenty-one (21) days after receipt the act shall be considered approved, and the District Administrator shall immediately send the Act to the High Commissioner. In cases where, in the opinion of the District Administrator, the approval or veto of an act will require consultation with the High Commissioner, the District Administrator shall so inform the Speaker, in writing, in which case the District Administrator shall have an additional thirty (30) days in which to take action. Acts vetoed by the District Administrator shall be returned to the Legislature with his objections. By a three-fourths affirmative vote the Legislature may submit the vetoed act to the High Commissioner through the District Administrator and the High Commissioner shall act within sixty (60) days after receiving the act. If he takes no action the act shall be considered approved and shall become law. All approved acts shall be known as Public Laws of Palau.

Section 10. The District Administrator and/or the High Commissioner shall have authority to exercise item veto on revenue and appropriations bills.

Section 11. The Legislature shall keep a journal of its proceedings and publish the same.

Section 12. Members of the Legislature shall, in all cases except felony or breach of the peace, be privileged from arrest during their attendance at the Legislature and in going to and returning from the same. No member shall be held to answer before any tribunal other than the Legislature itself for any speech or debate in the Legislature.

Section 13. As incidents of its legislative authority, the Legislature may conduct investigations, hold public hearings, subpoena witnesses and documents and administer oaths.

ARTICLE V

Section 1. There shall be four standing committes: Political, Social, Economic and Appropriations. Chairman and Members of the committees shall be appointed by the Speaker. Measures introduced by legislators shall be assigned to the appropriate committee by the Speaker. Measures reported out by committee shall be in written form either as bills, resolutions, or memorials. Measures shall be numbered and placed on a calendar in the order in which they are reported out.

ARTICLE VI

Section 1. The Legislature shall have the power to levy taxes and grant licenses and appropriate funds.

ARTICLE VII

Section 1. Compensation of the members of the Legislature and its employees shall be established by law.

ARTICLE VIII

Section 1. Amendments to this Charter may be made upon an affirmative vote of three-fourths of the members of the Legislature and approved by the District Administrator and the High Commissioner, or by the High Commissioner on his own initiative.

Given under my hand and seal this 25th day of July 1963.

/s/ M. W. GODING
High Commissioner
Trust Territory of the Pacific Islands

CHARTER OF THE
CONGRESS FOR THE ISLAND OF PONAPE
1952

Whereas, the representatives of the people of the Island of Ponape in the Trust Territory of the Pacific Islands have stated their desire for a

Congress to express the will of the people in the government of their island; and

Whereas, the United States of America has agreed, by ratification of the Trusteeship Agreement for the former Japanese Mandated Islands, to promote the development of the inhabitants of the Trust Territory of the Pacific Islands toward self-government;

Now, therefore, I, Elbert D. Thomas, High Commissioner of the Trust Territory of the Pacific Islands, do hereby charter the people of the Island of Ponape, Trust Territory of the Pacific Islands, to convene a Congress to assist in the government of their islands as hereinafter provided:

Section 1. *Establishment.* The Ponape Island Congress is established to express the will of the people in matters of law and government in the Island of Ponape and to act in an advisory capacity to the District Administrator, Ponape District.

Section 2. *Composition.* The Ponape Island Congress shall be composed of two Houses, the Nobles' House, and the People's House.

Section 3. *The Nobles' House, Composition.* The Nobles' House shall be composed of not more than five Nobles from each of the five *wehy* of the Island of Ponape: Net, Uh, Jokaj, Metalanim, and Kiti. The Nanmarki, Wasai, Naniken, and Nalaim of each *wehy* of Ponape Island shall be representatives for their *wehy* in the Nobles' House. The Nanmarki and the Naniken of each *wehy* shall jointly appoint to the Nobles' House one high ranking title holder outside the Nanmarki and Naniken lines. The Nobles' House shall provide the District Administrator with a record of all persons eligible for membership in the Nobles' House.

Section 4. *The People's House, Composition.* The People's House shall be composed of a representative, or representatives, from each municipality of the Island of Ponape. Each municipality shall elect by secret ballot on the basis of universal and equal suffrage of adult citizens, one representative to the People's House for each three hundred inhabitants, or fraction thereof, of the municipality as determined by the last official census taken by the District Administrator. Persons holding the rank of Nanmarki, Wasai, Naniken, and Nalaim may not be elected to membership in the People's House. All other Nobles are eligible for election to the People's House, but may not hold concurrent office in both houses.

Section 5. *Representation for Out-Island Colonies.* Either House may seat as non-voting delegates one representative from each colony of residents from other islands than Ponape. A majority vote by the members of the House concerned is required to seat any of these delegates.

Section 6. *Regular and Special Meetings.* The Ponape Island Congress shall convene in regular session on the second Tuesday of each May and November at Kolonia, or in special session at such other times or places as the Congress or the District Administrator may designate. When duly convened the Congress shall remain in session until adjourned by consent of both Houses.

Section 7. *General Rules of Procedure.* Each House shall prescribe its own rules of procedure.

Section 8. *Procedure, Presentation of Proposals, Resolutions.* At all sessions of the Congress matters for the consideration of either House may be presented as a Proposal by any member of that House or by the District Administrator. A Proposal, upon approval by a majority of the House, shall be passed as a Resolution of that House for consideration by the other House. A Resolution that has been adopted by a majority vote of both Houses shall be presented to the District Administrator as a Resolution of the Congress. A Resolution that fails to gain the approval of a majority of the second House considering it, upon two-thirds vote of the originating House, may be presented to the District Administrator as a Resolution of that House.

Section 9. *Resolutions, Presentation.* Resolutions presented to the District Administrator shall be in writing and shall be signed by the Chairman of the House presenting the Resolution or, in the case of a Resolution of the Congress, shall be signed by the Chairman of each House. Copies of all Resolutions will be furnished the High Commissioner.

Section 10. *Qualification of Members, Age.* No person shall become a member of the Ponape District Congress who is not at least twenty-five (25) years of age.

Section 11. *Qualification of Members, Residence.* No person shall represent a Municipality or a *wehy* who has not lived continuously in the Municipality or *wehy* for the three (3) years immediately preceding his election.

Given under my hand this 14th day of May 1952.

/s/ ELBERT D. THOMAS
High Commissioner
Trust Territory of the Pacific Islands

PONAPE DISTRICT CONGRESS CHARTER
1958

PREAMBLE

Whereas, the people of Ponape District of the Trust Territory of the Pacific Islands have expressed their desire for representation in the government of their district; and

Whereas, they selected and entrusted delegates from their municipalities to meet together in a Congressional Convention to draft a charter for the establishment of a district congress; and

Whereas, the Congress of the United States of America has agreed by ratification on July 18, 1947, of the Trusteeship Agreement between the United States and the United Nations Security Council to promote the development of the inhabitants of the Trust Territory of the Pacific Islands toward self-government;

Now, therefore, I, Delmas H. Nucker, High Commissioner of the Trust Territory of the Pacific Islands, do hereby charter the people of Ponape District to assemble a Congress of their elected representatives to be known as the Ponape District Congress to assist in the government of the district in accordance with the laws of the Trust Territory and the provisions of this charter.

Section 1. The legislative powers of Ponape District herein granted by the High Commissioner of the Trust Territory of the Pacific Islands shall be vested in a unicameral house to be known as Ponape District Congress.

Section 2. The Ponape District Congress, hereinafter referred to as Congress, shall be composed of representatives chosen every four years by the electors of the municipalities of Ponape District. The qualifications of electors shall be as Congress shall establish by law.

Section 3. Municipalities with less than four hundred population shall have at least one representative. Other municipalities shall be allotted one representative for each four hundred people. Those municipalities having an excess of at least two hundred people over multiples of four hundred shall be allowed one additional representative. Congress may by law increase the ratio of one representative for each four hundred people, but may not deprive any municipality of having at least one representative.

Section 4. Apportionment of representatives among the municipalities shall be in accordance with the official municipal census report as of June 1958, whereby Kusaie Municipality shall elect six; Madolenihmw Municipality, six; Kitii Municipality, five; Net Municipality (including Kolonia Town), five; Sokehs Municipality, five; Uh Municipality, three; Kapingamarangi Municipality, one; Mokil Municipality, one; Ngatik Municipality, one; Nukuoro Municipality, one; and Pingelap Municipality, one.

Section 5. Reapportionment of representatives shall be made in 1960, then every five years thereafter.

Section 6. No person shall be elected as a representative who is not a citizen of the Trust Territory of the Pacific Islands; is not a resident of the municipality at the time of his election; and has not reached twenty-five years of age; or has been convicted of a felony.

Section 7. Where a representative is removed from office by death, resignation, disability, or by action of Congress, another shall be appointed to fill the remainder of the term by the Chief Magistrate of the municipality, with the approval of the Municipal Council. In the event a representative-elect is unable to assume office, then there shall be a special election in the municipality in order to choose another in his place. Any person who assumes office as a representative under this Section shall not be exempted from the provisions of Section 6.

Section 8. Election of representatives shall be by secret ballot, and Congress shall set the time of election by law. Municipalities shall enact ordinances prescribing the manner and places of election, although Congress may change them at any time by law.

Section 9. Congress alone shall determine the qualifications and judge elections of its members. Congress may by a three-fourths vote expel any member or refuse to seat any representative-elect.

Section 10. Representatives to the first Congress shall be divided into two groups, one-half of whom shall hold their office for two years and the other half for four years; thereafter all representatives shall be chosen for four years. Congress shall maintain at all times the division whereby the term of offices shall expire every two years for one-half of the members of Congress. Unless otherwise changed by Congress the division of offices shall be as provided with the convening of the first Congress, whereby representatives holding their offices for two years shall be in accordance with the following schedule: Kapingamarangi, one; Ngatik, one; Mokil, one; Uh, one; Kusaie, three; Madolenihmw, three; Kiti, two; Sokehs, two, and Net, three.

Section 11. Election of representatives to the first Congress shall be held within ninety days of the approval of this Charter by the High Commissioner.

ARTICLE II

Section 1. Congress shall convene twice a year in regular session during March and September at dates to be fixed by Congress prior to close of the previous session; provided, however, that the first Congress shall be convened in September 1958 at a date set by the District Administrator.

Section 2. Congress shall be considered as being continuously in session from the date convened, but no session of Congress shall exceed twenty days. Sundays shall not be counted, otherwise, each day of the week shall be counted as one.

Section 3. The first Congress shall be called into session upon the approval of this Charter by the High Commissioner. The District Administrator shall act as chairman and examine the credentials of each representative-elect prior to calling the initial Congress together. Credentials shall be in the form of a statement from the Chief Magistrates of the municipalities presenting the votes cast for all candidates. Congress as its first order of business shall elect from its members a chairman who shall be called President. Congress may elect other officers as it desires. Hereafter all credentials of representatives-elect shall be presented to the President and examined by Congress as its first order of business of each regular session. No person may take the place of or be a substitute for a duly elected representative to Congress.

Section 4. Congress, by a majority vote of its members, shall establish its own rules of procedure not otherwise specified in this Charter.

Section 5. Each member of Congress shall have one vote. A majority of the members of Congress shall be required to pass a bill. Three-fourths of the members of Congress shall constitute a quorum.

Section 6. Any member may introduce a bill. Each bill introduced shall be read in its entirety before Congress, and Congress shall determine by a vote of the majority whether to accept it for deliberation or reject it. Any bill not rejected shall pass to the Legislative Committee for drafting and shall be submitted to Congress for consideration at the next regular session. Congress may by a two-thirds vote of its members consider any bill during the session at which it was introduced.

Section 7. Upon passage of a bill by Congress it shall be forwarded to the District Administrator as a Ponape District Congress Resolution and shall be signed by the President of Congress.

Section 8. All resolutions shall become law of Ponape District upon approval by the High Commissioner and shall become effective sixty days thereafter, unless otherwise specified therein. The District Administrator shall cause to be posted an English copy and a translation of all resolutions in the municipalities of the district and a copy filed with the Clerk of Courts along with the translation. Any resolution described herein returned by the High Commissioner as disapproved shall not become law of Ponape District.

Section 9. Any resolution upon which the High Commissioner has not taken action within one hundred eighty days from the date of acceptance by the District Administrator of an English translation thereof, shall be considered as having his approval and shall become law of Ponape District as provided for in Section 8 of Article II of this Charter.

Section 10. Questions may be submitted to Congress by the District Administrator for consideration by Congress.

Section 11. Municipal Ordinances shall have the full force and effect of law insofar as they are not in conflict with any law promulgated under the provisions of this Charter. District laws shall have the full force and effect of law insofar as they are not in conflict with the Trust Territory Code or any laws or regulations promulgated by the High Commissioner by Executive Orders.

Section 12. The District Administrator may convene Congress into special session.

ARTICLE III

Section 1. During sessions of Congress each member shall have equal rights and privileges and no member of Congress shall be honored or respect paid to him in address or manner because of title.

ARTICLE IV

Section 1. There shall be a Legislative Committee, and bills of Congress shall be committed to it in accordance with Section 6 of Article II of this Charter. The Committee shall maintain a permanent or semi-permanent staff to assist in the drafting or redrafting of bills as may be necessary. The Committee and its staff shall provide services to the members of Congress as may be required by them in the performance of their office. The Committee shall keep the records of Congress and copies of all laws which are applicable to Ponape District. It may keep such other records or documents as it may deem necessary to provide assistance to the members of Congress, or any other records or documents as Congress shall desire. Congress shall appropriate funds, which shall be a part of the approved budget, in order that the Committee may function properly.

ARTICLE V

Section 1. Congress shall have the power by law to levy and provide for the collection of taxes and fees in conformance with provisions of the Trust Territory Code.

ARTICLE VI

Section 1. Compensation of the members of Congress and employees whose salaries or wages are from district revenues shall be as Congress establishes by law.

ARTICLE VII

Section 1. Expenditures of district revenues shall be in accordance with the budget of Congress as established by law.

ARTICLE VIII

Section 1. Congress shall pass no laws which contravene the Trust Territory Bill of Rights.

ARTICLE IX

Section 1. All laws enacted under the provisions of this Charter shall be promulgated as Ponape District laws.

ARTICLE X

Section 1. Amendments to this Charter may be made upon the concurrence of three-fourths of the members of Congress and the District Administrator, and approval by the High Commissioner. No amendments shall be made which shall deprive any municipality of representation in Congress.

ARTICLE XI

Section 1. Any provision of this Charter which is construed to be in conflict with duly enacted Trust Territory law shall be null and void and the law of the Trust Territory shall have precedence.

Given under my hand and seal this 16th day of July 1958.

/s/ D. H. NUCKER
High Commissioner
Trust Territory of the Pacific Islands

CHARTER OF THE
PONAPE DISTRICT LEGISLATURE
1963

PREAMBLE

Whereas, the Ponape District Congress was established under the provision of a Charter granted on July 16, 1958, by the High Commissioner of the Trust Territory of the Pacific Islands in order to provide a representative legislative body for the people of the Ponape District; and

Whereas, the elected representatives of the people of the Ponape District, meeting as the Ponape District Congress pursuant to the term of that Charter, on April 19, 1963, by unanimous vote, requested that the existing Charter be replaced by a revised one, the provision of which they recommended;

Now, therefore, I, M. W. Goding, High Commissioner of the Trust Territory of the Pacific Islands, hereby rescind the Charter of July 16, 1958, and grant to the people of Ponape District this present Charter, giving them the right, in accordance with its provision, to participate through the Ponape District Legislature, in the government of Ponape District. The Ponape District Legislature is the successor in all respects and in every way, and in accordance with this Charter, to the Ponape District Congress.

ARTICLE I

Section 1. The legislative powers of the Ponape District herein granted by the High Commissioner of the Trust Territory of the Pacific Islands shall be vested in a single house to be known as the Ponape District Legislature.

Section 2. The Ponape District Legislture, hereinafter referred to as the Legislature, shall be composed of twenty-four (24) legislators elected every four years by the electors of the Ponape District.

ARTICLE II

Section 1. There shall be eleven (11) electoral precincts, as follows: Kapingamarangi, Kiti, Kusaie, Metalanim, Mokil, Net, Ngatik, Nukuoro, Pingelap, Sokehs, Uh. Apportionment of legislators shall be as follows: Kapingamarangi, Mokil, Ngatik, Nukuoro, and Pingelap shall each have one member; Net shall have four members of whom two shall be from and elected by the people of Kolonia Town, and two shall be from and elected by the people in the remaining area of Net: Uh shall have two members; Kiti, Metalanim, and Sokehs shall each have three members; Kusaie shall have four members.

Section 2. Reapportionment on a population basis shall take place every ten years, beginning in 1970. Regardless of population change, each precinct shall be guaranteed at least one legislator.

Section 3. To be eligible for election or appointment, a person must be a citizen of the Trust Territory of the Pacific Islands, have resided in Ponape District for a three-year period immediately preceding his election, be a resident of his electoral precinct for a period of not less than one year immediately preceding his election; must be twenty-five (25) years of age or over; and must never have been convicted of a felony.

Section 4. Where a legislator is unable to perform the duties of his office due to physical or mental disability or death or who resigns or is impeached by the Legislature, another shall be appointed to fill the remainder of the term by the Chief Executive of his municipality. In the event a legislator-elect is unable to assume office, there shall be a special election in his electoral precinct in order to choose another in his place.

Section 1. No person may sit in the Legislature who holds a public office in the executive branch at the municipal government level or who holds a judicial office.

Section 2. The Legislature alone shall determine the qualifications of its members. The Legislature may by an affirmative three-fourths vote of its members impeach any member. A legislator may be recalled by a majority vote of the registered electors in his precinct.

Section 3. Qualifications of electors shall be as follows: Each shall be eighteen (18) years of age or over; a citizen of the Trust Territory of the Pacific Islands; have been a resident of his electoral precinct for a period of at least one year immediately preceding the election; not be serving a criminal sentence at the time of the election.

Section 1. The Legislature shall convene twice a year in regular session on the third Tuesday of January and the third Tuesday in July if possible. The District Administrator may convene the Legislature into special session, whose proceedings shall be confined to the subjects stated in the District Administrator's convening call. A special session of the Legislature may be called upon petition of one-third of the membership.

Section 2. Each Legislator shall present credentials which shall be in the form of a statement from the Chief Executive of his municipality authenticating his election. There shall be an oath of office which the Speaker shall administer to each elected member individually. The Legislature shall organize annually at the beginning of each January Session selecting a Speaker and Vice-Speaker.

Section 3. The Legislature, by a majority vote of its members, shall establish standing rules of procedure.

Section 4. An affirmative vote of a majority of the members present, shall be required to pass a measure. Three-fourths of the members of the Legislature shall constitute a quorum.

Section 5. Any member may introduce a measure. Measures introduced shall be read before the Legislature two times on different days, before a vote may be taken.

Section 6. Communications and draft measures may be transmitted to the Legislature by the District Administrator for consideration by it.

Section 7. Upon passage of a measure by the Legislature it shall be signed by the Speaker.

Section 8. Each bill shall have an enacting clause as follows: Be it enacted by the Ponape District Legislature, that, etc.

Section 9. Each act shall be submitted to the District Administrator. If he approves he shall sign it and transmit it promptly to the High Commissioner. If the High Commissioner takes no action within sixty (60) days after receipt, it shall become law. If the District Administrator takes no action within twenty-one (21) days after receipt the act shall be considered approved. In cases where, in the opinion of the District Administrator, the approval or veto of an act will require consultation with the High Commissioner, the District Administrator shall so inform the Speaker, in writing, in which case the District Administrator shall have an additional thirty (30) days in which to take action. Acts vetoed by the District Administrator shall be returned to the Legislature with his objections. By a three-fourths affirmative vote the Legislature may submit the vetoed act to the High Commissioner through the District Administrator, and the High Commissioner shall act within sixty (60) days after receiving the act. If he takes no action the act shall be considered approved and shall become law. All approved acts shall be known as Public Laws of Ponape District. The Legislature by act, may repeal or amend District Orders with the exception of those designated Emergency District Orders in accordance with Section 29, Trust Territory Code.

Section 10. The Legislature shall keep a journal of its proceedings and publish the same.

Section 11. Members of the Legislature shall, in all cases except felony or breach of the peace, be privileged from arrest during their attendance at the Legislature and in going to and returning from the same. No member shall be held to answer before any tribunal other than the Legislature itself for any speech or debate in the Legislature.

Section 12. As incidents of its legislative authority, the Legislature may conduct investigations, hold public hearings, subpoena witnesses and documents, and administer oaths.

ARTICLE V

Section 1. There shall be four standing committees: Political, Social, Economic, and Appropriations. Chairmen and members of the committees shall be appointed by the Speaker. Measures introduced by legislators shall be assigned to the appropriate committee by the Speaker. Measures reported out by committee shall be in written form either as bills, or resolutions. Measures shall be numbered and placed on a calendar in the order in which they are reported out.

ARTICLE VI

Section 1. The Legislature shall have the power to levy taxes, grant licenses and appropriate funds.

ARTICLE VII

Section 1. Compensation of the members of the Legislature and its employees shall be established by law.

ARTICLE VIII

Section 1. Amendments to this Charter may be made upon an affirmative vote of three-fourths of the members of the Legislature and approval by the District Administrator and the High Commissioner, or by the High Commissioner on his own initiative.

Given under my hand and seal this 17th day of October 1963.

/s/ M. W. GODING
High Commissioner
Trust Territory of the Pacific Islands

TRUK DISTRICT CONGRESS CHARTER
1957

PREAMBLE

Whereas, the magistrates of the municipalities of the Truk District assembled in Council at Moen on the 23rd day of July 1957 have resolved that a Congress of the people should be convened to assist in the government of the district; and

Whereas, this Council has demonstrated its ability to exercise certain responsibilities of government under our laws;

Now, therefore, I, Delmas H. Nucker, High Commissioner of the Trust Territory of the Pacific Islands, do hereby charter the people of the Truk District to assemble a congress of their elected representatives to be known as the Truk District Congress to assist in the government of the district in accordance with the laws of the Trust Territory and the provisions of this charter.

ARTICLE I

This charter and all amendments hereto constitute a part of the laws of the Trust Territory of the Pacific Islands.

ARTICLE II. POWERS AND LIMITATIONS OF POWERS

Section 1. The Congress is empowered to enact laws not in conflict with the laws of the Trust Territory for the Government of the District, which shall acquire the force and effect of law in the District when approved by the District Administrator and the High Commissioner. The Congress is also empowered to levy taxes and to disburse funds subject to the approval of the District Administrator and the High Commissioner.

Section 2. In the event an Act of the Truk District Congress is in conflict with a municipal ordinance, the Act shall supersede and take precedence over the ordinance.

ARTICLE III. MEMBERS OF CONGRESS

Section 1. Each Municipality of less than 500 people shall elect one representative to sit in the Congress. Each municipality of more than 500 people shall elect one representative for each additional 500 people. Population shall be determined from the most recently published territorial census.

Section 2. Representatives to Congress shall be citizens of the Trust Territory, thirty or more years of age and of sound mind and shall have maintained official residence in the Truk District for a period of ten years or longer.

Section 3. Representatives to Congress shall be elected in accordance with the laws of the municipality represented to serve for a term of three years, except that municipalities entitled to elect more than one representative may elect, to the first two annual sessions of Congress only, one representative to serve for one year and one to serve for two years.

Section 4. Each municipality in a reasonable time after election shall issue a certificate signed by the island council or the island magistrate and the Secretary of the municipality to each member or members of Congress elected from the municipality which shall include: the name of the municipality; the name of the congressman; the fact that the individual named in the certificate has been elected to represent the municipality in the Congress; and the period of time which the congressman shall hold office. This certificate shall be presented to the Credentials Committee to show that the holder of the certificate is authorized to sit in Congress as representative of a particular municipality.

If any municipal officer signs a certificate as required by Article III, Section 4, of the Truk District Congress Charter, knowing that the person to whom the certificate has been issued has not been duly elected by the municipality as a member of the Congress, he shall be guilty of misconduct in public office and upon conviction shall be punished in accordance with Section 417 of the Trust Territory Code.

Section 5. In the event a representative dies, or becomes incapacitated to the extent that he cannot perform his duties, or is otherwise disqualified, a substitute may be elected or appointed as provided by law of the municipality represented to serve the remainder of the unexpired term.

Section 6. A representative may be removed for cause by a two-thirds majority vote of a quorum of the Congress.

Section 7. Members of Congress may receive pay, or other benefits as determined by Congress.

ARTICLE IV. OFFICERS AND EMPLOYEES OF CONGRESS

Section 1. At the opening of each session, the Congress shall elect a Chairman. The Chairman shall preside over that session and shall remain in office until a new Chairman is elected by the Congress.

Section 2. The Congress shall elect or appoint a Secretary who shall maintain a record of all proceedings of the Congress.

Section 3. The Congress shall elect or appoint a Treasurer who shall be responsible for the collection of taxes and the disbursement of funds. He shall maintain fund in his custody in a safe place and shall maintain an account of all funds received, expended, and due.

Section 4. The Congress may appoint such other officers or employees as may be necessary for the conduct of its business.

Section 5. The Congress may elect as advisors such persons as it may desire.

Section 6. Officers and employees of Congress may receive salaries or other benefits as determined by act of Congress.

Section 7. At each Congress the Chairman shall appoint a credentials committee of five members. The members of the committee shall serve until a new committee is appointed by the Chairman of the succeeding Congress. The committee shall meet and receive the credentials of each member of Congress before the opening session of the Congress and shall certify to the Chairman an official list, signed by each member of the committee, of all members eligible to sit in the Congress and the municipality they represent. Only those persons whose names appear on the official list shall be permitted to vote in the Congress. The official list shall be entered into and become a part of the permanent record of the proceedings of Congress.

ARTICLE V. MEETINGS OF CONGRESS

Section 1. Congress shall meet annually during the month of August or at such times as may be determined by act of Congress or the District Administrator.

Section 2. Except as herein provided the Congress shall determine its own rules of procedure for the conduct of meetings.

Section 3. A quorum shall consist of two-thirds of the elected membership.

Section 4. Legislative actions of Congress shall be entitled Acts of Congress (Nopung or Nomopung).

Section 5. A two-thirds majority vote of the quorum shall be required to pass an action of Congress.

ARTICLE VI. BUDGETS AND THE COLLECTION, CARE AND DISBURSEMENT OF FUNDS

Section 1. The Treasurer shall be responsible to the Congress for the collection, safe-keeping and disbursement of funds.

Section 2. Funds shall be disbursed only as authorized by the budget.

Section 3. Unexpended revenues shall not be accumulated from year to year except for funds placed and held in a separate account for a specified purpose. Such accounts shall be authorized by Act of Congress and their balances reported annually as a part of the budget. Except for funds held in separate account as authorized by this section, carry-over funds shall be applied to the budget for the following year.

Section 4. The budget shall be adopted as an Act of Congress. It shall not be amended except by Act of Congress.

Section 5. Records and accounts of the Treasurer and funds in his custody shall be made available for audit upon demand of the Congress or the District Administrator.

ARTICLE VII. AMENDMENTS TO CHARTER

This charter may be amended by Act of Congress and upon the written approval of the High Commissioner or by the High Commissioner on his own initiative.

Given under my hand and seal this 9th day of August 1957.

/s/ D. H. NUCKER
High Commissioner
Trust Territory of the Pacific Islands

CHARTER OF THE TRUK DISTRICT LEGISLATURE
1963

PREAMBLE

Whereas, the Truk District Congress was established under the provision of a Charter granted 9 August 1957 by the High Commissioner of the Trust Territory of the Pacific Islands, in order to provide a representative legislative body for the Truk District; and

Whereas, the elected representative of the people of Truk District, meeting as the Truk District Congress pursuant to the term of that Charter, on 7 August 1963 by two-thirds majority vote requested that the existing Charter be replaced by a revised one, provision of which they recommended;

Now, therefore, I, M. W. Goding, High Commissioner of the Trust Territory of the Pacific Islands, hereby rescind the Charter of 9 August 1957, and grant to the people of Truk District this present Charter, giving them the right, in accordance with its provision, to participate, through the Truk District Legislature in the government of Truk District. The Truk District Legislature is the successor in all respects and in every way, and in accordance with this Charter, to the Truk District Congress.

ARTICLE I

Section 1. The legislative powers of Truk District herein granted by the High Commissioner of the Trust Territory of the Pacific Islands shall be vested in a single house to be known as the Truk District Legislature.

Section 2. The Truk District Legislature, hereinafter referred to as the Legislature, shall be composed of twenty-seven legislators elected every two years by the electors of Truk District.

ARTICLE II

Section 1. There shall be fifteen electoral precincts, as follows: Number 1. Namonouito (Ulul, Magur, Ono, Onari and Pisarach); Number 2. Ta and Satawan; Number 3. Tol and Fala Beguets; Number 4. Lukunor and Oneop; Number 5. Namoluk; Number 6. Udot, Ramonum and Eot;

Number 7. Moch, Kuttu and Ettal; Number 8. Uman; Number 9. Manwunpattiu (Pulap, Tamatam, Puluwat and Pulusuk); Number 10. Lukeisel (Nama, Losap and Pis); Number 11. Fefan, Parem and Tsis; Number 12. Polle, Patta and Wonei; Number 13. Dublon; Number 14. Moen; Number 15. Namwin Pafeng (Ruo, Murilo, Fananu and Nomwin). Apportionment of legislators shall be as follows: Precincts 1, 2, 4, 5, 7, 9, 12 and 15 shall elect one member. Precincts 8, 6, 10 and 13 shall each elect two members. Precincts 3 and 11 shall each elect three members. Precinct 14 shall elect four members.

Section 2. Reapportionment on a population basis shall take place every ten years, beginning in 1970. Regardless of population change, each precinct shall be entitled to have at least one legislator.

Section 3. To be eligible for election or appointment, a person must be a citizen of the Trust Territory of the Pacific Islands; have resided in Truk District for a three-year period immediately preceding his election; be a resident of his electoral precinct for a period of not less than one year immediately preceding his election; be twenty-three years of age or over; and never have been convicted of a felony.

Section 4. Where a legislator is unable to perform the duties of the office due to physical or mental disability or who dies or resigns or is removed by action of the Legislature, another shall be appointed to fill the remainder of the term by the District Administrator. In the event a legislator-elect is unable to assume office, there shall be a special election in his electoral precinct to elect another in his place.

ARTICLE III

Section 1. No person may sit in the Legislature who holds an elected public office in the executive branch in a municipality, who holds a judicial office, or who holds a staff position in the district administration.

Section 2. The Legislature alone shall determine the qualifications of its members. The Legislature may by an affirmative three-fourths vote of its members expel a member for cause.

Section 3. Qualifications of electors shall be as follows: Each shall be eighteen years of age or over; be a citizen of the Trust Territory of the Pacific Islands; have been a resident of Truk District for a period of at least one year immediately preceding the election; be a registered elector in his precinct at the time of the election; not be serving a criminal sentence at the time of the election.

ARTICLE IV

Section 1. The Legislature shall convene twice a year in regular session. These shall be on the third Tuesday of February and on the third Tuesday of August, if possible. The District Administrator may convene the Legislature into special session, whose proceedings shall be confined to the subject stated in the District Administrator's convening call. A special session of the Legislature shall be called upon petition of one-third of the membership.

Section 2. Each legislator shall present credentials in the form of a statement from the chairman of the Truk District Election Board certifying his election. The Legislature shall organize annually at the beginning of each February session electing a Speaker and Vice-Speaker. There shall be an oath of office which the Speaker shall administer to each legislator individually.

Section 3. Members of the Legislature during their attendance at the Legislature and in going to and returning from the same, shall not be subject to civil process and shall, in all cases except felony or breach of the peace, be privileged from arrest. No Legislator shall be held to answer before any tribunal other than the Legislature itself for any speech or debate in the Legislature.

Section 4. As incidents of its legislative authority, the Legislature may conduct investigations, hold public hearings and administer oaths.

Section 5. The rate of compensation for the members of the Legislature and its employees shall be established by law.

ARTICLE V

Section 1. The Legislature shall, by an affirmative vote of two-thirds of its members, establish rules of procedure.

Section 2. Three-fourths of the members of the Legislature shall constitute a quorum. An affirmative vote of a majority of the members of the Legislature shall be required to pass a measure.

Section 3. Any member may introduce a measure. Measures introduced shall be read in the Legislature two times on different days before a vote may be taken. Measures shall be titled as either bills or resolutions.

Section 4. Communications and draft measures may be transmitted to the Legislature by the District Administrator for consideration by it.

Section 5. Upon passage of a measure by the Legislature it shall be signed by the Speaker.

Section 6. Each bill shall have an enacting clause as follows: Be it enacted by the Truk District Legislature, that, etc. Each bill passed by the Legislature shall be known as an act of the Truk District Legislature.

Section 7. Every act of the Legislature shall be presented to the District Administrator. If he approves or disapproves he shall so indicate on the act and transmit it to the High Commissioner. If the District Administrator does not take action within sixty days the act shall be considered as having his approval. If the High Commissioner approves he shall sign the act. If the High Commissioner neither approves nor disapproves the act within thirty days, it shall be a law in like manner as if he had signed it. Both the District Administrator and the High Commissioner shall have item veto power on appropriation acts. Each approved act shall be known as a Truk District Law. The Legislature may repeal District Orders with the exception of those designated Emergency District Orders in Section 29, Trust Territory Code.

Section 8. The Legislature shall keep a journal of its proceedings and publish the same.

Section 1. There shall be four standing committees: Political, Social, Economic and Appropriation. Chairman and members of the committees shall be appointed by the Speaker. Measures introduced in the Legislature shall be assigned to the appropriate committee by the Speaker. Measures shall be numbered and placed on a calendar in the order in which they are reported out.

Section 1. The Legislature shall have the power to levy and collect taxes and appropriate money.

Section 1. Amendments to this Charter may be made upon an affirmative vote of three-fourths of the Legislature and approval by the District Administrator and the High Commissioner, or by the High Commissioner on his own initiative.

Section 2. The Truk District Congress shall be automatically dissolved upon the convening of the first session of the Legislature. An election to select members of the Legislature shall be conducted no later than 31 December 1963.

Given under my hand and seal this 25th day of September 1963.

/s/ M. W. GODING
High Commissioner
Trust Territory of the Pacific Islands

YAP ISLANDS CONGRESS CHARTER
1959

PREAMBLE

Whereas, the people of Yap, Western Caroline Islands, through their duly elected representatives, have expressed their desire for greater representation in the government of their islands in accordance with the principles proclaimed in the Trusteeship Council and under the laws of the Trust Territory of the Pacific Islands; and

Whereas, their elected and entrusted representatives have met together to draft a charter for the establishment of an island congress; and

Whereas, we have confidence in the demonstrated ability of these people to discharge certain responsibilities of government under our laws and the provisions of this charter;

Now, therefore, I, Delmas H. Nucker, High Commissioner of the Trust Territory of the Pacific Islands, pursuant to authority vested in me, do hereby charter the people of Yap, Western Caroline Islands, to assemble a Congress of their elected representatives to be known as the

Yap Islands Congress to assist in the government of their islands in accordance with the laws of the Trust Territory and the provisions of this charter.

ARTICLE I

Section 1. The legislative powers within Yap, Caroline Islands, herein granted by the High Commissioner of the Trust Territory of the Pacific Islands shall be vested in a unicameral assembly to be known as the Yap Islands Congress.

ARTICLE II

Section 1. The Yap Islands Congress, hereinafter referred to as Congress, shall be composed of two representatives, who shall be known as Congressmen, from each municipality on Yap, chosen by the electors within each municipality to serve for a term of four years, except that in the first election of Congressmen, to be held within sixty days after granting of this charter, one Congressman from each municipality shall be elected for a term of two years and one Congressman from each municipality shall be elected for a term of four years. Thereafter, elections will be held at two-year intervals to elect successors to the Congressmen from the respective municipalities whose terms of office are due to expire.

Section 2. Any vacancy in the membership of Congress shall be filled by election held in the municipality concerned to elect a Congressman to serve the unexpired portion of the term of office vacant provided that, if less than three months of such term remain unexpired, Congress may determine that the position shall remain vacant until the next regular election of Congressmen.

ARTICLE III

Section 1. Any person who is a citizen of the Trust Territory, not less than twenty-five years of age, resident for not less than three years in the municipality in which he or she is nominated, has never been convicted of a felony, has not been legally adjudged mentally incompetent, and does not hold office in a municipal government at the time of elections, may be elected a representative to Congress.

Section 2. Any Congressman who retains the qualifications stated herein may succeed himself in office if duly reelected by the electorate of his municipality.

Section 3. Any member of Congress may be impeached and removed from office by resolution of Congress for cause determined by a hearing before Congress meeting in closed session at which the impeached and all parties who are witnesses thereto shall be heard. An affirmative vote of three-fourths of the total membership of Congress shall be required for removal from office.

ARTICLE IV

Section 1. Qualifications of electors shall be as Congress shall establish by law, provided that no person otherwise qualified shall be denied the right of suffrage because of sex, race, or religious creed, and provided that qualifications of electors which prevail in the municipalities of Yap at the time of granting this charter shall prevail in the first election of Congressmen hereunder.

ARTICLE V

Section 1. As the first order of business at the first session of Congress following regular elections of members, Congress shall elect from among it members an officer to serve as President of Congress for a term of two years, provided that, at the first session of Congress after granting of this charter, the District Administrator shall convene the Congress and preside until the election of a President as the first order of business.

Section 2. Following the election of President of Congress in accordance with Section 1, next above, Congress shall elect from among its members an officer to serve as Vice-President of Congress for a term of two years.

Section 3. The President shall appoint, and Congress shall confirm by majority vote of the members present, an officer to serve as Secretary of Congress for a term of two years or such shorter period as Congress may determine.

Section 4. When a vacancy occurs in the Presidency or Vice-Presidency of Congress, Congress shall elect among its members, at the the next regular or special session, an officer to serve the unexpired portion of the term of office vacant.

Section 5. Duties of officers shall be as determined by Congress, and shall include:

(a) that the President shall preside at all regular and special sessions of Congress, except that in the absence of the President, the Vice-President shall preside, and in the absence of the President and Vice-President, the Secretary shall preside;

(b) that the Secretary shall make and maintain or cause to be made and maintained records of all sessions of Congress;

(c) that the Officers of Congress shall comprise an Executive Committee whose function it shall be to prepare and publish before the convening of each regular session of Congress an agenda of business for the forthcoming session.

ARTICLE VI

Section 1. The President of Congress shall appoint from among the members a Legislative Committee, among whose functions shall be the drafting of bills and resolutions of Congress; other functions of the committee may be specified by Congress in its rules of procedure. The Legislative Committee may employ under the provisions herein, such employees as are necessary to perform its proper functions.

Section 2. The Congress may appoint or elect from among its members such other committees as are deemed necessary. Advisors and consultants not members of Congress may be appointed to non-voting membership on such committees.

ARTICLE VII

Section 1. Congress shall convene in regular session twice yearly, convening on the first Monday in May and the first Monday in November.

Section 2. Special sessions of Congress may be called by the President, the District Administrator, or by petition of a majority of members of Congress.

Section 3. In any session of Congress, regular or special, Congress shall be considered continuously in session from the date convened, but no session of Congress shall exceed ten days duration, excluding Saturdays, Sundays, and official holidays established by Congress by resolution.

ARTICLE VIII

Section 1. Compensation for services of members of Congress shall be as Congress may determine and enact as resolution provided that all Congressmen shall be compensated equally for actual days service in attendance at regular or special sessions of Congress.

ARTICLE IX

Section 1. Congress may employ such persons as are deemed necessary to proper conduct of its functions. Funds for the compensation of such employees shall be provided in an annual budget enacted by Congress as a resolution.

ARTICLE X

Section 1. At any regular or special session of Congress, each member shall have one vote on any resolution or representation introduced. Three-fourths of the membership of Congress shall constitute a quorum at any regular or special session. An affirmative vote of two-thirds of the members present at any regular or special session shall be required to pass a resolution of Congress unless otherwise specified herein.

Section 2. Congress shall, by a majority vote of its total members, establish its rules of procedure not otherwise specified herein.

Section 3. Any member of Congress may introduce a bill. Each bill introduced shall be read in its entirety before Congress, and Congress shall determine by a vote of the majority of the members present whether to accept it for deliberation or reject it. Each bill accepted shall pass to a Legislative Committee for drafting and shall be submitted to Congress at its next regular session for consideration. By an affirmative two-thirds vote of the members present, Congress may determine to consider a bill during the session in which it was introduced or at any subsequent special session prior to the next regular session.

Section 4. Upon passage of a bill by Congress, it shall be signed by the President and the Secretary and forwarded to the District Administrator as a Yap Islands Congress Resolution.

Section 5. Any resolution not approved by the District Administrator shall be returned to Congress, together with a statement of his reasons for disapproval and recommendation for reconsideration by the Congress, copies of which shall also be forwarded to the High Commissioner. At any regular or special session, Congress may, by an affirmative vote of three-fourths of its total membership, confirm such resolution and forward it through the District Administrator to the High Commissioner.

Section 6. Resolutions approved by the District Administrator shall be forwarded to the High Comissioner by the District Administrator and Congress shall be notified of such action. Resolutions approved by the High Commissioner shall become law of Yap, Caroline Islands, effective thirty days thereafter, unless otherwise specified within the resolution or approval, and shall be promulgated according to law.

Section 7. Any resolution upon which the District Administrator has not taken action within thirty days after acceptance by him of an English translation thereof shall be considered as having the District Administrator's approval, and a copy of the resolution together with a translation shall be forwarded by Congress through the District Administrator to the High Commissioner.

Section 8. Any resolution upon which the High Commissioner has not taken action within one hundred eighty days from the date of acceptance by the District Administrator of an English translation thereof shall be considered as having the High Commissioner's approval and shall become law of Yap, Caroline Islands, in accordance with Section 6 next above.

Section 9. No resolution or enactment of Congress shall have the force and effect of law except as provided herein.

Section 10. No ordinance of any municipality of Yap, Caroline Islands, which contravenes laws enacted under the provisions of this charter shall be accorded the force and effect of law.

Section 11. Acts of Congress constituting opinions and not intended to have the force and effect of law may be presented to the District Administrator as Representations of Congress.

ARTICLE XI

Section 1. Congress shall have the power to enact resolutions to provide for and maintain the welfare of the residents of Yap, Caroline Islands.

Section 2. Congress shall have the power by law to levy and provide for the collection of taxes and fees in conformance with provisions of the Code of the Trust Territory, amended.

Section 3. Congress shall establish by law an annual budget to provide for the use and disbursement of revenues collected under authority contained herein, under the Code of the Trust Territory, amended.

ARTICLE XII

Section 1. Amendments to this charter may be made by resolution upon the affirmative vote of three-fourths of the total membership of Congress or by order of the High Commissioner, provided that no amendment shall be made which shall deprive any municipality of Yap of Representation in Congress.

ARTICLE XIII

Section 1. Nothing within this charter shall be construed as contravening the Code of the Trust Territory, as amended, or any other laws, orders, or directives promulgated by the High Commissioner of the Trust Territory of the Pacific Islands.

Section 2. No act of Congress which contravenes the laws of the Trust Territory shall be accorded the force and effect of law.

Given under my hand and seal this 9th day of February 1959.

/s/ D. H. NUCKER
High Commissioner
Trust Territory of the Pacific Islands

Other Documents

MODEL CHARTER
DISTRICT LEGISLATURE

ARTICLE I

Section 1. The legislative powers of _____ District herein granted by the High Commissioner of the Trust Territory of the Pacific Islands shall be vested in a single house to be known as the _____ District Legislature.

Section 2. The _____ District Legislature, hereinafter referred to as the Legislature, shall be composed of _____ legislators elected every _____ years by the electors of _____ District.

ARTICLE II

Section 1. There shall be _____ electoral precincts, as follows:

Apportionment of legislators shall be as follows:

Section 2. Reapportionment on a population basis shall take place every ten years, beginning in 1970. Regardless of population change, each precinct shall be entitled to have at least one legislator.

Section 3. To be eligible for election or appointment, a person must be a citizen of the Trust Territory of the Pacific Islands, have resided in _____ District for a three year period immediately preceding his election, be a resident of his electoral precinct for a period of not less than one year immediately preceding his election; must be twenty-three years of age or over; and must never have been convicted of a felony.

Section 4. Where a legislator is unable to perform the duties of the office due to physical or mental disability or who dies or resigns or is removed by action of the Legislature, another shall be appointed to fill the remainder of his term by the chief executive of his municipality. In the event a legislator-elect is unable to assume office, there shall be a special election in his electoral precinct to elect another in his place.

ARTICLE III

Section 1. No person may sit in the Legislature who holds a public office in the executive branch at the municipal government level, who holds a judicial office, or who holds a staff position in the district administration. (Since conditions vary in the districts, the provisions in this section are optional.)

Section 2. The Legislature alone shall determine the qualifications of its members. The Legislature may by an affirmative three-fourths vote of its members expel a member for cause.

Section 3. Qualifications of electors shall be as follows: Each shall be eighteen years of age or over; be a citizen of the Trust Territory of the Pacific Islands; have been a resident of _____ District for a period of at least one year immediately preceding the election; be a registered elector in his precinct at the time of the election; not be serving a criminal sentence at the time of the election.

Section 1. The Legislature shall convene twice a year in regular session. These shall be on the _____ and on the _____, if possible. The District Administrator may convene the Legislature into special session, whose proceedings shall be confined to the subjects stated in the District Administrator's convening call. A special session of the Legislature shall be called upon petition of one-third of the membership.

Section 2. Each legislator shall present credentials in the form of a statement from the chief executive of his municipality certifying his election. The Legislature shall organize annually at the beginning of each _____ session electing a Speaker and Vice-Speaker. There shall be an oath of office which the Speaker shall administer to each legislator individually.

Section 3. Members of the Legislature during their attendance at the Legislature and in going to and returning from the same, shall not be subject to civil process and shall, in all cases except felony or breach of the peace, be privileged from arrest. No member shall be held to answer before any tribunal other than the Legislature itself for any speech or debate in the Legislature.

Section 4. As incidents of its legislative authority, the Legislature may conduct investigations, hold public hearings and administer oaths.

Section 5. The rate of compensation for the members of the Legislature and its employees shall be established by law.

Section 1. The Legislature shall, by an affirmative vote of two-thirds of its members, establish rules of procedure.

Section 2. Three-fourths of the members of the Legislature shall constitute a quorum. An affirmative vote of a majority of the members of the Legislature shall be required to pass a measure.

Section 3. Any member may introduce a measure. Measures introduced shall be read in the Legislature two times on different days, before a vote may be taken. Measures shall be titled as either bills or resolutions.

Section 4. Communications and draft measures may be transmitted to the Legislature by the District Administrator for consideration by it.

Section 5. Upon passage of a measure by the Legislature it shall be signed by the Speaker.

Section 6. Each bill shall have an enacting clause as follows: Be it enacted by the _____ District Legislature, that, etc. Each bill passed by the Legislature shall be known as an act of the _____ District Legislature.

Section 7. Every act of the Legislature shall be presented to the District Administrator. If he approves, or disapproves, he shall so indicate on the act and transmit it to the High Commissioner. If the District

Administrator does not take action within sixty days the act shall be considered as having his approval. If the High Commissioner approves he shall sign the act. If the High Commissioner neither approves nor disapproves the act within thirty days, it shall be a law in like manner as if he had signed it. Both the District Administrator and the High Commissioner shall have item veto power on appropriation acts. Each approved act shall be known as a _____ District Law. The Legislature may repeal District Orders with the exception of those designated Emergency District Orders in Section 29, Trust Territory Code.

Section 8. The Legislature shall keep a journal of its proceedings and publish the same.

ARTICLE VI

Section 1. There shall be four standing committees: Political, Social, Economic and Appropriations. Chairmen and members of the committees shall be apointed by the Speaker. Measures introduced in the Legislature shall be assigned to the appropriate committee by the Speaker. Measures shall be numbered and placed on a calendar in the order in which they are reported out.

ARTICLE VII

Section 1. The Legislature shall have the power to levy and collect taxes and appropriate money.

ARTICLE VIII

Section 1. Amendments to this Charter may be made upon an affirmative vote of three-fourths of the Legislature and approval by the District Administrator and the High Commissioner, or by the High Commissioner on his own initiative.

HIGH COMMISSIONER'S EXECUTIVE ORDER NO. 83
August 9, 1962

Subject: An Order Establishing the Office of District Treasurer, and amending the Charter of the Palau District Congress, the Yap Islands Congress, the Truk District Congress, the Ponape District Congress, and the Marshall Islands District Congress

I. Pursuant to the provisions of Section 36 of the Code of the Trust Territory of the Pacific Islands and the authority vested in me as High Commissioner, it is hereby ordered that:

1. The Office of District Treasurer be and it is hereby established within the Office of each District Administrator.

2. *Appointment and Compensation*
(a) The District Treasurer shall be appointed by the District Congress for a term which shall be specified by the Congress, subject, however, to removal for cause at any time by the District Administrator.

(b) The District Treasurer shall receive a salary for his services, from the appropriate District funds, in an amount and under such conditions as the District Congress shall provide.

3. *Duties*

(a) The District Treasurer shall receive, maintain, and disburse funds under the authority of the District Congress and under the direction and supervision of the District Administrator.

(b) The District Treasurer shall keep complete and accurate records of all funds received, maintained and disbursed by him in such manner as prescribed by the District Administrator. Such records shall be open to inspection and audit by the District Congress and the Trust Territory Government.

(c) The District Treasurer shall analyze the receipts and disbursements under the authority of the District Congress and, under the supervision of the District Administrator, prepare for presentation to the Congress an annual budget in a manner and at such times as the Congress may by law prescribe.

4. All District Treasurers presently acting as such pursuant to any law in effect prior to the date of this Order are hereby authorized to continue to act until the appointment of a District Treasurer at the next regular or special session of the respective District or Island Congress, subject, however, to removal at any time by the District Administrator.

5. The Charters of the Palau District Congress, the Yap Islands Congress, the Truk District Congress, the Ponape District Congress, and the Marshall Islands District Congress, respectively, are hereby amended to conform with the foregoing provisions with respect to the office of, appointment and duties of the District Treasurer.

6. Any District Laws or Resolutions in conflict herewith shall be of no further force and effect.

II. The above and foregoing order is subject to and is to be construed in accordance with Presidential Executive Orders numbered 10408 and 10470, dated November 10, 1952 and July 14, 1953, respectively.

/s/ D. H. NUCKER
High Commissioner
Trust Territory of the Pacific Islands

Index